Crimson Rose

Carolyn S. Tanner

STUDIO
OF BOOKS
THE SPACE FOR YOUR MESSAGE

STUDIO
OF BOOKS
THE SPACE FOR YOUR MESSAGE

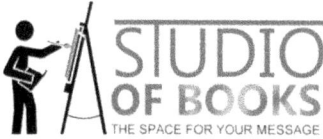

Studio of Books LLC
5900 Balcones Drive Suite 100
Austin, Texas 78731
www.studioofbooks.org
Hotline: (254) 800-1183

Ordering Information:
Special discounts are available on quantity purchases by corporations, associations, and others. For details, contact the publisher at the address above.

Printed in the United States of America.

ISBN-13: Softcover   978-1-964928-64-7
          Hardcover   978-1-964928-65-4
          eBook   978-1-964928-66-1

Library of Congress Control Number: 2025911731

DEDICATION

In remembrance and with continued love for my momma, Corene Tanner, who was more than a mother—she was my best friend and confidant, and for her youngest brother, my uncle Bobby Sellers, a stern man with a heart of gold, who in a lot of ways, I developed my main male character to resemble. We miss you!

To all my readers, thank you and my love goes out to you. No matter how our world changes, each of us has at least one thing in common—a need for someone to love us for who we are, with the positive and negative aspects of our personality. May you always find that special love.

AUTHOR'S NOTE

Using the writer's prerogative, I took historical characters out of the annuals of history and gave them a fictional part in the story. There were many colorful people who pioneered the Texas Panhandle whose lives were stranger than fiction, but regretfully, I could not fit them all into this story.

The Red Rivers Wars between the southern plains Indians and the U.S. military began in 1874 and ended in 1875. The Red River Wars were fought within the depths of the Texas Palo Duro Canyon and Panhandle region. The main incident sparking the wars was the attack on Adobe Walls where the buffalo hunters had gathered for needed supplies and exchange of information. Many famous hunters were at Adobe Walls at that time, including Bat Masterson and Billy Dixon. The war basically ended when the military slaughtered thousands of the Plains Indians' horses. Many tribal chiefs, leaders and warriors were imprisoned in Florida with many dying in captivity before they were released years later.

Billy the Kid and his gang were in Tascosa in the winter of 1878-1879 trading stolen horses with the ranchers, and again in 1880. He was also part of the reason the Panhandle Stock Association was formed in Mobeetie, Texas in 1880. In the winter of 1878, Dr. Henry F. Hoyt and Billy the Kid became good friends. Dr. Hoyt won an elegant lady's watch in a poker game, and knowing the Kid was searching for something special for his current sweetheart, presented Billy the watch as a gift for her. The Kid reciprocated by giving Dr. Hoyt a beautiful chestnut sorrel racehorse named Dandy Dick, branded B.B. on the left hip. The Kid tore off a piece of paper and made out a bill of sale at the McMasters and Howard store. Years later, it was discovered that the horse had been stolen from James Brady, sheriff of Lincoln County, when the Kid had shot his way out of Brady's jail, then shot and killed the sheriff and made off with his horse.

Henry Brown, an ex-member of Billy the Kid's gang, was a deputy or constable, and was fired a couple of months later for his aggressiveness and temper. He worked on the LIT ranch for a short while and was fired for the same reason. Several years later, he drifted toward Caldwell, Kansas, and became a peace officer. In

April 1884, Brown and three of his cronies rode into Medicine Lodge, Kansas with the intention of robbing the bank. The attempt failed and Brown was captured. He was killed a short time later while escaping from the Medicine Lodge jail.

It wasn't until 1882, under the direction of Texas Ranger G.W. Arrington, that the cleanup of Mobeetie and Fort Elliot began. Large numbers of fancy women, gamblers, men accomplished in robbery, cattle and horse theft, con games and similar practices, descended on the wild town of Tascosa.

Cape Willingham was sheriff of Tascosa and Frank Leigh was killed in the way described. McCullar was a mean cuss, best known for his cowboy shampoos (beating someone over the head with the handle of their gun). McCullar was ambushed and received the same treatment he had given many luckless men and lost his complete memory for three months. The beating changed his personality, and he became a peace officer for the law until Mexican Frank, probably because of his derision of his changed state, shot and killed him.

Sam Houston's youngest son, Temple was the first district attorney for the area, and one of the Southwest's most brilliant, eccentric and widely known criminal lawyers. He defended the most notorious: murderers, cattle thieves, gunfighters, buffalo hunters and prostitutes. He was one of the first whom the cliché 'silver-tongued orator' was applied. Temple not only served as the District Attorney for the Panhandle area, but two terms in the Texas State Senate and died of a brain hemorrhage at the age of forty-five.

Tascosa was a thriving town until the railroads bypassed it and laid its tracks toward Amarillo, Texas. The residents left, and the land and the old stone courthouse are now a part of Cal Farley's Boys Ranch.

It was not until the 1960s that the sexual revolution ended the holdover beliefs from the Victorian era. It released the men and women, who were usually kept in the dark about sex, and believed sex was meant for procreation—not for pleasure. However, that did not mean everyone previously believed those dictates.

We all have idealized assumptions about the growing west, but the more research I do, the more disturbing information I find. I often use the new information with hopes of making the west more realistic, though it may be information none of us imagined. Whether I agree or disagree with the practices is not relevant. It's the timeframe and how the people during that time perceived it.

In today's world, our history is being hidden, statues destroyed and a growing disdain for our great forebearers. Here's the issue—they were a different people with different value systems. We should be learning from their mistakes and adapting their wisdom into our lives, not judging them. We cannot grow by erasing history. Otherwise, we will be condemned in making the same types of mistakes and errors, never evolving into a better people.

TABLE OF CONTENT

Chapter 1
Early Spring, 1877
Verboten Love

THE POP of bullets and the twanging of arrows from the Kiowa hunters resounded throughout the prairie. Focusing on the last buffalo cow, Eyes-of-the-Sky pulled back the bowstring. With his arms straining, the string snapped, one end stinging his arm with the other end nearly hitting him in the eye, and the arrow nock still clamped between his fingers.

A grunt slipped between his clenched teeth as he watched Walks-a-Ways down the last cow with his old-fashioned rifle he had reengineered and decorated with feathers and paint. Walks-a-Ways was one of the few who still owned a white man's weapons. The rest had been confiscated after the Red River Wars, leaving most of the warriors with ancient weaponry.

The strong whiff of acrid gunpowder hit Eyes-of-the-Sky's nostrils and they flared with the caustic stench. His gaze briefly skimmed over Walks-a-Ways sitting upon his pony near the slain herd before he shifted and surveyed the land around them.

Walks-a-Ways sent a triumphant yet condescending glare toward Eyes-of-the-Sky. "Even a rabbit makes sure his bowstring is strong."

1

Eyes-of-the-Sky disregarded the braggart Walks-a-Ways' arrogant dialogue of his killing the bull and a cow, and his pointing at the younger warrior Eyes-of-the-Sky who made one kill. Ignoring him and the warriors' laughter that inferred he was still a young boy belonging with the Rabbit Warrior Society, Eyes-of-the-Sky kept his focus on the slain animals. He learned long ago avoiding Walks-a-Ways' constant baiting kept the peace, a lesson he learned the hard way, which started the day he stumbled into the camp searching for his father Red Eagle. Being half white and half Kiowa set him apart, and at the time, he only knew white ways. He still blushed with resentment remembering being grouped into the Rabbit Warrior Society where the boys were much younger than him.

They had been hunting buffalo for some time, crossing the plains and discovering fields of slaughtered buffalo without hides rotting in the hot sun or bleached bones drying in the wind. Many times, the women's wails split the air, heartbroken their main livelihood was decimated by the government-sanctioned buffalo hunters. This was the first herd they found, though a small one: two bulls, ten cows, and seven calves. It would barely supply enough meat through summer.

His heart heavy, he scrutinized how their lives had drastically changed from a freedom-loving, self-supporting tribe into a broken, government-reliant people. He snarled at his hand clutching his broken bow, fighting himself from throwing it on the ground and yielding into despair at the obfuscated oppression of his people. But his anger went deeper, deeper into the divide of his blood and for a woman who could not be his.

There was so much anger living within him that it made the first months living with the Kiowa hard while he tried forgetting his white ways, and of Walks-a-Ways' and his close-knit group of friends' incessant chiding to almost bullying. It was his father who taught him how redirection of his anger helped him excel in all his teachings. Perhaps his stubbornness of expecting something better sharpened his prowess as he relentlessly learned Kiowa hunting and fighting skills while absorbing the complex ways of the Kiowa culture, and therefore quickly advanced into four of the five warrior societies.

His horse shifted underneath him, reminding him part of his duty after downing the beasts was scrutinizing the area for outside threats while the women descended upon the slaughter field, gutted the animals, stripped hides, and cut meat for processing and storage, providing a hint of their previous life. By the time they completed their chores, barely a piece of bison would be left. Every portion—hide, tongue, meat, fat, tendons, bones and internal organs were exploitable.

It was watching the woman, who carried his unborn child, join the other women on the field. One side of his mouth quirked with his half smile, watching her slender, lithe form expertly strip the hide off a cow with her razor-sharp knife. Her body moved in graceful motions skinning the animal, emphasizing her beauty and displaying her confidence, which set her apart from others. After many years of their secret meetings, her appearance still sent flutters through his heart and stomach.

Another grunt slipped between his teeth, pulling his attention from her. Though she had his heart, the child she bore would be claimed by another. It was a sore spot, one he had trouble accepting. Glancing up, he spotted Walks-a-Ways scowling at him, his mouth tight against his teeth, his dark eyes filled with hate.

Eyes-of-the-Sky nonchalantly scanned the area around them, aware of the older man's contempt. The sentiments were mutual and began the day he first entered the village and was accepted by his father. He never understood their instant dislike toward each other. Perhaps he recognized the cruelty hidden underneath Walks-a-Ways' personality. He had seen and experienced it from others before.

Among the four social classes, Walks-a-Ways' was of the highest social caste, the *onde,* and he was also one of ten members of the *Koitsenko,* the most skilled and elite warriors who were selected from every society and branch of the Kiowa federation. One did not insinuate Walks-a-Ways only gained access in the *onde* and was selected for the *Koitsenko* when most of the elite leaders and warriors were either killed or imprisoned in Florida after the defeat of the Plains tribes.

Eyes-of-the-Sky's eyes narrowed, briefly wondering if Walks-a-Ways was suspicious of his second wife's infrequent encounters with him.

A shiver of dread slipped over his happiness as he studied the green grass sprouting among the dried golden-brown grasses, which grew during the warm spring days along with cold days splattered through them. The small herd had grazed near water, a small river branch where some trees grew along the river shore. There were white flowers blooming among the near leafless bushes, wild plum, grape and choke cherries, and would bear fruit in the midsummer unless another freeze or snow hit.

The land was bare and desolate but had many unusual spots, including the great Palo Duro Canyon, the thousand rolling hills, the large mesas or tablelands of the Llano Estacado and the flat plains spread across the area known as part of the Great American Desert or as the Tehans called it, the Texas Panhandle. Though water was scarce, the Plains Indians knew where it hid its water sources and the seasons they flowed.

Though many things were outlawed by the Indian agents, it was not unusual for Plains tribes to leave the reservation for hunting expeditions, supplementing the meager government-issued supplies or performing tribal rituals. With their freedoms taken away, disappearing from the reservation periodically provided some measure of liberty. It was a false liberation, though they had learned to avoid the white man and live in a measure of peace among them.

Watching his frail father Red Eagle help his elderly wife load the travois, shame filled him. After the bitter wars, which decimated many tribal members, along with the last few years living on the reservation, had drained his father of strength and vitality. With his father and stepmother's elderly age, it was he, his son, who was the primary family provider for survival food, and that was getting harder by the day.

His father often encouraged him to take a mate and keep their family strong, but his heart belonged with another woman from the *onde,* a mated woman who would never be his unless he found a way of changing tribal law. It was hard knowing his child would be raised by a man who hated him, and it was not a trouble-free circumstance. Something within him knew time was short, especially if he did not find a way before her pregnancy began showing.

Eyes-of-the-Sky suppressed his dark thoughts, shutting down

the reality of his people constrained on the reservation and being compelled to learn white ways such as farming, which few had interest in acquiring. The children were strongarmed away from families into mandated government-controlled schools, and along with their Christian indoctrination, could eventually wipe out memories of their indigenous ways. Was this how he wanted his child or children raised? This situation was as much a prison as his former life had been.

Turning away, he rode toward camp, worried about his father and his people. It was disheartening knowing that as a half-breed, if he wished, he could leave the reservation and live among the whites. The only thing keeping him with the Kiowas was the woman carrying his unborn child.

❧◦⟨◉⟩◦❧

THE WARMTH of the early spring day caressed Eyes-of-the-Sky's back and shoulders, the sunrise filled with the joyous laughter of children playing outside the camp with their bellies full, belonging among the few families who fought against placing them in the government-controlled schools. The winter had been long and hard, and they were facing starvation, the government rations insufficient in sustaining them until the next irregular issue of provisions.

By the next full moon, the tribe would finish storing the bison portions before returning and receiving their government allotments at the reservation. He hated the endless time lost while waiting impatiently in line to receive their allocations. It took away their manhood, their pride in supporting their families the Kiowa way.

With the hastily built racks containing thin strips of bison meat drying in the wind, the sounds of women's voices and laughter mingled with the children's distant enjoyment as the women dressed and prepared the precious food source. The lightheartedness was welcomed for it was a reminder of past times before the Red River wars.

Eyes-of-the-Sky averted his gaze downward, carefully working the fresh buffalo tendon by scrapping off meat and fat before letting the sun and wind dry it. It occupied him when thoughts of connecting with Sun-is-Setting invaded his mind. Instead, his thoughts drifted, remembering the life he lived in the white world with his mother, who had been captured by the Kiowa and then married Red Eagle. She was recaptured while she still carried him within her womb. Life had been hard and when she died, he was twelve years old. Finding his father had been the easy part. Learning Kiowa's way of life had been much harder.

Though life with the Kiowa was better, he still was not fully accepted. With his impure blood, he had already advanced as far as permittable within the Kiowa social and military organizations. He was of the second social order *ondegup'a,* which contained the lesser influential subchiefs, warriors and wealth. He worked hard honing his skills and wealth with the goals of elevating his status, but since he was of mixed blood, he could not advance farther, and there was no incentive for being selected as one of the ten *Koitsenko* or the *Real Dogs* as they were referred, for only pure-blooded Kiowa were eligible.

He stood, stretched, then hung the stripped tendon in the wind. After it dried, he would separate the fibers, rewet them, then twist them together until he had the length he needed for a strong and supple bow string.

Stretching, Eyes-of-the-Sky walked around his tepee, then stopped. Little Hare, her arms wrapped around a slumped Sun-is-Setting, who had her arms crossed over her midsection, stumbled out of their tepee and headed for the smaller one where women in their monthly cycle were housed, isolating them from warriors.

Black rage and concern crossed his features, but he quickly slipped back into his unreadable mask. Sun-is-Setting's face was pale, and she was obviously in pain. Was she miscarrying their child or had she been mistaken about her pregnancy? He watched Little Hare glance over her shoulder, her eyes narrowed, her mouth drawn into a straight line and her body tense before she turned back toward the woman she was guiding. Walks-a-Ways had left their tepee and stood tensely with his arms crossed over his chest, his face and jaw hard lines, glaring at his wives.

Walks-a-Ways turned and eyed Eyes-of-the-Sky, sending him a piercing, hate-filled glare. Eyes-of-the-Sky dropped his gaze and walked away toward the river, an uneasy shiver racing along his spine. He had no choice but act unconcerned. No one interfered with another's household issues, but it was not easy pretending he did not care and remain detached from the drama unfolding before him. And with her going into the bleeding lodge, it would prevent their planned encounter tonight.

With his high status, Walks-a-Ways had the privilege of acquiring more than one wife. Little Hare was his first wife, and after many years when she had not provided him with a child, he took another much younger second wife, Sun-is-Setting. Sun-is-Setting glanced back behind her before entering the door flap, and their gaze locked as he strode by before they guiltily looked away.

His jaw tightened and his teeth grinded together with his steady strut toward the river. He wanted and needed her. She was his life, his soul. She should be *his* wife, celebrating their love without sneaking around and hiding, but she was from the *onde* caste and married to another, and no one could mate outside their social group.

Eyes-of-the-Sky shuddered remembering his last meeting with Sun-is-Setting, one of happiness when she informed him she carried his child. Their secret rendezvous began many years ago, and within the little time they had, they shared their secret thoughts and desires. Sun-is-Setting had many times decried her husband's treatment of her, especially when he mounted her and quickly filled her with his seed. Still wet from filling Sun-is-Setting, he would lay beside his first wife and make love with her. Walks-a-Ways left no misinterpretation of his regard for his first wife, their moans and rustles of pleasure filling the tepee after he had spent just minutes with Sun-is-Setting, her grunts more of pain and dissatisfaction. Sun-is-Setting understood her husband regarded her as nothing more than a broodmare. He treated his first wife with respect, his second with disdain.

No matter how many times she begged her brother's return of her marriage price, he refused. Mayhaps if he returned her marriage price, their social status of the *onde* would be reduced to the *ondegup'a.* It was possible but not probable since it was rare for the *onde* having the same condemnation and retributions for misdeeds as the other classes, if any at all.

The disrespect her husband showed her was troublesome for Eyes-of-the-Sky. He found Sun-is-Setting a delightful, intelligent, caring and rebellious woman. It was her rebellion that sweetened his life and their infrequent unions. It was him she preferred, and he reaped the benefits. She was the bright point of his life, the spark that kept him striving to be the best.

They were both young and had become friends along with becoming lovers. Walks-a-Ways and Little Hare were much older than Sun-is-Setting. Sun-is-Setting proclaimed it was Little Hare who forced Walks-a-Ways into acquiring a second, younger wife. Little Hare wanted children and blamed herself for being barren.

The exhilaration of sneaking away brought them closer when discussing their lives and problems, and both their dreams of one day being mated. There was also Eyes-of-the-Sky's mixed blood keeping him from being elevated into the *onde* caste.

But that had all changed when last they met, and she giddily told him she was pregnant. They both knew it was his child though her husband spilled his seed within her womb every night he was not leading a war party, on a hunting expedition, in tribal meetings or keeping night watch.

There were no rumors or bits of information Eyes-of-the-Sky could construe that indicated Walks-a-Ways suspected she had a lover. However, no one spoke about this incident of the bleeding tepee for no one interfered with a mated couple and their private lives, and especially not him. If he reacted or spoke, it could prove their affair and could cost Sun-is-Setting's life.

◦◦◦◦◦◦◦◦◦

TOSSING and turning, unable to sleep from worrying about Sun-is-Setting, Eyes-of-the-Sky rose from his sleeping rug and left the tepee. The moon gave scant light with its sickle-thin appearance in the dark, starry night, but his night vision was good as he made his way toward the rushing river. Perhaps if he walked awhile, he would find rest tonight. Nodding at a warrior policing the encampment, he slipped among the trees.

With the crisp spring wind cutting through his clothing, he walked faster. He had gone a good distance from the encampment when he heard someone crying. Stopping, he listened closely, a chill racing along his spine, his heartbeat erratic and his breathing somewhat labored. *Who was crying? Could it be Sun-is-Setting?*

8

Surely not, though they had arranged a meeting tonight, she would not have left the women's tepee even after Walks-a-Ways left with another hunting party. His feet making no noise, he angled toward the sounds and stopped when the dark figure of someone kneeling on the ground, their hands covering their face, the form small and slender, and their clothing female.

"Do you need help?" he whispered, alarmed. Her cries stopped and she looked up in surprise, the tears cascading down her cheeks catching the feeble moonlight in soft, muted streams.

"Eyes-of-the-Sky? I was afraid you had forsaken me too. My heart is broken and broke more when you were not waiting for me." Sun-is-Setting swiped at her tears, sweeping away the moisture.

He took several steps toward her, needing her in his arms. She threw up her hands, stopping him. "No, do not come closer!"

"I saw you and Little Hare enter the women's tepee. Are you not carrying my child?" He paused with her drawing in a sharp breath and fresh tears appearing down her cheeks. He moved a little closer with her whispered words.

"I no longer carry the child."

"I do not understand," he whispered, crouching in front of her, fighting himself from reaching out in desperation and holding her, giving her comfort within his arms.

Her voice was broken, carrying a suffering which thickened the air around them. "Little Hare noticed I had not visited the women's hut in three moons. As we went toward our beds, she happily told our husband I was with child."

She took several deep breaths, fighting the sobs tearing from her throat, her words erratic and hesitant. "Our husband glared at me with hatred before he hit me many times in the stomach. It was Little Hare who made him stop before he could kill me."

Sobbing, Sun-is-Setting took another painful breath. "Little Hare found me bleeding at sunrise. I lost our child." Her shoulders shook with her soft cries. "I am sorry. I could not prevent it."

The anger shooting through him forced him to his feet, his eyes blazing deep black in the night. "I will kill him!"

"No, you cannot! It will destroy us both!" she exclaimed, her eyes beseeching his. "I beg you, please do not confront him or he *will* kill us both."

Eyes-of-the-Sky ran his hand across his brow, his eyes narrowed, his heart breaking, his words low and pleading, "Go beg your brother again to return your bride price. It is the only way we might have a chance of becoming mated."

A helpless sob sounded before she answered, "I have asked several times, and he refuses. He fears the *onde,* and us being demoted lower."

"Your brother is useless," he growled, frustrated.

"Do not," Sun-is-Setting begged, "do not speak so about my brother. We must find another way."

He sat down in front of her again, fighting the need of pulling her into his arms and comforting her while his mind searched for a solution for their problem. "We will leave here and find another tribe who will accept us or we will go live with the white eyes," he reasoned, his mind racing for a solution. "Gather what you need. We will leave at the next darkness while your husband is gone."

Chapter 2
Stolen Moments

RESTLESS, Eyes-of-the-Sky sat cross-legged in front of his tepee, a lilting voice and sudden laughter piercing his heart. He had been on several hunting trips and had brought back deer and antelopes that his stepmother was processing, plus other small animals and storing them for the coming seasons. It was imperative he provide them with sufficient food before he left with Sun-is-Setting, but that had been delayed.

His bow lay across his lap as he observed Sun-is-Setting's willowy body bend and twist while working beside Little Hare as they scraped and smoothed a fresh buffalo hide. Heavy-hearted, he and Sun-is-Setting had not met again since the night she escaped from the women's tepee, and he found her crying by the river. While working, she remained sober faced, no smile tugged her lips though Little Hare gaily tried lightening her mood. Her sadness and grief were palpable, her moves sluggish and her eyes always cast downward.

Seeing her thus broke his heart, yet at this point, there was nothing he could do. After Sun-is-Setting's miscarriage, Walks-a-Ways stayed close by when they were not hunting, shrewdly scrutinizing his wives. The chiefs had ordered one last major hunt for either bison, deer, antelope, elk, bear or any animal sufficient for food. Time was short and the camp would be breaking soon after the last hunt and heading for the reservation.

His lips formed a grim line knowing in the close-knit encampment, whether here or at the reservation, it was only a matter of time before their illicit affair was discovered, so quick action was needed. Walks-a-Ways had been in camp the same nights as Eyes-of-the-Sky, preventing their union during darkness. It had been so long since he was able to touch her, hear her melodic voice when they spoke or make love with her, so long ago his body and heart ached for her.

Standing, he left the camp and meandered along the free-flowing stream searching for a place for his morning absolution. Finding a secluded spot, he untied his long black hair and slipped out of his mixture of white man and Kiowa clothing before stepping into the water. The coldness took his breath away, nevertheless he waded toward midstream and scrubbed his body with sand, his memories spilling over.

Before the Red River Wars during the annual Sun Dance where he triumphantly proved himself during the gathering of different tribes, sexual promiscuousness, if not caught, was also part of the celebration. Stealing another man's wife anytime without his knowledge was a game and counted as coup—a big joke on the husband.

It was during the celebration Sun-is-Setting approached him, whispering her desire for him and offering herself. She was a little older than him and claimed she was captivated by his light blue eyes. She lured him toward a well-hidden place among the trees surrounding the river far from the different tribal camps.

They both knew their meeting outside their castes was forbidden except during this time, but maybe it was the forbidden, the thrill that enhanced their encounters.

With his memories of their first night together, Eyes-of-the-Sky lowered his hand underneath the water, teasing the heat springing below his belly. Many full moons had passed since they had been together and his need was great. Moving his hand slowly along his jutting erection, he remembered their laughter until he reached for her, tugged her against him and captured her soft, inviting lips with his.

Sun-is-Setting stiffened until his kiss softened and he stroked her lips with his tongue. Opening her mouth, she swiped hers between his lips, encouraging him. It was her first white man's kiss and she quickly adapted, her moans filling his mouth while his hands traced the curve of her waist until he captured her breasts.

With the sounds of drums beating in the distance, the trees blocking the moon and stars, they relied on touch, their bodies dark blots within the darkness. She stepped back from him and undressed, nodding her approval of his eager shucking of his own clothing.

The memory of her pressing her naked form against his, her skin smooth, soft and warm felt so right. Her fingers skimmed along his chest downward until she reached his hardness. The warmth of her small hand moving along his hard member sent shivers of longing through every nerve ending, and he felt himself engorge firmer with her fingers encircling it. She moaned against his mouth, "My husband is rough and has no care for my pleasure. Let me teach you the ways of satisfying a woman and show you greater joy."

While remembering the feel of her soft, warm naked flesh against his, his hand tightened around his shaft, feeling it enlarge and his testicles constrict. She had whispered, "You are a man now, but is this your first time with a woman?"

Speechless, he nodded. He felt her smile instead of seeing it in the darkness, and when she bent her knees toward the ground, he knelt with her. Lying on the grass, she pulled him down with her, took his hand and placed it between her legs, guiding it until his finger slipped inside her wet channel. "You will mount me and quickly experience your first time, then you will go slow afterwards."

He scooted between her legs, and she reached for his erect staff, positioning it at her hungry entrance. When the head was barely in, she stiffened and whispered, "Go slow for you are much larger than my husband."

It took all his willpower not to slam into her but enter her slowly. He eased into her, enjoying the wonderful sensation of moist softness enveloping tightly around his shaft until he was buried deep inside her.

She sighed, lifting her hips toward his. "I will make you into a wonderful lover."

Remembering how they took pleasure from each other, his hand tightened and his motions increased in speed. It was after their second round and when they were lying in each other's arms, he asked her, "Why did you choose me?"

She giggled softly, pressing herself closer and running her hands over his buttocks. "When you first came, your eyes spoke to me. Such anger, such passion, but we were both young. I have watched you become a strong and proud warrior and knew I would have you."

"And now that you have me, what now?" he asked.

She shifted back from him and dropped her hand, caressing and coaxing his soft member hard again while her low voice whispered in his ear, "You will give me the passion I need and a person I can share my life with though we must do it in secret."

"Walks-a-Ways has never accepted me as Kiowa. Why do you bring such danger upon us?"

"You were not born into our tribe and you threaten my husband with your quickness of becoming an excellent warrior and hunter. He believes you will somehow eventually take his place in the *Real Dogs,* and he is not pleased. Besides, does it not make the passion burn brighter? See, you are already hard again. And you are young and strong, which with me teaching you, you will make a good lover who can satisfy me in ways my husband cannot."

Their infrequent, yet fulfilling meetings, quickly progressed into a deeper connection. For the past several years, he gave her the full benefit of her patient teachings: how to love and cherish the delicate vessel of a woman's body, be patient and heighten her pleasure and thereby increase his own. She was his teacher, his safe haven, his life, his nemesis, his compensation *and* his only lover. The bond remained unbroken and now they were trapped in a vicious cycle of their own making.

It was remembering again of her telling him she was carrying his child, then her losing it when Walks-a-Ways '*accidentally*' punched her multiple times in the stomach, not only killing the unborn baby but seriously injuring her. And he could not say a word or react against the incident. That hurt—his inability of claiming and protecting her. Prying his hand loose from his aching, unfulfilled extremity, he ducked under the chilly water, his last memory dousing his desire.

❦

FROM HER peripheral vision, Sun-is-Setting watched Eyes-of-the-Sky skirt around the tepees and disappear into the surrounding trees along the river. Waiting a bit longer, she made a feeble excuse and left the women's company. Her action bold, she could no more stop herself from following him than she could stop the sun rising each morning. She prayed each day that the Great Spirit would release her from the torment of loving a man not her husband, yet she was unable and unwilling to halt their forbidden trysts.

She needed Eyes-of-the-Sky's arms around her so she could heal from the loss. With her husband constantly watching her, secret contact between her and Eyes-of-the-Sky had been impossible after she lost their child. Soon they would be packing up and leaving. Time was running out and their coming together would be more infrequent once they were back on the reservation. She flitted with the idea of stopping their rendezvous, terrified they would eventually be caught, and recognizing she was also being careless. Saving both their lives was imperative—they must end their connection. Only once more would she meet him before they broke camp in two risings of the sun.

With winter ending when it had been too cold and harsh for their meetings, spring brought warm days along with the cold. It was a warm day and she needed him, ached for him and too impatient for the cover of night.

Glancing furtively around her, she followed him into the trees along the sandy riverbank, her desire growing when she spied him totally immerse his body underneath the water, then soar through the surface with clear water shedding from his slim body. Shaking his wet, raven black hair, silver droplets spread in all directions and his copper skin glistened, accenting his slender, muscular form. Taking a deep breath, she stepped from her hiding place.

❦

WADING toward the shore, Eyes-of-the-Sky froze and glanced around them, irritated with her careless disregard for caution showing in his ice blue eyes. "Go back."

Holding his gaze with hers, Sun-is-Setting stepped closer and slipped out of her clothing. Prickles of danger racing along his spine, Eyes-of-the-Sky was fascinated by his first glimpse of the sun dappling her naked body. They had always made love in the dark of night, away from prying eyes, ashamed yet needful of each other. He knew her body more intimately than his own, the feel of her, the taste of her, her soft voice and low moans.

The last time he mated with her was when she told him she carried his offspring, and his desire rose sharply with her physical image and the glory of her nakedness. He had often fantasized about her nude in the light of day, and she proved more sensual than he dreamed.

She pressed her bare, petite form against his, but with the warmth radiating from her naked body, his resolve to send her away vanished. He captured her uplifted lips and deepened the kiss, the one white man's custom he kept. His hunger burning hotly as hers, he lowered her on the grassy banks, and they dispensed with preliminaries, mating like animals, taking and receiving, plunging toward fulfillment and release, an aura of danger, of expectancy heightening their passion.

Their encounter quickly concluded with each hastily dressing. Working tangles from his wet hair, he tied the length at the back of his head and walked away, saying, "Tonight. Since it appears your husband suspects us, we leave at dark. It is the only way we can be together."

Sun-is-Setting nodded her agreement and hurriedly gathered wood, obscuring her illicit rendezvous with Eyes-of-the-Sky and excited about escaping, though discombobulated about how they would survive.

A shadow fell over her and she glanced up, shock and guilt crossing her face. Her husband Walks-a-Ways stood over her, his legs splayed, his hands clenched against his hips, his face tense and his black eyes blazing. Fear clutched her in its unrelenting claws; he reached down and roughly jerked her toward him. The dried tree branches in her arms dropped forgotten at her feet.

Silent, his fingers bruising the tender flesh of her arm, Walks-a-Ways dragged Sun-is-Setting toward the village, then shoved her in front of the gathered, curious people. "I have caught my second wife

Sun-is-Setting preforming wifely duties with another man. For her betrayal, I declare a feast upon the prairie for all the warriors of the Taupeko Society."

Sun-is-Setting froze in disbelief, her face drained of color with her husband's pronounced sentence—inviting all the unmarried men of the *Crazy Horses* warrior society, except her family, where she would be any man's wife. She had prepared herself, if caught, by expecting her nose cut off or killed outright, but not this. This retribution was so rare, she had not remotely considered it. The declaration was decreeing an agonizing death sentence.

Eyes-of-the-Sky watched Walks-a-Ways force Sun-is-Setting into the village and stop in the center of camp. His heart hammering and painfully knocking a wicked tattoo against his chest, he hurried toward them, hearing Walks-a-Ways' proclamation. The people were stunned into silence, and Eyes-of-the-Sky's shocked voice rang throughout the encampment. "No!"

His black eyes flashing against the interruption, Walks-a-Ways pointed his index finger in his direction. "You, with your white ways, have disgraced me, and I demand payment when I return."

"Take everything I own and give me Sun-is-Setting. Do not punish her this way." Eyes-of-the-Sky leveled his voice, keeping the unmanly sound of begging from it.

"No other man shall have my wife. She broke tribal law of our union, shaming me with a white eye who is of the lower caste. I have spoken," Walks-a-Ways growled, his oblique eyes glaring at Eyes-of-the-Sky.

With the second slur against him, Eyes-of-the-Sky reached for the knife at his waist. Someone grabbed his arms and forced them behind his back, holding him motionless before he could fully draw his weapon.

"Be still, Brother. It is his right."

Recognizing his friend Flies-Like-An-Eagle's voice, he strained unsuccessfully against his friend's arms. The pounding of a pole being driven into the ground reverberated through his skull, shouting the uselessness of fighting the whole tribe.

Warriors fastened his hands with a leather thong and tied it around the pole. Helpless, he watched Walks-a-Ways drag Sun-is-Setting toward the open prairie, the members of the Taupeko Society whooping and hollering behind them, her blank, lifeless expression foreshadowed in her black eyes.

Holding back his sorrow and his eyes flaming with fury, he stared straight ahead, neither flinching nor speaking while women and children taunted him, poked and pinched his stiffly held body all through the morning until late in the day. A feast upon the prairie was tantamount to death with the warriors repeatedly violating her body until all were sated. His only hope was she survived and he could help her later, but what devastated him the most was his inability of protecting her. He was being shamed, not so much for stealing another man's wife but for being caught.

A slow-burning rage emerged within him that demanded Walks-a-Ways' life for his cruel punishment of Sun-is-Setting. And yet, he denied tribal law giving Walks-a-Ways the right of disciplining his wife however he deemed appropriate. Right or wrong, he could not accept the judgement—would not accept it!

The shadows lengthened toward sunset before the warriors arrived back at the encampment. Walks-a-Ways and the braves of the Taupeko society were met with taunts and jeers from the women. The men ducked their heads abashedly, ignoring them. Walks-a-Ways walked with his head held high and his black eyes mirroring his satisfaction. His first wife Little Hare briefly glared at him before lowering her head and slipping back into the tepee.

His hands freed, Eyes-of-the-Sky dropped his upper appendages and rubbed his wrists, restoring circulation—the tingling, piercing needlepoints shooting through his arms and hands as blood flowed freely through his veins. Glaring at Walks-a-Ways, his light-colored eyes blazing hatred, he shifted his attention and faced his father Red Eagle, waiting for his condemnation.

Red Eagle, a lesser influential chief, watched his son, his own eyes mirroring sadness. "Fire shall consume your possessions and your horses forfeited. You have dishonored your name and warrior status."

With his father speaking the harshest castigation, Eyes-of-the-Sky stood straight and proud, refusing humiliation for his loving Sun-is-Setting. "I regret my actions dishonor you, Father. The punishment is severe, too great against Sun-is-Setting and me."

"It is not enough," shouted Walks-a-Ways. "He has sullied the whole tribe with his adulterous white ways."

"Enough! He is Kiowa. Has he not proven his worth in giving gifts and counting coups? You are angry, but do not tear down his worth. He is my son and I have passed judgement." Red Eagle turned from Walks-a-Ways and back toward his son. "I have spoken."

More words useless, Eyes-of-the-Sky recognized his status had been dropped to the *kaan,* the next lowest caste. Now he had no wealth and was disgraced. It was his warrior experience that prevented his caste changing to the lowest level of *depone.* "You have passed the harshest sentence upon me; therefore, I ask for my war pony, nothing more, and I will leave."

"So be it," Red Eagle proclaimed in a dispassionate voice, feeling dead inside. The words brought more disgrace upon him— his son was running away like a dog with his tail stuck between his legs instead of facing the tribe like a man. His son, who was the fiercest of warriors, fighting more battles than just men, took the coward's way out.

Red Eagle took the knife hanging by his side, quickly chopped off his gray hair and threw it at his son's feet. Turning from him, he staggered toward his tepee while pulling his gray army blanket around his ragged-cut hair. Kneeling in front of his lodge, he sobbed, his thin shoulders shaking in grief.

His wails signaled the others, and women keened and wept for the two dead people—Eyes-of-the-Sky and Sun-is-Setting.

Eyes-of-the-Sky turned from the people, his heart heavy with his losses. His father cutting off his long hair signified his son was dead. His earthly belongings and tepee were set on fire, and unemotionally, he grabbed the bridle of his war pony while watching the yellow and red flames leap toward the center and black smoke curl toward the sky. Likewise, he also burned with suppressed rage and vengeance, his Kiowa life vanishing with the smoke.

Leaping gracefully on the back of his pony, he turned it toward the direction Walks-a-Ways had taken Sun-is-Setting. The pounding of the horse hooves matched the pounding of his heart, each beat crying out against fate. Half-remembered prayers to a God nearly forgotten drummed through his brain while he mentally prayed for

Sun-is-Setting's life, and at the same time cursed her brother for his selfishness. Her brother had avoided all the drama, his shame almost as great as Sun-is-Setting's.

Chapter 3
Shirt Off His Back

SPOTTING Sun-is-Setting's prone form lying lifeless on the green prairie grasses near the twin hillock, Eyes-of-the-Sky jumped from his pony before it stopped. The ground, saturated with her blood, was black underneath her. He silently screamed at the cruel fates for allowing this punishment against the woman who cherished and loved him, whose unbridled love provided him the necessary strength of excelling as a Kiowa warrior.

He groaned out loud and ripped off his shirt, placing it between her legs in a futile attempt to staunch the flow of blood. Her sweet body, covered with red marks now transmuting into dark bruises, had given him her unboundless love and pleasure. He picked up her skirt lying beside her and tenderly covered her nakedness. Tears flowing freely down his copper cheeks, he lifted her head in his arms and cradled her, crooning soft words of love and encouragement.

With his tears falling over her face, her eyelids fluttered open, revealing dimmed eyes. Smiling, her pale face momentarily brightened. "Eyes-of-the-Sky, I prayed I would see you again. Promise me you will bury me on the hill facing the rising sun."

"No, you will not die," he denied strongly, pressing her cold face closer against his bared chest. "I will carry you away and seek out the white man's doctor. He will help you."

Her spirit draining from her and soaking his shirt with her

21

lifeblood, Sun-is-Setting lifted her hand and caressed his cheek, smiling tenderly at his foolishness. "My heart is filled by seeing you again. Now I can leave this life. The Great Spirit has answered my prayers and has freed me from my torment. Just kiss me one more time," she whispered, her voice growing weaker with each word.

Bending, he took her lips with his, tasting his salty tears on them and seeking to breathe life back into her. With a soft, contented sigh, she gave him her last breath.

He released her still warm lips, his tears forming rivulets down her cheeks. With unsteady hands, he closed her sightless eyes, then lifted her slender body in his arms.

Trudging toward the twin hillock overlooking the stream where they last made love, he laid Sun-is-Setting gently on the ground, dropped beside her with his knife clutched in his hand and dug her grave in the hardpacked ground. With the earth awakening with life, he was burying his dead love, the very actions screaming out how short and futile life is.

He lowered her into a sitting position, drew her knees up against her chest and faced her toward the east. Rising, he cut off his long, black hair above the leather thong holding it and threw it into the grave with her, giving her his pride and unsurmountable grief. After he filled the grave and placed rocks over it, he lifted his arms toward the fiery ball of the setting sun and sang his death song for her, the low, sorrow-filled rhythmic sound resonating throughout the hills.

Chanting toward the lowering sun which cast his bronzed chest in red highlights, his song filled the air with sadness. The air grew colder, prickling his bare flesh, but he felt nothing while pouring out his grief to the silent stars and the cold face of the pale moon. A lone coyote cried out his lonesome, wistful song and intermingled with the rhythmic voice of Eyes-of-the-Sky's rising and falling throughout the hillsides.

Dawn lighted the world in golds, dusky purples and pinks, and he turned toward the east, his face drained of emotion, his voice hoarse, his lean frame straight and proud. His heart a heavy burden in the pit of his stomach, he made a mocking salute before vaulting on the back of his pony and heading toward the morning sun, not once looking back as he left his death song and Indian heritage with the one woman who had given his life meaning. Feeling nothing, thinking nothing, he was once again propelled into the white man's world.

❧❧❧

EYES-OF-THE-SKY traveled through the Texas Panhandle, the last hunting ground of the proud Plains Indians, in search for a tie with all he had lost in one short day. Leaving Sun-is-Setting's lifeless body and his Indian birthright was the hardest thing he had ever done. For a long time, he cared not if he lived or died, but some hidden instinct kept him functioning.

He left his tribe with his war pony, white man's blue army pants, moccasins and hunting knife. An inner well of determination kept him going during the first weeks of cool days and cold nights. He lived by instinct alone, falling back on his early training; a warrior living off the sparse offerings of Mother Earth and a few hapless rabbits snared in his crude traps. This period of being alone without another human being for miles around sapped the listless, emotionless mindset and the full blow of all he lost hit him with a crushing weight. Pure, consuming hatred at the fates burned through his soul and from the hate, he cared naught for anything.

All that had been sweet and pure in his short life had been mercilessly stolen, the tender core of his soul torn from him cruelly and suddenly. Though they both knew they might be caught, it still could not prepare them for the climactic consequences. His world's existence stopped with her death, his breath stolen from his body and thrown into the white man's hell. He wondered if fate was conniving on how much more he might bear until he completely broke apart.

His gentle mother, captured by the Kiowas when she was a young girl and raised by them, honorably married Red Eagle. While she carried him within her womb, she had been recaptured by the white eyes, and her short life was one of ostracism, cruel taunts and injustice. From the beginning of his memory, the suffering in her face haunted him. Her silent sobs of hurt, grief and remorse shook her thin frame when she thought he was asleep. Her own race treated her like she had a dreaded disease while her adoptive race treated her with the honor of a warrior's woman.

He was born fighting. He was a breed, a mixed blood whom the white man despised. His days were filled with loathing for the very ones who taunted and abused him, but most of all for the cruel words and actions toward his beloved mother. When his mother died of a broken heart, he was left with mingled feelings of hatred and love for her race.

The easy part was finding his father whose tribe was located near the Indian reservation south of Kansas. Thankfully, his mother had taught him the Kiowa tongue along with English, and which proved useful for his father and the Kiowa when they needed an interpreter. He also became a mighty warrior, learning skills that were foreign, but seemed somehow ingrained as he proved very skillful within a short period of time. It was his natural ability that propelled him as one of the best hunters and warriors within the tribe, closely rivalling Walks-A-Ways' status. The older warrior had a driving hatred toward him. Eyes-of-the-Sky's quick elevation challenged his own status as a warrior and hunter.

It was during the Red River Wars between the southern Plains Indians and soldiers that food became more scarce. Buffalo hunters, with the government's sanction, destroyed the mighty American buffalo, the Plains Indians' primary food source and almost everything they needed for survival, which by their destruction, forced them on the reservations. Truthfully, some tribes went willingly before the war, and some were forced later after their leaders and best warriors were captured and imprisoned in Florida.

His depression increased the further east he traveled and passed the putrid remains of rotting buffalo without their hides. His anger grew exponentially watching the big, black beast with smoke erupting from its nostril that some called a train, and men riding its back with some men along its side shooting at a large herd of bison for sport. The animals dropped and lay in waste along the railroad track.

Cresting a hill, he stared at the hundreds of bleached white buffalo bones scattered across the valley, reminding him of not only the desolation of their food source, but the desolation of his heart. He jerked the reins and turned his mount, heading back toward the west, wondering why all the females he loved with his whole heart but in different ways, he lost to the one thing he could not fight.

Death! The very word sent shudders of fear racing through his slender frame.

Thunder clouds in varying shades of gray covered the vast skies and the sun slipped behind a cloud. Toward the northwest, the clouds grew black, giving advanced warning of worsening weather. Jagged lightning split the skies and danced along the dry grasses, sending acrid smoke into the air. He apprehensively watched the ominous clouds and the black funnel drop lower toward the ground. The tornado jumped and whirled along the prairie for several seconds before rising and disappearing once more into blackness.

The weather kept in tune with his emotions: the ominous clouds—the deep hurt in his soul, the rain—the unshed tears he kept back, the tornado—the turbulence inside of him. His wrath kept his insides warm though his vulnerable body shivered in the pouring rain, and yet, his ingrained habit of scanning the land with eagle-sharp eyes was still an undeniable part of him. He saw the lone rider's blurry form through the gray downpour: the man hunched over his mount's neck and his face covered by his bowler hat. The horse stumbled on the sharp incline of rocks, and horse and rider fell, tumbling down the slope.

Without thinking, Eyes-of-the-Sky edged his pony toward the fallen man. He leaped lightly from its back and landed on cat-like feet beside the stranger. Kneeling beside him, he put his hand against the man's chest. The shallow rhythm and fall assured him he still lived. He checked him over for broken bones and found none, instead discovered the man had a raging fever.

The man's roan gelding, his massive head bent against the rain, stood close by. Eyes-of-the-Sky took the reins and hooked them on his war pony's saddle horn. He lifted the unconscious man's dead weight, slung him across his pony's back and mounted behind him, holding the man in position as he rode toward the river.

Eyes-of-the-Sky wondered why he bothered with this white eyes. He was more dead than alive, and even so, what could he offer? He had neither shelter nor food. Why should he try when he could not save the woman he loved?

The fates laughed down at him in rumbling clashes, calling him less than a man, shouting they controlled destiny, not him. The jagged flash of their eyes streaked across the sky, brightening the way momentarily before rumbling with laughter, daring him to save this one, one he did not know or care about. *'Leave him, leave him,'* the wind screeched the closer he neared the Canadian River. *'Let us decide whether he lives or dies. You are not man enough to change his fate for you were not man enough to save the woman you loved.'*

"Be still, crones!" he shouted, but the wind threw his words back into his face.

The stinging spray of the rain forcing his eyes and mouth closed, he kicked the sides of his war pony and edged him into a stand of trees. Kneading his mount into the respiteful haven, he ducked his head underneath the low hanging branches. The leaves softened the downpour, but the screeching wind grew louder like so many voices of fate ridiculing him.

'Fool, you cannot win. You belong to no people. Give up and die with the one you carry across your saddle.' Soul weakened, Eyes-of-the-Sky violently shivered, the enclosure of trees cold as a grave. His pony stopped when the gentle pressure at his sides trembled and cocked his head around looking inquisitively at his rider.

His eyes dull patches within his dark copper face, the uselessness of life made Eyes-of-the-Sky wonder why he was trying. Had he not tried twice before and lost?

'Eyes-of-the-Sky, my beloved,' a gentle, loving voice whispered. *'Fight them. Do not let them win. I shall always be with you for I am a part of you and you of me. Give this white eye a chance for life,'* Sun-is-Setting's voice whispered through his tormented brain, beseeching him as her sweet face rose before him. Her spirit flooded his soul with warmth, and his shivering lessened, igniting a determination of saving this white-eye for Sun-is-Setting.

Selecting a sheltered place, he jumped lithely from the pony's back and walked toward the roan gelding. He found a bedroll, coffeepot, skillet and some food supplies from the gear stowed behind the saddle. After spreading the bedroll on the wet ground, he took the unconscious man, laid him on the bedroll, stripped his wet clothing from him and rolled him snugly in the warm tarpaulin-surrounded blankets.

After he unsaddled the roan and placed the saddle underneath the unconscious man's head, he built a crude shelter over him, then found pieces of dried wood and built a fire. The fire crackled and popped, and smoke rose. He rubbed his hands over it, hoping it would restore warmth through his sparsely clad body.

The smell of ground coffee teased his taste buds until he reached for the blue and white speckled coffeepot. Braving the pounding rain, he filled it at the fast-flowing river, then settled the coffeepot on the fire. While waiting for it to boil, he cut jerky into small chunks and threw them in the skillet, the actions distracting his overactive mind.

Eyes-of-the-Sky sat back, crossed his legs and tore the man's already ripped shirt into strips, then held them out in the rain before placing them over the man's fevered forehead.

The aroma of beef jerky stew and coffee scented the fresh air while the rain slowed to a steady drizzle, then stopped. The stranger slept fitfully and mumbled incoherently. Kneeling over the stranger, Eyes-of-the-Sky changed the wet rag over his forehead. The stranger opened his eyes and stared at the dark face above him, his gray eyes mirroring confusion.

"Who are you?" the stranger croaked, his heartbeat increasing when he saw the wild-looking young man with the jagged edges of his raven black hair plastered around his head, lean over him. Only the light blue eyes alleviated his fear a stray band of Indians had captured him.

"Eye..." Eyes-of-the-Sky stopped, realizing his Kiowa name was now inappropriate. "Landon Wade, and you?"

"Kerby Olsen." The stranger fell back onto the saddle placed underneath his head. His throat burned and his tongue felt three times too big for his mouth. It was a strange feeling, especially when the last he remembered rain was pouring down in thick sheets.

Landon slowly nodded greeting, and the man closed his eyes. "Drink," he ordered, squeezing fresh rainwater over the man's lips. The water droplets splattered over Kerby's mouth and dribbled down his chin. At first, Landon did not think he heard him, but after a matter of moments, the stranger's tongue snaked out and took in the wetness.

⌒◉⌒⌒◉⌒

FOR THE next couple of days, Landon took care of Kerby Olsen, and Kerby gradually gained strength. Landon spoke few words while Kerby kept a steady conversation going until his eyelids closed in sleep.

"I own the KO Ranch about thirty miles from here. I was after some strays when the downpour started. I was in such a hurry to catch the bastards before the rain washed the tracks away that I didn't take time to put on my coat or slicker." Kerby looked at the strange young man who sat Indian fashion and stared into the fire. He shook his head, wondering if the youngster had heard him. Landon was a strange one, hardly speaking yet always interpreting his every need. He owed him a debt of gratitude which could never be repaid. If Landon had not come along when he did, he might be dead, and it was something he would never forget.

Even though Landon seldom spoke, Kerby would eat his hat if the young man did not have Indian blood in him. The man's very silence and faraway eyes bespoke and invoked curiosity, leaving unanswered questions preying on Kerby's mind. It was nothing Landon did or said for he was the very essence of kindness. It was more what he did not say. It was the very sullenness intriguing Kerby, and at the same time, appeasing him into trusting him. He could not explain the strange feelings toward the young man; they were something evoked, not understood. At the same time there grew a feeling of trust between them and grew still more when Kerby searched through his saddlebags for an extra shirt and found his money and personal belongings untouched.

Kerby regained most of his strength, and assuming his wife was probably worried about him, gathered his belongings. After he saddled his roan, he put his foot in the stirrup, then turned toward Landon. "You saved my life and I owe you a debt of gratitude. Ask anything you wish of me, and I'll grant it if it's in my power to do so."

"I want nothing," Landon stated flatly.

Kerby stared at him, his mouth gaping open. "Nothing? Well, I'll be a son of a bitch. No man wants nothing. Come, tell me what you want."

Landon stared through Kerby, his mind screaming, *'You cannot bring back Sun-is-Setting and nothing else matters.'*

Kerby waited for an answer, but Landon remained silent. Lifting himself into the saddle, he turned back toward Landon. "If you ever need a job or anything else, you come to the KO Ranch and I'll take care of it, you hear? The ranch is west of here."

Landon focused on Kerby and repeated, "I want nothing."

Kerby glanced at Landon's expressionless eyes and his bare chest. In a moment of compassion, he unbuttoned his shirt and threw it at Landon. The blue shirt fluttered toward the ground and landed at Landon's feet. "It's yours. It's the least I can do for you now." He kicked his heels into the roan's flanks before Landon could refuse and headed home.

Landon watched Kerby until he was nothing but a speck in the distance before he bent and picked up the shirt. Kerby did not know it, but his one small act of kindness was enough to breach the rugged bridge across his tormented brain. By giving him the shirt off his back, Landon swore then and there Kerby Olsen had a true friend in him.

The rest of the summer spent in loneliness; he avoided human beings until he gained control over his burning rage. He lived off the land and conversed with nature, becoming one with it.

Winter came with a vengeance, and he nearly froze and starved during the first weeks. Frozen cattle spotted the stark landscape, and he made his living by stripping the hides and selling them. He knew all too well a man could not live without the white man's gold. The venture did not last long with winter's progression and grew worse with his war pony succumbing to the cold weather and starvation. He found himself afoot on the KO Ranch, and swallowing his pride, he walked on near frozen feet and asked Kerby Olsen for a job.

Chapter 4
1880-1881
A Ruby Among Emeralds

HER HAIR flying out behind her in a silken, auburn-red banner, Crimson Rose McFarlin leaned over the mare's neck. Blackfoot galloped across the prairie grass that stretched out before her in an incessant waving, golden-brown sea interspersed with green surges occasionally sprinkled across the flat plains.

As far as she could see, the bountiful rich grasses met azure skies in everlasting eternity. Small canyons, beautiful in their starkness, sparsely dotted the land like a mighty fist had plummeted the earth in anger. It was as if God spent all his skills creating the mountains and trees, then saw this land and made it more beautiful with its simplicity. She loved this harsh land. It matched her spirit—simple, and in some ways, hard and unpredictable.

She treasured these infrequent morning rides when she could skip work around the ranch without her family's insistence she be accompanied by another rider. Living with her married sister, brother-in-law, their two small sons and her two older brothers left her with little alone time, and she craved intervals without human interruptions. The peacefulness of nature was liberating, especially feeling God's presence smiling upon the land.

Slowing her mount near the river, she rode toward the only real trees in the Texas Panhandle. Lining the riverbanks, cottonwoods and willows budded out in the greenery of spring along with wild plum, grape and chokecherry bushes clothed in white, fruit-giving flowers nodding with the wind.

Leaping from Blackfoot's back, Crimson patted the sleek, solid white mare with one black stocking on the right forefoot before leading her toward the trees for a drink of water. This was one of her favorite places, particularly during the summer with the wind soothingly rustling through the green and silver leaves accompanied by the rich morning sounds of whippoorwills. Moving through the tangle of trees and bushes where her booted feet made little noise, she neared the river, then stopped dead in her tracks.

Clear, living water burbled over the sand in tinkling, flowing motions, and in midstream, a man stood bathing. Intrigued instead of frightened, she dropped the reins and knelt behind the bushes for a better view. She had never seen a grown man naked before, and though he was obviously an Indian was irrelevant. Besides, sometimes her curiosity was greater than her common sense and this was one of those times. Shrugging off her guilt, she peered over the bush, fascinated by the man a short distance down the river from her.

Seemingly unaware of her presence, he scrubbed his hairless chest with sand before he slipped underneath the water. Standing, he shook his head, his raven black hair sparkling with silver droplets and sending sprays in all directions. She drew in a sharp, startled breath watching the man stretch and preen like a peacock displaying his feathers. While running his fingers through his wet, near shoulder length hair and turning toward the west, she observed his slender physique laced with muscles along his broad back and narrowing into tight, nicely rounded muscular buttocks. Her fingertips itched to run across his skin and feel the hard muscle and bone beneath it. She rubbed them together, amazed at the inclination. It was a foreign reaction but one she desired to experience.

He shifted his position toward her hiding place, and she recoiled slightly when he looked straight at her. Even from her viewpoint, his strange colored eyes, such a light blue they rivaled the sky for color, caught her attention and held it, revealing her mistake in believing him an Indian.

The hypnotic effect of his entrancing orbs disintegrated when he looked away. Her breath ragged and her stomach knotted up, a strange tingling began in the pit of her stomach while she studied his muscular chest down past his flat stomach and the vee starting below his naval along his hips and ending where she received her first glimpse of a man's softened privates nestled in a patch of coal black hair. He was absolutely exquisite and wondrously made, his male physique a work of art she never imagined in male form. Perhaps the difference was the men she was around usually wore loose fitting clothing that hid their shape, although none had ever captured her full attention or interest.

Her stomach clenched harder, an unusual tickling grew between her legs and swelled with intensity while scrutinizing him, observing every movement, each sensuous progression of him washing his body.

Intently watching him, she did not perceive his slow movement downstream and now he stood midstream almost directly in front of her. She stopped breathing. With a sharp gasp, she rose, stepped back and a twig snapped. Frozen in place, her eyes locking with his, she smothered a startled yelp. He headed toward her, breaking the spell keeping her motionless, then he cleared the water and ran along the sand.

Crimson turned and fled toward her mare who had wandered off. She struggled through the bushes, the slender branches snagging her clothes and stinging her exposed flesh. Something grabbed her arm, stopping her in midstep before she was swung around face-to-face with her captor. With panic widened eyes, she glanced up at him and his piercing blue eyes.

"What have we here?" His black eyebrow cocking in amusement, he seized her other forearm with his free hand to still her struggles against him.

A tinge of fear crept along her neck, and she fought against his strong grip, wondering what she had gotten herself into this time. "Let me go!" she screamed.

"Not until you tell me what you're doing hiding in the bushes." His voice carried a hint of laughter.

Her blush nearly matched the flame color of her hair with his indelicate reminder and her temper flared. "Let me go! I ain't doing nothing wrong."

Becoming aware of his wet hands holding her forearms and keeping her from fleeing, her voice faltered. Trembling, she felt the heat from his body penetrate through her clothing, and she turned her face away, avoiding looking at any part of his bare body.

"Do you make a habit of spying on men bathing?" he asked, sarcasm tingeing his voice. Normally he would have laughed the whole thing off and given her a show, but seeing her sparkle like a ruby among emeralds intrigued him.

Against her will, she met his ice blue eyes. "I do not!"

Green sparks flew from her eyes, and he softly laughed. "I suppose you've seen lots of naked men before."

"I have two little nephews and two brothers," she replied tartly, for some reason hoping he would believe she was more worldly-wise than she was. "It's nothing new."

"So that's why you were spying, making comparisons? I assure you male bodies are made much the same way, but that isn't the body part you're interested in, is it?" Her face turned a deeper red than her hair, and he bit back a chuckle before adding, "Anyway, I wasn't talking about boys."

Her generous mouth narrowed into a white line, angry that not only had he caught her spying on him, but his nudity was distracting. "They're all the same except for the si..." Crimson stopped, aghast. Here she was conversing with a naked man about the differences between men and boys' private parts. *What's the matter with me?* she asked herself, feeling her face growing hotter and wanting to sink completely below the sand, especially since she had no other concept for comparison except her little nephews.

No less shocked than she, her outburst tickled his fancy and enchanted him, wondering who this tantalizingly bold young woman was, and why she would put her life in danger to satisfy her curiosity. He released one arm and pulled her toward the stream. "Come with me and tell me more about the differences."

He forced her toward the cold stream, and she dug her heels into the sand, his exigence mingled with her embarrassment of being caught, making her resolute in refusing his demand. "Let me go! I know nothing!"

Biting back a grin, he stopped and turned toward her. "So, you admit it."

"Let me go!" Furiously near tears, every muscle in her body tensed and her eyes grew hard, yet a stubborn need to deflate his overgrown ego filtered through her next words. "There ain't much difference between you and my little nephews. Yours is just a lot bigger and contains hair."

Groaning inwardly, she wondered why she did not let the subject go. It was so silly and so against propriety. Never would she have dreamed of discussing this with a friend, if she had one, much less a total stranger and a naked one at that. Flaming red crept up her face with his laughter, and she screamed again, "Let me go!"

"I think not." Grabbing her shoulders, he held her motionless. "Look at me. Look enough so you'll know the differences between men and babies."

Crimson looked down, avoiding his eyes, but his loins were there, and she hastily raised pleading eyes. "Please let me go."

"Oh no, little one. You're going with me until I get to the bottom of this."

Refusing, she struggled against his arms. Had he not caused her enough embarrassment? His grip was like bands of steel, but it was the change against her thigh and stomach when brushing against him that stopped her struggles. Looking downward against her will, she saw the difference in his manhood. Where it was soft and nestled over a hairy patch before was now big, hard and jutting upward toward his stomach. She drew in a surprised breath but could not help asking, "What happened? Does it hurt?"

A grin Landon could not force back lifted his grim lips. "It will if you don't be still. That, my little spy, is a major difference between men and little boys."

Shock widened her eyes and seeing his smile, fury overcame her concern. "Let me go, you polecat!"

Sudden anger pierced him with her name-calling and continued reticence. "You're going with me. If you don't go on your own, I'll pick you up and carry you over there."

A tick throbbed in his cheek, and she realized he meant exactly what he threatened. Debating further refusal, the thought of him holding her in his present condition sent a fresh rush of red over her face from either embarrassment or something she did not understand or most likely both. "Why should I? As far as I am concerned this conversation is finished."

"No, it has not. Would you rather I question you while I'm as naked as the day I was born and in my present condition? I might do more than question you if you don't start moving." A crooked smile replacing his tick, he contemplated folding her into his arms and carrying out his threat. She was beautiful, enticing, with her green eyes narrowed in anger.

Glancing at his nakedness again and blushing fiercely, she forced her gaze toward the river, realizing she had no other choice. "I'll go with you this time, but let me warn you, the first chance I get, I'm leaving."

"You'll leave when I'm ready for you to leave," he replied harshly, pulling her toward the stream and fighting against the smile tugging at his lips.

Splashing through the chilly water, Crimson glared at him—her riding boots would be ruined. "I hate you!"

He shrugged off her venomous declaration. "If you hadn't been spying on me, you'd have no reason to hate me."

"Ooooooooow..." she screamed, knowing full well he was correct.

Pushing her none too gently forward where his clothes lay on the other side of the small river branch, he stopped, grabbed her by the waist and lifted her, setting her on the top of the boulder.

Ignoring her sputtering anger, he dressed and kept a guarded eye on her at the same time. With her lips compressed and facing away from him, he studied her profile. Her heart-shaped face was accented by high cheekbones, finely defined eyebrows and a pert upturned nose. Her lips were the color of the white woman's pride and joy, the rose, and were full and generous. Though her mouth was set in a stubborn, compressed pucker, there had been brief sparkles of curiosity in her green eyes suggesting she had never seen a naked man before, much less had ever been kissed. His loins tightened with thoughts of forcing the stubborn, angry set of her mouth into submission and giving her a taste of the forbidden.

Forcing the picture of the captivating fantasy away, he asked,

35

"What's your name?"

Crimson turned and met his extraordinary eyes, thankful he had on pants. "That's none of your business," she answered crisply.

"I'm making it my business. Now tell me your name." He advanced toward her, leaving no room for refusal.

While pulling on her earlobe, she studied the symmetric planes and angles of his face, the high cheekbones, the narrow nose that broadened at the end, his oval face, his lips, wide and soft, and the fathomless blue of his eyes lined with thick, black lashes, his handsomeness not eliminating her concern. "I'm embarrassed enough without giving you my name too."

"Tell me your name or must I force it out of you?" he snapped, suddenly irritated and smothering the laughter rising simultaneously.

Releasing a bitter sigh, she huffed, "Crimson Rose."

"Bramble Rose fits you better because you have enough thorns to prick a man sorely."

Why am I always so curious, especially watching this man bathe? More angry at being caught than regretting watching him, she wondered what she had gotten herself into this time. "You're not funny," she remarked acidically and at the same time wary.

Shrugging, a quirk of a smile pulled up one side of his mouth. "It wasn't meant to be funny. I only told the truth."

She jerked on her earlobe and slipped down the boulder, but his whiplash tone stopped her from leaving.

"Sit down! I'm not finished with you yet."

The sharp command in his voice sent fear prickling her spine. She suddenly realized she had very little knowledge, well really, none about the interactions between men and women. It was never spoken about in polite society and her family ignored her questions. With reservation Indians hunting throughout the vast Panhandle, her family was against her riding out by herself. And when her family could not escort her, an older ranch hand accompanied her. It was the echoes of her brothers' snide remarks they thought she could not hear *'they were too old to get it up anymore'* that had her face flushing hot again and remembering the stranger's hardened member brushing against her stomach. Realistically, she had no idea what that meant until now, and she still did not understand the full significance.

She had heard little about the interaction between men and women. The few times she had been around married women, they sometimes had whispered conversations when they thought she was not listening, though for the life of her, she was more confused about the subject. She heard one woman state men were like rutting beasts when they mated, though the picture it created was sickening, and that was vague. Sure, she knew about mating animals, but everyone always sent her running back to the house like it was an unnatural act. Their actions only increased her curiosity, and it was more infuriating since no one would answer her questions regarding it.

The strange tingling between her legs slowly filtered through her consciousness and her face flushed as the pieces began falling in place. "What do you plan on doing with me?" she almost whispered, hating the fear quivering her voice.

He slipped his shirt over his arms, leaving it unbuttoned before closing the short distance between them. With his movement, one side of his shirt blew toward his back revealing the white scar blazing starkly across his right side.

"That remains up to you." When she met his eyes, he added, "eventually."

"Who are you and by what right do you have keeping me here?" She desperately needed to escape, embarrassed he had caught her spying on him, especially now with the sensation intensifying between her legs and the moisture building there, escalating her confusion.

"By what right did you have watching me bathe?" It was her apparent innocence and beauty with the sparkling green eyes intriguing him, and at the same time, her boldness capturing his interest.

Her eyes glistened with tears, and she blinked several times, keeping the moisture back, irritated her embarrassment was so great. "You didn't answer my question."

"I'm Landon Wade."

"You ain't all white. You're a half..." His eyes turned cold, reminding her of the stream's icy water and stopping her in mid-sentence.

"That's right, Crimson Rose, *I am* a breed." The angry tick back in his cheek, Landon glared at her with the reminder of his mixed heritage.

"I...I'm...sorry. I didn't mean it that way," she stammered, taken back by his fierceness and wondering why she did not run away when she first had the chance. "You won't hurt me, will you?"

"What I oughta do is bend you over my knee and paddle your bottom for spying on a grown naked man. Don't you know how dangerous it is for a young woman such as yourself or any woman in a situation like this?" Watching her shrink back against the boulder, he bit back a smile.

"If...if...you touch me, I'll kill you," she declared with more bravado than she felt. There was something dangerous about him, yet she did not perceive he would harm her. Given her precarious situation, she could not stop herself from gazing at his full mouth, watching it tighten, then slightly curve upward with humor, and wondering how it would feel if he kissed her. *Stop! Your curiosity has already gotten you in trouble. Why borrow more? And why am I so fascinated with the relationship between men and women? But then, no man has tempted me before.*

"Those are harsh words, Crimson Rose. Say it too many times and it'll get you into trouble." Landon stepped closer, blocking off any hope she had of escaping. Reaching out, he fingered a lock of her auburn hair, watching the sun's rays sparkle in its red highlights and the soft tress curl around his digits with a life of its own.

She cringed against the cold hardness of the boulder. "You ain't gonna scalp me, are you?"

Swallowing his laughter, Landon kept his face grim while green pools of fear widened her spring green eyes. "If I was still living with the Kiowas, I just might. This would make a pretty trophy, but since I'm living as a white man, it would only cause trouble."

The dancing lights sparkling in his light blue eyes betrayed his teasing. Abruptly pulling back, her quick temper rose though her scalp stung where he still held her hair. "No man's gonna make a fool of me, especially not you."

With her jerking away, he tugged on her hair between his fingers and held her motionless, his attention on the soft, silky strands. "Your hair is the color of a well-ripened cherry. It's like you, well-ripened and ready for harvesting. I wonder if you will be sweet or sour?"

Meeting his intense eyes, she guessed his intention and drew back, her face stiffening in fury. "Don't you dare touch me!"

Her words slashed through his soul, and he decided he would show her how well he did dare. "Is that a challenge, Crimson Rose? I threatened to paddle you and teach you a well-deserved lesson. I believe that lesson is now justified."

Before Crimson could scramble out of reach, he grabbed her by the waist and lifted her into his arms. Sitting where she had been previously, he threw her across his lap and held her down with one arm across her lower back. She kicked up her legs, screaming insults at him as he brought his hand down hard against her backside, his reward her cries of outrage, but her name-calling had stopped. Pounding her backside, he appreciated the soft, firm cheeks underneath his palm until he grew exhausted. Uncomfortably aware of the ache in his groin, he pushed her off his lap.

Glaring at him, she crouched at his feet and rubbed her smarting posterior. Being the youngest child in her family, she had never been spanked. "Damn you, you enjoyed that. I hate you!"

A small smile creased Landon's narrowed lips. "Yes, I did. It's a lesson learned for your impropriety and your lack of decent manners. You deserve another one for your language."

She rose unsteadily, still rubbing her stinging rear end and wondering why she thought about kissing him. "I swear if you ever touch me again, I'll kill you."

"I told you once before those were awful strong words, Crimson Rose," he reminded grimly, rising slightly on his hands against the boulder before jumping off. Grabbing her arm before she could stalk away, he swung her around and pressed her struggling body against his.

She kicked out, her booted toe connecting with his shin, and heard his sharp intake of breath. "Let me go!"

"You're a regular little hellcat, ain't you?" Landon gasped, her aim true and his ankle throbbing where she struck him.

Struggling in his arms, Crimson became aware of a hardness brushing against her stomach each time she turned. She stopped and met the darker hued, strange gleam reflected in his eyes.

His eyes impenetrable, he released his hold and tangled his

hands in the curly mass of her hair. Her body erupted into tingling shocks and her stomach fluttered as he lowered his head. One thought crossed her mind, *finally he's gonna kiss me*. His lips moved over hers caressing them, molding them against his. She could not move; his kiss invoked unfamiliar yet not unpleasant sensations.

Clenching her fists, Crimson fought against the strange yearnings of her body and wanting her arms wrapped around him. She hated him, hated him for the way her body was reacting, and she had no control over it, but it did not stop her lips from softening underneath his.

The fire of his kiss eliminated the fire in her bottom. Her fists unclenched and her hands rose upward over his stomach and slipped along his sides, touching his smooth, hot skin where his shirt opened. Caressing his flesh and feeling the puckered scar on his side, her hands slipped around his back, caressing the rugged hardness of roped muscles underneath silken skin.

Her being caught fire like flaming arrows were shooting through her veins, and she grew breathless and weak as if inhaling too much smoke while at the same time becoming a mindless object. His soft lips playing with hers was all that mattered, wiping away the memory of his spanking, his insults, her embarrassment and hatred.

Landon lifted his head and stared into her smoldering eyes before drawing her closer. Brushing his lips across her cheek, he whispered huskily in her ear, "Little spy, you are beautiful, like a morning rosebud opening up under the sun's rays."

His bared chest felt good underneath her cheek, but his subtle reminder of why she was here in the first place created an adverse reaction. Stiffening, she stepped back from the circle of his arms, raised her arm and at the same time, swung it forward.

He caught her wrist in mid-swing, his softened face of a moment before all hard lines. "Don't ever slap me, Crimson Rose, whether you think I deserve it or not."

"I hate you!"

"That's three times you've said that, little spy, and I almost believe you," he grumbled, forcing her hand down.

"Then believe it." She rubbed her wrist where his fingers had been, flinching at the red fingermarks marring the whiteness of her skin. Looking up, her eyes hard and brittle, she whispered, "You are a slimy, lowdown snake in the grass and this conversation is now ended." Turning, she half expected his refusal, perhaps wanted it, but when he did not, she stalked toward the stream, his voice following her.

"We shall meet again, Crimson Rose."

Chapter 5
Complexity of Being Woman

CRIMSON ran across the stream without feeling the icy cold water splashing up and soaking her clothing. Cleared of the trees, she jumped lithely on her mare's back and raced home.

Hurrying toward the rambling, two-story ranch house, she hurriedly unsaddled her mount before heading for the privacy of her room. His brilliant blue eyes were still with her, and she could not shake the sensation they were watching and laughing at her, daring her. But whatever the challenge was about, she did not understand.

Sitting on the edge of the bed, she placed her hands between her knees, wondering if she was trying to smother the sensations or keep them in. Closing her eyes and squeezing her knees tightly against her hands, it was his eyes and remembering the sensation of his lips against hers playing havoc within her mind and body.

There was an emptiness, an aching demanding fulfillment, and wondering if the strange hardness of his manhood would fill this privation she was experiencing. There was so much she did not understand about the interactions between men and women. The few times she had approached the subject with her sister, Honeysuckle's face always turned beet red, and she would giggle nervously, telling her she would find out about it after she married. She attempted to speak about it with her brothers who scoffed at her and told her one day after she was married, she would find out and it was not up for discussion. So, what was the big secret and why was she curious?

The loud voices of her nephews' crying argument drew her attention from her bewildered thoughts. With a soft, confused moan, she opened her eyes and stood, hoping that surrounding herself with family would exorcise him from her tormented memory.

~◎⁊◌⁊◎◜~

HE CRESTED the hill and spotted three men standing at the bottom. Before they noticed him, he turned his horse around and rode back toward the bottom of the valley, then left his horse in a dry gulch. Climbing the hillside, he knelt and crawled until he gained a better view of the men below. A slow-burning rage seared his soul when he recognized the three men below as the boys who had once tormented, taunted and ganged up on him any chance they had when he was younger. After not seeing them for nine years, their features had not faded from memory. They were like rats, attacking in a pack, and he surmised they had not changed.

Archie Montgomery, the leader of the bunch, had been the worst. He never let an opportunity pass in attacking him either verbally or physically, mostly physically. He heard Archie was a gambler in Mobeetie and known for his sleight of hand. His gaze slipped toward Tom Martin—Tom always struggled and fought for leadership, and only by Archie's superior strength was he stopped from gaining control. And then there was Harvey James—the follower, mimicking the others' actions.

He watched them with narrowed eyes, wondering what kind of deceptive plans they made and vowed he would keep a close eye on them. When the men split up, he slipped down the hill and headed toward Mobeetie.

~◎⁊◌⁊◎◜~

WHILE cooking supper, Honeysuckle glanced at her little sister numerous times, a concerned purse on her lips. Crimson was strangely quiet and preoccupied with occasional soft sighs slipping from her lips. "Crimson, is something bothering you?"

Crimson jumped, torn from her forbidden thoughts of the man at the stream. "No."

"Are you sure? You seem kinda pale," Honeysuckle insisted, staring at her, her silence unusual for her normally chatty sister.

"Nothing's wrong," Crimson snapped, pulling her gaze from her sister's all-too-knowing violet eyes.

"I guess it's your monthly curse. You usually get moody during this time." Honeysuckle looked worriedly at her sister, then shrugged when Crimson turned and walked toward the sideboard. Sighing, Honeysuckle dished up the red beans.

Crimson remained silent. If she admitted it, Honeysuckle would soon discover her dishonesty when no used rags appeared for washing. She had her first monthly when she was nine years old. Honeysuckle had seen the blood on the back of her skirt and forced her upstairs, walking behind her and covering the visible evidence of her clothing with her body. After showing her the rags and explaining their purpose, she quietly proceeded telling her she was a woman now with the arrival of her bloody curse that would last a few days a month. *A woman?* was her first thought. *How could she be a woman at this age?*

The thought was terrifying. When she asked how that made her a woman, Honeysuckle just laughed, then seriously commented, "It means you can have babies now."

"I don't want babies!" she cried.

"Clean up and we'll discuss this at the kitchen table."

After cleaning up as directed, Crimson ran down the steps to the kitchen, full of questions. Pulling out the chair, she plopped down, her face filled with curiosity. "I still don't want babies. I don't wanna be a woman yet."

"As long as you keep the handle out of the churn, you won't get pregnant," was Honeysuckle's sage advice and would not elaborate further.

"Good, that means you get to do all the churning now. Does that mean you'll get with another baby? Though I don't understand how it puts a baby in your stomach." Honeysuckle's laugh only made the situation worse.

It did not help when Buck came through the back door about the time Honeysuckle spoke about butter churns, and supplied his comment, "When you're around a boy or man, put a pebble between your knees and don't you drop it for any reason!" They both chuckled while she glanced at them totally confused.

So, curious, she tried it. Her brothers watched her walk with her knees close together, keeping the small pebble between them. She could only manage small inept steps, and they both laughed at her awkwardness and teased her unmercifully when she refused to give them an explanation of why she was walking so funny. Her face flaming from embarrassment and anger, she stalked off, the pebble falling from its place between her knees. The whole thing was impossible and still did not make sense, especially if she was riding a horse. There was no way she could keep a pebble between her knees with a horse between them. Without the ability to get real answers, she kept her mouth shut about the apparently secret parts of life, but it only strengthened her curiosity.

Crimson still wondered how keeping the handle out of the churn prevented her from getting with child, though she was still required to churn butter. Besides, how did making butter create children anyway?

The whole logic did not make a lick of sense, and she still did not have an answer! Why was there so much secrecy concerning becoming a woman? The only thing she could ascertain from her memory was Honeysuckle and Buck were making fun of the whole process, and she would be required to figure things out for herself when she married. Perhaps it would not have bothered her so much if she had not met Landon Wade. Watching him bathe created a slew of questions and no one to answer them.

At the sideboard, Crimson opened the door and took bone china plates from the shelf as the men came stomping through the back door, tearing her from her confusion.

"I saw the half-breed crossing the L Heart range again. Reckon he's responsible for part of the rus..." Cotton never finished his sentence—a crash interrupted him. He turned toward the sound and Crimson staring mutely at the broken shards of china lying at her feet, and at the same time, caught Buck's warning glance.

"Crim, are you alright?" Cotton grasped her shoulders, worried by the distraught expression on her face and knowing his fiery-tempered, headstrong little sister never accidentally dropped dishes.

Shaking her head, Crimson raised her eyes and stared into the deep violet ones of her brother. "I'm fine. It just slipped from my fingers." Facing her sister, tears she could not keep back sparkled on her lashes. "Honeysuckle, I'm sorry. It was your favorite china."

"My word, Sis, there's no reason to cry over a broken plate." Honeysuckle draped her arm around Crimson's shoulders and guided her toward the table. "Here, sit down and I'll clean this up and finish setting the table."

"No, I'll clean it up and finish," Crimson argued, requiring some sort of distraction from her interaction with Landon Wade.

"I insist you let me finish. You haven't been acting like yourself today. I'm hoping you're not coming down with something." Honeysuckle pushed her back in the chair and turned toward the men. "Stop gawking and wash up for supper."

Crimson idly pushed the food around her plate only half listening to the men's conversation, the other part of her mind solely focused on Landon Wade. He was more than handsome, beautiful in a manly sense, and everything about him was perfect, but his eyes were the most remarkable and were indelibly printed on her mind. His clear, sky-colored eyes challenged her, taunted her and devoured her at the same time. After he found her watching him and their subsequent argument with him spanking her, he somehow still fascinated her. He was an enigma and admittedly the most handsome man she had ever seen, and it demolished any sense of security she had previously felt, reminding her she was no longer a little girl but a woman. But she still had no idea what that meant and why her body reacted so peculiarly when he kissed her!

She wished she had female friends, but girls and women were rare in the vastness of the Panhandle Plains or at least proper young ladies. Perhaps if she had female friends, they would discuss private matters and surely someone would have a clue. The few young women living in the Panhandle were not close enough to visit, much less become friends with, so that only left her sister who never spoke about things between men and women's interactions. She felt stupid with her very limited knowledge, or perhaps, imagination.

Crimson admitted her attraction for Landon was a forbidden thing. People pretended half-breeds did not exist and ignored them, but she found not thinking about him impossible. In one short afternoon, he turned her world upside down, evoking feelings and sensations she had never experienced before and creating a greater mystery of what happens between men and women.

Once her impetuous inquisitiveness settled on something, she would not be satisfied until she discovered the truth, which today had already proven itself with her watching him bathe in the river. It was a part of her personality she had never conquered, perhaps she did not want it conquered. How many times had she heard the saying *'curiosity killed the cat?'* It was another part of the colloquial that she heard years later that verified her prurience *'but satisfaction brought him back.'*

Sighing, Crimson rubbed her fingers across her eyes and forehead, desperately trying to erase him from her memory and her continued bewilderment. The room grew silent. Crimson lowered her hands and lifted her eyes. Her family was staring at her. A blush crept up her neck and face, and she wondered if the others knew her thoughts.

"Crimson, you're awfully quiet tonight," Buck commented, concerned she had not spoken since placing supper on the table.

Aware that she must never let them guess what happened today, Crimson smiled awkwardly, her face deepening in color while meeting her brother-in-law's round blue eyes.

"I saw you talking with a drifter this morning. Did you hire him?" Red asked, breaking the tense moment and sparing Crimson from answering Buck's question. His curly red hair fell across his greyish-green eyes, and he moved it back from his face.

Buck broke his curious contemplation of Crimson and answered, "Yeah. This time of the year we need all the ranch hands we can get. He says he's experienced and experience is in high demand. I'm hoping he works out. If he does, I might keep him on through winter."

"He does seem to know his business," Cotton interrupted, nodding his light blonde head toward Buck. "And talking about business, me and Red have decided it's high time we got out on our own. Wyoming's opened up and we're figuring it would be a good place for us. They say the grass is rich enough to fatten out even these longhorns."

Torn from her disturbing thoughts, Crimson stared at her

brothers. "Wyoming?"

"Yeah. There's lots of free land up there." Red smiled at his little sister, glad she awakened from her dark mood.

"How many mavericks have you branded as yours?" Buck asked.

"Around fifty. We figured it would give us a pretty good start," Cotton answered.

"During roundup, cut out two hundred more and put your brand on 'em. Find a good young bull or two and add them to your herd. Call it payment for helping me get this ranch started." Buck glanced over the coffee cup's rim at his brothers-in-law.

"Thanks, Buck, but there ain't no call for that. You paid us regular wages same as the others as well as cattle every year for extra money."

"I know, but without ya'll's help, me and Honey might still be working on getting this ranch started. Ya'll deserve some gift of appreciation."

Cotton slowly nodded, accepting the cattle. "Thanks. It'll help. It might be touch and go for a while. We heard the winters up there are brutal."

"We're thinking after the cattle drive, we'd leave from Dodge City and head for Wyoming." Red glanced out of the corner of his eye, anxious how his sisters took this piece of information and was dismayed when tears slipped from Honeysuckle's violet eyes before she ducked her head, her blonde hair falling across her cheeks.

"That would be mighty fine. It'll get ya'll there before the snow sets in." Buck took another sip of coffee before laying his cup on the table. "Got any men helping ya'll herd them there?"

Cotton and Red glanced at each other before Cotton spoke, "Well, we thought we'd ask if a couple of your new temporary hands might wanna hire on with us and wrangle our cattle there. Afterwards, they could either stay or head back here, whatever."

Nodding, Buck met each of his brothers-in-law's eyes. "I always hire several extra hands during the cattle drive. Take as many as you need. I'm sure some can use the extra money."

Red glanced at Cotton before speaking, "If it's gonna leave you short of men, we can go next year."

A bare smile swept across Buck's lips before he shook his head.

"Nah, it's time ya'll had your own place and land. Just remember, if for any reason you wanna come back, you're always welcome."

The brothers nodded and mumbled, "Thanks."

With the men talking about business, Crimson stood and gathered the dirty dishes from the table, helping her sister clean the kitchen.

She headed for her bedroom. Far from sleepy, brilliant blue eyes haunted her, invading her peace of mind. Throwing her nightgown fiercely on the bed, she left the room and headed for the corral, desperately trying to rid herself of Landon's haunting image.

With conflicting emotions rising within her chest, Crimson walked across the wooden porch, her shoes making little noise, and headed toward the barn and the fenced corral. With her approach, the horses nickered. Her mare Blackfoot met her at the fence, nuzzling her hand for the tidbit she always had for her.

"Sorry, girl, I haven't anything for you." She held out her empty hands, then patted the mare's muzzle, her thoughts once again plaguing her.

It shook her core when Cotton mentioned he had seen a half-breed crossing the L Heart range again. *What did it mean? What was Cotton implying?* Just the mention of a half-breed and her whole body went numb, the plates falling from her nerveless fingers and shattering at her feet. There had been an ominous quality threading through Cotton's voice which sent warnings shooting through her spine.

Pulling on her earlobe, she shook off the warning and allowed her daydreams replay Landon's kiss, how it made her feel like half-set jelly and provoking quivering sensations previously unbeknown. She ran her fingertips across her lips, remembering his soft, firm mouth on hers when receiving her first kiss from a man she memorized from the top of his head to the bottom of his feet. Perhaps it was wicked thinking about his nakedness, but that did not keep her from musing on the planes and angles of his body, muscles straining against a sleek frame or the harmless appearance of his softened organ or the more threatening appearance of it hard.

She bit her bottom lip until a dull pain drew her thoughts back from the naked man. Convincing herself she hated him and should not remember the rest, she violently shook her head, shaking the memories free.

It was after Buck rescued Honeysuckle from the Kiowas who captured her during the Red River uprising that their parents died in Kansas not long after she returned home. Their mother went crazy witnessing the endless Indians curiously watching them, seemingly always there at their small sheep ranch. She would sit for hours staring into nothing until she mercifully died in her sleep. Their alcoholic father spiraled out of control, and they found his body near the outhouse not long after the passing of their mother.

After verifying that each brother and sister wanted to live with him and Honeysuckle, Buck arranged for the sale of their small sheep ranch and packed their meager belongings. Buck had already claimed some land and was determined to homestead in the Texas Panhandle where he had previously hunted buffalo and built the ranch into what it was today. Though Buck was always generous, even splitting the little money received from the sheep ranch between the siblings, she did not blame her brothers for wanting to build their own places. They had no claims on this land, though Buck and Honeysuckle never said otherwise. It was assumed the ranch would be inherited by Honeysuckle and Buck's children.

Even before their parents' deaths, her brothers and sister fended for themselves, relying on Honeysuckle and her no-nonsense personality for almost everything, then on Buck after their marriage. Cotton was the eldest, a year older than Honeysuckle, then Red, two years younger than Honeysuckle, then herself, the youngest, three years younger than Red. Now her brothers were cutting the apron string, and she envied them.

Rubbing her earlobe between her index finger and thumb, a habit she had when troubled or in deep thought, she watched the closeness Honeysuckle and her family shared, the way Buck and she would glance at each other, touching so lovingly, and the way they held their two small sons. The family scene was a sharp pain through her heart. She wanted what her sister had in her own life: a husband and children along with the closeness and sharing they had. She gradually grew restless, especially after today, which pierced her subconscious more sharply. She was seventeen, nearly eighteen, and no longer a child. Landon's discerning image popped into her mind once again, but she forced it away.

With the barn doors opening, yellow light spilled into the yard, and Cotton and Red, slicked down, cleaned up, and wearing their Sunday-go-to-meetin' clothes, came out leading their saddled horses, dispelling her troubled thoughts. "Where ya'll going?"

"To the baile in Tascosa. Pedro Romero's throwing a big shindig tonight." Red's grin said more than his words.

"That sounds like fun! Hold on and let me change so I can go with you." Conveniently ignoring Cotton's frown, her excitement grew.

"Oh no, you don't!" Cotton's scowl deepened. "We don't need a tag-along. Just go on back into the house."

"I ain't a little girl, Cotton. I'm going and nobody can stop me." Crimson faced her brother, her mutinous chin thrust up and her hands anchored on her hips.

"Now look here, Crim, you ain't going, and we can stop you. Go on back into the house like I done told ya. We're going on men's business and it ain't got nothing to do with you." Cotton's face was stubborn as his sister's, and his shoulder tensed against the fight he knew was coming.

An impish grin sliced Crimson's full lips. "I know what ya'll got planned and I won't interfere. You can have your fun while I dance." She only had a vague idea of what happened between men and women, but she would die before she let her brothers know any different.

If her brothers were shocked, neither showed it. "You ain't going with us and I ain't telling ya again," Cotton growled. "The last time you went with us, you nearly got us into a shooting scrape, and I ain't standing guard over ya tonight."

"Oh pooh, you're blowing everything out of proportion. Those cowboys were drunker than a skunk, and they both decided they wanted to dance with me at the same time. It doesn't mean I nearly got ya'll into a shooting scrape." Crimson shook her hair over her shoulder, haughtily minimizing his concern.

"Sure, Crim. If you hadn't been flirting with both of them and leading them on, none of it would've happened. Me and Red wouldn't of stepped in and stopped it 'cause it was our little sister they were fighting over. Me and Red looked like we had been in a cock fight afterwards, and they told us we couldn't come back. That was over two years ago and they finally said we could come back tonight. All we'd need is having you messing it up for us again."

Crimson realized Cotton was resolute and there was no way he would relent but allowing him the last word was against her nature. "Red, you don't mind if I go, do you?"

Seeing the humor in everything, Red could not force back his grin. "Well now, Sis, if ya had more of Honeysuckle's collective calm instead of a fiery temper, I wouldn't mind quite so much, but every time we let ya go with us, ya either end up threatening some senorita or slapping some cowhand. Now mind ya, I don't mind ya putting some man in his place, but every time ya feel slighted?"

Red bit back a grin, his attempt at being serious now fruitless. Giving up, he threw back his head and guffawed. "The last time ya slapped a cowhand was 'cause he was watching a senorita instead of paying attention to you. I ain't seen him around since."

"I did not!" she denied strongly, a hot flush burning her face, glad her brothers could not see it. "He was talking to me but called me by that...that...girl's name."

"It doesn't matter anyhow. You ain't going and that's final!" Having had enough arguing with his headstrong sister, Cotton mounted his waiting horse and ignored her. "Come on, Red, or we'll miss the best part."

Red shot Crimson an apologetic smile before mounting and following his brother. As soon as they were out of earshot, Red replied, "She gave up too easy."

"I know and it worries me."

Chapter 6
Ornerier Than a Mad Boar

CRIMSON turned on her heel and rushed into the house. How dare her brothers forbid her from going to the party! She would show them! Her brothers were not her parents! Quickly throwing on a blue party dress and riding boots, she pulled a brush through her unruly hair and tied it back with a ribbon. Grabbing her party shoes and brush, she snuck out of the house and saddled Blackfoot.

A grim, determined smile on her lips, she mounted and headed toward Tascosa, the unsettling knack of doing the exact opposite of what someone demanded she do, stiffening her resolve in riding the long distance while the sun lowered and darkness descended.

She was glad for the full moon. It helped curb her fear. The night sounds were amplified and the areas where the moonlight did not reach held ominous shadows. She should kick Blackfoot's sides and hurry her along, but there was always the danger of prairie dog holes. Why risk her mare breaking a leg, then be afoot? The thought of walking any long distance at night made her shudder.

Cresting a knoll and stopping, she glared at the blackness where the moonlight did not reach, hating where she could not see. Fighting back her fear, she swallowed once, then started forward.

Near the bottom, the shadows deepened, and she gripped the

reins. Blackfoot danced nervously with the tightening of the bit in her mouth. The pitch-black bottom waited for her, and she leaned forward across Blackfoot's neck, kicking her flanks. Suddenly, the reins were grabbed, and Blackfoot reared, her tight grip barely keeping her from being thrown.

"Damnit, Crim, you were told you couldn't go!" she heard Cotton snarl.

"You lowdown, stinking coyote!" Fury pierced every part of her. "You could of gotten me killed!"

"You're too damned ornery to kill," Cotton retorted, throwing the reins at Red.

"I knew she gave in too easy." Red caught the reins Cotton threw at him from the other side of her horse.

Cotton grabbed Crimson and hauled her out of the saddle, setting her none too gently in front of him. "Damnit, why in the tarnation didn't you stay at home like I told ya?"

"You think just because ya'll are boys, ya'll can go and leave me sitting at home. Well, let me tell you, you're loco. Don't you think I get tired of staying around the ranch all the time?" Crimson clenched her hands at her hips, desperately fighting against hitting her brother.

"You're the most pigheaded, stubbornest, mulish person I ever met. Why in the hell don't you act like other young ladies your age?" Cotton shook her until her teeth rattled.

"Stop shaking me, Cotton!" After her brother released her shoulders, Crimson hissed, "I ain't never gonna be like those primping, soft-voiced, cow-eyed heifers! I ain't gonna be all mealymouthed and obliging when some smelly ole man flatters me. No siree! That ain't me! I'd be bored to tears and one thing I ain't never gonna be is boring."

"For God's sake, I wish for once ya would be!" The fine thread holding Cotton's temper nearly snapped.

"I don't know what you're getting so all fired huffy about. I ain't done nothing wrong."

"You call this doing nothing wrong, Crim? You snuck off and I bet you didn't tell Honeysuckle and Buck where you were going." Cotton slapped his hat against his thigh, fighting for some semblance of calm.

"So?"

"So? You don't find nothing wrong with that? I wish to God you were more like Honeysuckle." Setting his hat back on his head, he glared at his little sister.

"Well, I ain't Honeysuckle. I'm me!"

"I wish ya'll would quit arguing," Red interjected. "Both of ya have such hot tempers that neither one of you can talk without yelling at the other."

"I wouldn't be yelling if she would listen." Cotton fought the urge to clamp his hands around his little sister's skinny neck and choke some sense into her stubborn head. "Get on your horse. I'm taking you back and I'll hogtie you if I must."

"You can make me go back and you can tie me up, but I swear I'll find some way of getting back," she tensely informed him, stiffening her spine.

"She's right. Ya know as well as me if we force her back, she'll follow us anyway." Red realized Crimson would carry out her threat. She had proven it in the past. When they dunked her in a horse tank to cool off her temper, she ended up following them and sloshing all the way behind them, destroying their planned fun with her spouting off colorful language that would make an old degenerate ranch hand proud.

"I don't give a damn what she does, but she ain't going with me," Cotton retorted.

"I done told you can have your fling and pleasuring with the senoritas, and I'll stay out of your way." She tried convincing her brothers she would stay out of trouble. She needed a distraction to erase the disturbing image of Landon from her mind.

Cotton stepped closer and grabbed her shoulders in a bruising grip. "Watch your mouth or I swear I'll shut it for you."

"Don't get tough with me or I'll turn you from a stud horse into a gelding so fast, it'll make your head swim."

Cotton gave her a rough shove toward Red. "You talk some sense into her stubborn head. She's got a mouth like a stinking outhouse." Cotton stalked off several feet from them.

"Look, Sis, me and Cotton was wantin' one last fling before we leave. Can't you be a sweetheart and let us go on into Tascosa without ya?"

"Red, please let me go. I promise I won't cause any trouble. You and Cotton can do whatever you want, and I won't bother you." She held out her hand and touched his shoulder, her voice cajoling.

"Why don't you piss in her ear so she'll have something in her head," Cotton muttered.

"It wouldn't do any good. It'd just make her eyeballs yeller." Red suddenly laughed, knowing his headstrong sister would follow them regardless what they did. "Ah hell, Cotton, we might as well let her tag along. We ain't got much choice."

⁂

TASCOSA, a town made up of two stores, a blacksmith shop, and an adobe house, though small, was already the center for supplies for the big cattle ranches surrounding it. The bailes were held at Mexican plazas and were not considered part of Tascosa but went by the name of the owner. The Romero Plaza, built around a large central building, was where the baile was being held tonight.

The faint strains of the guitar and fiddle playing a Mexican quadrille reached the trio as they reached the small settlement. After tying their horses at the hitching post in front of Howard and McMaster's store, Cotton and Red left their weapons inside before walking the short distance to the social gathering.

A high, protective adobe wall encircled the hacienda and contained a tiled courtyard where oil lamps hung from wooden pegs high along the sides and some suspended by their metal handle across ropes crisscrossing the patio. The still night air was a bonus and gave comfort against a random gust of wind rocking the lighted glass lamps. Several chairs were placed near one wall and highlighted a couple of young ladies fanning themselves while flirting with several young men vying for their attention. Small tables and chairs sat closer at the back of the terraza where food and drink were served, and older, married couples ate, drank and enjoyed the revelries.

Crimson's steps grew lively, keeping in time with the music, the closer they neared the back patio gate. Repeating her promise of staying out of trouble, her brothers dubiously left her in the care of one of the older L Heart ranch hands, knowing if anything happened or if she decided to leave early, he would take her home.

The couples swirled in time with the music, men in cowboy boots wearing their Sunday clothes with their hair slicked back, twirled young Spanish women in bright colored silks, their hair fancily dressed, and the tinkles of their giggles mixing with the lower laughter of gentlemen. Dancing with one partner, then another, Crimson smiled, enjoying the rare party and interaction with other young men and women, some she barely knew, but most she did not.

It was several hours later before Cotton claimed her for a waltz. "I'm proud of ya, Crim, for acting like a lady this time."

"A compliment from you? What brought this on?" Cocking her head, she glanced up into his dark violet eyes sprinkled with touches of grey, and ran her tongue over her lips, surprised her hotheaded brother was praising her.

"Well, this is the first time we've been here this long without ya getting in some kind of trouble. I just thought I'd let ya know I appreciate it."

"Thank you. That means a lot since you rarely compliment me." Swept along in a waltz, she spied Red returning to the festivity, his arm wrapped around a young woman, his face holding a satisfied look, and repeated what she had often heard Cotton say before about similar situations, though she wondered what the pleasuring part meant. "Red better be careful unless he's prepared for a shotgun wedding."

Cotton glanced in Red's direction while dancing Crimson around the other couples. "It wouldn't be the first time."

"It wouldn't be too smart right now with ya'll planning on moving to Wyoming."

He shrugged, dismissing her observation. "That's *his* business."

They were interrupted when couples quickly dispersed, giving way for a man racing through the patio fence's outer door and running full tilt toward them. The stranger tripped and fell, sprawling in front of Crimson and Cotton. Suddenly, four men with drawn pistols surrounded the prostrate form.

Cotton gripped her sides, suddenly tense. "That's Billy the Kid."

All the stories she had heard about this legendary killer had not prepared her for the sight of the tall, slender figure with brown, curly hair sprawled at her feet. The image of a man lying prone before her with his hands above his head angled toward her with two men on each side with drawn weapons, not only shocked her but struck her as hilarious, and she emitted a giggle. Her giggles burst loose when Billy stood and ordered his men to holster their weapons.

Cotton's hand tightened around her waist in warning. Red hurried toward them, protectively positioning himself in front of his sister. Her giggles turned into full-out laughter, and she doubled over, her flaying hands having little effect of dislodging Red from his position in front of her.

"Senorita?" Billy's grin did not ease her brothers' anxiety.

Wiping tears from her eyes, Crimson straightened. The music had stopped, and everyone except her was tense with men protectively pushing their partners behind them. The smile never leaving her face, she stepped in front of her brothers and studied Billy, liking what she saw and instantly recognizing the charming smile emphasizing his two slightly protruding front teeth and the smile lines around his mouth, giving her a hint of his personality. She recognized his smile was as much a part of him as his fabled quick temper. "I'm sorry, sir. I've never had a man sprawled at my feet before." She ignored Cotton's warning look.

"Ah, Senorita, I see you kept your sense of humor for my clumsy entrance. My men get carried away sometimes. They thought I was in trouble, though I was havin' a foot race with the good Dr. Hoyt." He took her hand and bowed gallantly over it. "William Bonnie at your service, Senorita."

"It's a pleasure meeting you, Mr. Bonnie. People call me Crimson Rose, but my friends call me Crimson." She smiled, immediately aware of his piercing blue eyes with strange brown spots swimming through the blue.

"Senorita Crimson Rose, you have a delightful name. I assume you were named after your hair."

"You're very astute, sir."

Billy squeezed her hand before releasing it, then smiled wryly when she examined him from head-to-toe in much the same way he had studied her. "You like what you see, Senorita?"

Never mincing words and unaccustomed with proper protocol, Crimson pleasantly voiced her observation, "I think so." She smiled faintly at the shocked gasp of several women close by her. "You're very charming, but from the stories I've heard about you, you should be at least ten feet tall and ornerier than a mad boar."

Throwing back his head, Billy laughed loudly, loving such a beautiful woman was so forward and unintimidated by him. "Ah, Senorita Crimson Rose, you have made my day!"

He made a courtly bow. "You please me with your honesty. I will always be at your service. Anytime you need help, call on me."

Billy bowed again. "It's a pleasure meetin' ya, Senorita, but Senor Romero is motionin' at me. He appears angry with us, so I will join him and make my apologies."

After Billy walked off, Cotton growled, "Damnit, Crim, do you know what could have happened with your damnable laughter?"

"It didn't happen, brother dear," Crimson remarked patronizingly, shrugging off his anger. "What will happen now?"

"I imagine the same thing that happened with Red and me. They broke the unwritten law of not carrying weapons during the get-together."

"Oh well, at least I met him."

"I hope it's not at our disadvantage, Crim. He's very unpredictable." After his warning, Cotton motioned for Red, leaving her in his oversight for a few hours.

"I'm so excited I met Billy the Kid." Crimson's eyes shone with mischief.

"Yeah, Sis. I just wish ya meet him in a better way than laughing at him."

"Oh pooh, you're getting bad as Cotton, always worrying." She watched Billy and his men talk with Pedro Romero. After a few minutes, with Billy being very polite, he and his men left the party.

"Bad as I hate admitting it, Cotton's right," Crimson commented, watching the outlaw and his men disappear through the adobe wall's wooden door. When she saw Red's eyes straying toward the young women along the patio, she commiserated, "Oh, go on. I'll be good."

Red planted a kiss on her forehead. "Thanks, Sis."

Crimson danced several sets before Dr. Hoyt claimed her. "Miss McFarlin, the Kid said he enjoyed meeting you and hopefully would see you again. There's not many young women who'd laugh at his inelegant entrance, giving his reputation and all."

"I couldn't help laughing, Dr. Hoyt. It was just so funny having a man sprawled at my feet." Crimson giggled, thinking again of his prostrate form before her on the dance floor. "Besides from what I understand, he might very well be within the bounds of rightness for all he's done."

"Not too many people will agree with you," Dr. Hoyt replied thoughtfully, meeting her during the next call of the American quadrille.

"Is he so much different from the other men around here?" Crimson asked, meeting him again and sweeping her head toward the other men at the party. They all had reputations; it was just some were better known than others.

With the quadrille ending, Dr. Hoyt took her arm, leading her toward the edge of the dance floor. "No, not much different, but history will tell."

"May I have this dance, ma'am," a man slurred at her elbow.

Dr. Hoyt gripped her arm in warning. "That's Charlie Sorrel and he's a bad one, Miss Crimson. It's best you refuse."

She cocked an eyebrow at the intoxicated man, stifling her uneasiness. He was unkempt, had a strong body odor and his breath stank of liquor and cigar smoke. She wondered if he had cooties by the way he scratched at his unkempt beard. He made a mocking bow toward her and held out his arm. She had the distinct impression that no matter whether she accepted or not, he would cause trouble. Hoping it would cause fewer problems if she accepted the dance, she shrugged off Dr. Hoyt's warning and accepted.

"Ya have a lot of gall laughin' at Billy that way." Charlie clumsily stepped on her toes during the waltz.

"Were you sent back in here to tell me that?" Crimson asked tartly.

"Nope." Charlie's grip on her waist was very strong considering his inebriated state.

"In other words, you took it upon yourself," she surmised. "I don't appreciate it, sir, in the least little bit. He didn't seem mad."

"Ya think yore smart, don't ya, little lady? From ya bein' the only white lady here, I'd reckon you're not objectin' to makin' a little money on the side. I've got a gold eagle in my pocket, and you can earn it after we go outside for a bit." His hand traveled from her waist toward the side of her breast.

His insinuation eliminated all coherent thought, and without a second's hesitation, she brought her knee up sharply between his legs.

Charlie doubled over clutching his groin and screeching like a wounded animal. Swirling couples stopped and curiously stared at them while standing back in a circle around them.

Hands on her hips, enjoying his pain, Crimson stood glaring at Charlie. "No one propositions me, mister!"

Senor Romero, Red and Cotton hurried toward the disturbance. "Senorita McFarlin, what is wrong?" Senor Romero asked in concern.

"This slimy snake tried to touch me and propositioned me as well!"

"You've done it now," Cotton sighed disgustingly, sure their days of attending the bailes were over. "I swear, Crim, you've got a temper that would make a tornado turn tail and run."

Senor Romero waved some men forward who escorted Charlie out of the patio. His usually passive face concerned, he advised, "Senorita McFarlin, find you an hombre who can handle you and marry him quick before all of the available men who come around you are crippled for life."

"Senor Romero, I'm truly sorry. Please don't throw my brothers out because of this," Crimson begged, seeing the expressions on their faces. Cotton was so angry his face was blotched in red while Red bit back a laugh.

"Senorita, if he inappropriately touched or propositioned you, I will not hold you responsible this time nor your brothers. Just please try constraint next time."

"I will, sir. I promise."

"It's time we made a hasty exit, Cotton." Red looked worriedly around and nodded toward the gate of the fenced enclosure. "Charlie Sorrel is not one who will let this go by lightly."

"I agree." Turning toward Senor Romero, Cotton made their excuses. He grabbed Crimson by the arm and propelled her toward the door. "I hope you're satisfied, Crim. I knew ya couldn't stay all night without something happening. You better hope we're not all gunned down soon as we reach the door."

"What did you expect from me, Cotton? He tried touching me where he wasn't supposed to and then treated me like I was one of those painted ladies."

"No, of course not. It's just trouble always follows you."

Clearing the door, they headed the short distance toward Tascosa. Cotton ordered, "Red, pick up our weapons at the store while Crim and I get the horses. There's no telling what might happen if we linger."

Red ran ahead while Crimson and Cotton followed. Rounding the corner of the store, Crimson pulled back and stared. "Blackfoot, she's gone!"

Cotton raced toward the hitching post, cursing under his breath. "Damnit, Crim, now you've done it! Someone's taken our horses and I bet ya Billy the Kid and his gang stole 'em."

Red came out of the store and heard Cotton. Without a word, he handed Cotton his holster while he buckled his around his waist.

"What'll we do now?" Crimson wailed.

"How in the hell should I know? We can't go after them." Cotton desperately fought against taking his little sister by the throat and shaking some sense into her. It was her fault after all. None of this would have happened if she had obeyed him instead of coming with her normal tendency of attracting trouble.

"I guess we may as well walk." She fought back the tears.

"The hell I will!" Cotton yelled. "If you wanna be into next week gettin' home, then *you* walk, Crim!"

"Maybe Senor Romero will loan us some horses," Red suggested.

"I'll go ask! Ya'll are blaming me anyway." She was already walking back toward the baile.

Senor Romero readily agreed, knowing the McFarlin men and Buck Leathers' reputation for honesty. Staring over the dancers, wishing they were not leaving so early, Crimson waited while three horses were saddled. The gala lasted all night, and the night was only half gone. Her eyes were pulled toward a silent figure leaning against the wall, reminding her of Landon Wade. Her heart beating erratically, she sharply drew in her breath and hurried out the other door.

"Did you get the horses?" Cotton asked as she stumbled around the building.

"Huh? Oh yeah, they'll be here soon." Crimson wondered if it was Landon and what he was doing here, hoping at the same time he had not seen her. Her night would have been worse if he had cornered her, brought up their previous meeting and made it known she had spied on him bathing. She swore if he had, she would have done him the same way she had Charlie Sorrel.

Chapter 7
Stars and Diamonds

COTTON and Red both checked their pistols before snapping the bullet chamber back in place, each surreptitiously skimming the area around them, their talk subdued and quiet. Crimson jumped with Cotton's soft growl, spotting one of Senor Romero's men leading three horses toward them.

The man handed over the horses' reins. No one spoke a word, only nodded understanding. There was a noticeable tension—the night appeared darker, the black shadows hid unimaginable danger and the music drifted across plains like some kind of death dirge.

Crimson shivered with the tingling of her spine and took one of the reins, hoping it was her imagination working overtime. With her left foot in the saddle stirrup, Red stopped her.

"This one's yours, Sis." Red handed her the reins.

Shrugging, Crimson lowered her foot and handed Red her reins before taking his, unaware of his sly smile. She started to mount before noticing the funny shaped saddle. "What is this?" she asked, her brow wrinkled in confusion.

"A sidesaddle. It's what all the proper ladies ride," Red chuckled, breaking the tension engulfing them.

"I can't ride this! I don't know how to sit on it." She threw the reins at her brother. "You ride it."

"What is it now?" Cotton caustically asked.

"A sidesaddle, brother dear," Crimson replied sourly, "and I can't ride it."

"If it ain't one thing, it's another." He unsaddled the horse, threw the offending saddle over one shoulder and stomped toward the barn. "I'll be back in a minute after I exchange this or we'll be here all night."

"Thanks, Red. Now Cotton's gonna be a bigger sour puss going home," Crimson grumbled, staring at her brother's retreating back.

"You're welcome. I didn't figure he was mad enough already," Red chuckled.

"Yeah, always mad at me," she complained, petting the horse's blanket-covered back.

For some reason, the ride home seemed longer than normal. Cotton and Red spoke among themselves, excluding her, and she did not blame them. She had insisted on following them with the result being she had once again triggered trouble for them. Why was she so pigheaded? But could anyone really blame her for wanting more time with her brothers?

She might not ever see them again after they left for the cattle drive. Already there was a hole driven in her heart with her brothers' plan of leaving Texas and heading toward Wyoming, a great distance that did not bode well for future visits. It was possible that after the cattle roundup, it would be the last time she would see either one of them, and already she was feeling the sting of loneliness and missing them.

Topping a hill, the subdued glow of campfires ahead gleamed against the night sky growing brighter the nearer they approached. "Think they might share a cup of coffee?" Crimson asked, breaking the silence.

"Let's find out." Red kicked his heels against the gelding's sides, his brother and sister following.

A piercing screech, bloodcurdling whoops and explosive barks of gunfire broke the stillness. Far enough away with the night blackness shielding them from the camp, Crimson and her brothers watched in horror as painted, befeathered Indians raced through the camp causing havoc and shooting indiscriminately at the scattering people.

"What the hell?" Cotton jerked on the reins, pulling his mount to an abrupt stop.

"Indians," Crimson breathed, shock racing through her spine. "We can't stay here while those people get killed."

Before Cotton and Red realized what she was doing, she plucked Cotton's gun from his holster and raced toward the scene, shooting at the attacking Indians. Her brothers raced after her, anxious for their sister's safety, shouting, "Stop! Stop, Crimson!"

Racing in defense of the small wagon party, she leaned against the gelding's neck, aimed the pistol and pulled the trigger. The Indians shuffled about in confusion, surprised by the extra guns coming out of nowhere.

Grabbing hold of her horse's mane, she jumped him over the wagon tongue. Cleared, she aimed her pistol at the Indian in front of her and fired. She saw the bloody crease in the savage's upper arm as she raced past. In a blur, she perceived women and children underneath the wagons and men in various degrees of undress firing at the Indians. She pulled sharply on the reins, turned the gelding around and raced back into the circle of wagons.

The same Indian she had shot earlier blocked her way. Before she could swerve her mount to avoid him, the firelight reflected in his eyes, and she heard him mumble something before he aimed his pistol at her. She pulled off a quick shot, dismay filling her with the chamber clicking harmlessly. Realizing his intent, she felt the first tinge of terror. Jerking the reins, the horse reared and threw her off, the bullet intended for her slamming into the horse's neck.

She landed on the hardpacked ground, the breath knocked from her, the empty pistol still clutched in her fist, and barely rolled in time before the gelding fell. With the gunfire dying down, the fight ended in a matter of eternal seconds, and Red and Cotton were both at her side.

"Are you hurt?" Cotton quickly checked her over, worry showing on his face.

"I'm fine." Gasping, she drew air into her tortured lungs.

Assured she was unharmed, Cotton helped her into a sitting position. "Damnit, Crimson, ya could of gotten killed!" His concern for her safety made his voice louder than he intended.

"Please don't start." She almost cried, realizing how precarious the situation had been. The tortured screams of her mount did not alleviate the situation and she cast a grief-stricken glance in its direction.

Red patted her arm, his face pinched with concern over her falling off her horse and the surprise raid on the wagon train. "The main thing is you're not hurt." Giving her another pat, he rose and put a bullet through the injured horse's head.

The explosion rented the air and she jumped, drawing back into Cotton's arms.

"Damnit, Crim, ya nearly got killed and the fault's all mine for not making ya go back. Ya stupid, hotheaded, little fool! And that's not the worst. Ya took my pistol to carry out your idiocy."

"Oh, shut up, Cotton!" Crimson disengaged herself from her brother's arms and quickly rose. "Here's your dang gun!" She thrust it at him, her fury at his criticism helping her gain control over her fear.

"Let her be, Cotton," Red demanded, his perpetual smile gone with their continued argument.

"Hell, I might as well. Ya can't get nothin' through her thick skull."

Their timely entrance saved the immigrants' livestock and their valuables from being stolen, though there were several injured men whose women were patching them up. After retrieving the borrowed horse's saddle and the men moving the dead horse out toward the prairie, there was nothing more the trio could do, so they headed home.

While Cotton and Red discussed the raid, Crimson remembered the Indian she shot. "This whole thing is odd, don't you think? I mean, I've never known of Indians attacking at night before, and I could of sworn the Indian who shot my horse out from under me had blue eyes. I distinctly remember him saying 'shit' just before he pulled the trigger."

"Are you sure?" With her hands nervously tightening around his waist, Red was immediately alert.

"I'm almost certain. There was so much confusion going on, but with the firelight catching his eyes, they did appear blue," she mused, looking straight ahead over his shoulder into the dark landscape and replaying the chaotic scene in her mind.

"Indians intermingle a lot with whites or it could of been a reflection of the fire and made his eyes appear blue. And of course, the Indians learn our cuss words before they learn anything else." Cotton realized his explanation sounded unconvincing.

"It might not be a bad idea if we tell someone about our suspicions just in case," Red introspectively replied.

THE LIVING room never seemed small until today. It was a big room, but with Buck pacing back and forth in front of the fireplace where his Sharps .50 caliber buffalo rifle was displayed over the mantel, and the whole family standing around the large circular coffee table in the middle of the room surrounded by a large leather sofa and three big leather chairs, it did appear small.

"Damnit, Crimson, I pity the man who marries you if you can find one who'll put up with your headstrong ways." Pacing back and forth in front of her, Buck ran his hands through his flaxen-colored hair.

"Maybe that's what I oughta do—find some foolish man and marry him so ya'll won't worry anymore. I'm sure there are lots of fools around here that would take someone like me," Crimson pouted. *I'm probably a fool for contemplating marrying a stone-broke cowhand who rarely bathes and has lice running around his nasty beard and hair!* You could smell most of the men working the cattle ranches a mile away. *Why am I thinking about marrying when all I wanna do is—what? What do I want? One thing I want is ending this over an hour-long argument.* She was weary of it.

"I believe you've already damaged the biggest fools around here. Before we left, Senor Romero commented about you getting married real quick afore you injured the rest of the available men around."

Buck glared at Cotton, giving him a *keep-your-mouth-shut* look before turning back toward Crimson. "You should of let us known you were going, but I suppose that was too much of a hassle for ya. Even that wouldn't of prepared us for the other messes ya managed gettin' into. My God, I can't believe you raced into an Indian attack and had a borrowed horse shot out from underneath ya." Buck was at his wit's end. She never listened but seemed to run pell-mell into trouble. He often pondered if they should rename her Crimson Trouble McFarlin. It was more apt than Crimson Rose.

"Ya'll act more concerned for the horse than you do me." Crimson fought the tears filling her eyes.

"That's not true. We're concerned for your welfare and cringe at the thought you might of been seriously injured," Honeysuckle assured her, placing a quieting hand on her husband's forearm.

Absentmindedly, Buck patted her small hand and nodded at her two brothers. "You scared us half to death when we found you missin', Crimson, and then hearin' Cotton and Red relate what happened last night, didn't help matters."

"We worry about you. I'd be devastated if you were injured or worse." Honeysuckle's tender face creased with concern for her headstrong sister.

Realizing the truth of their anxiety, Crimson was immediately contrite. "I'm sorry, Honeysuckle. I never meant to worry you. It's just I get so tired of being cooped up on this ranch all the time. And I promise I'll earn the money and pay Senor Romero back for the gelding. I just wish Black..."

"I know." Honeysuckle put her arm around Crimson. "I feel bad as you. I know how much you loved that mare."

"Ya'll's horses and the gelding is the least of our worries." Buck stopped his pacing and stood in front of Crimson, his disquiet evident. "We're mainly concerned about your safety."

Crimson fought back tears and stiffened her spine against the urge. She had sworn after her parents died, she would never cry again, but she suddenly realized it was probably an impossible pledge. "Can I please go now?"

Honeysuckle glanced at Buck, and when he shrugged his shoulders, she squeezed his arm and replied, "Go on, Sis."

Before she left the room, Buck ordered, "Cotton, you and Red cut out our best gelding and return it with Senor Romero's other horses with our apologies."

❦

CRIMSON stepped outside and leaned against the porch rail, staring off into the distance without really seeing anything until she noticed spiraling dust clouds heading toward the ranch. Curious, she shaded her eyes with her hand and watched the riders trot closer. Her heart beat a little faster when she recognized Billy the Kid and four of his men leading three horses behind them. A smile lifted her lips, spotting Blackfoot distinct coloring among the riderless horses.

Billy stopped his mount in front of her and tipped his hat in greeting. "Senorita Crimson Rose, I've brought your horses back. We hid them for a joke and planned on givin' 'em back later, but you left quicker than we thought. After I found out what Charlie Sorrel did, I decided it'd be best and bring them out here instead of leavin' them with the blacksmith in town."

"We could of made some good money on 'em, though. Ya got some fine horses here," one of Billy's men added.

"Thank you for not selling them and bringing them back instead. You don't know how much we appreciate it!" Crimson thanked Billy, walking past him and running her hand along Blackfoot's sleek white neck.

"My pleasure, ma'am. I'm also gonna apologize for Charlie. I can assure you he'll never do it again." Billy's statement was grim, insinuating he had administered his own form of punishment.

"May I offer you a cup of coffee for your trouble, Mr. Bonnie?"

"Thanks, ma'am, but we best be gettin' back. I'm returnin' these and offerin' my apology." Billy handed her the horses' reins and tipped his hat before turning his mount and heading out, his men following.

Absently stroking Blackfoot and scrutinizing the men's retreating backs, she did not hear Cotton and Red come up beside her.

"I can't believe he really returned them," Red's disbelieving comment sounded near her ear.

"Well, he did," she stated softly. "Now ya'll don't need to worry about him anymore."

"Let's hope not," Cotton replied darkly.

CRIMSON was so tired, her bones hurt, but still she had trouble sleeping. All the night and day's assorted dramas did not clear Landon Wade from her tortured brain. She tried hating him, but it still did not banish her strange attraction for him. There was something intriguing about him—maybe it was his mixed bloods rendering him unattainable. Or perhaps he was the most handsome man she'd ever met, *and* he had this wonderful man smell—clean and musky, so alluring. And his skin—dark, feeling of silk wrapped around the fascinating bulges of muscle and bone along his body. She ran her fingertips along her lips remembering his on hers, uprooting strange sensations and emotions from within every part of her.

A ragged moan slipped between her lips, and she turned over on her stomach, imagining the warmth of his body against hers. Whatever these feelings were rampaging through her body, she craved more. It was his haunting eyes that gazed at her with an intensity she'd never experienced before.

Disturbed by her errant thoughts, she flipped over and rose from the bed, dressed, then left the room.

Stepping near the porch steps, a cool breeze pressed her skirts against her legs and caressed her cheeks with light fingers. She stared at the stars, hearing the chirping cicadas sing in symphony. The moon was a pale circle in the dark sky with the stars hanging so low it was almost as if she could reach out and touch them. In a fanciful moment, she imagined the stars as diamonds and reached out making believe she stole one for an imaginary necklace around her throat.

"Yes, ya were made fer diamonds and silks," a soft mumble sounded behind her, startling her. "I didna mean to scare ya."

"What are you doing here?" Crimson snapped, embarrassed at being caught in a whimsical moment. "And who are you?"

Taking a drag of his cigarette, the tip glowing orange, he dropped it at his feet and crushed it underneath his boot's toe. "John Sullivan's the name, ma'am, and you must be Crimson Rose. I've heard a awful lot 'bout ya. Seems like all the ranch hands are singin' yore praises. They didna come close to the truth though. Yore much purtier." Quickly raking her slender, rounded form with his eyes, his smile broadened and his eyes gleamed with appreciation.

"You're a flatterer, Mr. Sullivan, but you still didn't answer my question." She stepped back as he walked around the porch, leaned against the railing and hooked his boot heel on the bottom rail.

"Jist out for a breath of air."

"You're the new ranch hand Buck hired." He was a pleasant enough looking young man with curly, sandy-blond hair framing a round cherub face with freckles standing out against the deep tan of his face which the darkness could not hide, and his smile crinkling at the corners of his dark eyes.

"Yes'um, I am."

Crimson stared out into the night, rubbing her earlobe. She shifted her gaze from the silent house toward the ranch grounds. The only light was a feeble glow from the bunkhouse and soon that would be out, and beyond that were the dark outlines of smaller buildings. She did not really refuse this stranger's company, if a stranger he was. She had the persistent impression she should know him.

They talked for a while longer discussing the ranch. "It's a beautiful night, ain't it? 'Specially without the wind blowin'. This will probably be the last night I can enjoy it 'cause in the next week or two we start roundup. I know we jist met and all, but I was a'wonderin' if we might go on a picnic or sumthin' after the cattle drive."

Crimson looked at him, searching the dark shadows hiding his expression. She should curtly turn away but instead she lingered. Quite surprised, she heard herself agreeing, "Yes, it might be nice if we knew each other better, but until then, Mr. Sullivan."

Walking off, she was amazed at her audacity in accepting a proposal from a man she just met. There was something about him that felt familiar or was it her wish of blanking Landon Wade from her mind? Or was she so lonely she would grab at any offer thrown her way? Unable to analyze her reaction, she reentered the house and headed for her bedroom.

Chapter 8
All in a Day's Work

FORT ELLIOT was silent except for the muffled voices of the sentries. Shafts of dim light shone from a few buildings where officers burned midnight oil while finishing their endless paperwork and correspondence. The lights and lively sounds from Mobeetie a scant mile away, was a beckoning beam, gesturing toward the sinful pleasures of man and where a good part of the garrison spent their hard-earned money on gambling and ladies of the evening.

The lonesome howl of a coyote cried out toward the half-moon obliterated a few moments by a quickly passing cloud and the incessant screeching of the wind pushing the man closer toward destiny.

As he drew near Feather Hill, the lower section of Mobeetie, the lights from various saloons, dance and billiard halls only suggested what lay inside. The tinny sound of a lone piano came in gushes with the blustery wind. The drunken laughter of men and the tinkling giggles of women were enhanced by the sounds of knocking billiard balls and shuffling cards.

He tied his horse at the first hitching post before going the rest of the way on foot, glancing casually at the long, darkened spaces between the buildings. He was a wary animal, instincts highly geared, footsteps soft as a bobcat's from his years of experience with Indians. Avoiding the wooden sidewalks, he walked on the hardpacked dirt street instead.

The nighttime ribaldry sounding louder and light spilling out onto the sidewalk, he shifted his cautious gaze toward the man who staggered out of the saloon, stumbled and fell down the steps. The door closed behind the drunken man with a bang, muffling the sounds inside. The comfort of the knife inside his boot and the weight of the pistol on his hip assured him he was ready for any confrontation that might come during his visit.

A wooden sign suspended on an iron pole and bearing the name Silver Saloon, screeched in protest with each wind burst. Climbing the wooden steps, they groaned underneath his weight. He opened the door, the muted glare of coal oil lamps momentarily blinding him with the stale odors assaulting his sensitive nose. He did not hesitate at the door for his vision's adjustment but made his way steadily toward the bar.

After ordering whiskey, he watched the bartender pour him a shot glass full, then with a hand motion, he indicated for the bottle be left behind. He flipped a coin onto the bar and picked up the glass before leaning against the bar's side, his elbow on the top and the other holding the small glass of amber liquid. Glancing around the room, he studied the poker tables surrounded by men with gray clouds of smoke hanging around them while glasses of beer and whiskey sat at their elbows. The oppressive smells of stale smoke, liquor, unwashed bodies and the strong stench of cheap perfume made breathing difficult, but the men sweating over the cards seemed insensitive to the disgusting combination of odors.

Something elusive briefly flickering in his eyes, he took a sip of whiskey, letting the harsh liquid wash the taste of dust from his mouth while he searched the faces of the men. Unruffled, he finished his drink and poured another.

He would wait.

Another drink later, the storage door of the saloon opened, and a man dressed in a black suit with a white ruffled shirt and black string bow tie came out, his arm wrapped around a petite blonde wearing a gaudy red dress. The man's half-closed eyes and his face mirroring satisfaction bent down and whispered something in her ear while caressing the exposed tops of her breast. She loudly giggled.

The stranger's mouth tightened. He watched Gambler and his doxy stand at the opening and share intimate pats before they parted. She went out the back door while Gambler walked toward the poker table. The stranger followed, carrying his half-empty glass and whiskey bottle.

Known simply as Half-breed, a colloquial attached to any person with mixed blood, the stranger and his reputation preceded him. The men at the table quickly made room for him while two men cut their losses, left the game and stood behind the other players.

Suspenseful tension building, players dropped out of the game one by one with none taking their places, leaving Gambler and Half-breed facing each other.

Half-breed watched Gambler shuffle the cards in front of him, aware Gambler was a card shark with many tricks up his sleeve.

"Five card stud," Gambler announced softly in the quiet room, placing the deck in front of Half-breed.

Tapping the cards with an index finger, Half-breed signified the cards remain uncut. A fine sheen of sweat broke out on Gambler's forehead, and he masked his uneasiness by rolling his handlebar moustache between a thumb and forefinger.

Half-breed kept his face carefully immobile. Vigilant observation of the man in front of him told him exactly what kind of hand he was holding. His own hand was not much better, he assumed, with a pair of deuces, but it was logical the way Gambler twirled his moustache, his were worse. He was right when Gambler turned up a hand with nothing but a queen high.

Gambler retrieved the cards, his long, lean fingers caressing them like a lover before he spread them in a neat line in front of him, then flipped them over with one deft stroke of his finger, biding for time by showing off his ability. His stack of coins had dwindled sharply in the last hands, and if he did not recoup some of his losses with the next, he would be broke—something he did not appreciate. Without winning, he could not keep his woman up in high style. He was a dealer for the Silver Saloon, but with the heavy loss of his own money plus the saloon's, he might not be for long. He shuffled the cards a few more times, keeping his eyes riveted on the dark man in front of him before placing the stack of cards down on the table in front of Half-breed.

Half-breed cut the pile near the bottom and laid it beside the other stack. Plunking the piles together, Gambler dealt the cards, his sober voice piercing through the soft murmurs, "Draw poker, nothing wild."

Waiting until all the cards were flipped out, Half-breed picked up his scattered pile and systematically placed them in order. He carefully scrutinized the ten of diamonds, seven of hearts, two treys and the ace of spades. Keeping the two treys, he threw in the other three and made his bet.

Gambler's mouth twitching in the barest of smiles, he dealt him three more cards. He matched the bet and raised it before throwing in two cards from his own hand, then dealt himself two replacements. Taking them, he tensed slightly. For the untrained eye nothing seemed out of place; it was the barest hint of tightened knuckles.

Quickly estimating how much money Gambler had in front of him, Half-breed raised the bet. It would leave Gambler with approximately twenty dollars if he called it. His face and eyes bland, he glanced at the last three cards he received—another trey and two fives, a full house.

Gambler met the scorching eyes of his opponent while calling the bet, feeling a chill of fear go through him while allowing himself a triumphant smile before laying down his hand; a full house, aces over fours. He reached out, raking in the money, but Half-breed stopped him by laying a hand on top of his.

"Not so fast, Gambler," Half-breed rasped in a steely voice. He reached out and flipped his discard pile over, revealing an ace. "You're getting sloppy, Gambler. There can't be two aces of spades." The menace in his voice made his accusation very clear— Gambler had cheated.

The faces of the men around the table grew hard, and silence surrounded the saloon so complete, a drop of spilt liquor sounded loudly in the room. The rest happened in a blur. Gambler raised his arm, the hidden derringer popping into his hand like magic. Half-breed saw the change of expression in Gambler's eyes and barely slipped the pistol from his hip while dodging the bullet careening past his ear. He fired at Gambler a split second afterwards.

Acrid smoke filled the room and billowing gray clouds of gunpowder spouted from the guns. The rest in seemingly slow motion, the recoil from the bullet blew Gambler and his chair backward. The table tipped over from his uplifted feet while blood and gore splattered across the room. While falling, his face registered shock and he sharply drew in his last breath.

The crashing chair and table sounded muffled after the loud shooting. His hand was on his chest, covering the wound of bright crimson blood seeping between his fingers. The bullet wound in front was small, but where it went through and exploded, there was a gaping hole in his back, and blood quickly spread across the hardpack dirt floor.

Half-breed rose from the chair and dispassionately watched the man die before his eyes, then retrieved the scattered coins and pocketed them.

◦◦◉◦◦◉◦◦

EXAMINING the calf again, a grim white line appeared around Landon's mouth, an angry tick working in his cheek and his eyes narrowing into mere slits. The calf's tongue had been split and kept it from nursing. Kerby Olsen stopped beside him, but Landon did not spare a look at his boss.

"Another one?" Kerby's heavy white brows drew down in a frown. At Landon's nod, he let loose a string of explicit curse words.

Landon spoke, his voice carefully modulated against the anger erupting through him, "Looks like the same rustlers doing the rest of the cattle mutilations I've found lately. I've run across calves with the muscles supporting their eyelids severed so they can't backtrack where they last spotted their mamma, and some burned between their toes with a hot iron so they couldn't walk for several days."

Kerby let off another string of curse words. "The damn bastards are getting worse every damn season. There's no telling how many damn cattle they've made off with this year, not counting the unbranded calves."

Landon tried shrugging off his cold anger from the cruel and inhumane treatment of calves. Turning, he walked toward his horse, then mounted.

Kerby followed him, still cursing with each breath, mounted and kicked his heels against the gelding's sides, imperceptibly shaking his head. There was no telling how many hundreds of cattle they had lost this season, and it would sharply cut into his profits.

Landon rode in front of him, his back rigid with anger. Though Landon seldom spoke and kept his opinions mostly unspoken, Kerby trusted his life and his livelihood in Landon's more than apt hands. He had proven his trustworthiness several times and Kerby admitted he was the best hand he'd ever hired. Though men rarely spoke about their past, some slipped a little and revealed tidbits, but Landon was more secretive.

Everything about Landon was disparate, seemingly appearing he came from two completely different worlds. Perhaps he had, he thought, remembering his first meeting. He stared at the young man, trying without luck to glimpse past the emotionless face into the man it harbored, and only when they started the sharp descent into the canyon did he avert his gaze.

His mouth tightening into a white line, Landon spied four cows butt or kick their calves who tried suckling their mothers' swollen udders. He vaulted off his horse with the grace of a panther, his stride silent and purposeful, walking toward the cows.

Kerby was not far behind him, and Landon looked back at him. He suppressed an uneasy shudder at the sharp, cold anger glinting from Landon's strange colored eyes. Shifting his gaze quickly away from Landon's, he stepped closer, his face turning all shades of red, then white, and for the first time, he was at a loss for words. The udders of the cows were slashed, keeping the calves from nursing. Ugly red wounds, some oozing with the pus of infection and flies droning around the lesions, proclaimed the rustlers had devised a new cattle-stealing technique.

Pulling off his hat, Landon slapped it against his thigh, then ran his hand through his raven black hair. "The L Heart brand. I'll notify the owner and let him decide whether he wants the cows destroyed. It ain't my call."

Backing up a step and turning, Kerby headed for his gelding. "I'll go. I know where they're camped. 'Sides, Buck Leathers is a friend of mine."

Nodding slowly, Landon watched Kerby ride toward the west. Spying a boulder along the vast plains, he sat upon it, waiting while the pitiful bawls of the calves' frustration and misunderstanding pierced the air around him.

Green shoots of grass bravely peeped their heads out from the golden grasses, the first stirring of blooming wildflowers adding color against the monotonous landscape. His thoughts, always in times of trouble or withdrawal within himself, reverted to memories of Sun-is-Setting. The pain in his heart was still a heavy burden after all this time. He felt guilty and responsible for her death. If only they had stayed away from each other, maybe she would still be alive.

Landon shook his head, dislodging the thought. It had been impossible. Their love had been too strong. She had taken him into her heart and taught him everything: tenderness, desire and love, the most important ingredients for loving a woman. And she had been his! She had given his life substance, taking the young man who fought for acceptance in the Kiowa nation and who fought the division of his white and red bloods. She was the only one who recognized the inner turmoil he kept carefully hidden behind a stony mask. In some ways, she offered him the motherly affection he cherished before his own mother died. She had become all things: friend, lover and infrequently mother with her maternal advice.

Her face was growing dim in his mind's eye, yet her spirit still lived within him. He tried recalling her back into his heart, but her black hair turned auburn with the sun sparkling off the red highlights, and her dark eyes turned meadow green. His grim mouth lifting one corner into a semblance of a half-smile, he remembered the little imp of the creek bed fauna, wondering if he would ever see her again, what her reaction would be or if she remembered him.

Sitting Indian fashion, his face hard as the stone he sat upon, once again his confusion masked by his changing personality—he was a man straddling the fence, belonging to neither of his parents' people. He was neither white nor red, and until he could merge the two successfully, he would always be an outcast among both groups.

He felt the vibration of the horses pounding the prairie long before he heard or saw them. Standing on top of the rock, he pushed back his hat and shaded his eyes with his hand. He recognized Kerby and the owner of the L Heart Ranch, but the other two riders were strangers.

Buck vaulted off his horse, his face an inflexible mask, his normally cheery voice subdued with his greeting. "Well, if it ain't Sky Eyes."

Landon nodded greeting. "Buck, I wish we were meeting each other again under happier circumstances."

"Yeah." Buck pulled off his hat and ran his fingers through his straight flowing, flaxen hair. His quick examination of the cows told him soon enough the actions needed. His anger was impotent and curled up inside of him like a rattler. If he knew who was involved in these despicable acts, they would be good as dead, but he did not and it tore at his guts. He withdrew his rifle from his scabbard and nodded when Landon looked questioningly at his rifle hanging at the side of his horse.

Buck loaded the rifle, a deadly look in his dark blue eyes. "That's a hell of a way of weaning calves so they can come back later and steal 'em." His mouth a white slash in his tanned face, he glanced at the other two men with him. "I don't have much manners today, Sky Eyes. That's Honeysuckle's two brothers, Cotton Wood and Red Cedar McFarlin."

Landon nodded at the men, his normally expressionless face quirking a bit at their strange names and held out his hand. "Landon Wade."

After the stilted introductions were made, Red built a fire while Cotton retrieved the branding irons. Buck and Landon reluctantly put the cows out of their misery. The calves were branded and driven toward the main herd.

The liveliness and hard work of the roundup soon obliterated the grimness of the mutilated cattle. The air was heavy with dust clouds, the stench of burned hair and hide, and the bawling, frantic pleas of calves calling for their mothers. Gales of laughter and ribaldry filled the air when a cowboy ran from a charging cow answering the call of her young one's cry for protection from its persecutor. The horns caught his shirt and nearly ripped it off his back. Before the roundup was over, many would have shirts and pants shredded by running from a mad mama cow.

After the last animal was tallied and the cattle scattered on grass and water, cowboys, their faces masks of sweat and dirt, raced toward the chuckwagon, riding and screaming like banshees. Huge amounts of beef, beans, sourdough biscuits, stewed dried fruit, and coffee were consumed. The cowboys' stamina was amazing as they rose at first light, worked hard all day, came in at dusk, ate, and then took turns watching the cattle during the night. After their meal, they rolled one last cigarette and smoked before dropping into their bedrolls and instantly falling asleep.

The night before the cattle drive started for Dodge City, Kansas, Buck approached Cotton and Red. "We better head back and ya'll can say goodbye to your sisters or they'll never forgive us."

༄ঔৎঌৎঌৎ৶ৡ

WATCHING the three men ride off into the night, he slowly rolled a cigarette. He could not believe his good luck. The boss left for the night, and he had first watch at the farthest point of the herd. The match flared up and he cupped his hand against the wind, lighting his cigarette. Shaking out the match, he flipped it off into the darkness before striding toward his horse. Mounting, he rode off into the dark night.

Chapter 9
Stormy

WITH THE rolling golden-brown prairie grasses stretching out in front of her, Crimson urged Blackfoot into a run. The morning sun was at her back, gilding her long, auburn hair in bright red streaks and flowing behind her with the wind blowing it back from her face, exposing a healthy glow on her high cheekbones and cooling the perspiration from her forehead.

An unidentified tension filled the house these last few days with Buck back from the cattle drive. Buck's face held a pinched, worried look, and he kept running his fingers distractedly through his hair. Even Honeysuckle did not know what bothered him. It only intensified the distant feeling Crimson had experienced with her family lately. It was not only her brothers who had left the family nest but something more subtle, something within herself.

Urging her horse faster, she leaned over the mare's neck. Her dissatisfaction lately had grown more pronounced, and she did not understand why. Maybe it had been John Sullivan's attention after they met every night on the porch before he became busy with the roundup, branding longhorns and then driving cattle toward Dodge City. He made her feel alive, and yet there was something elusive and intriguing about him. Some long-ago memory flitted around her head, but she could not put her finger on it, and it disturbed her.

She thought of him often while he was on the cattle drive and contemplated the idea of marriage with him several times. The summer was nearly past and he had not come back with the others but had left for a couple of weeks. She heard some ranch hands say he was back and out in the west pasture. She tried picturing his face, but the image of the man she had seen bathing at the creek intruded instead.

With a hearty packed lunch of biscuits and ham left over from breakfast and freshly baked cookies, she headed toward the west pasture and a planned chance meeting. Though he promised several times before the cattle drive he would take her on a picnic, her impatience grew when he never contacted her afterward.

She slowed Blackfoot after spying three men ahead. She recognized John Sullivan's stout frame, but she could not see the other two well enough for identification. They were so engrossed in their conversation that they did not hear her coming.

John instinctively looked over his shoulder. Seeing the lone horse and rider draw near, he swept off his hat and muttered a foul oath. "What the hell is she doin' here?"

"I know her," Harvey breathed suddenly. "Ain't she the McFarlin girl?" At John's annoyed nod, Harvey swore. "Why didna ya say sumthin'? Has she recognized ya yet?"

"If she has, she ain't said nothin'. Let's jist hope she don't either." His frown deepening and anger sweeping across him, John glared at the young woman riding toward them. What was she doing this far from the ranch? "It might be better if ya'll left."

The other man mounted his horse and kicked his heels against its flanks, damned if he'd let a snip of a girl see him with these two. It was imperative he kept his association with these men secret.

Nearing the men, all Crimson saw was his retreating slender back and the Stetson perched on his head, briefly reminding her of the half-breed Landon Wade. She stopped her mount in front of John while the other man mounted.

"Hey, wait!" When he lifted his face, recognition crossed hers. "I remember you. You're Harvey James. You always pulled my pigtails when we were in school. Do you remember me? I'm Crimson Rose McFarlin."

"Howdy do, Miz McFarlin. 'Course I remember ya. Been a long time," Harvey nervously answered.

The elusive memory that kept appearing on her mind's edges suddenly materialized, and her eyes widened. "I knew I should know you, but your name ain't John Sullivan. It's Tom Martin." With memories of long ago flooding her mind, she missed the tightening of John's mouth. Why hadn't she recognized him before? They had sworn a childish oath promising when they grew up, they would marry. And how many times had she thought about marrying him when she believed his name was John Sullivan? Too many times! After all these years it seemed impossible that they would meet again, especially so far from their former home in Kansas.

"Ma'am, nice seein' ya agin," Harvey replied, anxiously wanting away from the silent confrontation going on between his partner and the McFarlin girl. John's color turned a murderous red and his eyes were narrowed. Harvey had witnessed his killing look too many times. Turning his mount, he headed out, damned if he was getting involved with killing a woman.

John grabbed Blackfoot's bridle in anticipation of Crimson leaving, but she just stared at him, her face revealing a mingle of shock, happiness and confusion.

"Why did you lie? Why didn't you tell me straight out who you were? Our friendship goes way back, Tom. Do you think I would've broken our friendship by telling someone your real name? Whatever the reason you had for changing it, I'm sure it's a good one."

Relaxing slightly, John released the mare's bridle and ran his hand down the mare's neck until he was beside her. He helped her dismount, purposely holding her close and letting her front slide down his body. He tightened his grip on her shoulders, fighting with himself whether to caress or squeeze them while at the same time struggling with his anger and his desire of strangling her. "I did, but I dinna know if'n ya'd keep yore mouth shut. It's been eight years since we last saw each other."

Unaware of his inner turmoil, she smiled. "Tom, we might have been kids, but the things we promised each other is still as special now as they were back then. Or have you forgotten?" she softly inquired, her meadow green eyes capturing his.

Before answering, he took a moment, forcing his anger down. "I remember. I promised ya I'd marry ya when we got older. It was a long time ago and we were nothin' but silly kids."

Bitter disappointment filled her, and she glanced down, hiding it. "Yes, I guess that's true." Hurt, she stepped back from him, flinching when his fingers dug deeper into her shoulders. "Tom, why did you change your name?"

He relaxed his grip when he saw the pain cross her face. "We cain't talk 'bout it now. Just believe me, it was for a good reason and maybe one day I'll tell ya. If ya value our friendship, then trust me." She opened her mouth, but before she could speak, he laid his index finger across her lips. "Trust me."

A thousand questions filling her eyes, the rough texture of his finger felt cold across her full lips and stopped her from speaking.

Tom's hands crept around her neck, tenderly caressing the slender column with his hands jerking involuntarily every few seconds while debating whether he should wring her pretty neck or go with another plan. With no immediate decision, he dropped his hands and clasped her shoulders.

"Tom, don't worry about me telling anybody who you really are or maybe I should say John."

"Crimson, for old times' sake, I wish ya'd keep this to yoreself. We'll talk later, but right now leave so I can git back to work."

"But…I packed a lunch for us."

"Thanks, but not today. Go afore ya git me fired."

❧◦⊙⊱⊙⊰⊙◦❧

LANDON glanced at the sky, his forehead wrinkled in a worried frown. The sun wove in and out of the gathering clouds and the wind steadily rose. The sun slipped behind another cloud, outlining it in silver and brilliant white, its center gray with patches of blue fleetingly peeking in between the varying shades of gray rolling clouds, and in the west, the skies grew into a near solid mass, growing darker. The long grasses undulated like millions of brown snakes racing across the prairie. Lightning streaked sideways across the skies with wicked glee, reminding him of a devil's pitchfork, and seconds afterward boomed with thunder.

Pressing his knees against the stallion's sides, he urged him faster. The trail he followed would disappear within a matter of seconds with the coming rain unless he outran it, but the wind increased rapidly, proving the hopeless impossibility of beating it.

Cresting the hill, he looked down at the small tributary of the Canadian River. Wind whipped the dry sand in blasts, bringing stinging sprays with each gust. Pushing back his Stetson, he stared at the small figure sitting on a rock along the dry riverbed, instantly recognizing the young woman who haunted his dreams. She sat with her arms wrapped around her legs and her chin lying on top of her knees, oblivious to the increasingly bad weather and him.

He kneaded Ebony down the sandy banks, and with the ready ease of self-confidence and complete control, kept his seat when the stallion stumbled, then righted itself.

Nearing Crimson, he saw tears marring the perfection of her ivory face, and his heart ached for her and yet, simultaneously, cried out against it.

Dismounting, he tied his unpredictable stallion several yards away and stealthily approached her before stopping directly in front of her. Tears coursed down her cheeks, and he barely refrained from reaching out and wiping them away. He fought the urge of comforting her and telling her everything would be fine, but he could not.

Instinct, not any sound, brought her eyes up. "It's you!"

A semblance of a smile crept along his stern lips; she answered a question that preyed upon his mind. Would she remember him and the day at the stream?

Crimson had been so immersed in her own bitterness against John, along with memories of Landon and their interaction, which was always at the forefront of her memories, she had not noticed anyone approaching her. She could not forget him, though she tried. Their unconventional conversation, him spanking her for daring him once too often, his copper body glistening with water, and the wildfire searing her soul from his kiss. There was something about him that was unforgettable, and she desperately fought against her attraction to him. "What do you want?"

Sweeping off his hat, he made a mocking bow. "Nothing." He straightened and watched her wipe away the tears with the back of her hand.

"What are you doing here? This is L Heart range."

He shrugged and answered sardonically, "One might ask you the same."

Her lips compressed into a thin white line and marred her normally open face, annoyed and angry at the same time he caught her in a moment of weakness. "My brother-in-law owns this land."

This was the one who haunted her, his sky-blue eyes mocking her, disturbing her dreams and emotions when she should be thinking about Tom, no, John Sullivan. She must remember that.

Even more handsome than she remembered, his raven black hair whipped in alluring disarray across his forehead, his heavy black brow uplifted with amusement, one side of his mouth cocked, his eyes strangely lit and holding her motionless. Tearing her eyes from his, her gaze traveled down his broad chest, slim waist and below his belt. Her face suddenly flamed, remembering what lay underneath his clothing, and she hastily tore her eyes away when his mocking laughter erupted.

"You are a little spy, my dear," he teased, amused her face turned nearly the same shade as her hair. The curious, intent traveling of her eyes along his body told him easily enough she remembered the day very well. "I must admit you are the first white woman who ever watched me bathe, and I did enjoy giving you a show."

"I did no such thing!"

He threw back his head and laughed, a deep rumbling sound coming from the depths of his soul. "I think the maiden does protest too much!" He wondered briefly where such silly words came from. They were totally alien, but he quickly rationalized he must have heard them in school long ago in some form or another. "Come now, admit it. There's no shame in it. Had it been you taking a bath in the stream, I would of done the same."

"Why you...you..." There were no adequate words describing how horrible she thought him. She rose in one fluid motion, the embarrassed red of a moment ago transversing into fury. "You low down, stinking buzzard, and I will not stand here and take your crude wisecracks." She turned abruptly, her riding skirt billowing out, then slapping against her legs.

Grabbing her arm, he held her firmly, refusing to let her leave. "Not so fast, my little spy. You're coming with me. A storm's a brewing overhead and those black clouds yonder look like they might hold a tornado."

"Don't touch me!" she screeched, jerking back from him. "I don't give a damn about those clouds and I'm not going anywhere with you!"

"The hell you ain't! I'll be damned if I let you refuse me when the storm is getting closer."

Crimson looked up and large drops of rain splashed over her uplifted face, her objection dying before uttered. As if in keeping with the truth of Landon's words, a spiraling funnel dropped from the blackness, descending toward the ground.

Seeing the tornado drop from the mass of rolling black clouds, Landon realized its destructive force was headed straight toward them. Grabbing her arm, he pulled her toward her mount. "Hurry up!" he shouted against the whipping blasts of wind. Grabbing her by the waist, he threw her on her saddled horse before jumping on the back of his stallion and motioning her to follow him. He remembered the sod remains of a house close by built by Mexican farmers long ago. It may not protect them much, but it was better than being caught in the midst of certain disaster.

Landon leaned low over Ebony's neck, clutching the reins. The stinging rain and sand nearly blinded him, and the wind seemed determined to blow him off his horse. Looking back once and seeing her still following, he did not turn around again.

Clutching the reins and leaning forward, ragged breaths and choked cries escaping from her compressed lips, Crimson grasped the horse's mane, fighting against being blown off its back. The wind spiraled around them, shifting directions as quickly as a woman changed her mind, and picking up debris with each mighty gust. It took her breath away, threatening to tear her from Blackfoot's back, and tore her favorite hat from her head along with ripping the pins from her haphazard hair she pinned up while sitting at the river. The wild tresses lashed at the tender flesh of her face, almost blinding her.

The furious wind sounded like a freight train rushing toward them. The rolling clouds completely obliterated the feeble shafts of sun and the lightning's wicked, jagged streaks speared the blackened skies, followed seconds later by the explosive crash of thunder, shaking the ground underneath them.

In their harrowing race against the raging storm, Blackfoot's sides heaved with the effort of obeying her mistress' commands. Crimson silently prayed, crying in ragged breaths of fear they found shelter before the tornado caught up with them.

As the storm darkened around them, she followed blindly, afraid if she lost sight of the man in front of her, the destructive, whirling mass would suck her up into its massive center where she would swirl forever lost inside. Blackfoot's muscular flanks tightened and relaxed each time she hit the ground, and both fought for breath, but her fear kept them blindly following the man in front of them with the trust of a child.

Time passed in utter slowness before they reached the dim outlines of the almost forgotten building. Part of the walls and roof had caved in, but in one corner there was enough roof left for shelter from the downpour.

With a mingle of relief and fear, Crimson slid off Blackfoot. Landon grabbed the reins of her horse and shouted above the roar, but the wind snatched his words away. His wild gesturing toward the adobe building propelled her toward it.

Entering the dark interior, the brunt of the wind lessened. Her sodden clothes clung to her clammy skin and violent shivering possessed her, as much from fear as from the cold wind. The interior pitch black, she timidly stretched out her hands toward the crumbling walls and felt it shake under the onslaught of the storm. Feeling along the wall, she found the far corner and collapsed, sliding down the damp mass. She sat down, clasping her knees and laying her chin on top, huddling there while Landon brought in their mounts.

The horses fought the bits, screaming in terror and pawing at the wet ground. Crooning soft, calming words, Landon struggled with the frightened horses until his arms bulged with the effort. The animals calmed a bit, still uneasy but enough to be tied down without them breaking free and running.

He tested a fallen ceiling beam, found it sturdy and deftly tied the reins around it. After patting their flanks, he reached behind his mount and took the slicker and bedroll from behind his saddle.

Sensing Crimson's terror along with the animals, though she

said not one word and no sound escaped from her tight lips, he suppressed the desire of dropping everything, enclosing her in his arms and comforting her. With the bedroll and slicker under one arm, he reached out and took Crimson's hand, forcing her on her feet. He spread the bedroll on the ground and pulled her beside him, then covered them both with the slicker.

The oilskin coat succeeded in blocking off a better part of the blowing rain, but the cold fingers of wind found tiny crevices and crept through, chilling their bones. Cold and frightened, and her teeth chattering, she almost sighed in ecstasy when Landon's arms snaked around her shoulders and pulled her closer against the warmth of his body. No thoughts of it being right or wrong for his arms around her and his embrace entered her mind. They were together under unpredictable circumstances, and she needed his warmth almost as much as she needed the air she breathed.

The slight figure in his arms intoxicated his senses. He gave her his warmth and took from hers, smiling in satisfaction when her trembling lessened. Her soft breast pressed against his side warmed his blood and teased his body. She relaxed against him and laid her head against his shoulder, tendrils of her hair snaking across his face, tickling his nose, and the faint smell of vanilla filling his nostrils, the scent reminding him of sweet cinnamon rolls. Her wet hair clung around his face and he brushed the red tendrils from her cheeks, her skin silken underneath his touch. His crooked smile widened when she sighed softly against his neck, her breath a soft caressing breeze sneaking through the turbulent storm.

Crimson snuggled closer against him, aware of the scent of woodsmoke and horses emanating from his clothing and the outdoorsy smell of his skin. It lulled her into a type of calm. His fingers touching her face burned her skin, and his breath fanned her ear and the surrounding area, sending a strange tingling along her spine when he bent close.

"You never did tell me your last name."

She turned her head toward his ear and came within a bare inch of his lips. "McFarlin."

"Crimson Rose McFarlin," he repeated, saying it like a caress, rolling it around his tongue. "Are you any kin to Honeysuckle Leathers?"

"She's my sister."

They moved their heads back and forth, speaking in each other's ear.

"Don't you have some brothers with names like trees? Yeah, Cotton Wood and Red Cedar. Right?"

She nodded against his shoulder, hearing the slight chuckle in his voice, and a smile lifted her mouth. They did have strange names.

An uprooted tree crashed several yards away, shaking her out of her false calm. The wind picked up volume and thunder exploded overhead. His arm tightened around her, and he patted her shoulder while crooning softly in her ear in much the same way he had the horses.

Crimson changed from a hellcat with the first meeting into a frightened little kitten, intriguing him with her fiery temper, her reticence and fear, and how she cuddled against him, seeking his warmth and protection, all soft and womanly.

He spoke loudly in her ear over the storm surrounding them while he regained his composure, forcing his attention from her softness pressed against his side. "Tell me about your strange names."

Worried about her family, fear ate at the edges of her mind. Was her sister and the kids safe? She silently thanked him for his attempt of softening her fears, but he only succeeded in reminding her of them. Her lips trembling and tears misting her eyes, her words breathed across his bent ear. "My father had a strange sense of humor before he drank himself to death. He wanted sturdy sons able to bend with the harshest times, and girls sweet and lovely as flowers. He would tell us the story about our names, but it was Honeysuckle who kept the story alive by retelling it."

Fierce pride and a touch of embarrassment filled her voice. Hers and Honeysuckle's names were not so bad, but Cotton and Red? She knew of several who had sported more than one bloodied nose and blackened eye when they made fun of them.

Catching the anxious tone in her voice, he reassuringly squeezed her shoulder. Her mouth moved past his, and their lips briefly brushed. He heard her sharp intake of breath and felt the sudden tremor in her limbs, the brevity of those soft lips touching his own and igniting his blood. His lips thinning into a straight line, he fought the hunger boiling in him, his instinct warning him she was an innocent, untouched maiden.

It was hard keeping his emotions banked. He had never allowed another woman close enough for his emotions to become involved. It was simple relieving his loins with the few prostitutes he had visited and afterwards fleeing like a frightened deer when they attached too much significance with his desire, but for some reason, this young woman tugged at his heart. "Why were you crying?"

Denying the obvious, Crimson shook her head against his shoulder. What did she know about him? How could she trust a total stranger with her hurt reaction with John's crude dismissal of her planned picnic? He was delving into her mind, shaking her control, warming more than just her outer body. A storm built inside her, hysterical laughter building in her throat, but at the same time, her lips desired a closer examination of the warm ones that had touched hers so briefly, producing pleasant sensations throughout her body. A strange aching developed inside her, a loneliness needing comfort, something crying out she was a woman now. Shaking her head against his shoulder, she fought down the wayward emotions.

To dispel some of the tension building between them, she turned toward him. "You never did tell me why you're here."

A crooked smile lifted his full mouth, and he cocked an eyebrow in teasing mockery. "No, I didn't, but then you didn't either."

"I did so. I said my brother-in-law owned the land."

Her answer insufficient, he shrugged his shoulder, a half-smile playing about his lips. They were once again shifting their heads, their lips near the other's ears. Those full lips tempted him, and the next time she moved close, he did not move back but allowed his lips brush across hers.

Chapter 10
Begging Eyes

THE WORDS died unspoken. Her tongue flicked along her trembling lips, gathering the touch unto herself, and her lowered lashes hid her uncertainty. Crimson shivered and Landon pulled her closer against him. Lifting her eyes, she lost herself in the baby blue depths and watched the corners of his eyes crinkle with his smile, his eyelashes drooping while capturing her mouth with his.

He licked along the outer edges, teasing, evoking strange sensations along her spine, then slipped his tongue between her lips, probing until she unclenched her teeth. Their tongues met in an unexpected sensual dance, his tongue exploring the inside of her mouth and eliciting sensations in her breasts begging for his touch. Encircling his neck, her fingers entwined in the thick hair at the nape, she shifted closer, wanting her body molded against every inch of his.

His fingers caressed along the velvety softness of her jaw and tangled in her unruly auburn-red hair, his kiss deepening as he held her tenderly against him. The rain grew stronger, blowing into the corner where they sat, the stinging wet drops interrupting them. Slipping the slicker over their heads, he eased her entirely onto the ground while his hand slipped over the gentle curve of her breast.

Sighing with his gentle pressure massaging the mound, she shifted her hips until she felt his hard bulge pressed against her stomach. With her hands growing warmer around his neck, she pulled him tighter against her.

Straining for control, he released her lips and found her emerald-green eyes mirroring the same confusion and desire he was experiencing. Hail hit the ground slowly at first, then picked up speed. Fighting for some semblance of control over their towering emotions, they sat up and watched the white marble-sized pellets hit the soggy ground and bounce around like rubber balls. He had not totally released her, and when a small shiver went through her, he pulled her snuggly back into his arms.

"Why did you kiss me?" she asked softly.

"Do I need a reason?"

She pulled back from him and studied his face, searching the emotionless mask for an answer. "Yes, I hate you." Her words did not carry conviction.

"Do you, Crimson, or are you just mad I caught you watching me bathe?"

Reminded of the spanking, she completely withdrew from his arms. "No man has ever touched me before and what you did deserves my hate."

Landon smiled, remembering the soft breast momentarily underneath his palm before the hail hit and interrupted them. "Maybe I should have left you at the creek instead of bringing you here."

He said the words warmly, softly conveying a different meaning, and a little shiver ran down her back, alarming her. "You would have liked that, wouldn't you? Well, I don't care what you do and...I'll never forgive you for spanking me." Crimson moved over a little further, leaving several inches between them, the cold seeping through where his body had touched hers only moments before.

"You ungrateful, little twit! If you'd leave your temper at home once in a while you might see things differently." His pleasant tone of moments before carried traces of anger.

"You damn...damn..."

"Half-breed," he supplied coldly. "What I should do is bend you over my knee, young lady, and beat some gratitude into you. If nothing else, someone needs to beat those words out of you. Your language is bad as the sporting ladies in Mobeetie." He reached toward her, indicating he would carry out his threat.

"Don't touch me! I'm warning you, Mr. Wade. I ain't submitting this time. You did it once, and I swear you ain't gonna do it again." Her voice was low and menacing, telling him she would fight tooth and nail this time. Already her hands were drawn into claws.

He should prove his threat and show her who was the strongest, instead he icily retorted, "You couldn't carry on a civil conversation if it meant your life."

"I could if I had someone civil to talk to."

"Alright, let's try." He was already weary of her hot temper yet fought his attraction and yearning of having her completely, compliantly, willingly beneath him. Suspecting he was the only man who had ever kissed her, especially after coaxing her clenched teeth apart, his loins tightened again remembering how their tongues met, her body turning soft and hot at the same time, her arms closing around his neck and her body searching out the length of him with a hunger matching his own.

Shifting her knees against her chest and clasping her arms around them, she eyed him suspiciously, wondering what new game he was playing. She squeezed her thighs tighter together against the funny pressure between her legs, fighting the desire of lying down and discover the reason and possibly the cure for the unfulfilled ache. It did not help they had been at dagger's point from the very beginning, and she saw no reason of stopping at this late date. But then what did she have to lose?

Drawing in a shuddering breath, she changed her mind—anything that would stop the strange sensation between her legs demanding something she did not understand. "Where do you work?"

Landon smiled crookedly. "Depends on where you're talking about. Wherever you mean, it's still too far from here."

His vague answer had her struggling for his comment's meaning. Was he implying that he lived too far away and would never see her again or he had no desire for another encounter with her? Or perhaps he was hiding what type of work he did? "That's what I mean about not being able to talk civil with you. You haven't given me a straight answer yet."

"Then try me again," he encouraged, realizing his mistake.

Searching his face, she studied it, determining if he was willing to have an amicable conversation. "Were you at the Romero baile?"

"I was. I caught a glimpse of your flaming hair, but you were gone before I could speak with you."

He answered one question, so she tried another. "What were you doing there?"

Crossing his legs Indian fashion, he leaned his elbows on his thighs. "I was riding toward Mobeetie and stopped there for the night."

"But why?"

"Crimson, I said we'd try to have a polite conversation. I didn't say I'd tell you everything." Her eyes shot emerald sparks, and he regretted his answer of not explaining more.

"I knew you wouldn't tell me a damn thing."

"And I should of known you couldn't control your damn temper."

"Why should I?" she cried, standing and walking toward the opening of the shelter.

Rising swiftly, he caught her arm and whirled her around, his eyes pinpoints of chilling lights. Instead of a sharp retort, he caught her by surprise when he lowered his mouth on hers, pulling her forcefully against him until she felt every angle of his hard body against hers. The anger of moments before quickly drained out of her and was replaced instead with liquid fire. Her knees grew weak and she leaned against him, wanting the kiss to last forever, intrigued by his rod-iron stiffness pressing against her stomach, but almost as quickly as it began, it ended.

He pushed back from her, his mouth a white slash against his copper skin. "Go home, Crimson, before I decide I want more from you than just a kiss."

Flustered, she turned away from him, despising him and the all-too-familiar ache between her legs that started the first time she watched him bathe.

The hail stopped and the sun bravely peeped its head out from behind a cloud, the fingers of sudden light blinding her. As her anger boiled near the breaking point, still a strange sadness engulfed her.

For some reason, she turned back toward him, the obstinacy of her eyes turning into a soft, liquid green silently begging him for something she had no words for nor understanding.

Reading her silent plea, a muffled groan tore from his throat. He closed the distance between them in one long stride and took her in his arms. Lowering his mouth until his lips brushed against hers, his harsh whisper breathed across her lips, "Damn you, Crimson Rose, for your begging eyes." He captured her lips, molding and probing hers until she opened her mouth and accepted his tongue.

Like a gunpowder keg, something exploded between them that no amount of sanity could extinguish, the hate she so often uttered nothing but a spoken word, a phrase keeping her from admitting what she truly felt for this man. Her arms snaked around his neck and she tugged him firmer against her. Putty in his hands, she whimpered when he slid his hand from the curve of her waist and lifted her into his arms, not breaking their kiss, and carried her back into the ramshackle haven.

Gently lowering her onto the bedroll, Landon broke the kiss and laid beside her, one side of his mouth lifting into a half smile with her hungered whimper, and her hands fastened around his shoulders. His hand rested at her waist and his lips were near the shell of her ear. "No matter how much we try, my little spy, we cannot deny this attraction between us."

He nibbled on her ear, sending delicious tingles through her. "I gave you a chance to flee and now it's too late."

She weakly shook her head, whether refuting him or herself, she never knew. The chemistry between them kept them fighting their temptation for each other while at the same time giving into it. "Damn you for the half-breed you are, I want you near me, but I still hate you," Crimson groaned through clenched teeth, but her words carried little conviction.

Landon nuzzled her neck. "Perhaps, but you desire me more." With the fullness of her breast filling his hand, the sharp sensation cut off her rejoinder. A yearning, fierce as her anger and red hot as her hair, swept like wildfire through her entire being. She grabbed his head, entwined her fingers in the blackness of silken strands and aggressively pulled his mouth down hard against hers.

The fervor of her kiss surprised and pleased him, heating his body until he pressed his aching hardness against her soft stomach. Her body smelled and tasted of vanilla mixed with the scent of desire. Though he believed her a virgin, she proved as passionate in desire as in anger. He ground his mouth against hers, taking everything she gave, and she giving it back, trembling and pressing herself against his body. His hands played upon her soft breast, feeling the nub stiffen underneath his palm. Their breathing ragged, he pulled back and stared at her through slitted, burning eyes. He trailed his finger teasingly along her jaw, over her passion swollen lips along her cheekbones.

She placed her hand over his, moving it over her mouth and kissed his palm without opening her eyes. "Is this all? Is there more?"

Moving his thumb across her plump lips, he caressed her cheek, along her neck to the tender hollow in the front before lowering his hand down the front of her blouse. Unbuttoning her blouse, he mumbled against her cheek, "Yes, little one, there's more, much more. I'll take you so far into the white man's heaven you'll never wanna return."

Drawing the edges of her blouse apart and revealing her breasts, he lowered his lips, kissed around her neck and dropped his face between her breasts, the taste of vanilla pleasant on his lips and tongue. Her whimper increased as he captured a breast and feasted on it. The cherry red nipples hardened against his tongue and a mellifluous, ecstatic moan glided across her lips, her hips shifting upward. He had never heard such pleasurable sounds from a woman before and his manhood stiffened more. His body demanded he have her, and unless the world suddenly ended, he would fulfill both their needs.

She instinctively opened her legs with his hand dropping lower toward the edge of her riding skirt and traveling up her leg. Another whimper escaped her when his hand touched her aching mound and her hips rose, chasing the sensation. With his mouth suckling her breast and his hand slipping between her legs exploring the wet apex between them, her eagerness increased with his fingers skidding between her nether lips. Her hips lifted, wanting more, and a sharp sigh escaped her with his finger landing on the hardened tip there and his gentle stroking. She could not stop her hips from moving with his finger, the sensation of pleasure commanding the natural movements. "Please don't stop," she breathlessly begged, wondering why the plea slipped from her mouth. Her body ached down there and needed some type of fulfillment, something she did not understand but wanted anyway.

He kissed down her stomach, whispering, "Only for a moment, Little Spy. Only long enough to undress you." He carefully slipped the tip of his finger into the wet warmth between her thighs, grinning with the increased movement of her hips as he gently nudged his finger back and forth, his satisfaction and excitement growing with her movements forcing his finger deeper. Capturing her lips again, he removed his hand from underneath her skirt, one corner of his mouth quirking with her disappointed groan.

Shifting upward, he quickly unbuttoned her skirt and kissed down her chest and along her legs as he tugged it past her feet. After removing her boots, he stripped them both without a word of denial being issued from her mouth.

With his hand propping up his head, he watched the light play upon her ivory skin and her small breast agitatedly rising, the dark cherry-red peaks hardening proudly. He touched a pert nipple, tracing along the upper curve down the indentation of her waist and over gently rounded hips riding atop long muscular legs. The sunlight caught the red highlights in the thick bush between her legs, sparkling like a ruby, inviting him to steal the precious jewel it harbored. Her hips squirmed uncertainly beneath his stare, the motion all at once innocent, inviting and teasing.

Her eyelids fluttered open when he removed his hands from her completely, her questioning eyes locked with his, silently begging him for more, and she raised her arms toward him in an open invitation.

He laid down beside her and cupped the side of her face. "You're like a goddess tormenting men. Are you real or are you a cruel apparition playing upon the emotions of mortals?"

Her laugh sultry, she pressed her cheek against his hand while lifting her own and stroking the side of his face. "I'm mortal, Landon, with an aching inside of me that demands something. Please show me what it is. I don't think I can stand this anymore without knowing."

The innocence of her words stirred his hunger higher and his manhood stiffened harder. While caressing her willing body, he fiercely kissed her. There was no reticence or virgin protestations he would have expected from another. She was liquid fire, waiting for his cooling touch. Dropping his head toward her breasts, he took one nipple in his mouth, gently suckling it while his other hand played upon her other breast, caressing it, then tweaking the nipple between his thumb and forefinger.

Her hips rose against his arm until his elbow touched the red bush between her legs. A moan slipped between her lips and she moved her hips against his elbow, searching for the pleasure point again. Giving her nipple another little pinch, he lowered his hand and settled it over the thick bush between her legs, tangling it there with his index finger slipping along the pouting lips. She opened up like a morning rose blooming with the rising sun and would blossom fully before the day was through.

She gyrated underneath his hand while many different sensations drummed through her, from her breasts to the secret part of her, meeting somewhere in between and erupting into a melting in her lower regions that demanded fulfillment. Sucking in her breath with the sensation, he teased each breast and his finger slipped along the pouting nether lips, touching the throbbing center of her.

A ravishing flame shot through her veins, intensifying with his gentle teasing. She subconsciously lifted her hips in time with his strokes, the crispness of his hair filling one hand, the other moving over the satiny, roped muscles along his back with an urgency steadily building within her.

Lowering his hand, he found the tight opening guarding her precious jewel. He probed higher, widening out the snug shelter with his fingers, struggling against his own need. Gently nipping at her nipple, he used his thumb to move with the intrusion of his fingers, her moans growing louder and her hips moving more quickly against his busy hand.

He released her nipple and whispered into her ear, "Let go, Crimson." Taking her nipple back into his mouth, he sucked and nipped it, and increased the speed and pressure between her legs. He felt the tightening of her channel and her hips shot upward and froze before she let out a mewling groan and exploded with pleasure. He slowed his movements, releasing some of the force, and worked her past the most intense parts of her climax.

An intensive fever propelled his hand free from between her legs before he moved over her. His own passion flaming hotter, his hardness unerringly found the opening. His hands moved between their lower bodies, and he tenderly moved the strands of hair away from the precious shelter before he pushed forward a little at a time, allowing her channel's adjustment for his hardened girth.

Reaching the barrier of her virginity, he paused, waiting for something more and enticing him further. She opened her eyes, the lids half closed and revealing the sensual depths of her desire, her hips gently lifting. He took her mouth, devouring it while breaking through the barrier.

Crimson stiffened against the tearing pain inside her but uttered no sound. Landon laid on top of her unmoving, gently brushing the tangled mass of hair from her face, his lips worshipping hers. The pain quickly passed and the sweet throbbing built once more. Slowly moving her hips against him, he matched her rhythm. The pleasure grew more intense, and more so when he dropped his hand between them, touching her sensitive area. He opened the swollen, lower lips further rubbing against it with his thrusts. Groaning with pleasure-seeking release, they both rushed toward culmination, exploding with blinding ecstasy.

It was the most beautiful sensation in the world, and if this was heaven, she never wanted to come back down. But the phenomenon disappeared too quickly, and she settled back down like a leaf slowly drifting on the wind. Languishment weighed her limbs.

Landon lay beside her and pulled her into his arms, nestling her head against his shoulder. Shafts of sunlight caught the fine sheen of perspiration on their bodies and sparkled like so many miniature diamonds.

A satisfied smile playing about her lips, Crimson traced a pattern across his finely muscled chest, the smoothness like the finest satin. She could stay this way forever with the warm fingers of sunlight playing across her naked flesh and the deep sense of security sweeping away her loneliness.

"Can we go back to heaven?" she asked softly, moving her hand toward his softening member, understanding now why it grew and hardened and its purpose. Closing her hand around his softened member, she gently coaxed it stiff again and wondered if this was what Honeysuckle considered a handle and between her legs was the churn. A smile tugged at her lips with the wonder of it all. Why did she wait so long? This type of churning butter was most delightful.

Chuckling against her mouth, he moved his hand between her legs and thrummed his fingers against her love bud before pushing a finger inside her. Watching her lips purse and the closing of her eyes, he gave her his full attention, stroking her, coaxing her again to chase her pleasure, amazed his manhood quickly hardened and swelled. After she relaxed some, he entered her and heard her soft sighing moan, and enjoyed her hips moving against his. He was in no hurry now and moved gently, evenly within her, surprised when he felt her tightening against his hardness. Her moans increased with the shudders of her body and her love tunnel pulsated around his member. He kept up his steady strokes, amazed she reached a third peak.

She fascinated him, teaching him a woman could have several climaxes instead of just one. Taking his time, he enjoyed feeling her pulse around his stiff organ with her tunnel fluttering around him with each move, and her legs clasping around his waist until he moved faster and harder, his own climax near. Soon as he felt her tighten against him again, he spewed his hot juice inside her, his groans mingling with her suddenly increasing moans.

Lifting slightly on his arms, he gazed down at her, noticing the tears squeezing past her closed eyelids and flowing down the sides of her face. He lowered his head and took her lips, gently kissing her and knowing he had no desire to leave her but knew he had no choice. It was better this way, he decided, running his tongue along the channel of her ear and whispering, "You'd better go home now. I'm sure your family's worried about you."

Reaching up, she stroked both sides of his face. "I like being in heaven with you. Will it always be this way?"

"Between us?" he asked softly. "Most likely yes, but perhaps not with other men, Crimson." He could feel his manhood stirring once again with her whispered words, and God help him, he wanted her again, realizing he would never get enough of her. He also felt a deep stab of jealousy at the thought of any other man touching her instead of him.

A blush crossed her cheeks, and she licked her lips. "I didn't know this could be so good, this going to heaven with you, and for some reason, I never wanna stop though I feel a little sore. Will you go home with me?" she asked, suddenly timid. Shouldn't there be more between them considering what they shared—this heavenly sensation of two people connecting in the most sensuous manner?

He rose on his elbow so he could read her eyes. There was a silent message in them, one he could not acknowledge. "No, little spy. We've shared something very special, but now it's time we go our separate ways."

Chapter 11
Oil and Water

HER PEACEFUL calm fled. Rising, Crimson crouched on her knees and glared at him. "You take what I so freely gave and leave, and that's the end of it? Is this all there is between us, Landon? Just this one time in heaven?"

His eyes glass hard, Landon rose with her. He grabbed her arms and pulled her back against him, her stiffly held body a barrier between them. She was constantly on his mind and in his dreams, but they could never be together. His mixed blood was a stronger deterrent in the white world than the Kiowa's. Her association with him would ruin her reputation. "What more do you want between us? Marriage? Will you marry me knowing I'm a half-breed? What about the hate you keep spewing at me?"

When she looked down between them, he roughly shook her. "Answer your own question, Crimson. Is it just one time in heaven? Is there something more? Answer me!"

"Damn you, Landon Wade, I should have known what we shared was too good to last." She fought the tears flooding her eyes, her teeth clenching as she pulled back from him, breaking his hold.

"You never answered your own question. Answer it!" he demanded harshly.

Reaching for her clothing, she angrily dressed. "I can't! I don't know what I feel, but it still doesn't seem right going our separate ways after what we just shared."

"Do you have a better way?" Landon watched her button her skirt, disgust with himself making his voice grate. *What did she want? Would she willingly admit she wanted a half-breed? Half a man? And can I accept it?* All he ever loved, he lost. Should he love and lose her too? Hate at the cruel twist of fate tore through him, shredding his heart. He could see in the narrowing of her eyes she would never accept him except for an occasional tumble in the hay. *He was a half-breed, and no white woman would be associated with one nor marry one without her being shunned by polite society, or by the rugged wilderness settlers.*

Dressed, Crimson stared down at Landon's crouched, naked form. He rose so swiftly she backed off a step as he threw on his clothing with as much fury as she had. Confusion roiled through her like the gray clouds before the tornado. *What do I want?* She could not answer the question any more than he could. "I hate you, Landon Wade." Tears streaming down her cheeks, she approached Blackfoot. Jerking the reins free, she led the mare out of the shelter and mounted.

Ignoring the soreness between her legs, she turned one more time and glared at him, searching for something but not knowing what. Why should everything end in anger? Should she dismount and fall into his arms? Everything within her screamed she should, but searching his cold eyes, she saw there was nothing more.

Kicking her heels into Blackfoot's sides, the tears she had been keeping back flowed down her cheeks. The wind snatched at her hair, her mount's hooves kicked up mud and her lips trembled with her cries, the pain of rejection twice today cramping her lungs and heart. *Is there something wrong with me? Twice today I have been rejected by two different men. What is wrong with me?*

He watched her ride off until she was nothing but a speck in the distance and his anger fell away from him like a snake shedding its skin. They were from two different worlds, worlds of oil and water, and never mixing. Turning toward the south, he noticed the sun was sinking toward the horizon. It was too late to find camp before dark, so instead he would retire for the night at the remains of the sod house.

Watching the skies turn a soft red, yellow, and pink, her name rolled off his tongue. "Crimson." She touched his life like the crimson highlighting the western sky and was just as beautiful.

⁕⁕⁕

"CRIMSON, thank God you're safe. We were worried sick about you." Honeysuckle pulled her sister into her arms and gave her a hard hug.

"I'm fine, Sis." Crimson abruptly pulled back. The pale lantern light sharpened the worry on Honeysuckle's face, and Crimson was immediately contrite for her sharp reaction. "Are the kids alright? Did the tornado hit here?"

Buck looked Crimson over, making sure she was unharmed. "We only got the wind, rain and hail. We were worried about you though. You didn't tell a soul where you were going, and we wouldn't of known if one of the ranch hands hadn't seen you heading out toward the west pasture. The main thing is you're safe, though I did worry whether you were in the tornado's path."

"Yeah, but I sheltered in the old adobe close by the creek and sat out the storm." She was not lying, but she was not telling them the whole truth, especially about the half-breed taking her innocence. She argued with herself all the way home whether she regretted her actions or not. Regret? No, she did not. She would do it again with him. He made her loneliness disappear, and she felt safe and desired by him, something she had never felt before. No, she wanted more with him regardless of his mixed heritage, but she must sort out the strange feelings she had for him and if it was worth destroying her family with her association with a half-breed.

"Come inside and I'll draw you a hot bath. You need out of those wet clothes before you catch your death, if you haven't already," Honeysuckle motherly scolded, reaching for her hand.

"I'll be there in a minute. I gotta get Blackfoot bedded down." Crimson hesitated, drawing back from the proffered hand. She needed more time, just a little longer. Her emotions were all over the place, and she must get them under control before she answered the million questions lighting their eyes. The memory of Landon

106

was still too fresh, his kiss still burned across her lips and his lovemaking a beautiful but distant dream.

"Go on in with your sister. I'll take care of Blackfoot." Buck reached for the reins.

Crimson jerked back the straps, her voice coming out sharper than she intended. "She's mine and I'll do it." She hastily added, "You taught me that I must take care of my own mount, remember? And that's what I'll do."

Buck searched Crimson's face, her attitude and swollen red eyes nagging him. Something was bothering her or she was still shaken from being caught in the storm. Crimson had always been headstrong and independent, and whatever it was, he would allow her the time she required to settle her emotions.

"Crimson, Buck will take care of Blackfoot. Come inside and warm yourself. The night air is chilly, and I don't want you down sick." Honeysuckle glanced at Buck and frowned when he turned aside her unspoken request.

"Go inside, Honey, and get some water heated and some warm clothing ready for Crimson."

"But Buck..."

Buck frowned at Honeysuckle, stopping her words. "Let Crimson take care of her horse if she wishes." Buck shooed his wife inside and followed behind her.

Crimson watched them disappear into the house before leading Blackfoot into a stall. It was surprising Buck seemed more astute to her emotional upheaval than his usually discerning wife. Silently thanking him for his understanding her distress, she promptly bedded down her mare.

Sniffing against the tears running down her cheeks, she rubbed Blackfoot down, then curried her. She must get herself under control before her family noticed her anguish and asked questions she could not answer. There was no logical explanation she could give nor why her heart ached, especially since she probably would never see Landon Wade again. He had made it clear that this was a one-time occurrence, but what they shared was beyond her expectations, beyond her understanding of why her body craved him.

Biting on her bottom lip, she knew he was right—no woman could marry a half-breed and have a regular life. And why was that?

She bit harder on her bottom lip until she tasted blood. *Why is life this way? But then, why should I care?* Landon was right—she could not marry a half-breed or be seen with him, but somehow the admission settled uneasily within her stomach.

Giving the mare an extra ration of grain, the task did not exorcise Landon from her thoughts and what they had shared from her exhausted brain. Rubbing the stray tears from her eyes, she forced herself to settle down and stiffen her spine for the interrogations she knew were coming. She closed the gate behind the mare and would request if Buck would release Blackfoot into the corral later. Picking up the lantern from the straw-strewn floor, she headed toward the big double doors, but stopped as snatches of conversation drifted toward her between two ranch hands just outside the partially opened barn doors.

"I threw in my hand and cut my losses fastern than a red skin on d' warpath when I saw Half-breed enter the game. That sidewinder Gambler turned a bottom deal and the breed was smarter than a fox after catchin' dinner on a Sunday morn. Gambler drew his hideout gun, popping lead, but that breed came up a smokin' and wearin' a shet eatin' grin as he blew Gambler to kingdom come."

"Hell, ya say? Gambler turned out to be belly up to a rattler on a freezin' day and it serves him right for bein' kicked into a funeral procession. Don' reckon the law got in the act, do ya?"

"Weren't nothin' the lawdog could do, it bein' a fair fight and all, though it's known Half-breed plays a lone hand and has snake blood that'a kill a buffalo at a hunert paces."

Walking away, their voices drifted off into the distance.

Crimson shifted through their long-winded, flowery conversation discerning they were discussing a gunfight. Putting her fist in her mouth, she bit down, choking back a strangled cry as disturbing memories of Salina, Kansas, assailed her. There were four of them who played together: Tom, Harvey, Archie and her, though the boys were a couple of years older than her. Archie hated his given name, Archibald, and demanded that they call him either Arch or Archie. She remembered it was a hot day and they were playing marbles when the boys told her about a killing in the saloon they had witnessed. The boys had peered under the swinging bar doors at the intense poker game going on inside. A disgruntled player pulled a gun and accused the fancily dressed gambler of cheating. The gambler raised his hands in a gesture of misunderstanding and a derringer popped in his hand so fast, the naked eye could not distinguish the motion, then he shot the accuser.

"That's what I'm gonna be when I git older, a gambler. Ya should of seen his clothes! They were all black and he wore a frilly white shirt underneath his coat and a black and red vest. Had a neat moustache too!" Archie exclaimed, excitement over the shooting lighting his dark eyes.

There was rivalry between the three boys though they were all good friends, and Archie was the leader, an arrangement Tom hated but could not change. As jealousy rose, Tom belittled Archie in his never-ending challenge for supremacy. "If you're gonna be a gambler, you gotta have a fancy name like he did."

"Yeah," Harvey agreed, mimicking Tom's lead. "What ya gonna call yourself? Archibald?"

His eyes burning like coal, Archie glared at Harvey. "Ya want your nose bloodied, Harvey? If ya don't, ya better watch your mouth."

"Don't start fighting," Crimson interrupted in disgust. Turning toward Archie, she repeated the question Tom asked. "What are you gonna call yourself when you become a gambler?"

His anger easily diverted, Archie pursed his lips, thinking about it. "Gambler, I guess. Seems fittin' 'cause that's what I'll be."

"That's stupid," Tom grunted. "Ya gotta have a fancy name."

"I don't know, I kind of like the name. It tells it all," Crimson replied.

Archie smiled at her, glad somebody took his side for once. "Yep, that's my new name—Gambler." He said the name over and over, relishing the sound.

Oh, my God, Crimson's mind screamed. *It can't be anybody else but Archie killed in the saloon fight, and they called him such terrible names.* A sense of loss filled her. They had been inseparable the year before they split up with Tom and Archie moving away. She and Harvey felt awkward around each other afterward and went their separate ways. She had forgotten about it—it was so long ago. But it was strange they were all in the same area and did not know it. Poor Gambler. He had achieved his dream and died for it. Tears misted her eyes. She wondered if Tom and Harvey knew about his death.

She rubbed her earlobe between an index finger and thumb as other bits of the conversation replayed in her mind. *Half-breed, half-breed!* They were playing marbles and an older half-breed boy walked across the street. All three of the boys had an aversion for breeds, especially Archie. His eyes lit up with malicious glee when the boy crossed near them. Throwing down his marbles, he picked up a large rock, stood and tauntingly shouted, "Half-breed!"

Tom and Harvey stopped playing too and joined him while Crimson hung back, hiding behind them, her face flaming from embarrassment and shame for their spitefulness. "If ya'll are gonna start again, I'm going home."

"Then go home, Crimson, if you're a Injun lover," Tom shot back, turning and ignoring her.

She backed up a few steps, then stopped when she saw Archie throw the rock at the boy and the projectile smacked him on the back of his head. The half-breed rubbed the back of his skull and turned his blazing eyes on them, growling in a menacing voice too old and mature for his age. "One of these days I'm gonna kill all of you for what you've done to me and my ma," he cried, his eyes glaring with such hatred, it frightened her.

How could she have ever forgotten those eyes? Eyes the same color as the sky and he had been a loner too, and his name was Landon Wade. She groaned out loud this time. It couldn't be! She remembered it all so clearly now. How could she have ever forgotten? They had come a full circle, their lives tied irrevocably together, bringing them all back into another place and time in some bazaar twist of fate.

Half-breed! Half-breed! Her mind kept crying over and over. It was the man she could not erase from her mind. The one who pulled her from her hiding place when she watched him bathe, the one who saved her from the tornado and kissed her until she was breathless, the one who took her innocence. *My God, he must have been the one who killed Archie! Is he after me too? Was his lovemaking some cruel jest, a start of worse things coming and he was punishing me for being with those three boys?*

Leaning weakly against the barn door, a muffled groan escaped her. Surely he must remember her and was saving her for something more, some cruelty only he could administer. Her heart beat an irregular tattoo and tears stung her eyes. Hadn't he evaded all her questions, neatly turning them back on her? He never told her what he was doing on the L Heart range or anything about himself, and she had broken the unwritten law of the West: never ask a man his name, occupation or what he was doing.

Trembling violently, she bit harder on her fist, stopping her choking cries. She could not face Honeysuckle and Buck this way. Furiously dashing the tears from her eyes, she slammed her fist against the wooden door, letting anger spill over her. She would not let him get the upper hand. She knew his little game now, knew it with as much certainty as she knew she was alive. It was unfair he should punish her too for being part of their group long ago, and she would not let him. She would make sure she was never anywhere near him so he could hurt her again!

With new determination, she opened the barn doors and walked toward the house. Stepping on the porch, she blew out the lantern and placed it beside the wall. While closing the door behind her, she heard Buck's and Honeysuckle's voices raised in an argument.

"Damnit, Honey, let it be! Why in the hell do you keep insisting on knowing something that ain't got nothing to do with you?"

"You're my husband and I have a right to know. I've waited until I'm sick of waiting for you to tell me what's bothering you. Don't you think I know when you're worried about something? Especially when you keep running your fingers through your hair like you're doing now."

"You're gonna keep on until you get every last damned detail out of me, ain't ya, Honey?" Buck's voice snarled.

"Yep. Now will you please tell me what's wrong?"

"Ah hell, Honey, it's the ranch and you don't need to know any more than that," Buck argued more softly.

"Buck Leathers, don't act stupid! Anything that concerns you concerns me. Now out with it!" Honeysuckle firmly demanded.

"Ah hell."

"And please watch your language, Buck. That's another thing when you're worried, your language is terrible."

"Alright, alright."

The voices stopped and Crimson imagined Buck running his fingers distractingly through his hair, his face pinched with worry while searching for the right words of telling his stubborn wife. After a few tense-filled moments of quiet, Buck's lowered, worried voice spoke.

"We've had a hellva bad year. The rustlers are becoming bolder and have devised all sorts of cruel ways of rustling cattle. They're stealing us blind and there ain't a damn thing we can do about it."

"My word, why not? You have enough men, don't you, to guard the range?"

"Hellfire, Honey, do you realize just how much land we do have? There ain't no way of guarding all of it. There's too damn much. They could be hiding stolen cattle on this very range and we'd never know it until it was too late."

Honeysuckle's voice was much subdued when answering, "Don't you know who's at the head of it?"

"Not really. There's been reports of a half-breed seen around here several times. We know he's got something to do with it, but we don't know if he's at the head or just the go-between. There ain't a damn thing I can do about it until I have more positive proof."

The words screamed at Crimson. *Half-breed!* Oh no! It couldn't be, but then it all made sense. Wouldn't Landon hate all whites for what he had suffered when he was growing up? Wouldn't this be the perfect way of getting back at her, by making her family paupers? A strangled cry escaped her lips.

Honeysuckle heard her and hurried from the other room. "Oh, Crimson, I'm so sorry you heard us. Don't worry about it. Buck will find a way out of this predicament. He always does."

Buck echoed her words. "It's nothing for ya'll to worry about. We're doubling our guards and praying for the best."

A daze enveloping her, Crimson nodded, letting them think their conversation had brought the startled cry. Her throat moved convulsively as she tried telling Buck her suspicions, but the words stuck stubbornly inside her.

Honeysuckle draped her arm around Crimson's shoulder and led her toward the warm kitchen where a steaming bath awaited her. She clucked in motherly concern with the paleness of Crimson's face, worried she was coming down sick by being in the wet elements for so long today.

The water grew tepid before Crimson decided she could no longer stay the inevitable. Sighing, she stepped from the hip bath.

Honeysuckle looked Crimson over more closely, observing the weary sag of her shoulders and a red flush on her cheeks. In her motherly, affectionate way, Honeysuckle lifted her hand and touched Crimson's forehead. "I hope you're not coming down sick. Best you get into bed now. We can discuss your adventures of this afternoon in the morning." Honeysuckle's concern rose by the minute.

Chapter 12
Proposal

CRIMSON'S relief at not being questioned was censored by the knowledge tonight's respite would last only a short time, and she needed some ready answers by then. She bit her tongue against the lies she was already forming. The thought of lying made her uncomfortable and did not sit too well on her shoulders. *Damn you, half-breed that you are, Landon Wade. Why? Why, when the power of your kiss makes me want...wanna what? I gave you my most precious possession in a moment of madness and now I find out you are after revenge. There's no other answer for it. The pieces fit only too well.*

She flung over on her stomach, buried her face in the pillow and pounded her fists against the mattress. Hot tears scorched her eyes, wetting the pillow in front of her. *He's not worthy of my thoughts, him being a half-breed.* But that did not stop his ice blue eyes from staring at her from the dark recesses of her mind.

Rational reasoning totally swept from her viewpoint, she rose and washed her eyes, the water burning the inflamed flesh. She grabbed the towel and wiped her face, then with a muffled oath, threw it down. *Addle-brained fool!* she berated herself. She totally forgot about asking Buck to let Blackfoot out into the corral. Now she must do it herself. Grabbing her shawl from the nail on the wall holding her clothing and draping it across her shoulders, she hurried down the stairs, grabbing the lantern and matches at the back door before leaving the house on silent feet.

The stars and moonlight lit her way until she reached the barn. She opened the doors and a yellow, subdued glow spilled out. Curious who would be in the barn at this time of night, she stepped inside, setting the lantern down and closing the door after her, not considering danger might be lurking in the shadows.

Her bare feet making no noise, she walked toward the source of light at the far stall. Blackfoot nickered softly, recognizing her scent. Sweeping past the pen, she absently patted the mare's nose as she walked by. Reaching the last stall, she stopped and silently watched John saddle his horse, unaware he had company.

The feeling of being watched crept along the back of John's neck, lifting the short hairs. He turned swiftly, his words uttered in harsh disbelief, "What in the hell are ya doin' here, Crimson?"

Confused, Crimson saw shock widened his eyes, then narrowed with relief. And was there also a menacing gleam in his eyes? She could not be sure, so she ignored his question. "Are you leaving because I know your real name?"

"That ain't got nothin' to do with it," John snapped, then thought better of it. "You're right. Ain't no use lyin' 'bout it. It's jist if ya let slip my real name, I could be arrested and hanged."

"So, you're running away like a wounded dog," Crimson assumed a bit caustically. She missed the hard glint appearing in his eyes before he turned around and fastened the cinch underneath the horse's belly.

"I gave my word. Doesn't it count for something?" she inquired a bit more softly.

Quickly turning around, he closed the few steps between them and took her shoulders between his square hands, fighting the anger tensing every muscle in his body. "And if ya accidently let slip my real name, then what, Crimson?"

"I would not," she hastily assured him. "Why do you run? Why did you change your name? Please tell me. You can trust me." She was almost pleading with him. If he left, she would be alone and helpless against Landon's wrath. This was the one person she could share her fears with and only he would understand why Landon would extract revenge against her.

A frown furrowing his brow and his mouth drawing into a thin white line, John dropped his hands and pulled out his pocket watch, checking the time while debating whether he could trust her. He clicked the watch shut and turned toward her.

Crimson reached for the watch, curious. She had never inspected one before and had only seen a few at a distance. But the ones she had seen men pull from their pockets were always silver and John's was gold. After he handed it over, she flipped the pocket fob and studied the ornate-designed gold with a picture of a crouching mountain lion with emerald eyes inside the round flourished design. It was beautiful and she suspected it was expensive. Placing her thumb against the release button to view the inside, John took it from her fingers and slipped it into the small side pocket of his pants.

"Welp, Crimson, I'll tell ya, but ya must swear ya will never tell a soul." At her nod, he captured her shoulders, then used his forefinger against her chin and lifted her head. He must convince her into believing him and the best way was him staring straight into her eyes.

"It ain't a pretty story, and I'm doubtin' my sanity by tellin' ya."

"Please, John, tell me the truth. We're friends, remember?"

Slowly nodding and letting the tense silence pass between them, he shrugged. "It was in Illinois where I worked on a farm for a while. There was this girl, Jenny…eh…Jennifer. We was a mite close, she carryin' my babe and all, and we was figurin' on runnin' away together 'cause her pa had forbidden her from seein' me agin."

He raised his hand and massaged his temples, his eyes taking on a faraway quality. Turning away from her, he continued speaking so softly, she strained to hear his softly spoken words. "We was up in the hayloft makin' plans, but we got into a little tiff. I should of remembered she had been mighty moody ever since she had gotten with child. I don't remember what the fight was 'bout now. Anyway, when I tried takin' her into my arms and kiss her anger away, she pulled back and ran toward the ladder. She slipped and fell."

He groaned, reliving the past and rubbing his face. When he turned back around, a suspicious moisture gleamed in his granite eyes. "Down below, the old man I was workin' for had his plow turned over and had sharpened the blades."

Crimson stepped closer and placed her hand on his shoulder in silent comfort, feeling his distraught and pain.

Sighing, he covered his face again, his words muffled, "She fell on it. There weren't a thing I could do. She was dead. I knew they would accuse me of pushin' her off the loft 'cause her father was well respected and he hated me. I had no choice but run afore they took me in for a murder I didna commit. At one point, I saw a poster of me nailed on a tree. Do you know how I felt seein' my picture on a wanted poster? It ain't a good feelin', Crimson. I didna have a choice but change my name too, don't ya see?"

"How terrible it must have been for you, but if it was an accident, you should have stayed and fought it."

Grabbing her shoulders in a painful grip, his voice rose with disbelief, "Fought what? The whole town? Don't ya understand I was almost a stranger there? Her father was rich and had lots of power. He would of had me hung jist 'cause I took his little girl away and she fell, gettin' killed. Cain't you understand, Crimson? I had no choice!"

"But if they have a poster of you…" With his fingers digging into the tender flesh of her arms, she cringed against his sudden anger.

He sighed heavily and released his hold. "I had a full beard and moustache back then."

Reaching out, she caressed his cheek, the roughness of his day-old beard pricking her fingers. "Poor John, it really must have been terrible for you. Don't worry. I promise I'll never tell a soul."

His steel gray eyes capturing hers in a resolute glare, he grabbed her hand and pressed it tight against his cheek. "Ya know more about me than anybody else in the world 'cept Harvey. From what I've told ya, it could put ya in the position of holdin' it over my head."

"I would never do that, and you know it," Crimson strongly denied, incensed he would think such a thing about her. She suddenly clicked on an idea, an idea that would protect her from Landon Wade. Before she could change her mind, she added a bit slyly, "'Sides, if we got married like we promised when we were young, a wife couldn't testify against her husband."

"Ya'd still marry me after knowin' about my past?" John asked incredulously. With her silent nod, he pulled her into his arms and brought his mouth down against hers, crushing her lips in a bruising kiss.

His thick lips grounded roughly against hers, and she felt nauseated, the feelings she expected and had experienced with Landon not forthcoming. *This is madness!* her mind silently screamed. *What is wrong with me? Am I so desperate for a man that I proposed marriage just for his protection?* Perhaps she was. John was strong and could safeguard her from Landon, and if she was gone, it would spare her family from the grief of cattle rustling. *Oh, please, dear Lord! Don't let me make a terrible mistake! I need protection from Landon Wade who is out to harm me and my family!*

Releasing her lips, John kissed along her jawline and around her ear while his hand traveled upward from her waist and cupped her soft breast underneath her nightgown. He breathed in her ear, "I've loved ya for so long, Crimson. I jist didna think ya'd have me now."

She stopped his hand and moved it away from her breast. "A promise is not easily forgotten."

He smiled down into her eyes and placed a soft kiss on her lips before speaking, "No, it ain't. In jist a few minutes when I thought my life had ended, ya succeeded in givin' me a new beginnin'."

Cupping her face, he captured her lips again, grinding his mouth and hips against hers. She tried moving away, but he lowered his arms around her waist and pressed his pelvis against her stomach, groaning with the softness pressing against his aching groin, her nightgown nothing but a thin layer of material hiding her naked body underneath. With a growl, he dropped his hands onto her buttocks and gyrated his hips against her stomach. "I've dreamed so many times about kissin' ya, lovin' ya so well ya'd do anythin' for me."

With his sudden, harsh invasion of her private parts, Crimson pushed hard against him, breaking his embrace. "John, stop!"

Grunting, he captured her hands and shoved her against the barn wall, then forced her hands over her head. Moving closer until his phallus felt the softness of her stomach again, he groaned while rubbing himself against her belly. "We're gonna be married, Crimson. There ain't nothin' stoppin' us from findin' pleasure with one another now. Ya don't know how much I want ya."

"Stop! We're not married yet!"

"Come on. Cain't you feel how much I want ya?"

"Let me go!" she cried, struggling against him.

He growled, "Keep it up, sweetheart. That feels mighty good."

"Let me go or the marriage is off," she ordered in a hard voice, fighting against his grip.

Even though she struggled against him, he forced her into an empty stall. "Ya put yoreself in this position and it'll look really bad on ya if either one of us tells somebody 'bout this."

If he told anyone or they were caught by one of the ranch hands, her reputation would be compromised and no man would want her. Landon could destroy her family along with John ruining her. How did she get herself in this position? She only came to release her mare into the corral. "This is wrong and you know it. Now move off me and forget about marriage. I made a mistake."

Releasing her hand he held above her head, John forced her harder against the wall, his face directly in front of hers. "It ain't no mistake! Ya didna ask me to marry ya 'cause ya felt sorry for me. I ain't that dumb, Crimson. So what ya wantin'?"

Her eyes glistening with tears, she dropped her gaze from his, hating herself and him. And not just John but Landon too. It was her fear of Landon forcing her into a situation she now realized she did not want, but John was the only one who would understand and protect her. It was also her flash of compassion for John who was running from the law, for she never doubted his story, that she was committing herself in marriage. Sure, she had grown up with him until he moved away, and she hopefully believed he would treat her right. Perhaps he could fill this aching loneliness plaguing her so often lately that was worse now after her encounter with Landon this afternoon. But why did she not melt with John's kiss and allow him the same privilege she had with Landon? With his manhood digging into her stomach, she only felt revulsion, not the melting of her body as she had with Landon.

"I'll tell you, but I won't do anything with you until after we marry."

"Then tell me the truth, Crimson. What are you wantin'?"

"John, did you know Archie was in Mobeetie?"

"I knew. He was goin' under the name Gambler. Why ya

askin'?" He stared at her, closely examining her facial expressions after he released her.

"He was killed. I heard some ranch hands discussing it. It seems he was shot by a half-breed. Remember the half-breed in Salina, Kansas ya'll always teased? He's here too. I think he's the one who gunned him down and I think he's after us too. Can you find out for sure?"

"What brought all this on? Archie was killed afore the roundup." Suddenly wondering why she really proposed to him, John studied her closely.

She bit on her bottom lip, her eyes wide pools of fear. "I just heard about it. Will you find out for me?"

"I'll find out," John agreed grimly. "If the breed is after us, ya need my protection."

"Yes, I do." She shrugged and turned, knowing this was all she could do.

He grabbed her arm and swung her around in front of him, then grabbed her hair, holding her head so she faced him. "We *are* gittin' married, so don't think ya can change yore mind. Ya will regret it if ya do. Ya understand me? Tell yore family soon unless ya wantin' me ruinin' yore reputation."

With a final, brutal kiss, he turned her loose. She bent down to pick up her fallen blue shawl from the hay laying along the barn floor. John grinned with the perfect view of her rounded, shapely derriere and slapped her hard on the bottom cheek. "Now git!"

◦✦◦

HE WATCHED the small, auburn-haired figure below, admiring the graceful way she sat on her horse, and felt a fleeting moment of regret. The spirited girl must die. Certain news had filtered through the intricate gossip network, and she now proved a danger against their well-laid plans. He watched her for a few more seconds, shaking back needless feelings, then squinted down the rifle barrel and squeezed off a shot.

Her mare reared, throwing the young woman from its back before it raced off into the broken landscape. The distant figure lay motionless. If she was not already dead, she would be soon. Satisfied she was out of the way, he replaced his Stetson over his head and slipped down the side of the rocky hill, mounted his stallion and rode away.

∾◦◉᠀᠀᠀◉◦∽

CRIMSON lay stunned, the air knocked out of her lungs, and too afraid to move while she painfully fought for breath. Common sense dictated she remain still. She did not know what made Blackfoot suddenly rear, but whatever it was, she was thankful. As she was falling, a bullet whistled past her ear followed a split second afterwards with an explosive boom. The fall had saved her life. If Blackfoot had not become frightened, she could be lying here either dead or dying. A silent prayer kept running across her brain—*please don't let the shooter check if I am dead!*

Forcing herself motionless and barely breathing, it seemed like hours before enough time had passed for the shooter to escape. She slowly sat up, every bone in her body aching. Glancing around the rugged terrain, she observed an area where her murderer would be hidden. When no more shots rang out, she surmised her would-be assailant was long gone.

Blackfoot had disappeared, and she hoped the mare had headed home. At least with her riderless mare arriving back at the ranch, Buck would know something had happened and send out search parties for her. Rising, she dusted off her clothes and started walking. She should be much closer to John than home. Maybe he had heard the report of a gun and was on his way here, but that was a long shot, or he could assume someone was hunting in the area. However, it was all she could hope.

In a state of shock, Crimson's confusion mulled out that someone wanted her dead, and she kept coming up with the same answer. Landon! Surely he was the only one who would want her dead. But why didn't he kill her those other two times? Was this a cruel type of revenge with some part of him wanting her to die in a lonely, desolate spot without friends or family around? If she had been wounded, help would have come too late.

Glancing frequently over her shoulders, she walked for hours. She had never been so afraid in her life. The thought of a bullet in

121

the back by an unknown assailant or at least one who kept hidden, made her nervous and anxious. She plodded along until she thought her feet would not lift one more time when she saw the outlines of a camp in the distance. The joy of someone up ahead might help her, lifted her spirit and gave new strength to her tired limbs.

She stumbled into camp and collapsed in Billy the Kid's arms.

Chapter 13
Imprint in Time

"SENORITA Crimson," Billy called, holding her close and ordering someone bring him a canteen. He eased her on the ground and sat beside her. Raising the canteen, he placed the rim against her lips.

Crimson placed her hands around the canteen and drank greedily, the warm water like ambrosia, until he took the canteen away.

"Slowly, Senorita. If you drink too fast, you will be sick," Billy admonished her.

She nodded, willingly obeying his command. With her thirst sated, she glanced around at the curious faces surrounding her.

"Senorita, what do we owe for the untimely honor of your company?" Billy asked, swiping off his bowler hat, wry amusement with a touch of concern pulling up his brow.

Brushing back the stray lock of hair, she eyed Billy, debating how much she should tell him. "I think someone tried to put my lights out. My horse spooked before the shot and threw me off. It saved my life. My horse ran off afterwards and left me afoot."

"I can't imagine anyone wantin' to harm you, Senorita," Billy confessed, strangely looking her over. "Are you sure they were aimin' at you and not some game?"

"I'm not a senile, imaginative person, Mr. Bonnie," she retorted. "If they were shooting at game, wouldn't they check and see if they killed it?"

"I'm not sayin' you are, ma'am, but you could of been mistaken."

"There was no mistake, I assure you," she replied crisply. Glancing at each of the men surrounding her, she inquired, "Perhaps you saw someone around here today."

"It would take someone coldblooded to kill a woman," Billy thoughtfully remarked.

"Yeah, coldblooded as Half-breed," Henry Brown commented.

Immediately alert, Billy probed, "What do you mean?"

"I saw Half-breed this mornin' when I was out huntin'. He weren't in too big of a hurry if'n I recall."

"Half-breed," Crimson gasped, her fears strengthening and a vice painfully squeezing her heart. "What did he look like?"

Henry Brown pushed back his hat and scratched his head, seeking a faint description. "Well, I ain't never looked at a man that much, but I can tell ya he's a little under six feet tall, I reckon. Slim built, dark complexion, black hair, and cold blue eyes. He always wears one of those expensive Stetsons and rides a stallion. He's gotta reputation for being a cold-hearted rattler."

Her breath hitched in her throat and her lungs felt they were crushed underneath a tremendous weight with Henry describing Landon and solidifying her presumptions into fact. She fought for control over her reeling senses. Any doubts she might have had were completely gone.

Now more than ever, she must find John. She was hours late for their rendezvous. Surely, he was worrying about her since he was the one who demanded they meet today and would come looking unless he decided she could not get away from the house. She had argued with him about meeting him so far from home, but he had kept his promise and had not touched her inappropriately again. He had been sugary sweet, but she had seen him skeptically search her face and her body several times.

"I need a horse," Crimson whispered hoarsely.

"By all means, Senorita. Take any one of them." Billy jumped to his feet and offered her his hand, observing the deathly white of her face. "I'll ride with you a ways."

"Thanks, Mr. Bonnie, but there's no need. I'll just borrow one of your horses and have it returned later."

"Of course, Senorita. Take any horse you want and keep it. Call it a gift, a tribute to your beauty."

Crimson drew back from her troubled thoughts and stared at him. "I can't do that!"

"Please, Senorita Crimson Rose. It would please me knowin' a beautiful woman is ridin' my gift," Billy pressed, his easy smile lighting his eyes. He took her hand and pressed a lingering kiss on the back of it. "Please, it would give me much pleasure."

"Who could refuse such a gift when given this way?" She was overwhelmed—a horse was a valued commodity and a hanging offense if stolen. Without a horse in the sparsely populated areas, was a matter of life and death.

Selecting a bay gelding from the herd of horses they had, she thanked the men for their help and gift before riding off. It was over an hour later before she spotted John's camp. Kicking her heels against the bay's sides, she raced toward him before realizing John was bent over the prone form of Harvey James. Seeing Harvey clutching his bloody side, she hastily dismounted and hurried toward them. "What happened?"

Something flickered in John's eyes, and he and Harvey exchanged quick glances. "The son of a bitch Half-breed shot me. We was a' argu..." Pain shot across Harvey's face and he gasped for breath.

"We ran into the half-breed Landon Wade and had a shootout. You're right. He's out to kill us," John finished.

Crimson knelt beside Harvey, laying a soft hand on his arm. "He...he...tried killing me this morning too, but that ain't our main concern. Harvey needs a doctor now and the closest one is in Tascosa."

All business now, her own near-death experience pushed into the background, she ordered, "Cut off his shirt, John, and we'll use it as a pad over the wound." Looking around her, she asked, "Are there any bandages or maybe an extra shirt we can use for binding his wound?"

John nodded toward the horses. "We both have extra shirts in our bedrolls."

She retrieved the shirt while John cut off Harvey's bloody one. After stuffing the old shirt against the gun bullet laceration, she and John wrapped the other tightly around his midsection. With their combined efforts, she and John helped a weakened, injured Harvey mount his horse. With Harvey between them, they headed for Tascosa.

❧⟶⟵❧

"DR. HOYT, how is he?" Crimson asked.

"He's lost a lot of blood but he's alive. I advise him of staying with someone here for a few days. The long ride back just might do the trick and kill him."

"Thanks, doc. Send the bill to the L Heart," Crimson replied, hurrying after John.

After they had Harvey situated, she and John headed back, stopping along the way at John's camp and retrieving his gear. Crimson was packing supplies when John pulled her up against him. Moving her hair back from her face, he said, "We gotta get married soon as possible."

"Yes, I agree."

"Have you told yore sister yet?" John enquired, his pitless gray eyes boring into hers.

Crimson looked down at her dusty boots. "No."

"Tell 'em tonight. Landon is hot on our trails, and we'll both be a lot safer after we git married."

"It might be months before a traveling preacher comes around," she hesitated.

He cupped her chin and lifted her face, staring sternly into her eyes. "We can git married by the post adjutant in Fort Elliot."

"Not until after Honeysuckle has her baby."

Bringing his mouth bruisingly down on hers, he pulled her slight frame harshly against his. His full lips were like rubber and his slobbers ran down her chin. When his hand traveled toward her breast, she pushed him back. "No, John, don't."

"Damnit, I need ya. We're gonna be married, so whut difference

126

does it make if'n we do it now instead of waitin'?" he mumbled thickly.

"Let me go! You promised you'd wait." She stepped back from him, suddenly wary.

"Then let's head for Fort Elliot. We can git married by the end of the week," he coaxed, taking a step toward her.

She held out her hands, stopping his advance. "No, not until Honeysuckle has her baby, I told you."

"I'll wait jist a little longer, but remember, I'm a man, and I can't keep seein' you like this without wantin' ya," he throatily proclaimed.

"No, you promised we'd wait until after we got married."

"What ya 'fraid of, Crimson? That ya might want me afore we marry?"

He smiled cruelly, watching her face flush red as he rubbed the bulge straining in his pants. "Babe, yore a hot one and will be hotter after I deflower ya. I can barely wait puttin' this atween yore legs and hear ya groan with pleasure."

◈◦◦◈◦◦◈

"WHERE in the hell have you been? We've got nearly every ranch hand out looking for ya since Blackfoot came in riderless!" Buck cried, helping Crimson dismount, then taking her reins before motioning a ranch hand forward and taking her mount. "And where did ya get this gelding?"

"Enough, Buck! Let's at least get her inside the house before you start drilling her," Honeysuckle cried, placing her arms around Crimson and leading her toward the back door.

Honeysuckle settled Crimson at the table, then poured three cups of coffee and handed one to Crimson and Buck before grabbing the other one for herself.

She allowed Crimson to take a sip before she asked, "Do you feel like answering our questions now?"

"Start with why you were riding by yourself and not telling us where you were going," Buck interrupted.

Crimson sat her cup down and dropped her gaze, avoiding their eyes. "I know you're gonna be mad when I tell you, but at least let me get it all out before you scream at me."

"Ah, hell, Crimson! What have you done now?" Buck shouted at her.

"Hush, Buck. At least let her tell us what happened," Honeysuckle warned, shooting her husband a stern glance.

With Buck's under-the-breath mumbles, Crimson drew in a loud breath before raising her head and meeting their concerned, curious eyes, John's command fresh in her mind. "I don't know any proper way of explaining this except being honest about it. I've been meeting with John Sullivan since before the cattle drive. We decided we are gonna get married after Honeysuckle has her baby."

"Like hell!" Buck exploded, slamming his fist against the table, the strength sloshing the coffee cups' contents onto the top.

"You ain't got a say in who I marry, Buck. I'm eighteen now!" Crimson cried, suddenly wishing that she was only seventeen and he could refuse.

"He ain't worth it, Crimson! You can do much better than that piece of shit!"

"Buck, enough! Let her tell us what happened before you lose it again," Honeysuckle cried, placing her hand on his arm. "She is considered an adult now."

"Age don't make a adult," he growled and stared pointedly at Crimson.

Honeysuckle shook her head, wondering how Crimson would finish her story without Buck losing his temper again. "Please, let her finish before you utter another word. Afterwards, we can decide what needs done."

Taking a calming breath, Honeysuckle nodded toward Crimson. "Go on."

"I was meeting John, but something spooked Blackfoot and she threw me off just as I heard a gunshot. I was afraid to move for a while. I didn't know if the shot was meant for me or some kind of animal. I thought I was closer to John than home, only I stumbled into William Bonnie's camp instead. They had me drink some water and after I told them what happened, Mr. Bonnie gave me a horse. As I was riding back home, I ran across John and another ranch hand. The man with John had been shot. We patched him up, put him on his horse and headed for Tascosa. You'll be getting a bill from the doctor and maybe from someone who put him up for a few days until he can ride again without bleeding. After that, I hurried home."

"So, it's taken you all of two minutes of telling us what happened during the last sixteen hours? What are you leaving out?" Buck snarled, knowing it wasn't the complete story.

"Buck, at least she's alive! The rest is unimportant right now." Honeysuckle shot her husband a warning glance. "Have you eaten anything today?" With Crimson shaking her head, Honeysuckle rose from the table and fixed Crimson a plate.

Placing the filled plate and silverware in front of Crimson, Honeysuckle watched her eat while she rubbed the tense muscles in Crimson's back. "I'll fix you some bathwater and you can go to bed afterwards. We'll finish this discussion tomorrow. It will give us time to think about everything you've told us."

Buck sighed, a feeling of unease itching his scalp. "I'll arrange for the gelding's return tomorrow."

"No, Buck. The gelding is a present from Mr. Bonnie. It would be discourteous if we return it."

With Buck opening his mouth to reply, Honeysuckle shook her head at him. "It can wait until tomorrow."

CROSSING the desolate plains, the sharp, blustery wind cut through the serape Crimson wore. The monotonous golden-brown scenery tore at her already frayed nerves. She rode aimlessly, her wish—alone time. For the last few months, she did not wander far from the ranch house, afraid if she went too far, she would be shot in the back. She only ventured out when she was with some of her family or had an infrequent rendezvous with John.

With her teeth tugging at her bottom lip, she worried about the distance she kept between herself and John. What she so freely gave Landon would cost John the marriage price, and she was determined she'd never give into her baser desires again.

She leaned over the mare's neck, the wind tearing at the curly mass hanging loosely down her back. Blackfoot raced across the prairie, her strides lengthening out and moving through the stretch of land before them. *What am I doing? Am I ready for marriage and do I want it?* John's touch, so different from Landon's, turned her stomach, yet she proposed to him! Was the situation serious enough for such a drastic step? *Yes,* she defiantly determined. *Landon will destroy me if I don't.* Had he not already tried killing her and Harvey? Hadn't he already killed Archie? Wasn't he stealing cattle from her family? "Why are you doing this?" she cried fiercely into the blowing wind.

Marriage should not be too bad. There should be a certain amount of love between her and John. After all, she was marrying her childhood sweetheart. She loved him.

She shuddered involuntarily, convincing herself she did love John. It was the only way she would survive this marriage and his crudeness.

Like the shifting winds of a tornado, her mind kept switching from John to Landon. Had Landon really asked her to marry him? No, how could she be so naive? He only asked her *if* she could marry him. And could she? *No! No! A thousand times no!* Her heart palpitated unevenly, torn apart between her tangled feelings for Landon and knowing what he was, and the safety of marrying her childhood sweetheart. "Landon, why are you a half-breed out for revenge?"

Subconsciously, she reined in Blackfoot and eased out of the saddle. She stood a few moments, staring at the abandoned sod. Tying Blackfoot's reins around a sage bush, she walked toward it, a lone tear trickling unheeded down her cheek. Entering the broken sod, the cold wind was blocked off, and she placed her hand on the broken beam above her head, leaning against her arm and gazing at the place where she lost her virginity. She walked in further and stared at the spot where it had happened. There should be some sign, some imprint they had been here, but there was nothing except an inner turbulence tugging at her mind and body.

"Crimson."

The voice, an apparition from the past, spoke behind her and Crimson swiftly spun on her heels. Bright sunlight was at his back, haloing him in an unearthly glow and nearly blinding her, and his name was torn from her. "Landon."

He stepped farther inside until he was a couple of feet from her.

"I've been waiting and watching. I knew you'd come back."

Meeting the fire in his eyes, she mentally shook herself, her back stiffening, wondering what would happen now. Would he kill her? They were all alone, and nobody would discover her body for days, maybe weeks or months—maybe never. "What do you want?" she asked harshly.

"Is that a way of greeting me? I hoped you'd run into my arms after what we shared." His mouth twisted sardonically, a slow-building anger in his blood.

"Leave me alone! There is nothing between us." Crimson backed off a step as he neared. He stalked her like prey until she was backed up against the wall. Placing his arms on either side of her head, he succeeded in blocking off any hope of escape. She proudly thrust her head up, giving him a full view of her long neck and gritting her teeth from cringing when he caressed the slender column, his index finger rubbing against the inside hollow. She kept her fear hidden deep inside while his eyes grew cold as a blue January sky.

"But there is, little spy." His finger stilled, gently pressing at the base of her throat. Like a black panther ready to leap, every muscle in his body grew taunt. "Why are you marrying him, Crimson?"

His eyes grew cold, and she blanched, hating the chilling look. "John?" she asked innocently, then answered his question like he was a simple-minded fool while looking at a spot above his head. "Why I love him, of course. Is there any other reason for marriage?" Why didn't she accuse him point-blank and have him either deny or confirm her suspicions he wanted her dead?

"You don't love him. You'll never love him."

He spoke with such confidence, she was almost persuaded into believing him. Jerking away, she sidestepped around him and moved toward the fallen beam. Draping her arms around it, she held on like it was a lifeline, defying him. "I do love him!"

"Then turn around and look me in the eyes, and say it again, Crimson," Landon icily demanded, his voice low.

Her arms tightened around the beam. She could not look into his eyes or face. She couldn't! She did not believe it herself. Why didn't she tell him the real reason she was marrying John?

A bitter laugh tore at her throat and she quickly stifled it. My

God, he would only laugh at her. Her voice barely audible, she asked, "Are you saying I'm not good enough for him?"

"No, he is not good enough for you, but then I don't know. I've never met him much less seen him."

With his low voice sounding close behind her, she jerked her head around and stared at him, her heart tightening painfully within her chest. What was she doing standing before a murderer? If he was going to kill her, she would rather be looking him in the face, not shot or stabbed in the back.

Forcing herself to release her hold on the wooden beam, she lifted her eyes and glared at him. "It's none of your business who I marry! Can't you understand?" Her ardent words ended in a hopeless whine.

Chapter 14
For Better or Worse

"**YOU'VE** said it often enough I should believe it, Crimson, but I don't. Neither of us can go on denying this attraction between us. It's stronger than the both of us." Landon growled deep in his throat when she pulled away from his reaching hand.

"Don't touch me! Please don't touch me. I can't think when you're near me." She held her hands out, palm upwards, stopping him. "Go away, Landon. Just go away. There's nothing between us."

"There's nothing between us? Don't be a fool. If there's nothing, then why do you melt with my touch? Answer me!" His light blue eyes blazed into hers, commanding her answer.

"No! I hate you!" Her words, filled with frustration, sounded unconvincing in her own ears.

"We're both damned." He reached out and caught her, bringing her hard against him. Seizing the long length of hair at the nape of her neck, he held it, keeping her from turning her head away. "We're caught in a trap, and we'll never be free. This thing between us might be wrong, but we can't continue fighting it. If we do, it'll destroy us both or we'll destroy each other. Admit it, Crimson. Admit what you feel for me. Admit there's something between us that neither of us can fight. Damnit, whether we want it or not, we belong together."

"Let me be! I'll admit nothing! Can't you understand that?" she cried, banging her fists against his chest, not noticing the tears streaming down her cheeks.

He pulled her so tightly against him, her fists were captured between their bodies. "You don't hate me, little spy. You want me as much as I want you. We're like fire and ice together. We belong together, but we vaporize when we are."

"No," she moaned. "I do hate you."

His eyes grew cold. "Shall I show you how much you hate me?" Without letting her answer, he lowered his head and ground his mouth against hers.

She struggled at first, but soon her arms were wrapped around his shoulders, and she was wildly returning his kisses. Before she realized it, they were both naked and he was lowering her onto her serape, his hand exploring every inch of her with her honey dewing between her legs and fire lacing through her body. There was only a small whimper when he took her, taking her to such incredible heights, she nearly swooned. Breathless, she crossed her legs around his hip, keeping him on top of her.

"You can't deny it any longer. You're mine. Make no mistake about it," he savagely whispered in her ear.

Crimson balefully watched Landon dress. Was she insane falling so easily under the power of his kiss? She should not feel anything for him. It was all wrong. *Wrong! Wrong!* The words echoed through a tunnel in her brain, yet as she stood, she did not reach for her clothing.

"Crimson, promise me you won't marry him. Promise me!" he demanded, a fervent glaze in his eyes.

Her chin thrust up in defiance, her eyes emerald hard, she spat, "I'll promise you nothing, Landon. There can be nothing more between us." The final ring of her words tore at her heart, but she was not prepared for the violence of his words or actions when he grabbed her forearms and shook her.

"Is my mixed blood so repugnant?" A muscle twitching in his jaw, he drew her naked form against him. Before she realized it, his mouth descended once again on hers, and he lowered her on the serape, caressing her until she groaned against his mouth, wanting him once again.

Withdrawing, he drew back and stared into her half-lowered eyes. "Tell me again you do not want me," his voice a deep crooning while his hands played upon her flesh until she felt herself tightening against his finger, but before she found the release, he withdrew it. "Tell me, Crimson."

"Please," she moaned.

"Please what? What do you want?"

"You," she cried, reaching out for him.

He laughed softly and stood, quickly undressing before kneeling between her legs and filling her. "How much do you want me?"

"Please," she whimpered again. "Please, don't do this," she cried, moving her hips toward his, but he moved back from her, placing his hands along the sides of her hips, holding her still and only allowing the tip of his hardness inside her.

"Do you want me?"

"Yes," she cried before he filled her completely.

Pulling back until just the head stayed inside her welcoming entrance, he crooned, "Tell me again, Crimson. Do you want me?"

"Don't do this. Please, yes, I want you!"

He laughed softly before filling her again and again, pulling nearly out of her while watching her eyes close and the softness of desire sweeping across her face. "We'll never get enough of each other," he warned, slowly reentering her and watching her face each time he pulled back, almost out, before slowly reentering her again over and over, watching her mouth open and the moans erupt from her with each of her multiple orgasms. He could no longer contain himself and picked up the speed, spewing his love juices within her as she peaked once again, the strength of their climaxes racking their bodies.

He slowly rolled off her, moving his hand between her legs and hearing her groan. "You will never get enough of me nor I you." Laughing softly, he stood.

Standing over her, he admired her lithe form and how her legs were still splayed. "Do you want me again? Tell me how much you want me, then tell me you are still marrying this guy."

Tears slipping between her closed eyelids, she turned on her side, her sobs tearing through her. What had she done? This was so wrong, but she could no more constrain herself than she could fly to the moon. His very touch left her trembling with desire, nonetheless this manner of cruelty was more than she could comprehend. Was this a new torture, one that made her want him and he also wanting her dead?

Drawing her knees upward in a fetal position, she trembled with fear, desire, and a hurt she could not contain. She felt him kneel beside her and caress her leg, moving his hand until he was caressing her bottom. Through her tears, she answered him, "I want you, but I cannot have you. I will marry John."

"So, my mixed blood is repugnant." He pushed her away from him. Standing, he quickly dressed and stalked out of the sod, not waiting for her confirmation of his deepest fear.

Within seconds, she heard him leave by the sounds of pounding hoof beats and the emptiness filling her. The only man she could ever love just rode forever out of her life. She beat her fists against the ground, racking sobs tearing through her throat. "Why are you the one doing these terrible things?"

∾⦿⧓⦿∾

THE GRAND Central Hotel, a false-fronted wooden building, was where the wedding dinner would be held. The street sounds of Mobeetie occasionally drifted through the window with the March wind whistling through the structure, screaming like lost souls. The skies were heavily ladened, promising snow, the day seemingly against their marriage as much as Honeysuckle and Buck were.

With her teeth worrying her bottom lip, Crimson pulled the brush through the riotous waves of her hair. In another hour, she and John would be standing before the post adjutant of Fort Elliot repeating their marriage vows.

Laying the brush on the bureau, she leaned forward and placed her elbows on top, dully staring at her wavy reflection in the mirror, wondering why she felt so confused and detached. She was getting all she had wished for, wasn't she? Then why this nagging feeling of something missing? She loved John and he needed her. They had been childhood sweethearts; she told herself often enough she should believe it. He had been through so much and she felt sorry for him.

Pulling on her earlobe, she straightened, a sigh of resignation passing her lips. No matter how many times she rationalized this, the truth was always the same—she was marrying John to avoid Landon.

"You can still change your mind."

Crimson jumped. She had not heard Honeysuckle enter the room. "No, I will marry John."

"You always were the most stubborn person I ever knew, Sis. This whole marriage is wrong. I just feel it in my gut. It's too sudden. What do you know about him? Why doesn't every word you utter not have his name in it?"

"What would you have me do? Act like a schoolgirl having her first crush? Give me credit for having a little more sense than a schoolgirl," Crimson crisply interrupted.

"That's not what I meant, and you know it. Your eyes don't glow when you do talk about him. It ain't natural. There's something missing in the whole blasted thing." Honeysuckle used every bit of logic she could summon while carefully laying Crimson's freshly pressed wedding gown on the bed.

"Don't, please, Honeysuckle. We've been through this a thousand times." Crimson bit her bottom lip, keeping back the tears suddenly springing into her eyes. From the day she told Honeysuckle and Buck she was marrying John, Honeysuckle had cried and pleaded nearly every day against it. If she could only tell them she was marrying her childhood sweetheart and had planned it for years, it might alleviate their concern, but if she did, she would also reveal his secret. She hated lying. It was like a bitter gall in the pit of her stomach. Maybe she had not flat-out lied, but it was the same. Half-truths, that's what she had been telling them, and it started the night of the tornado.

Honeysuckle could not let her baby sister go through with this travesty of a marriage. She had a strange aversion for the man, something rare for her since she naturally mothered everyone and found good in all. She imagined her little sister as a rabbit thrown into a rattlesnake pit, and she would be too far away to protect her. It was more than Crimson being the last one leaving the family nest. It was something more, something she could not identify. "Please reconsider. You still have time. I'm begging you. Buck and I will stand by you through thick or thin. Buck is against this marriage as much as I am. In fact, he has done nothing but rant and rave about you marrying a...a..."

"A shiftless cowpoke," Crimson grimly supplied for her. "Yes, Sis, I know, but it still doesn't change my mind. I know what I'm doing. Can't you be happy for me?" Crimson gripped her hands at her side, forcing herself from shaking her sister and yelling she was doing it for her, for them, by marrying John so she could protect them from Landon.

"I would be if I felt he was the right one for you." Honeysuckle took a step closer until she was staring into her sister's eyes.

Fighting against her tears, Crimson bit her trembling lower lip. *What is the matter with me? I should be elated.* Instead, she wanted to sit down and cry out her frustration and fear. Her mind argued with Honeysuckle's words while her heart agreed. She did not love John, she finally admitted, but she had no choice in marrying him, and she would never let her sister know the truth. Uttering her first boldface lie, she cried in frustration, "I love him, Sis. I love him! What more is there?"

"Who are you trying to convince? Me or yourself?" Honeysuckle scoffed, challenging her sister to recognize the difference between real love and infatuation. She quelled at the thought of Crimson making a terrible mistake.

Crimson grabbed her sister's shoulders, angrily stopping herself from shaking her and clarifying her reasons, anything that would make her accept her lies. "Honeysuckle, I want what you have. I need what you have."

Releasing her sister's shoulders, Crimson stepped back, her face haunting and lonely. "Please understand. I want my own husband who loves me the way Buck loves you. I need my own home, my own children, my own happiness."

"You have time for all that," Honeysuckle interrupted, despair filling her. She never guessed this was at the root of Crimson wanting marriage. Surely Crimson was not jealous of her happiness, but then Crimson had been acting strange since last spring, withdrawing more and more from the family.

"Dang it!" Crimson snapped, uttering the words without thinking. "Please let it be! I am marrying John Sullivan for better or worse, and nothing will change my mind. Please understand!"

Tears sprang into Honeysuckle's eyes and ran unheeded down her cheeks. She closed the distance between them and hugged Crimson, her voice choked, "If this is so important for you, I'll try. My only wish is for your happiness, true happiness, but please reconsider your decision and make sure you are marrying the right person."

Crimson hugged her sister in return, tears blurring her vision, her heart screaming for her to listen and back out of this marriage before it was too late. But what did her happiness mean compared with losing the things she most loved in this world: Honeysuckle, her family and the ranch, which had been the only real home she had ever known. She released her sister and stepped back, wiping the tears from her eyes. "This is foolish. It's my wedding day and here we are blubbering like idiots. We should be happy."

Honeysuckle sucked in a trembling breath and nodded, Crimson's last words screaming through her brain, *we should be happy*. There was nothing more she could say. She tried and nothing worked. Giving up, she sighed, "I'll help you dress."

THE BLUSTERY, bone-chilling wind found places through the heavy wool cloak and through Crimson's clothing, freezing not only her but also the center around her heart. Her mind screamed she was doing the right thing by marrying John—protecting her family and herself. It also shouted she was deluding herself that she loved him. Her heart cringed with the knowledge she could never love John Sullivan or Tom Martin, one and the same man, and had settled on the dark, forbidden half-breed Landon Wade, a man whose very cerulean-blue eyes haunted her day and night. One touch from him and she would willingly, eagerly strip naked and enjoy those magnificent trips that carried her heavenward, safe, protected, yet dangerous.

Crimson sat on the edge of the front seat. Honeysuckle and the baby covered beneath Honeysuckle's cloak, sat between her and Buck. The boys were covered with a heavy quilt, their cries swept away with the steady, sharp fingers of icy-cold wind. The fort lay in the valley below Mobeetie, the ride slow but also too fast, carrying the wedding party toward the Post Adjutant's office. The wagon's slow creaking and rough ride made it through the fort and stopped at a small wooden building.

John stood in front, stepped forward and helped her from the wagon. An intense shiver shook her body with his touch.

Leaning close, his smile turning into a smirk, John whispered, "I'll warm ya up real good tonight, my bride. Jist wait."

When another violent shiver shook her body, his smile widened. Grabbing her hand, he placed it on the crook of his arm and leaned over close while patting her hand. "I see ya are as anxious as I am for tonight."

Anxious? Is that why my stomach is clenched, bringing a grimace of notable pain on my face? What am I doing? The very thought of his hands on her felt intimidating enough she almost turned and ran back toward the wagon—and drove away, far away from him.

Entering the small building, the brunt of the wind was lessened. The room was cold though a small potbellied stove burned in the corner. The room was stark with a small, almost bare desk with ledgers lining the shelf above it. A large open ledger was set on the desktop, and she imagined that was where their marriage would be recorded. John led her directly in front of a painfully slender, middle-aged man who stood in front of the desk, his arms clasped behind his back, his face unreadable. She heard her family file in behind her and the door close. Someone reached around her and took the cloak she removed from her shoulders.

Though the wedding party was small with only her family in attendance, the room was overcrowded, withdrawing the remaining oxygen from it. She drew in several short, sporadic breaths, hoping it stopped the painful beating of her heart while fighting for enough air so she could draw a full breath. *What am I doing?* Her legs were frozen in place although she wanted to run, be any place but here.

As if he felt her desire of escaping, John tightened his hand over her arm and squeezed it hard. He admitted Crimson was a fetching piece dressed in an olive-green gown with the darker green velvet jacket and carrying a small white Bible with green streamers. Her auburn hair waved around her shoulders and was tied back away

140

from her face with green ribbons. She had been resolute about waiting until their wedding night before she would let him touch her and had succeeded in making his loins ache by only allowing him a few kisses.

He impatiently played her little game, preferring he had taken her before now. Instead of forcing himself on her, he insisted on a quick wedding.

Buck was against their marriage and had treated him coolly, but it did not deter him. It had, in fact, increased his determination of marrying his precious little sister-in-law. The Leathers were one of the most respected families in the Panhandle, and with the aid of them and Crimson's sparkling reputation, his nefarious activities would be well shielded. Who would suspect them or him? And he would be part of the family.

Glancing at his bride, a sly smile lit his full lips. It would never have worked if he had planned it this way himself, and he choked back a laugh thinking how easy it was. She literally fell into his arms and suggested he marry her. After he weeded out her fears about the half-breed, he knew her fear of Landon propelled her into his arms. Next time he saw the half-breed, he'd thank him.

He had waited a few days before he had answered her question, verifying Landon Wade was indeed the one behind all her fears of retribution, and it had been a simple matter saying Landon had killed Gambler. He promised he would protect her against the half-breed, going so far as to say he loved her. The silly chit would believe anything.

Ah, the sweet smell of success. Now he would soon be brother-in-law to one of the most powerful cattle barons in the Texas Panhandle.

Reflexively licking his thick lips, he squeezed her trembling hand. Her virginity was like a sweet treat held out as temptingly as a carrot before a mule, and tonight he would taste it, savor it until he was sated. Surely she would be fiery as her hair with him between those sweet thighs.

Before he could dwell more closely into tonight's consumption, the post adjutant began the ceremony, pulling him from his pleasant imaginations.

Though Crimson repeated the vows in a strong voice, she was

unaware of what she said. Her whole body and mind were numb, not registering her actions. John's lips on hers were cold and unfeeling, lacking the fire and tenderness Landon's had. *God, what am I doing comparing John with Landon again? There is no comparison. John loves me and I love him. He will protect me, and in protecting me, save my family from certain disaster. I will be happy! John is my husband, and I owe him my loyalty and love. I will be the wife he wants, and he will always be first in my life,* she kept rationalizing and convincing herself during the ceremony.

"You're cold as an icicle, Sis," Honeysuckle murmured in her ear, hugging her. "Are you sure you're doing the right thing?" At Crimson's nod, she said no more.

The wedding feast at the hotel's restaurant was stilted and uncomfortable. Buck made no bones he was against their marriage, refusing any friendly overtures with John. Crimson was glad the whole ordeal was over though she cried when Buck and Honeysuckle, along with their new baby girl and their two little boys left town and headed home, a long journey where they would stay at neighboring ranches at night until reaching theirs.

Now she must face the night alone with John. Her stomach lurched sickeningly though a few times she eagerly anticipated the night. A wetness grew between her legs. She hoped the full pleasure Landon had shown her would also come true with John.

Chapter 15
Inch for Inch

JOHN politely left the room and smoked a cigarette outside while Crimson undressed. She hugged the traveling gown in her arms, her eyes misting, remembering Buck and Honeysuckle bought it for her and their planned trip up north, and instead, it served as her wedding gown. She carefully folded the dress and placed it inside her traveling bag, then slipped a cambric nightgown with its lace edged neckline and long sleeves over her head, buttoning it up under her chin. She fearfully eyed the bed, wondering if John would detect her lack of virginity, and if he did, what his reaction would be. Crossing the room, she turned the cover back, slipped between the sheets and pulled the quilt up under her chin, waiting for her new husband.

Her trembling began anew when John opened the door and closed it behind him. "Well, my little bride, tonight's the night." Licking his full lips in anticipation, he laid the things he had taken from his pockets on the top of the bureau and stripped down, leaving on his long underwear. Cupping the top of the glass lamp, he blew out the flame.

His clothes shuffled in the darkness as he slipped out of his undergarment, then eased onto the bed beside her and roughly pulled her into his arms, growling in her ear, "Now I shall have what I have been waitin' for so long. It'll hurt the first time, so I've heard, but after that, ya will want me as much as I want you."

His thick lips claimed hers, and she cringed inwardly. She tried returning his kiss, but his lips were hard and unyielding, bruising her mouth. It turned her stomach as his unsavory slobbers ran down her mouth and chin, soaking the lace of her nightgown and lodging with uncomfortable wetness.

Where was the fineness of Landon's kiss? She blocked her mind against her traitorous thoughts but could not enjoy her husband's kiss. John's rough fumbling of her breasts and his squeezing of them elicited cries of pain which he mistook as passion.

"Yes, yes, ya are fiery as yore hair, ain't ya, my bride? Jist wait. Ya will be beggin' for me to spear your precious little jewel. Yore mine. I'm the first and only one," he muttered into her ear, spittle running down his lips, thinking of the prize waiting for him. The thought was too much and he grew impatient. He grabbed the hem of her nightgown and pulled it over her chest, crudely spread her legs apart with his hands before he moved between them and shoved into her without preliminary.

The tearing, piercing agony sliced through her nether regions, and a scream was torn deep within her throat, lodging there with the feeling she was being ripped apart by his intrusion. Her fists clenching at her side, she automatically stiffened against the raw pain, preventing him from penetrating further. The first time with Landon had been so different and without the torment she was experiencing now. Tears escaped between her tightly squeezed eyes and ran into her hair. She hated this act of marriage, this intrusion upon her body, and at the moment, she hated him worst of all.

He groaned and shuddered, then laid limply on top of her. His ragged breathing slowly returning to normal, he moved from her, sat up and drew back his fist, slamming it into her face. "Ya lyin' whore. Who was the first? Who was it?"

Lights flashed before her eyes and explosive pain shot through her skull. It took several seconds before Crimson could recover from his blow. When she did, she pushed him away and crouched on her knees, pounding her fists into his chest, a low menacing snarl punctuating each blow. "Don't you ever hit me again! Do you hear me? Don't you ever lay another hand on me!"

His surprise was so great, he tried deflecting her blows, marveling at the power behind them before he shoved her from the bed. She landed in a heap on the floor. Jumping from the bed, he alighted with a foot on each side of her head. Reaching down, he grabbed her hair, pulled her up in front of him and swung his fist, striking her across her face.

Her body slammed against the far wall and she slid down it before slumping motionless against it. His snarl of anger broke the sudden silence as he tossed her limp form over his shoulder and tossed her onto the bed. Disgusted with his new wife, he picked up the pitcher of water from the washstand and threw it over her.

The cold water shocked her back to consciousness and she came up fighting. John caught her arms and forced them behind her back. "Ya damn whore, when I find out who had ya first, I'll kill him. And as for you, ya try hittin' me again, I'll beat ya so bad ya won't be standin' for weeks. Ya gave someone else your precious maidenhead, not even lettin' me touch ya afore we married, but no more, little wife. Ya will jump at my commands and strip when I say it's bedtime. Listen and listen well if ya wanna show yore purty face around town."

"Don't threaten me, John! I'm not a namby-pamby idiot who'll do nothing if you hit me again. I'll fight you with my last breath." Crimson was so angry, she felt no fear. With her head spinning and her nauseated stomach's threat of expelling what little she had eaten, she clenched her fists, determined nothing would deter her from giving him back inch for inch, slap by slap, punch for punch.

He released her arms and grabbed the front of her gown, holding her in place with one hand grasping the material at her throat while swinging the flat of his hand repeatedly across her face. She raised her hands, protecting herself, but it was ineffectual. Soon the ringing in her ears and the continuous slapping weakened her until she could fight no more.

"I'll slap ya silly every time you defy me, Crimson." John shoved her back on the bed, but before she could gain her senses, he ripped the gown from her body and took her once again, roughly, angrily, pounding into her and savagely loving her grunts of pain so much, he forced her more than once during their marriage night.

‿◦⁀◦⁀◦◦‿

CRIMSON turned on her side and clutched the edges of the mattress at the farthest edge of the bed, his very presence repulsive. She touched her face, the tenderness of flesh and swelling obvious underneath her fingertips. Moving her lips brought excruciating pain. Burrowing her head against the pillow, racking sobs tore through her. What had she done? She had jumped from the frying pan into the fire.

Landon, why didn't I listen to you? What was I thinking? She married John to escape Landon and had landed into another snake pit and wondered which one was the deadliest. Her heart was being ripped asunder, fighting the hate building within her for her husband and the feelings she had for Landon, and it was all wrong. She cared, oh God, she cared more for the man who was determined to kill her than she did her own husband. *What is wrong with me?*

Biting on her fist and smothering the choking cries, she admitted she hated sex with her husband, perhaps hated him more for forcing himself on her. Never had she been subjected to such pain and humiliation. Maybe she deserved his beating for giving into a half-breed murderer and cattle thief. But at least with Landon, he would kill her quickly with little pain—with John—the pain would last a lifetime.

What have I done? What will I do now? Accept John's dictate or continue fighting him and suffering what she suffered tonight? John was her husband and she had vowed to love, honor, cherish and obey him, and it left her with no option but be a good wife.

Crying until there were no more tears, she turned and glowered at his sleeping form who snored peacefully beside her, unconcerned. "I'll be your wife in all ways, but I can't promise I'll always be a submissive wife," she whispered, swallowing against the bile rising in her throat.

Aware of the uncomfortable stickiness and the lingering pain between her legs, she eased from the bed and stood in front of the stand holding the water pitcher and bowl. After pouring what little was left of the water into the bowl, she wet a rag and washed herself, sharply drawing in her breath with the icy cold water touching the tender, abused flesh.

Sighing, she placed the cloth on the edge of the washbowl and strode toward the window. Pushing back the curtain, she stared outside, ignoring the cold-inducing goosebumps rising along her skin. The nighttime sounds of ribaldry drifted through the window and the silvery glow of the quarter moon lit the street outside while the cold seeped through the windowpanes, whispering across her naked flesh.

Shivering, she almost let the curtain drop when she spied John's watch on the bureau. The watch had intrigued her from the start, and later she had been confused why John quickly took it away from her. Picking up the watch, she noticed there was a small bit of change beside it.

She made her way silently toward the window and pulled back the curtain. The dim light barely exposed the design of the mountain lion with emerald eyes within the gold, and she wondered briefly how John could afford such an expensive pocket watch. Pressing the latch on the side, she ran her finger along the inside cover. The smoothness changed into a raised center indicating an inscription, and she held it up toward the moonlight for a closer examination, but the inscription was blurred in the darkness, and she could not read it.

John shifted positions; she jumped and quickly turned toward the bed, afraid of him discovering her going through his personal belongings and beating her again. Quickly closing the watch case, she replaced it on the bureau and hurried back to bed.

❧⊙᠗᠔᠗⊙᠖❧

FORT ELLIOT, strategically located in a region offering water and timber, was most importantly located between the bulk of the Panhandle and the Indian reservation. There was a spread of wooden buildings and tall picket fences built around the main parade grounds, and on the outer edges were several Indian scout tepees and less important buildings and corrals. The area was crisscrossed with streams containing water throughout most of the year. The gently rolling prairies were covered with a fair amount of timber and brush containing wild berries and plums surrounding the fort. The soldiers hunted a variety of animals: buffalo, wild turkey, quail, deer, pronghorn antelope, an occasional black bear, and catfish and sunfish from the streams that complemented their meager diet.

A detail of soldiers returning after several weeks of scouting maneuvers, clattered into the fort. Their normally monotonous life held little excitement in their search for Little Robe's band of Cheyenne spotted in the area, which proved a fruitless quest. Instead, they hunted pronghorn antelope and brought in a large supply of meat.

Landon stepped down from the saddle and stretched the muscles in his back. He rode with the calvary at the request of Major Larner when the news reached the fort that reservation Indians roamed the Panhandle. Major Larner reasoned with Landon being familiar with the area, he would also possess knowledge of where the Cheyenne might be located.

"Come inside. I have a bottle of whiskey hidden inside my office," Major Larner revealed, handing the reins of his horse to a waiting soldier. "Private Williams, take care of Mr. Wade's horse."

"Yes, sir!" the private replied smartly, then tentatively added, "It's a shame that ya didna get back sooner. We had a righ' smart weddin' the other day. The sister-in-law of Buck Leathers, the owner of the L Heart Ranch, got hitched. She shore is a purty thang."

Landon stiffened slightly before handing the reins over. A mask slid over his face, hiding the emotions swirling inside of him. *Why did you marry him, Crimson? You haunt me, disturbing my dreams and intruding on my work.*

"Duty comes first, private," Major Larner quipped. He motioned with his head toward his office. "Come on inside. This weather's done chilled me to the bone and a little refreshment sounds mighty fine." He rubbed his left thigh, grimacing as he limped toward his office.

Nearing the office door, the major and he were stopped. Captain Pierce handed the major a thick leather pouch. "Just came for you, sir," the captain stated, saluting.

"Thanks, Captain." Major Larner opened the door, throwing back over his shoulder, "Maybe we'll make it inside before we're stopped again."

Landon closed the door behind him and gratefully took the ladderback wooden chair the major offered. For some strange reason, his legs felt like water, barely holding him up. A pot-bellied stove in the corner of the room had been stoked and took the chill out of the air, but the warmth did not penetrate the coldness wrapped around his heart.

Detached, he watched the major take his keys and unlock the desk drawer, then pull out a bottle and set it on the table. The major scrounged around for a couple of glasses and plopped two reasonably clean ones on the desk. He grabbed the bottle and pulled out the cork with his teeth, then poured them a liberal measure while speaking around it, "This oughta warm us up a mite."

Landon accepted the glass and took a drink. The whiskey burned his throat, spreading warmth through his stomach.

The major smacked his lips together after he drank. "This should have been a change of pace for you. Thank Kerby Olsen for us for lending you out. "

"Yes, I will and yes, it is a change of pace," Landon replied, pushing the image of Crimson at the back of his mind.

"Life here at the post gets mighty dull. It would have brought a little more excitement if the Cheyenne had been around here." Major Larner held his leg straight out in front of him and rubbed his thigh while he spoke, "Take back to the war. I got shot in this leg at Bull Run. I think those ornery sawbones loved amputating limbs. They sawed-off enough of them to fill a lake, and I sure wasn't gonna let them take my leg and add it with the growing pile. It's a miracle they didn't. It still gives me a little trouble now and then like today when it's so damn cold, but it sure is a lot better than having none at all."

He took another swallow of whiskey and grimaced. "I should've gotten married, but I never had time. Be nice having a wife on days like this. Might relieve some of the ache in this leg on cold nights if I had a nice warm wife cuddled up against me. I guess there's no use in regretting it. Hell, I'm not so old yet that I can't enjoy me a little filly now and then. How about you? You planning on getting married one of these days?"

Landon's smile was crooked. "Why get married? I'm still young and besides, there's not many decent fillies around."

"Reckon you're right, boy, but one of these days you're gonna get lonely like me and wishing you had a little filly waiting at home for you."

They changed the subject and spoke a while longer about the probability and improbability of Little Robe's Cheyenne in the area before the major opened the pouch and took out the missive. Reading it, his eyebrows knotted between his eyes.

Landon curiously glanced at the posters Major Larner laid on top of his desk. The name Tom Martin glared across the printed page, bringing painful memories of his childhood.

Seeing the frown on the usually emotionless face, Major Larner asked, "Know him? He's a deserter from the army and made off with several army horses and the payroll after he killed several squad soldiers. He's been sighted in this area, and the army is wanting him real bad."

"I'll keep an eye out for him." Landon smoothed his face, carefully omitting his knowledge of knowing him years ago.

"Let me know if you do see him." He laid the letter down beside the posters before speaking again. "Tomorrow, I'll have these posters nailed up around the fort and Mobeetie, but right now, let's head towards the mess hall for supper. We both could use a good meal." With Landon's agreement, Major Larner left the missive and posters on the desk.

It was several hours later before Landon left the company of Major Larner. The sun had lowered hours ago and the skies were coldly bright with stars and a sickle moon. He mounted Ebony and started toward Mobeetie whose subdued lights were hidden behind a hill. He needed a drink—no, several drinks, anything that would drown memories of Crimson and her damnable marriage.

Entering the Silver Saloon, he ordered a bottle of whiskey. He took it and the small glass before settling at an empty table. There was a poker game going on having the looks of continuing all night while saloon girls made regular rounds refreshing drinks. He was half through the bottle when a pretty, petite blond pulled out a chair at the table and sat down beside him.

"Haven't seen you in here before, Mister." When Landon remained silent, she continued undeterred, "You are a quiet one. My name's Rovin' Wendy."

Landon nodded greeting without answering.

She placed her hand on his thigh and smiled when the muscles jumped underneath her hand. "Buy a lady a drink?"

His cocked eyebrow in her direction conveyed he did not associate her as a lady, but nonetheless, he motioned for another glass and poured her one. Her small hand on his thigh was discomforting, reminding him how long he had been without a woman. Since meeting Crimson, no other woman held any appeal for him.

He nursed his drink while idly listening as Rovin' Wendy prattled on until his ears perked up at her last words.

"I heard this feller named John Sullivan got married a few days ago. I seen him on the street, but my man, Gambler who got killed several months back, said his name was Martin, Tim...no Tom. That's it. Tom Martin. Seems he married some girl by the name of a flower, Rose sumthin' or other."

Landon asked harshly, "Crimson Rose?"

She eyed the young man before answering, "Yeah, that's it. Mean anythin' to ya?"

Landon smiled crookedly. "It might." If she knew Tom Martin, perhaps he could glean information from her without seeming too eager and relay it to the fort major. If the man Crimson married was Tom Martin, this would free her from a known criminal. He took her hand in his, his smile never leaving his face. "How about you and me having our own party?"

She returned the smile and nodded. "Thought you'd never ask. I have a place not far from here. Just give me a minute so I can tell Joe I'm leavin'."

With her sauntering toward the bartender, Landon viewed the sway of her hips, his mind clicking on the possibility of Tom Martin being the man Crimson married.

Grabbing the bottle of whiskey, he followed Wendy out the back door, barely noticing when she took his arm. Her small shanty was a short walk away but far enough away they were both shivering with cold by the time they entered. Wendy took his bottle and set it on the small table before wrapping her arms around him and standing on tiptoes, pressing her lips against his. He slipped an arm around her waist and cupped her breast with his free hand.

Sighing, Wendy was taking a chance with this stranger, but he was the only man who had remotely elicited a slight interest in her tonight. Perhaps he could tell her what happened the night her man was shot. She still did not know the man's name who killed him or what he looked like, but it didn't stop her. She had sworn revenge for Gambler's killing, and she would get it, but it would take time and patience—and that was something she was long on.

Kissing her until she was breathless and leaning weakly against him, he drew back and undressed. In seconds, their clothes were piled at their feet on the dirt floor, and they tumbled onto the small bed. She was like a flower, small, fragile and smelling faintly of gardenias. He fought himself from taking her quickly. There was a heaviness in his heart and a burning rage at Crimson for marrying another man. He hoped having sex with another woman would wipe her from his memory.

Wendy was slender, her buttocks small, tight and nicely rounded, her waist tiny, her breasts the size of wild plums with large dark nipples. He played her body like a finely tuned instrument until she was on the brink of ecstasy, then subsiding until she begged him for completion.

Afterward, he lay beside her, a fine sheen of sweat covering their bodies. The wind whistled eerily through the building, the seeping coldness touching their skin with icy fingers. Landon pulled the heavy quilt over them and gathered her into his arms, acknowledging he had been deadly wrong—nothing could compare with Crimson's fiery passion.

"It's been a long time a man cared about my pleasure too," she commented, snuggling up closer against the warmth of his body. "Not since Gambler. He always made sure my pleasure was great as his own. I miss having a man take care of me. Perhaps you could take Gambler's place."

Chapter 16
Taking Care of an Itch

LANDON stiffened and curtly asked, "Are you wanting me as a protector?"

"Yes, and you'll get half of what I earn." Rovin' Wendy searched his face, expecting his acceptance, frowning when his body stiffened against hers.

Pulling her head back from his chest, his fingers tangled in the straight length of her blond hair. His eyes resembled shards of glass while hers pleaded, and he slightly relaxed his facial features. "Thanks for the offer, but I haven't the time you need for a protector."

He laid his finger on her lips, stilling her protest. "It's a nice offer, but I wouldn't be around often enough for the protection you need. You need someone around town, not a lone ranch hand. I rarely get into town, so what good could I do?"

Her mouth quivered and tears diamonded her lashes. "It was a thought."

He kissed her eyes closed, feeling like a heel. "It was a nice gesture and one I'll never forget."

"My Gambler was a good man. I sure do miss him."

"Tell me about him," Landon softly ordered.

153

Wendy complied, laughing silently at how quickly he took the bait. Here was a man who could help her extract justice. She traced a pattern around his nipple while she spoke. "My Gambler was the best card player around. He hailed from some place in Kansas. Salina, I think. He was good to me, always deckin' me out in the prettiest clothes and givin' nice little gifts. Tom Martin was certainly jealous of him, I can tell ya. They got into this argument over some business deal, and Tom threatened Gambler. He didn't know I heard him though. Anyway, one night this breed came in and began playin' poker with my man. I could tell there was sumthin' goin' on. This breed was agitatin' Gambler and makin' him do crazy things until finally the breed accused my man of cheatin'. Now let me tell ya, Gambler never cheated a day in his life, but that dinna make no difference 'cause the breed filled my man up with bullets, mortally woundin' him, and now here I am all alone."

Landon tensed slightly underneath her straying fingers when she mentioned *breed*. Was it possible that she did not know he was a half-breed? He let her ramble while he gathered his wits about him before asking, and using a voice bordering on boredom, "Do you know for sure who killed your man?"

"All I know for sure is he's a breed. I wasn't there when he gunned my man down in cold blood. I'm sure Tom Martin had sumthin' to do with it though." She turned her head slightly away, finally admitting she was not there, and all her assumptions were pure conjecture.

"Why is that?" he asked harshly.

"Boy, you sure got grumpy all of a sudden. Is Tom Martin some friend of yours?"

He brushed back a stray lock of her long blond hair in an apologetic motion.

Rubbing her cheek against his hand like a kitten seeking a good petting, she replied, "Gambler would tell me 'bout his business sometimes."

Landon forced his face into an impenetrable mask, hiding his emotions while Wendy told him tidbits of Gambler's other occupations.

✺❧❦❧✺

"YORE LIKE havin' sex with a damn hole in a wooden fence!"

"What do you expect from me, John? It hurts!" Crimson cried, fighting against the tears filling her eyes, and pulling the covers up under her chin.

"Hell, ya could at least move yore ass instead of layin' there stiff as a board. I'd be better off pleasurin' myself." John rolled off the bed and began dressing, his wife making him physically ill. She had the body of a siren but was passionless as a piece of wood.

"How should I know what I'm supposed to do if you don't tell me?" she screamed at him. "I'm new at this, no matter what you think."

She reached out a hand toward him, groaning when he evaded it. "Teach me, John. You're my husband, so show me how I can please you." Why was she begging him? She answered her own question. She could not take any more beatings and he was her husband. She owed him that much.

John paused in buttoning his shirt and stared at her a few moments, the sudden thought of making her act like the whore she was, pleasing him. He would break her high and mighty spirit and let her know she was subservient to him. Dropping his pants around his knees, his stiffened manhood jutting out, he growled, "Then come, little wife, and drop on yore knees in front of me and I'll begin yore lessons."

She watched him lick his thick lips, her stomach revolting when she realized what he was wanting. Trembling all over, she cowered under the quilt. "My God, John, I'll use my hands on you. Surely you don't expect me to...to..."

His grin was evil. "Take it in yore mouth, my dear? That's exactly what I'm a 'spectin'."

He almost laughed with the shock flaming across her face, her wide eyes glistening tears. "Maybe I'm goin' too fast, huh?

He pulled up his pants and finished dressing, throwing over his shoulder, "Ya make me sick with yore pure, holier than thou attitude, Crimson. Ya didna come to me pure, and I ain't never gonna let ya forget it, but I'll compromise with ya some and teach you how to pleasure me. In fact, ya will be beggin' for it afore I'm through with ya, but not now. I've had all I can stand of ya tonight."

His face screwed in revulsion, he grabbed his coat and slipped it on. "Cower in bed tonight, Crimson, for this is yore last night of actin' like a piece of wood. Tomorrow night we begin yore lessons."

Slamming the door behind him, his mocking laughter followed him, a lascivious grin pulling up his thick lips. *Ah yes, my little wife, tomorrow night ya shall learn the trades of a whore, but tonight I have other plans.*

❦

JOHN rode toward Fort Elliot and tethered his horse behind the embankment the army used for shooting practice. Walking the rest of the way on foot, he carefully skirted around the sentries. A light shone out of the Post Adjutant office and he silently headed toward it, cursing under his breath when stepping in some mud with bones crunching underneath his feet.

Crouching behind the first lighted window, he watched Major Larner count a stack of coins before putting them into a small metal box and locking it. After placing it in a desk drawer and locking it also, the major stretched lazily before rising and putting on his heavy coat. Blowing out the lamp, he opened the door and left his office.

John drew back into the shadows, listening as the major stopped and spoke a few minutes with a sentry, then smiled briefly when the major told the sentry he was headed for Mobeetie and the McLowry Saloon. When all was silent again, he rounded the building and carefully unlocked the door with his pocketknife.

Entering the pitch-black room, John stood against the closed door a few moments, letting his eyes adjust before walking toward the desk. He struck a match against his pants leg and it flared, giving him a small amount of light before he shook out the match and dropped it. He forced the drawer open with his knife and seized the heavy metal box from inside it. The metal box rattled when he set it on top of the desk. He broke it open, took the coins along with several silver certificates, and shoved them inside his pants pocket.

Striking another match, he glanced around, searching for something that might suit his fancy when his eyes fell on the posters. His face in a rough black and white sketch glared out at him. The match burned his fingers, and he shook it out none too soon when footsteps of the sentry passed by the building. Sneaking toward the door, he withdrew his pistol, cocked it and waited.

The footsteps passed by, and he slowly let out his breath. Assured the sentry had moved away, he turned toward the desk and struck another match. He quickly read the missive, noticing the received date was today and orders given for distribution of the posters in the surrounding area. The army was offering five hundred dollars for his capture. A cruel smile lighting his mouth, he grabbed a poster, folded it and put it in his pocket.

Taking the lantern sitting on a side table, he poured the coal oil around the room, then picked up the rest of the posters. He rolled them together before lighting another match and setting the posters on fire. Systematically, he ignited the office and desk. After the fire flared up and yellow flames licked at the woodwork, he snuck out of the office, silently laughing. The Post Adjutant office was next door, and he was sure they would both burn, especially his and Crimson's marriage information right along with it.

John was in good spirits by the time he reached McLowry's saloon. He had a pocket full of money, had destroyed all the wanted posters and his marriage information. Now only one man had knowledge of his past that could harm him and he would soon take care of him. With a glass of whiskey in his hand, he smiled at the pretty saloon girl with dark brown hair.

"Well, look what the cat's done dug up."

"Now, Jenny, ya ain't mad at me, are ya?" John cajoled, slipping his arm around her tiny waist.

Jenny shrugged his arm away and backed off a step. "The hell I ain't! I found out 'bout your marriage from gossip. You didn't have the decency of tellin' me yourself."

She slapped his hand away when he reached toward her. "Don't touch me, you bastard! I'm madder than a pole cat. I thought I was your woman."

"Ya are, baby, and ya always will be. You knew from the very start I'd never marry ya." John held his temper in check. Perhaps she was right being angry with him, but he needed her help.

"So, you up and married a lily-white bitch, and I bet she's as boring and cold as an old hat in bed." Jenny stood with her hands on her hips, her eyes angrily flashing that he attempted smoothing things over with her!

John ran his hand down her bare arm, smiling when she shivered. Certain of an easy win, he coerced, "No one can compare with ya in bed, babe, and everythin' ya said 'bout my wife is true. I only married her 'cause her family has lots of money, money enuff for me keepin' ya up in style."

Jenny relented, relaxing her pose, and blinked back her angry tears. "Oh, John, how could you do this? It's been ages since I've seen ya and my whole body has been achin' for ya."

"I'll take care of the itch soon as ya do sumthin' for me." He closed his hand on Jenny's arm and pulled her away from the group of men for a little privacy. Shoving her up against him so she could feel his hardness swelling in his pants, he maneuvered her until she could see the other men in the bar.

"See the major over there?" John tilted his head in the direction of Major Larner. "Go cuddle up real good with him and take him to yore place. Git him in yore bed, babe, and make sure ya keep his sole attention on you."

"What ya plannin'?" Jenny asked suspiciously.

"Don't ask questions. Jist do as I say if ya want some of this later." He guided her hand down and placed it on the hard bulge in front of his pants. Her groan of desire assured him she would comply. "Now go swing that purty little ass over there, smile real big and posture enuff to give him a real good view of these." He cupped her breasts and lifted them upward enough that they almost spilled over her bodice.

"You don't have to be so crude, John."

"Just do as yore told, Jenny."

"Alright, John, but I'm expectin' double my pay."

"I plan on it," John growled huskily, pushing her in the direction of the major. He watched Jenny sashay toward Major Larner, posturing prettily. The major smiled and his eyes lit up. Confident Jenny would get the job done, he finished his drink and left.

◦◦◦◦◦◦◦

JOHN secreted himself in the closet, leaving a crack in the door. Lust, strong and animalistic, whipped through him, watching his

158

mistress and the major have sex. He rubbed his painfully hard organ straining against his pants, saliva running down his thick lips and chin, his harsh breathing matching theirs. He removed his hand, clenching both at his sides and fought for control. He must not let his baser emotions destroy his chance. By force of will, he detached himself from the scene.

But the impact of watching his mistress having sex with another man, completely took him off guard, and he needed all his facilities. He could not take his eyes off them even if he wanted. He must strike at the exact moment the major reached culmination.

He watched the frenzied movements of the major's skinny hips humping his mistress. Slowly, he drew his pistol and opened the closet door. He crept out, his booted feet making no noise on the hardpacked dirt floor, and raised his pistol, holding the barrel end. He slammed the wooden grip against the major's skull as soon as the major hunched forward and froze a second before the major groaned and convulsed in climax. The major collapsed on top of Jenny, a rush of air spilling from his lungs and blood running down the side of his head.

It took a few seconds before Jenny overcame her erotic haze and realized what had happened. Her eyelids lowered with passion, her lips bruised and pouting, she focused on John standing beside the bed, and shakingly whimpered, "John, you coulda waited a few more minutes. I was almost there."

Pushing the dead weight of the major onto the floor, John leered at her and snickered, "Ya missed me, huh, baby? Ya little bitch!"

Jenny raised up her elbow and licked her lips, her eyes wide with surprise at his contempt. "John, I only did what ya told me. What do ya expect? Lie under him without feelin' a thing?"

"Not you, babe, not you. But don't worry, I'll take care of yore hankering in a moment soon as I have him tied up," John thickly remarked, taking in her hair, the sheen of perspiration on her naked body and the sensuous droop of her eyelids.

A slow smile spread across her lips, seeing the unmistakable proof of John's lust. She turned over on her side, running her hand up along her hip, waist and cupped the small mound using her finger to tease the areola of her breast. Watching John bind the unconscious major, she huskily encouraged him, "Hurry, John. I have a yearnin' that keeps just a 'buildin', and I don't like waitin' for ya. Ya know how much I like sex, 'specially with you."

John slyly grinned down at the bound major and the funny depiction with his hands tied behind his back, his feet strapped together, and naked. Satisfied with his work so far, John quickly stripped and joined his mistress. He took her roughly and cruelly slapping against her spread thighs and twisting her breasts, smiling chillingly with her groans of passion matching his own. A powerful orgasm ripped through his body, sending him over the brink into total darkness.

When he came to, Jenny was running her fingers through his wet hair, murmuring in amazement, "Oh, my. Oh, my, you were a total beast."

Nipping at her neck, John caught a thin layer of skin between his teeth before falling beside her. "Ya liked that, babe? We jist might do it agin sometimes."

"What do you mean?"

John turned over on his side and grabbed her hair, pulling her face closer. "I mean exactly what we jist did. Let another man mate with ya while I watch." As uncertainty crossed her face, he mercilessly pulled her hair. "Ya liked it, Jenny, so don't pretend otherwise."

Tears springing in her eyes, pain pierced her skull and fear leaped into her breast. "Anythang ya want, John. You're my man. I always like what ya do with me. You're always the best in bed."

He nodded in satisfaction before releasing her hair. He sat up and popped her smartly on the bottom before running his hand over the reddened cheek and slipping his fingers along the crack. Poking at her puckered back hole, he snarled, "I'm gonna take all your holes tonight, Babe, so don't ya go gittin' no more men while I'm gone 'cause I plan on ridin' ya hard, fast and rough all night long. "Now, git me his clothes," he finished, slapping her rearend again.

When she handed him Major Larner's clothes, he searched the pockets, transferred several coins into his own before he threw the clothes into the small potbellied stove, grinning maliciously when the flames caught and devoured them. "Throw the rest of his clothes and boots in there, Jenny. We don't want any proof he was here."

Jenny hurriedly obeyed him, nervously biting on her bottom lip.

John was acting strange and was being excessively violent. He had never been an easy man, but tonight was different, and she would not antagonize him further while he was in this mood. The one time she did, he beat her so severely she could not work for a couple of weeks. Lucky for her, he made sure he gave her enough money for survival. The only reason she kept him around was he was different than other men and was unashamed of trying different types of sex. She liked that, especially the rough stuff.

While she completed the task, John dressed. After buckling his holster, he pulled Jenny up against him, his hands traveling down her naked backside and shoving her front roughly up against him. "Keep yore fire goin', babe. I'll be back later for more, a lot more."

Savagely pushing her away, he slung the unconscious major over his shoulder. Heading for the door, he growled churlishly, "Clean up, Jenny. I don't wanna smell him on ya when I git back."

He paused a moment, a bizarre smile lifting his lips. "Perhaps the next time after you finish with another man, I'll lick that sweet thang atween yore legs, and then after I fill you with my seed, ya can take me in yore mouth and git me hard agin."

She gasped, slipping her hand between her legs. "The thangs ya do with me makes me willin' to do anythang ya want. Hurry back."

John headed for a small basin many miles outside of town. The frigid wind blew incessantly, creeping through each weave of his coat. The major was thrown over his saddle in front of him, his skinny bottom glaring blue in the pale moonlight. The major groaned with each step the horse took.

John's grin was malevolent as he moved his hand over the major's backside. "Yore ass is ice cold, but don't ya worry none, it won't be long afore ya won't feel a thang, 'specially after I bang this hole," John laughed, poking his finger into the major's rectum.

"Been a long time since I gotta feel a man's ass aginst me. Sometimes I like it jist as much as a lady's. And as horny as I got watchin' ya with my gal, I'll be that way all night."

With a maniacal laugh, John pulled the major's side closer against him so the major could feel his hard-on. "Ain't ya the lucky one! Ya know the best way to break a straight man is using his asshole like a woman's. And I will use it good afore I put ya outta of yore misery. Maybe I'll take the kerchief off yore mouth jist to hear ya scream."

Chapter 17
Not One Tittle

OPENING her eyes wide with surprise, Crimson felt the coins John pitched toward her fall onto the quilt around her. With tentative hands, she reached out and picked them up, her mouth hanging wide open in disbelief and confusion. The coins jingled in her hand as she closed her fist around them. She distinctly remembered the lone coins on top of the bureau several nights ago and knew there had not been many. "Where...where did you get these?"

"Won it in a poker game last night after I left ya. Take it and buy ya sumthin' purty. I'll be gone most of the day, so enjoy yoreself while ya can. We'll be leavin' in the mornin'." John robustly grinned at the shocked expression on her face.

Crimson stared at her husband, wondering at his cheerful mood, especially after the last stormy nights. "But...but there's over a hundred dollars here." She had never seen so much money at one time in her life.

John nonchalantly shrugged. "Enjoy it while ya can. Lady luck is fickle, and it might be a long time afore she smiles on me agin."

"But we might need it later," Crimson protested.

His mood swiftly changing, he glowered at her. "Do ya doubt my ability of takin' care of ya, Crimson?"

She hastily shook her head, nervously holding the coins in front of her. "No, John, never. I just thought…"

"Ya let me do the thinkin'," John interrupted.

"Fine, John."

Sitting on the bed beside her, he forced a jovial smile back on his lips. He lifted her heavy hair from her neck and placed a kiss behind her ear. "Get dressed and go have fun. I'll be back sumtime tonigh'. Eat in the restaurant downstairs while I'm gone. I probably won't be back until after supper." He patted her leg, frowning when she stiffened.

Rising from the bed, he left the room before he lost his temper. He must keep his stupid wife happy and prevent her from being suspicious. He could not afford her brother-in-law digging into his past.

Crimson stared at the closed door, a puzzled frown marring the perfection of her face. She was quickly learning her husband was a man of many moods, but it was either good or bad, hot or cold, and rarely warm. Shuddering in revulsion, she remembered the last week and did not want a repeat of those nights.

John had locked her in the room so no one would observe the bruises on her face. He occasionally brought her food, then made her strip and wait for his pleasure. Hatred was growing inside her and it scared her, the inclination foreign and terrifying at the same time. She reiterated a mantra over and over—*John is my husband to love, honor, cherish and obey till death do us part.* Did it help? Maybe some, but she made her bed and now she must lie in it. She had no other choice. The thought of failure was stronger than her fear.

Bringing the coins up toward her nose, she shook her head and sighed, her shoulders dropping in dejection. Her fighting spirit was almost gone, something she had never dreamed would happen. John was much stronger than her and fighting him only brought her more harm, and with that knowledge, it required a shift in her belief system.

A few days ago, he had thrown a package of rice powder onto her lap, demanding she use it and cover the last remaining discolored traces of the bruising. She was glad he did for the traces of yellow, green and blue markings of his anger still showed on her face.

CRIMSON slowly ate her lunch of buffalo steak, fried potatoes, black-eyed peas and tender biscuits with plenty of fresh butter and wild plum jam. She had already wasted most of the day just pondering her and John's marriage, and still had not come up with a suitable answer. Not that it mattered. She married him, and she would be a good, faithful wife.

Now with the money he gave her, should she buy dress material or something for her new home which she had not seen nor knew where it was located? All she knew was he had secured another job far away from her family and also found a home for them. A hundred dollars was a lot of money and there was so much she wanted and did not know what she would need. She decided she would pocket most of the money in case they needed it later.

She wondered whether the house had windows and what it was built of or how many rooms it had. Surely it had windows, and she would shop for curtain material. Maybe red and white checkered or a nice, flowered pattern material. She'd have a look at the mercantile stores. Maybe they would have a fairly recent Harper's Bazar or Lady Godey's book on the new eastern styles or...

Her thoughts were interrupted by the scrapping of a chair being pulled back from her table. A flicker of fear, then anger filled her face. A mocking smile on his lips, Landon sat down beside her without asking for permission.

"I did not ask you to join me."

"Hello, Crimson, mind if I have a seat?" At her silent incensed stare, he answered if she had spoken, "Don't mind if I do, thank you."

In a glance, she took in his cold, ice blue eyes, the rugged jut of his chin and the challenging smile. A shiver of fear or was it desire, swept through her slender frame. "Mr. Wade, you lack manners. I did not ask for your company. I am a respectable married woman now and you should leave."

His infuriating, crooked grin never left his face during her tirade. "And another thing, you can't call me by my first name. I am Mrs. Sullivan, Mrs. John Sullivan," she intoned distinctly, making sure her meaning was clear.

"I heard you got married, Crim... excuse me, Mrs. Sullivan, but I couldn't believe you got married so fast, especially after we..."

"How dare you!" she cried, not letting him finish, red rushing from her neck and flooding her face.

"That's twice you've said that, *Mrs. Sullivan.*" Landon slurred her name, curling up his lips in disdain. "You oughta realize by now I dare very well."

"I will not sit here and take your insults, Mr. Wade." He laid his hand on her wrist, pressing down on it and keeping her from rising. "Let go or I'll make a scene."

"Be still, Crimson, or I'll raise my voice loud enough so everyone in this room can hear what we did. I'll embellish it nicely, going as far as adding a little extra." His shaggy eyebrow lifted with amusement, remembering their first meeting.

She uneasily looked around the room and lowered her eyes, observing some of the diners curiously staring at them. Forcefully unclenching her hands, she eased her pose into a more companionable posture while lashing out at him, "You have no right treating me like this."

"Don't I, little spy? You're mine! I am your first. You belong to me, not this John Sullivan." His eyes turned murky blue, his jaw firm as rock. "Never doubt, Crimson. I shall have you."

"No, you will not! I never belonged to you!" she blustered, feeling helpless and lost by his overpowering presence. If he was not so handsome and masculine, and if she could catch her breath, maybe she could leave here with a little dignity intact. His hand burned through the sleeve of her dress, sending tremors down her spine. It was not fair his touch was enough for her to recant her marriage vows, especially when she knew he was the one rustling their cattle and trying to kill her. And his kiss? Would she ever forget it? She subconsciously licked her trembling lips and softly begged, "Please let me go."

He released her arm and smoothed out his face, the emotionless mask in place once again. "This is not why I'm here. I'm here to ask you a few questions."

Keeping her focus on her half-eaten plate of food, his smooth voice pulled her eyes back to his, those extraordinary eyes that never left her in peace. "What kind of questions?" she asked, her heart leaping into her throat.

Landon searched her face, feeling an almost overwhelming compulsion of pulling the pins from her hair and watch the wavy mass fall free down her shoulders. Her eyes widened in sudden alarm, turning a darker green.

He remained silent too long, and she grew uncomfortable staring into his aloof face. Increasingly uneasy, she finally blurted out what was uppermost in her mind. "Please don't steal any more cattle from my family. I'm not living there anymore. Please! I didn't have anything with them calling you names and hurting you!"

His eyes widened, then narrowed. "What are you blabbering about?"

"You don't know?" She sighed in relief, then grew tense once more. Was he playing some kind of cruel game with her?

"Hell, no, I don't know!" Landon harshly answered. "Pardon my language, ma'am, but you ain't making a whole lot of sense. Suppose you tell me about it."

She studied the hard lines of his face, searching for a clue if he was playing her for a fool or if he hadn't recognized her yet. But if he did not recognize her, who was killing off her friends and attempted killing her? She watched his lips narrow into a white line, his strange eyes never leaving hers while thinking, *he does remember! It's in his hard eyes and the tight line of his lips. I will not play his game! He'll only laugh at me and deny it!* "Nothing, I meant nothing."

"You keep mouthing inane things, ma'am, if you'll pardon the expression, without telling me a thing. Now, tell me what you were talking about."

"It's nothing, I told you!" she repeated, furious once again at his intrusion and the overwhelming memories of their times at the abandoned sod.

Captain Pierce interrupted them, and Landon never finished questioning her further.

"Mr. Wade, could I please have a little bit of your time? It's very important or I wouldn't be interrupting you. Ma'am, would you mind?" he asked, turning toward Crimson, his eyebrow lifted in question.

"You're fine, Captain. I was just leaving." She grabbed her

drawstring purse and rose from the table, nodding her head imperially toward them. "Good day, gentlemen."

Landon absently motioned toward an empty seat while he watched the gentle swaying of her hips. After the captain took a seat, the captain clearing his throat brought him back from his observation. He turned slowly toward him. "Captain Pierce, you have my undivided attention."

"I'm sorry about interrupting your chitchat with *Mrs.* Sullivan, but this is important army business, sir."

Landon's brow arched sardonically with the captain emphasizing Mrs. "There's nothing going on between us, Captain Pierce. We are old friends. In fact, we grew up together."

Captain Pierce's face grew red. "I stand corrected, sir."

"Good. Now what's so important?"

"Last night, you were with Major Larner?"

"I was."

"Well, sir, he's missing. We know he wouldn't have deserted or anything like that," Captain Pierce hastily added, "but one of the men who pulled sentry duty last night said the major headed for the McLowry saloon. We traced him there and him hooking up with a saloon girl named Jenny. She claims the last time that she saw him was when they both left the saloon, him going his way and she hers."

The captain paused and Landon impatiently waited for him to continue. "What's so strange about that, Captain?"

"Well, sir, his horse was still tied outside of the saloon, and you know how punctual he is. Well, it seems mighty strange he hasn't shown up yet."

Landon's whole attention was on the man now. "You're suspecting foul play?"

"It's possible, but we don't know for sure. His office caught on fire last night and several other buildings burned down before we got the fire out. Surely coincidental, maybe," his voice suggesting he believed them connected. "I just thought you might give me some sort of clue. It was reported you and he talked well into the night."

"I wish I could help, but we only spoke about trivial things, nothing important. If I was you though, I'd question this Jenny again. She might know more than she's telling."

"We have, but she hasn't changed her story one tittle."

Landon rose from his chair. "I suggest we head back to the McLowry Saloon and question her again. Stories change more than once when they're told by the same person."

The saloon was almost empty when they entered. There was a lone cowboy nursing a beer and two or three men passed out on the floor with one underneath a table, leftovers from last night. The bartender, a big, brawny fellow, polished glasses behind the bar.

"What can I do fer ya?" he bellowed.

"We'll take a couple of beers while we question one of your girls." Landon leaned against the bar, hooking his foot on the rail and placing his elbows on top.

The bartender drew the beers and slapped the glasses of golden liquid with white foamy tops in front of them. "I don't want no trouble, mister. You jist drink your beers and skedaddle, hear?"

Landon nonchalantly took the beer, downed it and wiped off his mouth with his shirt sleeve before answering, "We don't want any trouble either. This is government business, and we will be asking Miss Jenny a few questions."

"You're a cocky son-of-a-bitch, ain't ya? Well, you jist make it quick 'cause I don't want her any more upset than she already is. I cain't have her spillin' expensive liquor all over the customers tonight."

Landon cocked an eyebrow at the bartender. "Upset?"

"Hell yeah, those damn soldiers been badgerin' her all mornin' 'bout their major. She's done tol' 'em a thousand times she don't know nothin' 'bout it." The bartender wiped his meaty hands on his apron, eyeing them suspiciously. "I suspect yer here and doin' some more badgerin'. I don't know why ya don't jist take her word fer it. She's a good girl and if'n she says she don't remember nothin' more, then she don't."

"We'll keep it in mind." Landon flipped a few coins on the bar and followed the captain, steadily making his way toward a dark-haired young woman who distractedly wrung her hands together in her lap.

"Why don't ya'll just leave me alone! I don't know nothin'," she cried when they stopped in front of her.

"We're not accusing you of anything, ma'am. We need to hear your story again and perhaps question you, see if you might have left out something. Maybe you saw Major Larner visiting with somebody last night or you saw what direction he headed when he left or if somebody stopped him and you just forgot about it."

Landon watched her agitation continue to grow by the way she kept creasing the material of her gown between nervous fingers. She was too jittery and obviously upset for her not knowing anything, and instinct told him she was not telling all she knew.

"I told them all that this mornin'."

"Suppose you tell me all over again."

She futilely glanced over at the bartender, still wringing her hands in front of her. "He was in here last night drinkin' and playin' a little billiards. He was pretty drunk when he left, so I helped him out the door. He wouldn't tell me which one was his horse, so I jist left him standin' in front of the saloon. It was cold and I was tired and went home. I don't know where he went from there."

"Not one tittle," Captain Pierce stated under his breath so only Landon heard his comment.

Landon's brows drew together, unsatisfied with her answers. Her speech did not ring true. It was too practiced, too perfect, but before he could pursue the matter, they were interrupted. It was a day of interruptions.

"Captain Pierce, sir." The private saluted smartly. "Lieutenant Rawlins wants you back at the post hospital."

"What is it, private?" Captain Pierce stiffly asked.

"Well, sir." He eyed Jenny, a red flush creasing his face.

Captain Pierce curtly dismissed Jenny and watched her leave before fixing the private with a scowl. "You can speak freely now, Private James."

"There was a body discovered this mornin' while we were out on maneuvers. We think it might be Major Larner's."

"Think? Explain yourself."

Looking down at his shuffling feet before looking back up, the private's face grew a darker red. "Well, sir, the man's face was blown up in bits and he was buck-ass naked. We couldn't find hide nor hair of his clothes or personal effects, but that ain't all, sir…"

When the private hesitated, Captain Pierce prompted him, "What else?"

"Well, his…" The private looked down at the front of his britches and motioned toward his groin. "His privates, sir, somebody blew the dang thang off."

"Good, God, man! How in the hell do you think it might be the major if there's nothing identifying him?"

The private stiffened, his voice holding a tinge of anger. "The corpse is 'bout the same build as the major's and the hair 'bout the same color, but that ain't all, Sir. He has a scar on his left thigh. You know, the leg Major Larner always favored?"

❧◦❀◦❧

CRIMSON glanced dispassionately at the assorted packages strewn across the bed. She did have over half the money left, though she had gone on a shopping spree, buying indiscriminately in her desperate attempt of blocking Landon and whatever questions he might have from her mind. But what questions could he possibly ask?

She rubbed at her forehead, unsuccessfully erasing him from her memory. He was so beautiful, so totally male. John was infinitesimal as a cockroach compared with Landon. How could John's boyish face and pitless gray eyes equal Landon's exquisite, well-formed maleness and soul-penetrating eyes? And his hands, so different from John's square, meaty ones. John's elicited pain, but Landon's? Her body grew weak with longing, remembering his long, slender hands with the clean fingernails touching her so lovingly.

Picking up her brush, she drew it viciously through the tangled mass of hair, delighting in the pinprick's scalp pain. She was wicked, so totally wicked. She married another man, so why did she keep comparing the two? *What is wrong with me?* But the smarting tugs of the brush did not destroy his image from her mind's eye.

Her husband's body was stocky and unbending like a solid rock, but Landon was slim with roped muscles and a beautiful physique, supple and unbreakable. Darkness compared with John's lightness. He reminded her of a black panther with startling blue eyes, always watching, lean, mean and ready to spring, and with his mere touch, her bones lost consistency and her insides melted.

What was she thinking? He was her enemy, remember? Was he

171

not rustling her family's cattle? Had he not killed Archie and attempted killing her? Where and when would he strike next?

And he did remember her when they were young. She had seen it in his eyes. There had been a flicker of surprise, a faint widening of the eyes when she begged, *how could she have been so stupid?* no pleaded with him to leave her family alone.

She slammed the brush on top of the bureau. "I'm a stupid fool for letting him see my fear! Stupid! Stupid! Stupid!"

With a wide sweep of her arm, she scattered the packages covering the bed across the room. "Landon Wade, I'll not let you destroy me! I can't let you destroy me." Her voice ended in a hopeless whine.

With her hands over her head and closing her eyes, tears squeezed between her lashes. "Leave me alone! I can't think about you! I must block your eyes always before me! Please, just leave me alone! Let me live in peace with my husband."

Falling on her knees, she pounded the bed in impotent fury, hating she had made a mess of her life and married the wrong man, but the man she loved was the one destroying her and her family.

Her fingernails digging into the cotton mattress, she fought against the turbulent emotions swelling within her breast. Landon haunted her, dogging her every step with his ice-cold blue eyes. Straightening, she rose, speaking into the deathly still room, "Now you are really being silly."

She forced herself in picking up the packages and neatly stacking them against the wall. The shadows in the room lengthened with the quickly disappearing light. Exhausted, she nearly tore the buttons from her blouse in her bid to undress. Changed into her nightgown, she brushed her hair until wisps of hair attracted like metal to a magnet around her head and the brush. Carefully braiding the unruly mass, she drew back the covers and slipped between the sheets.

Rubbing her tired eyes, she was emotionally and physically drained. All day she surreptitiously looked for Landon, expecting him behind her, dreading it, yet strangely disappointed when he wasn't there. *This is foolish! I must quit thinking about him!*

No sooner had she thought it, when the room door opened. John entered like a dreaded nightmare, his very appearance taunting her and making her feel guilty thinking about another man.

"Ah, I see yore already in bed like a nice little wife. Take off that damn nightgown and git ready for yore next lesson." He chuckled, pleased with his own little joke. He had thought about her all day, scheming and planning on what he would make her do tonight. It tickled his fancy thinking about making her satisfy him like a prostitute would, and she would never guess he was using her.

After she tossed her nightgown toward the foot of the bed, he blew the lamp out and stripped, an evil grin on his lubricous mouth. Slipping into the bed, he pulled her roughly against him, placing a wet kiss on her resisting lips. "Another lesson, little wife, in pleasing me."

Chapter 18
Dangerous Secrets

JOHN'S steady breathing assured her he was asleep as Crimson shakily rose from the bed. She inwardly cringed at what he made her do tonight and wondered at her wisdom when asking for him to teach her how she could please him. She felt cheap and used, and at the same time, she had felt a familiar wetness between her legs while she was doing some of those things with him. There had still been discomfort when he took her, but near the end, a tingling, yearning had built inside of her. She was frustrated when he finished his pleasure, leaving her on the verge of tears with this unfulfilled aching between her legs.

Taking a rag and wetting it, she cleaned the stench of her husband from her body. Shaking her head, dislodging her random thoughts, she grabbed the towel sheet and dried herself.

Draping the towel around the top of her chest, she tucked the end between her breasts, glancing nervously at the sleeping form before looking back at the pile of coins he had withdrawn from his pockets and placed there earlier. She was not being nosy, just curious how much money he had. Then she saw it—a large, crumpled and folded piece of paper. Curiously picking it up, she headed for the window and carefully smoothed out the paper, glancing agitatedly toward him every so often. She pushed back the curtain and held the paper toward the waning moonlight.

Suddenly, the bed ropes creaked, and before she could react, the paper was torn from her hands.

"Ya damn, prying bitch! What in the hell do ya think yore doin' goin' through my personal belongin's? Ya may be my wife, but that sure as hell don't give ya the right to snoop into my stuff."

She cringed back toward the wall, his explosive temper reminding her of their first night together. "I wasn't pryin', Tom..."

She never finished. The power of his blow slammed her against the far wall. Sliding down it, she landed hard on her posterior, the towel sheet coming loose and falling around her. Pain and metallic blood filling her mouth and stars dazzling before her eyes, she pulled her knees toward her bared chest, stunned while she gingerly touched the cut on her upper lip, feeling it swell beneath her fingertips.

"Stupid bitch! I knew ya couldna keep from callin' me by my real name."

"But...but...we're in private. No one heard me, John." She shook her head, desperately clearing her vision. Was that high-pitched voice really hers?

"We're in private, John," he shrilly mocked her. "I don't give a damn if no one heard ya, Crimson. Yore to *never, never, ever* use my real name. Do ya hear me? A slip like that in public could get me hanged. Or is that what ya want?"

She stared at him, speechless, submissive as a simpering cow-eyed heifer. She, who deplored those types of women, was quickly becoming one. Not that she was afraid of pain, but somehow it had become a factor in her relationship with John. She could not admit her marriage was a failure before it started, and if she went back home, Buck and Honeysuckle would never let her hear the end of it.

But why should she take John's beatings? In the matter of seconds of this running through her mind, she clenched her fists, her fingernails cutting into the palms of her hands. Rising like a wrath of fury, she attacked him, fingernails extended in claws, a feline screech tearing from her throat.

"You low-bellied snake in the grass, never again will you touch me. Never! I'm going home and I'm telling Buck and Honeysuckle all about you beating me and treating me badly."

The flesh of his face ripped underneath her attack, bringing four, deep, red gouges along his cheek before he captured her wrists and pulled her arms tightly behind her back. He forced a calmness he did not feel with her screamed threat, realizing his mistake might cost him all he had diligently worked to accomplish. "Crimson, I'm sorry I hit ya. It's jist it makes me so damn mad when somebody goes through my personal belongin's, and then ya usin' my real name."

He pulled her naked, still struggling form tightly against him, enjoying her struggles against him and the swelling of his manhood. "Damn it, Crimson. Shut up and listen."

She grew still and cocked back her head, glaring at him.

"Look, I was wrong in hittin' ya. We started out wrong. Let's try agin. We'll be a proper husband and wife."

She nodded numbly, her whole body shaking with the sudden violence between them. He brushed his fingers against her cheek, gently coaxing her anger away. Agreeing with him, a harshness edged her voice, "One more time, John, one more, and then if it happens again, I'm going home and telling my family the truth."

His answer was a soft kiss on her forehead. She never saw the deadly rage shining behind his eyes when he edged her naked form on the bed and dropped his hand between her legs, stroking her until she was moaning with desire, then he took her again with a vengeance, the pain successfully quelling her craving.

⚜

AN ANGRY tick working in his cheek, Landon listened as the captain questioned the men one by one on the details of finding the body in the canyon. There was no way they could be certain it was Major Larner's body, but some sixth sense told him it was. Who would do such a cruel thing? Not only did the body sustain a lot of damage, but the fort physician also diagnosed he had been sexually assaulted as well. The cruelty and advert damage the body received spoke more of a personal vendetta. Major Larner had been well liked at the fort and in town, so the whole affair was illogical.

"Are you sure there were no Indian signs, private?" Captain Pierce probed.

"No suh, weren't no sign a'tall of no injuns. Been over that thar canyon several times and still weren't no signs. Thar weren't a print of nuffin'. D'wind was blowin' too hard las' nigh' to leave any. No, suh, nuffin' a'tall. Whoever dun it got out wid out a trace. Probably ne'er will fin' out."

"That'll be all, private." Captain Pierce watched him leave before speaking, "That's the last one and we still don't know any more than we did. How about you? Any suggestions?"

"Nope, nothing. I'm confused as you. I can tell you it wasn't Indians who did this. That I can assure you, but whoever it was had some kind of grudge and he's got a helluva way of showing it."

The captain ran his fingers distractedly through his hair. "Yeah, and we'll probably never find out. That's what bothers me the most, the not knowing."

Landon crammed the Stetson on his head, his face a grim mask. "There's nothing more I can do, Captain, but go out in the morning and scout around the area. Maybe I can find something the others missed."

Leaving the room, Landon stepped out into the cold night, desperately needing fresh air to cleanse the horrible scent of death from his nostrils. His jaws ached from clenching his teeth as he combatted the impotent anger steadily building inside of him. He was furious and saddened at the uselessness of the major's death. There was nothing left he could do tonight. He would get an early start in the morning.

⋗◦⊙⋖⋗⊙◦⋖

CRIMSON idly watched a spider weave its intricate web across the ceiling. A cricket chirped somewhere in the room, its tune screeching through her head in a steady cadence. Sunlight spilled through the window, blinding her and making star points behind her closed eyelids.

She kept telling herself she must get up and begin the day. It was already an hour past sunrise, but what was the use? Besides a little housework, there was nothing she could do on the ranch. John had hired someone who came every day to take care of the animals and do outside work.

John deposited her at the ranch, and she rarely saw him. He was gone on business for days at a time, he said. She pulled the sheet up closer around her shoulders. Buck had never been away from the ranch like this on ranching business during the winter, and now it was nearly summer, and nothing had changed. The whole thing was strange, but when she asked John about it, he just shrugged and told her it was none of her concern, just do her part. So she had done her part and for what? No one appreciated it, just her and the eerie howl of the wind.

Forcing herself from the bed, she made it, dressed, then swept the spider web from the ceiling. Rummaging around the room until she located the cricket, she squashed it underneath her foot. The sudden quiet was deafening, and she almost wished she had let it continue its nerve-racking song. Anything was better than this awful quiet with only the mournful wail of the wind blowing through the cracks of the house which only emphasized her loneliness.

Brushing a stray lock of hair from her forehead, she glanced around the sparkling clean sod or at least as clean as it could ever be with a dirt floor. It was not much different than the one she grew up in when she was young. It had one big room, a bed in one corner, and the kitchen and fireplace in the other. It was not much, but it was her home.

She tentatively picked up her hand mirror and peered at her face, then touched her black eye, nodding grimly. Why did she take his hair-trigger moods—his sudden violence always left an unpleasant taste in her mouth. The guilt she felt for giving the only possession that rightfully should have been his, her proof of virginity, constantly preyed upon both of their minds. John never let her forget she had given another man his prize. Their last argument had been over John demanding the man's name and her refusing.

His irrational temper exploded, and she borne the brunt of it, her swollen black eye was testimony afterward. And like all other times he had used her as his punching bag, he apologized prettily, begging for her forgiveness. Sometimes he pushed her on the bed and played upon her flesh, bringing her close but taking his pleasure without ever allowing her the same. She wondered if that too was done on purpose and was another form of punishment.

Maybe she was wrong in not telling him who took her virginity, but the thought of admitting she made love with her enemy kept her silent. How could she tell John she preferred Landon's touch and

178

not his? How could she admit it? But with blunt rationality, she did admit she preferred Landon's touch. In fact, John's frequent absences were heaven sent. She berated herself for her disloyalty and improper reflections. She was John's wife for heaven's sake. She should willingly submit, but something inside her revolted.

Opening the door and letting in the fresh midspring air and sunshine, the trill of birds singing steadily welcomed her and the new day. She stoked the fire, put on a pot of coffee, prepared a roast and stuck it in the oven, and began making a pan of biscuits just in case John came home today.

Everything was done automatically while her mind wandered to the day she and John left Mobeetie. They had left before sunrise, and the clip-clop of the horses and the rattling of the wagon were the only sounds in the early morning stillness. She glanced around the town one last time, imprinting it on her memory when she saw Landon slouching against a building lazily watching, his dark face inscrutable. She hastily faced forward and stared straight ahead all the while conscious of his eyes boring into her back.

Violently shaking her head against the persistent traitorous considerations about another man, she felt disloyal to her husband. Why did everything about Landon play upon her mind with such regularity? It was unnatural and wrong. She was a married woman! She had married her childhood sweetheart and he had given her everything she had ever wanted. Then why was she so unhappy? So dissatisfied? So lonely and unfulfilled?

She tensed slightly when she heard a steady clip-clop of horse hooves, the creaking of leather and the jangling of hardware breaking the morning quietness. Wiping her hands on the apron hanging around her waist, she walked toward the door, mentally unprepared for John today.

Sighing with relief, she watched Harvey dismount, tie his reins on the hitching post, and stride toward her, tipping his hat.

"Mornin', Miz Sullivan. Is that coffee I smell?"

"Come on in, Harvey, and have a cup. It's fresh made." Crimson stood back and let him enter before stepping behind him. She retrieved clean coffee cups from the shelf near the stove and placed them on the rough wooden table. Bunching the end of her apron, she retrieved the coffee pot and poured some of the strong black brew into the cups before placing it back on the small, cast-iron stove. "I have some biscuits in the oven. They'll be ready in a minute if you want some."

"Sounds mighty good, Miz... Is it alright if I just call ya Crimson since we grew up and all together? It jist don't seem fittin' bein' so formal and all."

"That'll be fine, Harvey." Crimson placed a crock of fresh butter and wild honey on the table. "I suppose John sent you with a message. How long will he be gone this time?"

He shifted while watching her bend over and pull a pan of golden-brown biscuits from the oven. The thin material of her skirt outlined her well-shaped backside, and his mental picture of him lifting the edges of her skirt over her waist was intriguing and pleasing. She was a mighty fine-looking woman with all the physical attributes he admired. "Three or four weeks. I'll catch up with him later in the week."

Sighing in relief, she placed the pan in the middle of the table, then turned.

Though Crimson's black and swollen eye startled him, Harvey had seen the evidence of John's beatings before, and mistook the meaning of her sigh. "I guess it do git mighty lonely out here all by yoreself and all so much." John was rarely around and Crimson was left here by herself most of the time without a man. And he had not been with a woman in a long time. *Just saying!* She turned back around with a couple of plates in her hand. He grabbed a biscuit and liberally spread it with butter and honey after she placed a plate in front of him.

"Ya know, it don't seem righ' for ya'll havin' so much trouble atween yoreselves so soon after ya got hitched." It took his full concentration of not lowering his hand down and shifting himself into a more comfortable position or preferably, 'choke the chicken' which he would do as soon as he left her. He couldn't remember how many times she and that sweet body enticed him into manhandling himself until he found a soiled dove and took his relief in her, which just wasn't often enough.

Sitting in front of him, Crimson dropped the hot biscuit on her plate and blew on her fingers while warily shooting him a sideways glance. "Whatever do you mean, Harvey? We aren't having problems. It's he's gone so much on business."

Harvey grunted before taking a bite, sarcastically grumbling, "Business, huh?"

Sipping her coffee, she studied Harvey over the rim. "What's going on?"

He wiped his hands down his pant legs before lifting his eyes up and meeting hers. "Ya really don't know?" He said it more as a statement of fact. "I hate seein' someone sweet and pure as you bein' made a fool of."

Slapping her coffee cup on the table, she stood, moving the bench back with her leg calves. How she hated those words, *sweet and pure!* They were in direct conflict with how she felt about herself. She hastily stepped back toward the stove before answering, "My marriage ain't got nothing to do with you, Harvey."

She piddled around the stove for a few minutes, hating herself for wondering what he was talking about. She was taken by surprise when Harvey grabbed her and suddenly whirled her around. Gripping her shoulders, he held her steadfast when she tried pulling back.

"Maybe yore marriage ain't none of my business, but I cain't stand by watchin' ya bein' made a fool of. It jist don't seem righ'."

"My marriage is not up for discussion," she fumed, suddenly angry at his insistence. She meaningfully glanced at his hands, and he dropped them quickly at his sides.

"I don't mean to git ya all riled up, but ya should be aware of what's goin' on. I mean, ya will be the laughin' stock of town if'n ya ain't a knowing."

Against her better judgment, her curiosity was once again piqued. "Then suppose you sit down here and tell me what's going on." She missed the sudden leer splitting his thin lips as she swept past him and was reseated. By the time she had turned back around with a delicate eyebrow raised, his smile was gone.

Harvey took the seat across from Crimson and cleared his throat. "Well now, I don't like bein' the bearer of bad news, but somebody's gotta tell ya."

"Get on with it, Harvey, since you're so all fired up in telling me anyway," she edgily snapped.

"Well, ya don't need gittin' so testy about it. I jist wanna keep ya from gettin' real hurt later on by John up and leavin' ya for good. It's better for ya to at least be a mite prepared."

"Then just tell me, for heaven's sake, and get on with it."

Green sparks flew from her eyes, and Harvey had the grace to lower his. "Well, ma'am, it's jist John has this doxy in town he's been keepin' up. They've been real cozy since afore ya'll got married. It don't rightly seem righ' and all. You see, he ain't been gone all that much on business. He's been with his mistress."

She felt deflated and hurt, and oddly at the same time, relieved. It was not so unusual for men to have a mistress or two. It kept her from performing her wifely duties quite so often. "Now that you've told me, what are you expecting from me?"

His mouth gaping open, Harvey stared at her, not expecting her resignation. He snapped his mouth shut. "Ya know, I expected ya'd git angry or sumthin', not this. 'Sides, I know yore not stupid, so why are ya actin' that way?"

"I'm not stupid, Harvey James, and I don't like you implying it either. Just what in the tarnation am I supposed to do? Cry, scream, rail at something I have no control over? That's not me, no sir, that's not me. If he wants his little...little...whatever she is, then it's his problem."

He shook his head in disbelief. "Whatever happened to that fiery girl I always knowed? I jist cain't believe you'd jist sit there and take all his crap. No, suh, ya sure had me fooled."

Staring down at her hands, she wondered the same thing. What was happening? Never had she believed she would have taken all the things John had doled out. She had submitted willingly: his beatings, his cussing, his belittling of everything she did, and his unusual sex training, forcing her into doing things she had never dreamed or imagined. Did she feel like she deserved it for making love with another man before marriage and could not forget him?

The last thought hit her like a thunderbolt. Of course, how could she be so stupid? She had let him run over her while she subsequently felt she was being disloyal and deserved his contempt. And why should she when he was actually doing what she had only done twice before they married? Was she any different than him?

Her voice soft, the words that left her mouth shocked them both. "What should I do? Take a lover too?"

Harvey stood quickly, his excitement growing harder and more obvious along the front of his pants. "Now, that can be arrange righ' now, Crimson. I've always wanted ya and will make it real good for ya. And I'll never hit or beat ya! No man should do that to a woman!"

"What?" Crimson cried, taken back when spying his swollen manhood bivouacking his pants. "You keep that dang thing in your pants, Harvey! I ain't gonna take on a lover. I am married to John for better or worse!"

"Oh, I can keep it in my pants and still pleasure both of us." Harvey took a step toward her, thinking about lifting her skirt.

"Ain't going to happen, Harvey. I ain't taking a lover." She must get out of this lonesome place so she could think. The last time she had seen her sister and her family was when they had brought over her and John's wedding gifts in the wagon months ago. "Tell John I'm going to my sister's for a while. I'll be back in a few weeks or so in case he decides on coming home before then."

Green sparks shot from her emerald eyes, and Harvey bit back a grin. He had succeeded in raising her ire. Perhaps soon she would accept him between her luscious thighs. "Sure will, Crimson, and ya jist remember what I said. It ain't righ' for him doin' this. Ya got rights, so use 'em."

Chapter 19
Deceiving Eyes

THE MORE Crimson considered John's infidelity, the angrier she became. Had she not been the prim and proper wife? Had she not done her wifely duty? It wasn't fair! John was her husband! They promised to love and cherish one another, and that's the way it should be. But right now, she must get away from this lonely place and put things in perspective.

She bid Harvey a tense goodbye and packed a few clothes. After cleaning the kitchen, she wrapped the left-over biscuits and roast in cheese cloths, then secured them in a saddlebag. After filling two canteens with water, she saddled Blackfoot and headed southwest. Her sister's place was over a hundred miles away, so she packed her thick woolen cloak for protection against the unpredictable weather, though she did plan on staying at neighboring ranch houses along the way during the night. The long ride would do her good. She had been idle way too long.

By the third day, her backside was so sore she wondered if her decision had been made too hastily. The food she had taken with her was already exhausted, but the ranch families along the way provided her with ample food until the next home came into view. Friendly families begged her to stay with them or at least provide an armed escort for her since there were rumors of Indians sighted in the area, but she refused. Surprisingly, no one asked about her black eye, which tended to show through the rice powder at times. Though several concerned eyes searched her face, along with people compressing their lips, stopped themselves from asking questions.

Crimson knew it was vital she took time alone and wrangled her thoughts in some type of order. However, her deliberations were on the rockiest road she had ever traveled with its ins-and-outs, ups-and-downs, and swirling around worse than a tornado. It seemed nothing held its place—each conjecture jumping around like a frog escaping from a scalding water stream.

She gauged her direction by the mid-morning sun, then kicked her heels against Blackfoot's side. With each step of the mare, Crimson rolled the problem over and over. On one hand, she was glad John's attention had been diverted so often from her, but on the other hand she was furious he was making it obvious. People would think she was not woman enough to keep her husband from straying, and that bothered her the most. She had been sliding along, letting things happen without raising a hand, but now it was time for her to take control of her own destiny and plan her future accordingly. She did not deserve his treatment of her. She was a human being too.

And why did Landon Wade pop into her deliberation again? His beautiful manly presence, memories of his sky-blue eyes and the way he looked at her like she was the sweetest, best dessert he could devour, swept through her reflections along with regrets—regrets he was the one causing the problems for her family's ranch. But…oh, her dreams of having his arms around her once again fluttered her heart.

She let Blackfoot pick her way across the flat plains while her mind drifted with daydreams of Landon worshiping her body. She had not realized Blackfoot stopped until a deep voice spoke and hands grabbed at her reins.

"What in the hell do you think you're doing out here all by yourself?"

Crimson violently jumped, shaken out of her reverie. "Let me go!"

"I ain't letting you go until you tell me what you're doing out here. Don't you know it's dangerous?" Landon kept a firm grip on the reins, his usually expressionless face pinched in anger.

Recognizing the voice, Crimson stiffened, masking her fright and berating herself for not being more alert. "Why should you care? You've already tried killing me once."

"Tried killing you, Crimson? If I wanted you dead, I would let you continue riding straight for the Kiowa encampment." He fought down his urge of reaching over and shaking some sense into her stubborn head. "Haven't you heard what Indians do with white women?"

"You can't scare me, Mr. Wade. The Indians are peaceful now since they've been put on reservations."

"You know that is not always true." Landon released her reins and sprang off his horse, landing lightly near her mount's side, then pulled her down in front of him. "Quit fighting me, Crimson. I ain't gonna hurt you."

She stopped struggling and looked up into his eyes. Drowning in the crystal blue depths was her first mistake. All anger slowly sapped from her, and she could not look away. They were like the eyes of a snake, hypnotizing its victim before striking. When she saw his face lower near hers, she could not move. Instead, she opened her lips slightly, wetting them with the tip of her tongue, and accepted his hard, demanding kiss, and with it, the rest of her energy and strength was stolen from her.

Her arms were imprisoned by him and she grew frustrated when she could not lift them around his shoulders. He softened his kiss, playing with her lips like a treasured toy, invoking pinpoints of desire racing through her breasts and lower belly. Her whole world stopped and her tormented reflections were frozen in a hidden part of her brain.

Releasing the tempting morsel, he murmured in her ear, "Damnit, Crimson, you scared me half to death with your mindless riding. I've been following you for several miles, watching you head straight for the Indian encampment. My silly little spy, what will I do with you now? They've spotted you. You can't go back and you can't go around them. You will now ride with me into their camp."

She tried making sense of his words, but she was only aware of his hard, slender body pressed closely against hers, and the manly scent all his own of woodsmoke and clean perspiration of the outdoors.

Gently moving back from her, he held her by the forearms. If he had not held her up, she would have fallen—her legs were weaker than undercooked cream pudding. He pushed back a wayward tress of hair, noting the sun reflecting in the red highlights. "Did you hear me, Crimson? You will go with me into the Indian camp—as my woman. It's very important you remember or it could be dangerous for you."

Numbly nodding, she did not comprehend his words. All the anger, disillusionment and hurt were gone by being in his arms again, and at the moment, she would go anywhere with him. There was no sense of right or wrong, how he rustled cattle from her family, killed Archie or tried murdering her—he answered all her dreams with him by her side. She lifted her free arm and touched his face, afraid he would disappear into thin air.

He kissed the palm of her hand before giving her a lift back into her saddle. "Don't be afraid. Just do what I tell you. Pretend you're my woman and everything will be fine. The tribe is just over the next rise, so stay behind me."

Her mind was once again functioning properly without his arms around her. She wondered what kind of idiot she was by giving in so completely. He was her enemy, yet he was like a habitual drug, destroying her will and swooping down like an eagle of fantasy, teasing, tempting and out of reach. He could destroy her if she let him.

Stiffening her spine, she stared straight ahead, crimson flushing her cheeks. She had a malady wantonness for a man not her husband, and only he could cure this aching void. Rubbing her earlobe, she nearly cried out with frustration, craving his arms around her, the only place she truly felt safe, comfortable and loved.

But how could she eliminate these urges, especially when she married another man? How did he create these longings, these fantasies every time she was near him? *They were not all sexual*, she bluntly admitted. There was more, but she could not fully admit nor accept it.

Her disturbing reflections were interrupted after cresting the hill and viewing the encampment directly in front of them. The wide spacing of the tepees gave the appearance of a larger village. However, what she did see shocked and shamed her. The people were undernourished, their clothing threadbare and their dogs' ribs protruded starkly against the ragged fur of their coats. Indian men, women and children stopped what they were doing and stared at the intruders. She glanced quickly at Landon's stony face as he guided them through the middle of the tepees toward the opposite end.

Stopping in front of a tepee larger than the rest, he lithely jumped from his stallion, not sparing a look in her direction. He solemnly greeted the tall brave waiting in front of his tepee. "Flies-Like-An-Eagle, it has been long. Much water has passed between us."

"Not enough to destroy our friendship, Brother. Come and make smoke with me, and we will renew our trust in one another." Flies-Like-An-Eagle entered his lodge and Landon followed him.

Women and children curiously fingered her riding skirt or touched her hair, making her uncomfortable with their strange guttural language. Crimson quickly scrambled from Blackfoot's back and hurried inside behind Landon. Sitting on the buffalo robes beside Landon, she glanced back and forth between the two men who spoke in Kiowa, their voices sounding like pebbles plunking into water.

"You have not forgotten our tongue, Brother. It is well you remember our native ways." Flies-Like-An-Eagle took a clay pipe from a leather pouch, filled it with tobacco and lit it with a burning branch from the fire.

"The people are not well." Landon watched while Flies-Like-An-Eagle inhaled deeply on the pipe and released a cloud of blue-gray smoke.

"The winter has been hard. Government's rations are not enough to appease our people's hunger." Flies-Like-An-Eagle passed the pipe to Landon. "We have not found buffalo in many moons. The white eyes have killed them all."

Landon inhaled before blowing out smoke. "Brother, I have information that the buffalo are being slaughtered in other tribal lands. The white eyes are determined to kill them all. However, I will bring you ten *wohaws* for the people. Though the meat is not as good as the buffalo we hunted, it will feed our people." Landon was certain Kerby Olsen would let him cut out ten cows as a tribute to his people and therefore keep the peace.

"You are still good Kiowa. Much has happened since last I saw you. Many people have left for the happy hunting ground. Some have taken new women. Children have grown into men. Our young men now count coup across the Rio Grande into Mexico. It is a sad time for us."

His face grim, Landon nodded agreement.

Flies-Like-An-Eagle glanced at Crimson. "She your woman?" Landon nodded. "She has fire hair and eyes of calm spring grass. I will give you many horses for her."

Landon turned and stared into frightened green eyes, his expression never changing, and cocked his head, contemplating Flies-Like-An-Eagle's offer. He faced his friend, saying, "I would not wish her on my worst enemy. Her temper matches her hair and her eyes are deceiving. In all the moons of your life, you cannot tame this one."

Flies-Like-An-Eagle guffawed, and Crimson's widened, fright-filled eyes traveled from one to the other. "In the old days we had much *Tehans* and they were the worst of all to tame. Keep your woman, Brother, and bear her thorns bravely."

Landon relaxed and smiled crookedly, enjoying the recounting of their old days. Women brought in food, and they ate, then began talking again.

Flies-Like-An-Eagle glanced at Crimson but directed his statement at Landon. "She has many feelings for you."

Landon's smile was self-deprecating. "Many and most are prickly as the bear plant."

"Keeps life interesting," Flies-Like-An-Eagle commented. "A warrior needs a woman in his old age to make him comfortable. Yours will prick you sore. Aaaaeeeiiii! Little brother, you have much to learn!"

Flies-Like-An-Eagle's frequent referral of Crimson had Landon growing uncomfortable. He admitted she was tantalizing with her face soft in sleep, her hair an unruly auburn mass and her head leaning against his shoulder. Carefully keeping his face immobile, he quashed his desire of shifting her into his arms and brushing her hair gently from her cheeks.

"It was a sad day when you left our tribe. We mourned long for you. The women never let Walks-A-Ways forget his cruel punishment of his second wife. His first wife was discontented afterwards. She died during a fight with the white warriors."

Landon shifted his gaze from Crimson. "I shall never forget it, but I now have other things taking my time." Landon accepted the pipe Flies-Like-An-Eagle had refilled and lit again.

"Yes, I can see this one takes much time."

After the pipe was finished, Flies-Like-An-Eagle knocked the ashes into the fire and replaced it in its special pouch. "Now that we have recounted past coups, why did you come?"

Landon leaned over slightly, increasing the effect of his words. "My heart is greatly troubled. It is rumored our brothers have been making war on the *tai-bos*. There have been many wounded and killed, and much horses and livestock stolen."

"It is not our people nor any of our brethren. I know of which you speak. It is the bad *tai-bos* who dress up like us. They do these things and blame us," Flies-Like-An-Eagle grunted, his eyes narrowing in anger.

Landon sat back, satisfied his assumption had been validated. "My brother always speaks truth. I will tell the *tai-bos* they must find the bad white eyes doing this." Never doubting Walks-A-Ways' word, he suspected who the men dressed as Indians were and who had been attacking the emigrants, stealing their livestock and murdering them.

⋯⦿⧉⦿⋯

LANDON shook Crimson awake after he and Flies-Like-An-Eagle finished their conversation. Soon as her eyes opened, he nodded toward the tepee flap, stood and headed out the door. Crimson quickly scrambled after him. He led her toward a different tepee and entered first. He did not look at her as she scurried behind him while he pointed at the area near the back where a mixture of army blankets and buffalo robes lay on the floor along the hide walls. "Undress and crawl in."

Fully awake now, Crimson turned on him, her eyes shooting green fire. "How could you act like I wasn't there!"

Taken by surprise with her outburst, Landon growled, "Shut up, woman!"

"I will not be quiet, Mr. Wade. You talked in that funny language all day, and I couldn't understand a word. And besides all that, ya'll were talking about me!"

Landon took a step closer, an angry tick working in his cheek. "I'll not tell you again, Crimson. Shut up or should I trade you to Flies-Like-An-Eagle?"

"You wouldn't!" She stepped back in alarm, unconsciously crossing her arms over her chest.

"He offered a mighty handsome price for you, but he would be getting the worse end of the bargain." Landon advanced toward her, the ice blue depths of his eyes chilling her bones and she retreated.

"He said you had hair like fire and eyes like calm spring grass. Hah! He oughta see you now. Your glare would set a prairie on fire." He grabbed her shoulders in a hard grip and held her motionless. "Is your pride so stubborn you would risk me selling you?"

Her eyes narrowed with her fury though her fright was greater. She gulped against the lump lodged in her throat. Staring into his hard, cold eyes, she wondered if he really would sell her, then decided he just might if she pressed her luck. "Let me go!"

Landon released her, dropping his hands and clenching them against his sides. "Crimson, don't push me."

She rubbed one forearm, then the other, massaging the discomfort away. "'I'm not. I don't like you treating me like I'm not here."

Fighting down his fury, he inhaled a deep breath and carefully repositioned his face back into its usual lines. "I treated you as was expected of me. These are a different people."

"Well, I'm not one of them. Just because you're a half..." She stopped, aghast with her partial words.

"Half-breed, Crimson? Yes, I am, but does that make me any less a man?" The angry tick was back in his cheek and his body took on a deceptive, loose-limbed appearance.

Noticing the change, she grew wary, not recognizing the man in front of her. After entering the Kiowa camp, he had become a different person. Salving her stinging conscious, she snapped, "I don't like you touching me."

"No, Crimson?" he asked sardonically. "I remember very well you begging me to take you. You were hotter than a mid-July sun. If I kissed you now, you would freely, nay, eagerly give me what I want. No matter how much you try and deny this thing between us, it takes one touch and you are mine."

"Oooooowww..." Crimson cried, but any retort she could offer was not strong enough, and the little devil at the back of her mind whispered he spoke the truth. She melted like butter in the hot sun when he touched her.

Turning away from him, she plopped down on the bed mat and began furiously tugging off her boots. Damn him! He had answered something bothering her since her marriage; she was no better than John and had no right judging his faults.

When Landon joined her on the mat, she moved toward the furthest edge, keeping her back stiff. Within minutes, his steady, rhythmic breathing informed her he was fast asleep. It was one more strike against him. It took her hours before she dropped off into a restless slumber, wishing, hoping he would take her into his arms again.

∾☙✿☙∾

GROGGILY, Crimson weakly pushed at Landon when he shook her awake. Only when he curtly told her they were leaving did she become alert. Furiously, she pounded her riding boots against the ground in case any night creatures had made their bed in them before pulling them on.

Sitting on her horse, her back ramrod straight, she dispassionately watched Landon and Flies-Like-An-Eagle grab each other by the forearms in goodbye.

Landon let his gaze slide over the people. Flies-Like-An-Eagle interpreted his look and answered the unspoken question in his eyes. "There is another hunting camp toward the rising sun."

Landon nodded his thanks and mounted.

"Brother, Walks-A-Ways is hunting in the same area. Both of you are filled with hate."

His face carefully blank, Landon leaned forward in his saddle. "Yes, and it will only end when one of us is dead." With those last words, he turned his mount and rode toward the morning sun highlighting the eastern horizon.

Her head held high, Crimson followed him until they had ridden far enough away that no one from camp would see them, then maneuvered her horse beside his. She was still processing their stay with the Kiowas and hesitant about asking questions. They had ridden for several miles without speaking before she noticed they were traveling in the wrong direction. She pulled sharply on the reins.

Stopping, Landon circled back. "What's wrong now, Crimson?"

"We are heading in the wrong direction. I was headed for my sister's ranch," she stated stubbornly, her anger not abated.

"I will take you there after one more stop." Landon carefully kept his temper banked.

"I won't go!" She mutinously cried.

"Crimson," Landon began patiently, "if you wanna risk being captured by the Kiowas, then go. Just one word of warning—without me beside you, you won't be protected or safe. Now on the other hand, we can stop at one more place and afterwards I'll make sure you get to your sister's safely."

She rebelliously lifted her chin but realized the truth of his words. Though the Indians were usually peaceful, it was no guarantee she would be safe from them or some other undesirables. The plains were vast. One could ride all day and not see a single person. However, all types of men, along with Indians, wandered through the prairies. She had no other choice but follow him.

They rode the next few hours without speaking, each lost in their ruminations. Arriving at the next Indian encampment, she noticed it was more wretched than the other.

Once again, Crimson dismounted by herself while Landon made his way toward an old, toothless crone bent with age and hugged her. Crimson hung back, watching them. The woman's hair was chopped in ragged strings, her face scarred and two finger joints on her left hand were missing.

"My son, I knew you would come again."

"Mother, you are well?" Landon asked his stepmother, a flicker of compassion rising within him. Time had not been kind to her.

She cackled. "Eeee...another winter like this last and I will not worry about being well again, but all is well now. Come inside, my son, and eat with me."

Landon followed her into a worn-out tepee, forcing back a smile as Crimson scuttled closely behind them. He crossed his ankles and gracefully seated himself in front of the fire, his legs crossed Indian fashion. He gratefully accepted the bowl of gruel and dipped his fingers into it, bringing it toward his mouth. He noticed while eating that Crimson trepidly stared at the food before her hunger got the better of her and she followed his example.

After they finished eating, his mother grabbed a large pouch hanging on a tepee pole and carefully took it down. Stepping behind her son, she placed it in his lap. "I made you clothes from the last buffalo your father killed long ago. I knew you would be back some day before I died." She grunted satisfaction as he withdrew the first piece, a yellow tanned shirt with fringes, followed by a breechcloth, leggings and short moccasins with long flaps and fringes on the bottoms.

Landon graciously accepted the gifts. "They are beautiful, mother of my childhood. I thank you." Landon glanced surreptitiously around the tepee, noticing his father's belongings, especially his warrior's shield and weapons, were missing.

His mother intercepted the look and brought out another pouch, quietly saying, "He was broken with sorrow when you left and gave up his spirit that winter. Before he left for the Great Spirit, he talked about you. He regretted his harsh judgement and mourned when you left. He asked that I give you some of his things if I ever saw you again."

Keeping his mask from cracking with grief, he accepted the pouch. In the Kiowa way, they carefully did not speak his father's name, Red Eagle, the same way Flies-Like-An-Eagle had carefully not used Sun-Is-Setting's name nor used his name since he was also considered dead. "It was a sad time for all of us, Mother, and I forgave him long ago."

"Son, you always were a proud and brave warrior. Now honor me and wear your new clothes. Your father will be content with you wearing them to mourn for him. And son, when you mourn, mourn for me as well for this will be the last time we see each other."

Nodding, his heart heavy, he barely turned his head and ordered Crimson, "Go with my mother."

With refusal on her lips, Crimson stopped, but turned and followed the old woman out of the tepee flap when he unbuttoned his shirt.

The clothes were soft against his skin and felt strange now. He had not worn the clothes of his people in a long time. It saddened him that his stepmother had sacrificed her own comfort by making him rich appointed clothes. Her own clothing, a mixture of Kiowa and white, were threadbare and worn.

He fastened a breastplate of pipestone painted light blue around his neck, which was one of the gifts his father left him. Fixing the sky-blue headband around his forehead, he then fastened the knife case around his waist. Against the people of his tribe, his clothing was rich indeed, and in the olden days before the reservation, they would have served as ceremonial garb.

As he left the tepee, he heard Crimson's frantic cry.

Chapter 20
Broken Lance

"**LET ME** go!" Crimson screamed at the burly Indian who laughed in a beastly manner and held her arm in a tight grip. Frightened out of her wits, she tried kicking at his shins, anywhere her foot landed.

"Let her go, Walks-A-Ways." Landon's menacing, low-pitched voice matched the intensity of his narrowed eyes.

Walks-A-Ways pulled the struggling woman up closer against him. "Ah, dead one, so we meet again." He slurred in contempt. "I have your woman and very pretty she is, but her skin is colorless as the winter snows."

"Let her go," Landon ordered again.

"We have come a full circle, dead one. You stole my woman and I steal yours. Maybe when I'm finished with her, you can have her back, if there's anything left of her." He laughed uproariously.

"You have no honor, Walks-A-Ways. You would steal my woman without a fight?" Landon taunted him, leaving no option— only the coward's way out if he refused.

Walks-A-Ways eyes flashed like burning coals. "I have much honor. It is you who have no honor."

"Then fight me as a warrior," Landon goaded.

Walks-A-Ways roughly swung Crimson away from him, grabbed his war lance from the side of his pony and threw it between

Landon's feet.

The war lance wobbled bare inches from his nose, but Landon did not move a muscle nor blink an eye. He slowly pulled the lance free, dropped it over his uplifted knee and broke it in half, then threw the pieces at Walks-A-Ways' feet.

"Call on your white spirits for help, for you are no man." Walks-a-Ways stalked toward his tepee and disappeared inside.

Crimson rushed into Landon's arms, her face abnormally white. "Mr. Wade, what is happening?"

Pushing her inside the tepee, he answered, "We fight to the death. Whoever wins, wins you."

"Oh, God, no!" she cried, throwing herself into his arms. "No, I won't let you!"

He grabbed her shoulders and gently pushed her back. "Do you care then, Crimson?" he asked gently, his heart leaping in his chest.

"No... yes...oh I don't know. I would carry the guilt of your death on my conscience the rest of my life if you lost," she stuttered, cringing with her cold words. The thought of him dying for her sake made her realize just how much she cared for him. Right or wrong, the truth was painful. He was her enemy, and if he knew her great affection for him, he would destroy her. Her breath left her, realizing she *was* unequivocally in love with him. It could never be! She was a married woman!

Her eyes mirrored her torment, and a sudden pain pierced his heart. He abruptly turned away, realizing she would never admit this passion drawing them together and separating them at the same time. He mumbled so low, she almost did not catch it. "Don't worry. If I do lose, my death need not be on your conscience. We have an old score that should have been settled long ago. Now leave me and go with my mother."

Struggling against her fear over his fighting for her, unconvinced there was an old feud between them, she stood motionless. Every nerve ending in her body vibrated and she should be in his arms telling him how much she loved him. It might be too late after the battle.

God in Heaven, she did love him, loved him so much she would willingly die for him. Apparently all her life she had searched for someone who could accept the abundant love she so desperately wanted to share, and here he was, her enemy. A soft inner glow penetrated through her eyes, watching him pull his shirt over his head and throw it on the ground. Reaching out toward him, giving into her secret, she softly spoke his name, "Landon."

"Get out of here, Crimson," he harshly ordered, not turning around.

Tears springing into her eyes, she swiftly turned and ran out of the tepee. The moment was gone, frozen in time.

Stripping until only his moccasins and breechcloth remained, he sat cross-legged in front of the fire and mixed his war paints, the ingrained habits of years gone by still strong. He painted a light blue slash on each cheek followed by a red streak. With the light blue again, he drew the outline of an eye in the center of his forehead and filled it in. On his chest, he drew squiggly lines and arrows. After he finished painting himself, he sat quietly, blanking his mind and gathering his strength about him.

The flap lifted, and a warrior stuck his head inside. "It is time."

❧⟨◉⟩❧

CRIMSON stared at Landon, the warrior he was, soaking into her memory. His appearance dramatically changed like there were two entirely different people living inside of him. He reminded her of a chameleon, swiftly changing in a twinkling of an eye, and all with different clothing. She had seen but had not been aware of his changed appearance earlier. The shock she received from the Indian brave cruelly grabbing her and speaking in a language she did not understand, and then Landon telling her they were fighting over her, had eliminated it from her conscious.

Staring at him, she felt a jolt of lightning dance along her veins from the top of her scalp and travel down to the tip of her toes. He emerged as some dark pagan god, and the war paint prominently brought out his primitive beauty. His graceful head encircled by a sky-blue band, matched the color of his eyes and emphasized the blackness of his hair. He was nearly naked, wearing only a breechcloth and moccasins, his torso hairless, his shoulders broad with finely roped muscles, and his legs muscular and gracefully formed. A pale scar, a couple of inches long on his right side, glared starkly against the dark copper of his skin.

Following the brave inside a circle drawn in the dirt, he did not spare a glance at her. Catching sight of his eyes, she shuddered. They resembled the finely honed blade of his knife; the color the blue glint of steel catching a ray of sun, and just as cold and hard.

She tore her sight from him and observed his opponent, really seeing him for the first time. He was a couple of inches shorter and many pounds heavier than Landon. He had the big belly of one well-fed, a startling contrast against the other undernourished people in the camp.

Morbid curiosity and fear kept her immobile while watching the men take one end of a leather rope and slip the knotted thong's end in between their teeth. Each held a knife and began a strange ritual of slapping the knife from one hand to the other while they circled each other like wary animals. They feinted, dodged and slashed in graceful acrobatic movements, each carefully staying within the designated area drawn upon the ground.

A glimmer of information surfaced, reminding her Indians admired bravery above all else. She bit down on her bottom lip, stopping herself from crying out, the metallic taste of blood filling her mouth as Landon jumped back, his stomach pulled almost against his back, swerving and avoiding the wild sweep of his opponent's blade.

The men danced around each other, jabbing with wicked gleaming knives. Walks-a-Ways turned, whipped out and slashed Landon's forearm, leaving a dark, almost black gash in its wake, then blood peeped above the slash and ran down his arm.

Back and forth like ferocious animals gauging their prey, they moved, never too far or they would be pulled up short by the thong. Landon feinted, ducked and twisted back, bringing his knife across Walks-a-Ways' stomach. A streak of bright red blood oozed out of the long slice.

Before Walks-a-Ways could recover, Landon caught him by the arm on a backward stroke, twisting until Walks-a-Ways' back was on the ground. Landon straddled him, forcing his knife closer toward Walks-a-Ways' throat.

Walks-a-Ways kicked upward and threw Landon over his head, jumping upright in almost the same movement. The leather rope sharply jerked Landon's head back, throwing him off balance a second before he recovered. He jumped lithely back onto his feet.

Again, they warily circled each other, each looking for an opening. Walks-a-Ways kicked out with his feet, catching Landon in the chest and knocking him on the ground. Landon's knife flew from his hand and landed outside of the circle. Walks-a-Ways dove on top of Landon. He drew his arm back to deliver the coup de grace when Landon caught his knife hand in midair.

They struggled, arms bulging, each pushing the knife toward the other. Landon kicked up, buckling his chest and dislodging Walks-a-Ways, landing back on his feet at the same time. Walks-a-Ways kicked at Landon's side, and Landon caught his foot, flipping him over and rolling toward him to stop the jerking pull of the rope.

Landon moved swiftly, straddling him and catching Walks-a-Ways' knife hand, forcing it toward Walks-a-Ways' chest. After several moments of intense struggle, Landon gave a loud war whoop, and with a mighty shove, pushed the knife through Walks-a-Ways' throat.

Crimson briefly closed her eyes when Walks-a-Ways' body spasmed a few times before he lay still. Covering her mouth with her hands, she choked back the gore rising in her throat and willed her stomach still.

A woman's wail screeched throughout the camp. Someone jerked Crimson's hand from around her mouth and roughly yanked her forward, dragging her toward the tepee. Suddenly in Landon's arms, she shook violently, releasing the tears she could not hold back any longer.

Landon brushed a stray lock of hair from her face, whispering, "It's over, Crimson. It's over."

After her trembling calmed and her tears stopped, she pulled back and stared into his sculptured face. If she ever had doubts about his ability of slaying another person, they were now gone. She watched him kill with as much compassion as someone slaughtering a cow. Terror, relief, aversion and a multitude of other different emotions swept through her.

Whatever Landon was expecting, it was not the loathing he momentarily glimpsed in her expressive green eyes. His victory a bitter taste in his mouth, he turned away and carefully washed the war paint from his face and body. He patiently stood while his mother smeared medicinal salve on his wounds, the salve pungent and smelling of rank buffalo fat and herbs. Still ignoring Crimson, he slipped into the remaining clothing his stepmother had so lovingly made and left the tepee without a word or a backward glance.

As soon as he disappeared through the tepee flap, Crimson hurried after him, afraid he was leaving her with these people, and caught his arm, crying, "Don't leave me here, Landon, please!"

His stance inflexible, he stared down at her. She called him by his first name again and had several times in the last two days, but it gave him little satisfaction. "I'm not leaving you. Go back and let me be!" His voice crisply cracking, he issued an apparent order. His stepmother grabbed Crimson's arm, cackling strange guttural sounds, and pulled her toward the tepee.

Crimson fought against the surprisingly strong hands while watching Landon head out toward the green prairie away from the camp, and only after she saw him stop on top of a hill, did she turn around and meekly follow the old crone.

Conflicting emotions tearing at her heart, she pulled on her earlobe. He was her enemy, yet he had fought for her. And if he had lost, what would have happened? *Is this another one of his cruel games?* Did he fight the Indian just so he could keep her all to himself and elicit his own form of retribution later? And what if he decided on leaving her here anyway?

The last thought jarred her. She watched and waited until the old crone nodded off by the fire and gentle snores issued from her open mouth. Silently, she carefully edged out of the tepee, skirted around the encampment and ran toward the direction Landon had taken.

The sun was a fiery ball hanging low on the western horizon, its glow eerie and blood red. She ran toward the man silhouetted within its bloody circle. His arms were outstretched toward the sky and his mournful, sorrow-filled rhythmic song broke the silence of the breezeless evening.

With the melodic beat of the song, a sadness she could not describe flooded her. The closer she drew near Landon, the slower her feet moved until she was nearly in front of him. She stopped short, her breath catching painfully in her throat. His copper skin glowed almost red with the sun, and his tears, reflecting the color of the blood red sun, ran in rivulets down his cheeks.

Blinding, scolding hot tears rose up, scorching her throat, and she turned sharply on her heel, running back toward the encampment faster than she had come. She had never seen a man cry before, and it was oddly tender and sad. This man, who had the face of a stone-cold killer and a cattle thief, was weeping. It did something within her heart she did not like, bringing back more sharply than ever how much she loved him, and yet, still denying it at the same time.

∽◌❧❦◌∽

LANDON silently slipped out of his clothes and glanced at the sleeping form. Crimson was sniffing and hiccupping in her slumber. A sudden tenderness filling him, he knelt beside her and saw the tear marks on her petal soft cheeks. Lying down beside her, he pulled the cover over them both and gathered her into his arms. She snuggled closer, moaning in her sleep. He kissed her forehead, murmuring, "Crimson Rose, don't cry, my little green-eyed spy. One day we will be together without shame or remorse."

∽◌❧❦◌∽

GRADUALLY coming awake, Crimson turned over, seeking the warmth she knew was there last night. When she found the pallet empty, she quickly sat up, blinking her eyes in confusion. She must have dreamed those arms around her last night and the sad voice speaking her name.

She combed her fingers through her hair, trying for some semblance of order before she rose and sat before the fire. The old crone handed her a bowl of gruel, jabbering something unintelligible. As she finished the last bite, Landon entered the tepee.

"We leave now."

She searched his face for an answer of her memory last night, but his face was bland, showing nothing of his inner thoughts.

Pulling her eyes from his, she noticed he once again wore his regular clothing. He turned, ducked under the flap and was gone before she could speak.

Landon watched her mount before turning and hugging his stepmother, his voice soft, "It's goodbye again, old woman. You have been as much a mother to me as my own. If I never see you again, know my heart is always with you."

His stepmother wiped tears from her eyes. "My son, find your way. You still do not know who you are. I pray every day the Great Spirit will allow you final acceptance of the great and kind man you are."

Gracefully leaping into the saddle, Landon pulled the reins around and rode off, never looking back. He had broken his vow when he sang his death song for the man who had given him life and for his father's wife. The fine thread keeping him bound with his former life was forever cut, and this time, there would be no going back. The one who had killed his beloved with his cruel punishment was dead, one last task completed. He mourned for them all: Sun-Is-Setting, his father Red Eagle, his father's wife and himself.

Sun-is-Setting's face was nothing but a blur, a faded memory, and he was now forever free. He salved his conscience when he avenged her, and it was now over.

Tearing himself from his grim, sad thoughts, Landon glanced at Crimson. "Do you still wanna go to your sister's?"

"No, I wanna go home." There was too much that needed sorted out, too many emotions requiring dissection before she could face her family. Her problems with John were the least of her worries. She had discovered something about this man, something she would not have believed if someone had told her. He was her enemy and deserved her contempt, and she was in love with him. She must examine these tumultuous emotions more closely before interacting with another human being.

They rode in silence for several miles before Crimson gathered courage and asked, "What do you do for a living?"

He taciturnly shrugged his shoulders. "I do many things."

"Like what for instance?"

Landon stared straight ahead. How much should he tell her? Could he tell her his secrets? Their bond was not strong enough and may never be. "Things you'd have no interest in."

She compressed her lips together. Without saying a word, he had affirmed her suspicions. He was a thief and a murderer. Then what was she doing here riding so peacefully beside him when any minute he could kill her too? Even as she thought it, she felt no fear. "I guess I shouldn't ask you anything. You never give me a straight answer," she sarcastically stated.

A strange, crooked smile on his lips, he glanced at her. "I'm glad you finally noticed."

With her back ramrod straight and her eyes staring straight ahead told him without words she was angry. An impish impulse forced a low laugh from him. "I remember you when you were a long-legged, skinny, freckled face, little redheaded girl. You've turned into a stunning woman."

Crimson glanced sharply at him; he just proved her assumption was correct. He did remember her. "You haven't changed. You're still the moody, brooding, icy eyed person you always were. You just grew up."

"Thank you," he responded a bit caustically.

They rode a while longer without speaking. Birds chattered angrily at their intrusion and a startled flock of blue and iridescent quail darted upward from their roosting place. The skies were clouding over, promising either rain or snow, one never knew in the Texas Panhandle. The wind increased, slapping Crimson's riding skirt against her legs. She retrieved her wool cloak and pulled it around her shoulders.

A chill swept through her and she shuddered, bracing herself against the blasts of wind. "It's getting colder. Looks like it might storm." It was an inane statement, but she was tired of the silence.

"Yep, it just might."

To keep the conversation going, Crimson stated, "You said you had questions for me."

"You answered those questions that day in the restaurant without me asking," Landon informed her.

"How...what?" she stammered.

"You married your husband knowing he was going under an assumed name."

"I said no such thing," she stuttered, wondering where he got such an idea.

"Perhaps not in so many words. It was when you declared you had no involvement with them calling me names and beating me that answered my question."

Her shoulders drooped in dejection. He was right. She had implied it. John made her swear against using his real name, but he could not make Landon do the same. "Are you gonna tell? He really had a good reason for changing it."

"I bet," Landon bit out caustically.

"No really. It was all a misunderstanding. It wasn't his fault," she asserted, then stopped. She swore she would not divulge John's past. "Please don't say anything."

He shrugged noncommittedly.

The silence stretched between them until Crimson broke it again. "I felt bad about how they treated you when we were younger. It was terrible what they did."

Landon studied her out of the corner of his eye, wondering what she was after. He could not trust her, at least not with this. "I never could figure out what you saw in them."

"They were my friends."

Dissatisfied with her answer, he probed none too gently, "Even friends need some redeeming qualities."

Thinking about his words, she could not analyze why they were friends. "We were all young." She knew her answer was lame when she said it.

Landon leaned forward in his saddle, a frown furrowing his forehead. Just how much she knew about her husband's activities, he did not know. "They all turned out for the worse."

Turning her head sharply toward him, her voice an octave higher than normal, she asked, "Are you saying I turned out for the worse too?"

"Only you can answer that." He shrugged and stared straight ahead.

"Just what are you getting at? How did the others turn out for the worse?" she bitingly questioned.

His eyebrow lifting mockingly, he turned toward her. "You wouldn't believe me if I told you."

"Then try me."

He studied her a moment before answering, "Archie Montgomery? Gambler? He was the head of the syndicate, the cattle rustling operation around here."

"Archie?" She lifted her finely arched brows in disbelief. "Not Archie. His only dream was playing big time poker."

Not disavowing her, he looked out over the landscape, his shoulders relaxing.

"What else?"

He glanced at her. "You didn't believe me the first time, so why should I tell you more?"

Crimson frowned. No, she did not believe him. "Why do you want me dead?"

"I'll repeat it again, Crimson. I never tried killing you." He stared at her, his heavy black brows knotted. "If I wanted you dead, you would be already. We've been together the last few days and I haven't harmed you, have I?"

Sharply glancing at him, she turned and stared in front of her. What he said made sense, but if he was not the one intent on killing her, then who was? And he was the only one who had a motive. "This fall, in October, were you on the L Heart range?" she asked softly, fearful of his answer. Was he lulling her into trusting him?

"Yes, several times. Why?" he asked more sharply, watching the changing expressions on her face. What was she getting at?

"Someone took a potshot at me, and I had it on good authority you were in the area at the time." She faced him, her eyes widened with fright. "It *was* you!"

Chapter 21
Whitewashing Conscience

"CRIMSON, it wasn't me who shot at you. I wouldn't have missed." Landon tried being patient when all he wanted was to pull her off her horse, shake her, then make love with her.

"You've never told me anything, so how could you lie?"

Sighing, he retorted, "You still don't believe me. Tell me what reason I'd have for wanting you dead."

His eyes grew cold and stormy with his words. Afraid of saying anything else, she snapped, "Just forget it."

He studied her for a moment, his eyes narrowed. It did not matter what he said, she would never believe him. He turned back and stared off into the distance.

She was glad he let the subject drop. If he wanted her dead, he would have already killed her, right? Deep down, she desperately wanted to believe him, but too many things pointed in his direction. And yet, if he was the one, why wasn't she frightened of him? Nothing made sense anymore!

Time stretched out between them with Landon brooding about their strange relationship. Neither trusted the other, but they were drawn together like sunshine to the earth that was sprinkled with cloudy days. He wondered many times what characteristic Tom Martin, alias John Sullivan had that attracted Crimson. They did not match—more a contradiction of opportunities. Crimson was from a prominent family and well-liked while Tom was the lowest scum of the earth far as he was concerned. He growled suddenly, "Why were you such a stupid fool and marry him, Crimson?"

"I'm not stupid nor a fool!" Crimson cried, bursting into tears. The words rang through her skull, reminding her of all the times John had called her stupid and a fool. And Harvey had spouted those very terms before she left. And yet, how many times had she called herself the same things? She wondered if it was true, especially with Landon spouting the same words. It really hurt coming from him. She did not know why, it just did.

Sorry for his hasty words, Landon plucked her from her saddle and placed her in front of him. Ebony skittishly fought the bit before he grew accustomed to the added weight.

Pounding her fists against his chest, she bawled, "I'm not stupid. I'm not! I wish everybody would quit calling me that."

Landon held her firmly against his chest, immediately contrite. "I didn't mean it that way, Crimson."

"Then why did you say it?" she sniffed, tears rolling down her cheeks.

"I just wanna know why you married him." Landon soothingly patted her back still wondering what brought the onslaught of tears.

"John?"

"We both know it's not his real name, Crimson."

"What difference does it make? It's already done and there's nothing I can do about it," she whispered, defeated.

Landon walked the horses toward the streambank and higher ground before stopping underneath the trees. The streambed below was dry, but a flash flood could erupt anytime without warning. He selected a place far enough away from the main water flowlines so they would not be in danger if the gray skies opened with heavy rain. He helped her down and dismounted. "I'm sorry, Crimson. I never meant to hurt you and make you cry. I just can't figure out how you could marry someone like him."

The tears would not stop. Never in her life had she burst into tears over something so trivial. What was the matter with her? Landon brought out all her worst traits.

She covered her head with her cloak, her shoulders shaking with sobs, wishing the earth would open up and swallow her. She was also embarrassed by her silly show of tears. *What is wrong with me?*

Giving her time to gain control over her emotions, Landon unsaddled the horses. He did not know what else he could do. Her tears had increased while holding her.

Walking away from him, she sniffed several times but nothing stopped the flow of tears. She sat on a fallen log, sniffling and wiping her nose with a lace handkerchief she had taken from her dress sleeve. Damn these tears! She *was* acting like a stupid fool! *Maybe everyone is right, and I am a fool and stupid. If only he had not repeated those words.* A shadow fell over her, and she lifted her face, rubbing hard at the flowing tears.

"Crimson." He caressed her name, gently breathing it. Without conscious thought, he sat beside her and pulled her into his arms. He tenderly wiped the silver droplets of water from her cheeks, murmuring, "Please stop crying."

"I can't!" she whined. "They won't stop! Now I really do feel stupid."

His laughter low and self-conscious, he drew off her hat and tangled his fingers in the wavy length of her hair, slowly bringing her face closer. She was dewy-eyed and the moistness revealed tiny brown spots in her emerald eyes, her brown lashes sparkling with silver and her lips, rose-red, pouted and moist. He captured those soft lips with his, molding them, tenderly searching, tasting their sweetness and the salt of her tears.

He only meant to brush her mouth with his, and the touch of those rose petal-soft lips ignited his blood and chased away all coherent thoughts. Gently forcing past her teeth with his tongue, he explored her satin inner mouth. Like a bee to nectar, he drank her sweetness while with gentle hands, traced her sides, following the curve of her waistline and back up, cupping the tempting mounds underneath her cloak. The firm, soft globes filled his hands and the twin peaks stiffened underneath his palms.

She should be experiencing shame or guilt, but there was none, only this weakening of her body in his arms where she was warm, cherished and cared for. Moving back only slightly, she allowed him access to the front buttons of her blouse. A muffled groan escaped from her with his velvety lips traveling over the corners of her mouth, the curve of her cheek and the hollow indentation at the bottom of her throat. She arched her neck backward, allowing him to nibble at the soft spot before he opened her blouse and bared the fruit of her bosom. Shock waves of desire lapped at her breast and washed downward past her stomach. Squirming on the log, strong melting sensations poured over her, settling with intensity in her lower region.

Landon slowly undressed her—she had no will, no strength, no power, no desire of stopping him. After he slipped her blouse off her shoulders and drew her chemise over her head, he knelt at her feet and tugged off her boots. Standing, he encouraged her onto her feet where he unbuttoned her riding skirt. The skirt whispered down her hips and landed between their feet.

Barely able to take his eyes from her, he spread the bedroll, then took her hand and gently laid her down between the covers, trembling like a green boy with his first woman—she had not been in his arms for so long.

Through desire laden eyes, Crimson watched him bare his magnificent body, astounded anew at how savagely beautiful he was. He lowered himself beside her, took her in his arms, and she shivered with anticipation. Only he could bring the satisfaction her body craved.

He played upon her velvety flesh, teasing, tasting and inhaling her womanly scent, filling his hands with her tender breasts, exploring the peaks and valleys, creating rivers of fire coursing through her veins. His hand moved lower and tangled in the thick bush between her legs.

The first pangs of guilt assailing her, she stiffened, stopping his hands and shifting her head back and forth in denial, yet unable to articulate her rejection. Her body ached for him, but the ominous words reverberated through her skull—*I am married!*

The unexpected reaction took Landon by surprise. He knew she was as hungry for him as he was for her. No! he violently denied, reading her thoughts. He would not let her change her mind. She was his! Capturing her lips, he teased them, drawing her essence into himself until he felt her relaxing again. He crooned into her shell-shaped ear, coaxing her as he would a skittish colt, "It's alright, my little spy. Let me love you and show you the joys only I can bring you."

He worked his magic on her, laying slightly on top of her, his hardness like a branding iron against her hip. Like a thirsty man drinking water, she yearned for more and began running her hands across the sinewy strength of his back, marveling anew at how surprisingly smooth and soft his skin was.

Tenderly nudging her legs apart, he found the button of her desire and her breath was torn from her. Fingers of yearning, hotter than a prairie fire, lashed through her lower belly and centered between her legs. The sensations became deep and penetrating, her breathing ragged and hoarse, her body yearning for his.

"Take me, Landon. Please," she moaned.

Bending, he kissed the heart-shaped mole on her inner left thigh, constraining himself against his own burning ache throbbing against her leg. His desire of showing her the joys of making love again was shadowed by his fear that once sheathed, he would lose control—he wanted her so badly. He gently parted the plump nether lips and gently probed the opening with the tip of his shaft. She trembled underneath him like a frightened doe.

The troubling sounds of horses broke through the haze of his passion, and he groaned in frustration. He was so close. He pushed in a little further, prolonging the moment until he heard a low growl and the horses rearing and whinnying. Cursing under his breath, he kissed her passion swollen lips and whispered huskily, "I must check on the horses. I'll be right back. Don't move."

She nearly cried when his warmth left her. Through half-closed eyes, she watched him slip into his pants and boots, then grab his rifle. After a few minutes, a rifle shot rippled through the air.

The loud explosion shocked her back to reality. *What am I doing? Have I gone mad? I'm married!* She sat up quickly, pulling the cover under her chin and shaking all over.

There was a shoosh of branches, then Landon entered the clearing. "It was a bobcat. We won't be interrupted again." He propped the rifle close by and began undressing.

"No!" Crimson screamed, disturbing a flock of birds nesting in the underbrush.

He stopped with one boot in his hand and stared at her. "What?" he bellowed, confusion cracking his voice.

"No! It's wrong! Please, I'm sorry. I shouldn't have gone this far. I couldn't help it. Landon, I'm married! I can't do this!" she wailed, burying her face in her hands, sobs shaking her slender frame.

"Crimson, I don't care if you are married. You are mine!" Landon dropped his boot on the sandy ground and took a step toward her, but she stopped him with her next words.

"No! Go away! Damn you and your eyes! I am a married woman!" She lifted a tear-stained face, her eyes green pools of troubled water.

He stared at her, his loins throbbing painfully, reminding him of how close he was to claiming her. Of all the damn times for her to remember she was married! It took all his control of staying rooted and not moving closer until he was shaking the unwelcome thoughts from her head. What did she think he was made of? Steel?

Sharp, liquid anger spreading through him, he hissed bitterly, "*Mrs. Sullivan,* have it your way. I hope to hell you're satisfied and your body aches as badly as mine."

Biting on her lower lip, she pulled the covers snugly underneath her chin. She *did* ache, ached so bad she could cry with this awful unfulfillment, this terrible longing savaging her body and leaving her as desolate and black as the aftermath of a prairie fire. Shuddering, she met his eyes, the blue depths resembling shards of glass, hard and impenetrable, and his face stone cold. She watched him turn away and dress. If only she could say something and break this angry tension between them. Instead, she remained silent for if she said anything, it would only make matters worse.

He threw her clothes at her, then left the camp, his long-legged stride stiff with fury.

Dressing quickly, she laid back in the bedroll and turned on her side, silent tears streaming down her cheeks, the lonesome soughing of the wind blowing through the trees matching the hopelessness of her soul.

❧❀❧

THE EXTRA weight against her waist was pleasant, and Crimson snuggled deeper against the circle of warmth, drifting in and out of dreams without fully becoming awake until the persistent drops of water pulled her from her slumbers. She tugged the covers over her face, then stopped, realizing the arm around her waist held her against a hard body and the stiff rod teasing her backside was Landon's. Easing her head around, she met his eyes. His face was bland, his tasseled hair softening the harshness of his eyes.

"I trust you slept well."

She struggled out of his arms and crouched on the bedroll beside him. "How dare you sleep with me!"

Lazily stretching, he reminded her once again of a black panther. "You never learn, do you, Crimson?"

He sat up, grabbed his shirt, slapped it out before slipping it over his arms. "This is my bedroll, and whether or not it was occupied, I was not gonna sleep on the cold sand."

Quickly rising, she stalked off, his chuckle following her. Her mind argued she should slip back into the bedroll, strip off her clothing and give into the raging desire that only he could satisfy. Though it was her secret wish, it was better to hang onto her anger. It was safer than forgetting her marriage vows.

Slipping behind some bushes several yards from camp, she answered the call of nature. Feeling human again and in more control of her emotions, she knelt by the fire and warmed her hands. She should apologize for her anger but could not force the words from her mouth. The light rain had stopped, the light sprinkling not enough to settle the dust which was now picked up by the slight wind and blowing into the fire.

He poured her a cup of thick, black coffee in the tin cup he pulled from his saddlebag. Handing her the hot cup, he waited for her to finish drinking so he too could have some before they broke camp.

She warmed her hands against the hot metal, her mind going over last evening. Oddly, there was no shame for what they had almost done—there had only been rapture in his arms. She did feel guilty! She was married and was aware if the horses had not acted up, she would have willingly made love with him. She had never wanted anything so badly and still felt the disquieting aftereffects of unfulfillment settling between her legs.

Pressing her thighs together, attempting to suppress the ache, she drank her coffee before throwing the grounds into the fire and handing Landon the empty cup. There was an awkwardness between them, an impression of things not finished.

Once again, she wondered about her sanity in marrying John. Their marriage was a shamble, a farce, and after what nearly happened last night, she was determined she would make her marriage change for the better. If her marriage was stronger, she would not be tempted by another man, she reasoned. When John came home, she would speak with him about trying again and making their marriage work. She would be a better wife and force herself in liking his touch while gritting her teeth against the pain. She had made her bed, now she must lie in it. It might not be a bed of roses, but it was all she had.

～◦৩৵ৎ৯ৎ◎৲～

THE RIDE toward Crimson's sod was made in silence, broken only by inane observations about the landscape around them.

Landon felt like he had come a full circle, ending one phase of his life when he killed Walks-A-Ways and the part of his existence that began with him falling in love with a married woman, Walks-A-Ways' second wife. Now the cycle was beginning again, and he could not deny he wanted this woman riding beside him. His balls ached, feeling shriveled up and sore from denied release. Soon as he delivered Crimson safely home, he would head toward Mobeetie, but the thought of having sex with Rovin' Wendy after he had nearly had Crimson, left him feeling disinterested and stale.

Stealing a glance at Crimson, he admired the way her hair waved down her back and how the sun picked out the red-gold highlights. Her hat shaded her eyes, hiding the dark green depths. Her lips were pouted and tempting, her chin, pointed and stubborn. She was a redheaded vixen, a temptress and the wife of a man known for his nefarious activities. He wondered how much she knew or suspected about her husband's business. For all he knew, she might be in the thick of it.

He grimly stared ahead, cursing the bobcat interrupting them last night. Given another chance, he would make love with her until she cried repeatedly with pleasure, and he would make sure there were no interruptions. But he could not help but wonder if they did become lovers, would he be put into a position of killing her husband

214

too?

⧫⧫⧫⧫⧫

EACH night was torture as Landon waited for Crimson to fall into a deep sleep before joining her in the bedroll, smiling when her unconscious form shifted closer, seeking his warmth. His smile deepened when he caressed her breasts, and she moaned in her sleep. It did not help with his own groin aching with frustrated need.

Tomorrow, they would arrive at her small homeplace. Waiting until she was in deep sleep, he laid down beside her and caressed her breasts, wanting a taste of the bared fruit within his hand. With her soft moans and her buttocks moving against his hardened manhood, he slipped his hand down her leg and moved it up under her riding skirt until he could touch the thick bush between her legs. Her moans deepened, her hips moving in time with his caressing finger, the movement of her soft buttocks teasing against his hardness.

His hips moved with her as her top leg moved over on top of his legs, giving him better access to her slick, wet upper inner thighs. He slipped a finger inside her while rubbing around the swollen flower of her womanhood and her hips moved harder against his hand. It took all his willpower of not stripping them both and having her completely. And he was determined to give her a taste of pleasure before he delivered her home. Feeling her tighten around his finger, he slammed harder against her buttocks and groaned as he spewed his own seed within his pants while she bucked against his fingers, releasing both their passion.

He knew she was awake, but instead of pulling away in horror, she grabbed his arm and held it against her waist, mumbling something he did not understand. She sighed, moved her hips back against him and fell asleep. A smile spread across his mouth, and he cupped her breast, falling into a slumber while wrapped around her body.

Crimson awoke with the comfort of his hard body spooned around hers and his hand gently holding her breast. Breathing deeply as in sleep, she wondered if he would again initiate what he had started last night. Instead, he squeezed her breast and placed a light

215

kiss on her neck before releasing her. She heard him move around the camp before walking further toward the streambed.

Neither spoke about last night. Crimson could not keep from remembering the early morning hours and a smile broke across her lips, thankful for the unexpected release he gave her. Lowering her eyes, she also knew he had discharged last night too when the wetness from the front of his pants soaked into her covered buttocks. It was a little thing, but one they both needed.

Why did I marry John when I could be making love with Landon, a man who satisfies my body, taking me to incredible heights I never dreamed, and yet I am denied the same release with my husband? If John satisfied my needs, would I be content as his wife or was there something more I should be considering about our relationship?

With her guilty emotions flipping back and forth, she knew if Landon had slipped her skirt from her last night, she would have willingly spread her legs for him, anything for the heavenly sensations he brought forth in her body. At least his actions helped release the frustration of him being near her, and surprisingly, she did not feel as guilty as she should. It was not really sex they shared—more a play of emotions and tensions that were brought about without penetration, she reasoned, whitewashing her reaction.

Chewing on her bottom lip, she almost begged him to stop and complete what he started last night—her body ached, yearned and screamed for him. She squirmed uncomfortably on the saddle, biting her bottom lip and stopping the words from issuing from her mouth, knowing if she so much as ask him and finish what he started last night, he would drag her from the saddle and devour her the way she dreamed.

Chapter 22
Family Affair with a Gun

STARING out over the monotonous landscape, Crimson spotted the sod house, the little speck in the distance, and she bit hard on her bottom lip. She was nearly home and a disturbing sadness engulfed her. She would be leaving the company of this strange man, her sworn enemy, and going back to the lonely life she had lived all winter.

Visibly stiffening her back, she was determined to save her marriage, and she could if Landon stayed away. She could not deny her love for him, but it was something she must put completely out of her mind. She was too vulnerable, too susceptible when around him, especially with his touch—it made her forget her marriage vows. Though unhappy leaving him, she tartly informed him through stiff lips, "I can ride the rest of the way by myself."

Landon leaned forward and lazily looked at her. "I said I'd see you home and I shall, right up to your doorstep."

"That's not necessary. I'm safe enough now," she insisted. With him around, her thinking was muddled.

He did not answer but kept riding beside her. She threw him a piercing glance, then shrugged. Just a little bit farther and she would be free of him, but the realization made her miserable.

They clattered into the bare yard, and she swung her foot out of the stirrup. John's drawl froze her in the saddle.

"Well, if it ain't the damn half-breed with my deceiving wife."

Crimson stared at her husband; the dangerous tone of his voice had her heart beating erratically. There had been no smoke coming from the chimney and she had seen no horses, but they could have been on the other side of the house. What disturbed her most was she had not seen nor heard John and Harvey until then.

"Ya stupid bitch, I knew I couldna trust ya. Harvey said ya were goin' to yore sister's, but I knew different," John growled.

Finishing her dismount, she willed a calm countenance to cover her anger. "John, I was headed for my sister's. The Indians are loose from the reservation again and Mr. Wade saved my life."

John sneered, his face showing disbelief. He glared at Landon, snarling, "I think we need to teach this half-breed a lesson about foolin' around with white women, 'specially married white women, even if they are tramps."

Sharply drawing in her breath, she blanched at his insult.

John ignored her. "Go get my whip, Harv, and we'll show this breed a thang or two."

Realizing his intention, Crimson rushed toward her husband, throwing herself in front of him. "John, don't be stupid! He saved my life! Doesn't that count for something?"

A stunning blow knocked her onto the hardpacked ground and her cheek stung. Shocked, she did not move but glared at her husband.

Landon reached for the gun at his waist, stopping bare inches from the handle as he heard a metallic click and Harvey say,

"Don't try it, breed, or I'll blow yore brains out or what little ya have." He chuckled at his little joke.

"Ya don't want him doin' that, now do ya, breed? It would take all the fun out of us teachin' ya a lesson." John spoke in an almost conversational tone, his boyish face drawn up in ugly, cruel lines. "Now very slowly, ease off the horse."

Her cheek stinging, Crimson maneuvered into a sitting position before standing. Her head rang from his slap, but she could discern his intentions. "No, John! You can't do this! Nothing happened between us. It's like I said about him saving me!"

"Shut up, Crimson," John snarled. "I'm a' aimin' to teach this bastard a lesson afore I git rid of him for good."

She watched in horror as Harvey, smiling in malicious glee, hand John a long black whip. Landon still had not moved, and his eyes were harder and colder than she had ever seen them. She could not stand back and watch her husband kill a man, especially the man she loved!

Turning on her heel, she ran toward the house. The whip cracked loudly behind her and piercing pain ripped through her back. Without breaking her pace, she gasped, tears stinging her eyes. She tore through the house and stopped in front of the fireplace, took down the loaded rifle, pocketed a few extra shells laying on the mantel and headed back outside.

Stopping just outside the door, she took everything in at a glance. Harvey was holding a pistol on Landon. Landon was still mounted, and John, the length of the whip curled up around his hand, was stalking toward her. Bringing the rifle up against her shoulder and pulling the gun's hammer back, she pointed it at John's chest. John stopped short, his face registering shock.

"I'll use it, John! Don't make me shoot you!"

"Ya'd shoot me over a damn half-breed, Crimson?" John asked, loosening the whip until the tip lay at his feet ready to strike like a deadly snake.

"I wouldn't have to if you didn't let your hate override your common sense." As she talked, she edged toward the solid wall and braced her back against it. She needed something solid behind her, especially from the recoil of the rifle if she was provoked into shooting her husband or Harvey. If her shoulder slammed into the wall, it could very well break it, but at least it was better than being thrown backward and landing on the ground. "It ain't right to punish a man for saving your wife's life, now is it, John? Or would you have preferred I'd been captured and tortured by Indians?"

His body was deceptively loose, Crimson noticed. "Drop the whip, John," she demanded softly.

John slowly smiled. "Now, Crimson, I ain't got no time for damned games." He motioned with his head in Landon's direction, moving his wrist back and forth as he coaxed, "This here breed..."

Seeing the change in his expression, she suddenly realized his plan of using his whip to snap the rifle from her hands. Without a moment's hesitation, she aimed the barrel between his legs and fired.

The explosion split the air.

Dirt billowed between his feet and her ears rang with the loud report. The recoil slammed her shoulder against the wall and throbbing pain flooded through her right shoulder. "Drop it, John, before I aim a little higher," Crimson demanded in a deadly voice, shifting another bullet into the chamber and leveling the barrel at John's chest anyway.

John dropped the whip, not at all certain what his wife might do next.

"Now step back from the whip, John. And, Harvey, drop your pistol on the ground real slow like. I'm mighty nervous and my finger just might accidentally pull this trigger again."

John jerked his head toward Harvey in silent command. Harvey laid the pistol at his feet and stepped back, a grim, amused smile on his lips.

Satisfied both men had carried out her instructions, her eyes strayed toward Landon. "Now just mosey on out of here, Mr. Wade."

Wry humor lighting his eyes, Landon watched the scene with interest. Crimson stood against the wall of the sod, her wavy hair whipping around her shoulders and head with each gust of the wind, her face a hard, determined mask, and pointing the rifle at her husband, keeping him at bay. He knew her shoulder was aching. He had seen it slam against the wall moments ago when she fired the shot. He had also seen the strip of wet blood along her back where John had used his whip on her, but nothing in her stance and determined face showed any pain.

He leaned lazily forward and speculatively eyed the trio. "I might oughta stay around, Mrs. Sullivan, just in case they get any idea about harming you."

"I don't need your help, Mr. Wade. This is a family affair and I can handle it quite nicely, thank you. You just get on about your business and let me attend to mine," she crisply stated, a hard edge strengthening her soft voice.

Landon's smile was crooked. "I reckon you can handle them, but if you need me, you just holler." He tipped his hat in a mocking salute, turned his mount around and galloped away.

Watching Landon ride off, Crimson was uncertain what her next move should be. She could not keep holding John and Harvey at gunpoint much longer; her shoulder ached abdominally and was growing tired from holding the heavy rifle, and her back stung from where the whip had ripped her blouse and skin.

"Ya stupid bitch, do ya realize what ya jist done? Ya let the only person who knows who I am ride off." John's hands curled at his sides while fighting his need of closing them around her skinny neck and throttling her for letting the half-breed go.

His words were like a bucket of ice-cold water thrown in her face. "So what, John? I doubt very much if he will tell anybody, but I just might."

He tensed with her words. "The half-breed is our enemy, Crimson. We came to a mutual agreement on that and ya let him go right when we had him in the palm of our hands. Jist what is goin' on in that stupid head of yorens?"

Crimson leaned against the wall, slightly relaxing her pose. "Maybe he is our enemy, but it doesn't make it any righter of killing him when he risked his life for mine. You don't pay a man back like that. 'Sides all that, I've had time to think about our marriage and come to the conclusion I'm tired of how you're treating me. Since I hold the upper hand, we're gonna get a few things straightened out."

"Why ya stupid bitch! I'm gonna beat some sense into that stupid head of yoren's as soon as ya lower the rifle." John took a menacing step forward and stopped when she repositioned the rifle toward his chest.

"Don't think about it, John. I'm tired, sore and in a terrible mood, and right now it wouldn't bother me a bit to blow a hole right through you. You see, I've been thinking about how you've been treating me. I've taken your beatings, cussing, belittling and just plain being ignored, and I'm flat tired of it. I am your wife and I plan on being just that. Ever since we got married, I've been used as nothing more than your housekeeper along with washing your nasty clothes. And when you do grace me with your presence, I cook your food. I'm nothing but a convenient piece of fluff to you and I'm tired of it. From now on you're gonna start treating me differently."

John threw back his head and roared with laughter before his eyes narrowed. "Ya think yoren bein' smart, don't ya? Well, let me tell ya jist how stupid ya really are. Soon as ya put that damned rifle down, I'm gonna beat some sense into ya."

She dramatically shrugged. "Well then, let me tell you something, John. If you lay another finger on me, I'll head straight for the laws and tell them who you really are. And if you think you can stop me, you just try. I told Landon before we got here to make a call at my sister's and tell her and Buck I need them here."

"Ya what? Ah hell, Crimson, yoren jist bullshittin' me. You didn't have the foggiest idea what was gonna happen here," John thundered, speculatively eyeing Crimson.

"I wouldn't be too sure, John. Mr. Wade knows the Indians are off the reservation and camped not too far from here, and there might be trouble. Now Mr. Wade knows about you slapping me and lashing me with the whip. When Buck finds out, he's gonna hit the ceiling."

Uncertainty crossed John's face. He had tried lulling Crimson and her family into trusting him. If what Crimson said was true, then he might oughta tread lightly. Buck was one man he did not want suspicious of him. And Crimson? Yeah, he could kill her, but then her family would hunt him through the ends of the earth. Besides, hadn't he been swaying Crimson into trusting him? "Ya will pay for this."

"Maybe, maybe not. All I know is I'm tired of living like this."

After a quick decision, John was faced with keeping peace with his wife just a little while longer, then... "Crimson, what ya wantin'?"

"It's very simple, really. Treat me with the respect due a wife which means if you hit me one more time, I'll blow a hole right through you." He nodded slowly in agreement, realizing she meant exactly what she threatened.

"You will not belittle everything I do. Instead, you will compliment me. And you will not cuss me or around me. The last thing I want is for you to get rid of your mistress."

"How in the hell...pardon me, ma'am, do you know 'bout her?" John snapped.

She shrugged. "It doesn't matter how I know about her. I am your wife, John, and I wanna be your wife in all ways. Do you realize you haven't spent a week with me? It gets lonely out here and from now on you're gonna stay around a little more."

John glared at her. She had the whole thing figured out and held all the trump cards. There was nothing much he could do without incurring the wrath of her family. He was afraid of no man, but her brother-in-law was one man he'd as soon skirt around very carefully. Buck's reputation as a deadly shot preceded him, and it was reputed at a hundred paces he could shoot a fly off a buffalo's head with a Sharp's .50 buffalo gun without moving a hair, the one he kept over his mantel as a trophy of his buffalo hunting days.

It wrenched his guts into an ugly mass thinking about conceding with her demands, but he did not see any other way around it. "Alright, Crimson, ya can have it yore way, but jist remember I cain't stay around all the time. I've gotta lot of outside businesses that need my attention."

Easing the rifle's hammer forward, she lowered it. "Just remember I won't hold with you messing around with the floozie. I'm your wife."

⌒◯⌒◯⌒◯⌒

LYING very still, keeping her breathing even, Crimson prayed John would think she was asleep. She wondered about her decision in forcing the issue in making her life with John into a real marriage. True, he did stay around for longer periods and treated her with some respect, but their conversation was stilted and polite like total strangers. She hated the nights worst of all when he still took her with violence, caring naught for her desires. Obeying his commands, she swallowed her revulsion and blanked her mind. But no matter how she tried, Landon's startling azure eyes popped into her inner vision at inopportune times, his sweet, fire-laden caresses lingering in the back of her mind, taunting her for all she missed by not giving into his gentle call of passion. It made the times with her husband harder to endure.

She was often plagued with crying fits overcoming her at silly, meaningless times like she had with Landon. Tears came into her eyes by an innocent word, when she became frustrated at some inane housework detail or for no reason at all, completely baffling her with its cause.

Feeling John ease out of bed, she was startled out of her thoughts. Through narrowed eyes, she watched him dress and leave, closing the door softly behind him. Hearing muffled voices coming from outside, she did not move. Her curiosity piqued, she thought about sneaking out of bed and listen to their conversation. Before she could move, the door opened. She held her breath, lying very still while John reentered the room with Harvey close behind his heels.

"Yore sure she's asleep?"

"Yeah, jist whisper so she don't wake up. We don't need her hearin' what we're talkin' 'bout." John motioned toward the table in front of the stove, and the benches were carefully moved, avoiding making any noise. They seated themselves before speaking again.

Their voices lowered more and she missed most of what was said. Harvey dug in his pockets and pulled out several coins, handing them to John.

"It's all we got 'sides a few horses and mules. Some of the settlers got…"

He stared at the motionless form on the bed before his voice trailed off with him moving from the table and walking to the stove. Hearing the sound of coffee pouring, his voice came out muffled with his back turned toward her.

"Thangs are gettin' purty hot. We had to hit hard and run fast with the damned breed fast on our heels."

John counted the coins in front of him. "Tell the men to lay low for a while. We'll meet in Mobeetie durin' court week."

Harvey finished his coffee, but before he left, John stopped him.

"Let's go to the barn afore ya go," John ordered, moving his hand over Harvey's backside.

"Whut for?" Harvey whispered, not wanting what John was demanding.

"I need yore ass," John tensely whispered. "Bet it's been a long time since ya had a good humpin' and we both need it."

"Hell, John, ya gotta wife," Harvey stammered.

"She ain't worth shit in bed. I only take her ass to hear her scream in pain. She don't know that's what gits me off 'cause every time she screams, her ass squeezes so tight, it gits me off real good. 'Sides, I like yore ass much better than hers, so come on, let's git to the barn. I've a hankerin' for ya. It's been a long time we had a good humpin' with one another. 'Sides, ya always been my bitch even when we were jist boys experimentin' with each other. I remember the first time I made you suck my dick. You sucked it like it was a lollipop." John rubbed his crotch, remembering how fast he had cum.

"I ain't a damn dog, you bastard," Harvey grumbled, opening the door.

John softly chuckled. "Yeah, ya are. Yore my bitch in heat and that mouth of yorens is still the best, so tonight I'm takin' both of 'em."

He grabbed Harvey's butt cheek and squeezed. "If'n yore really good tonight, I let you do the same with me. I haven't tasted that dick of yorens in a long time. Damn, I need a good screwing too until I'm walkin' bowlegged." Truth be told, he liked sex, a lot of different kinds of sex, and it didn't matter where it came from or who provided it.

After hearing the door close behind the men, Crimson sat up blinking her eyes several times, shocked hearing the last of their conversation. First, John lied to Harvey about anal sex. They tried once—the operative word *tried*. It was too painful and she barely let him penetrate before she refused to let him try it again. Second, she never dreamed two men could mate like a man and a woman. It shocked and disgusted her simultaneously, but a tickle grew between her legs, wondering if it was possible.

∽⃝⃝⃝⃝∽

JOHN softly closed the door behind him and eyed the still form on the bed. Crimson turned over, facing the fireplace. He waited a few moments until he was convinced his wife was sound asleep.

He moved a brick from the inside wall. Laying the brick on the cold ashes, he pulled a metal box out and lugged it toward the table. Unlocking it, he placed most of the coins inside and the rest in his pocket. Instead of relocking it, he threw the key in the metal box before replacing it in the hole and sliding the brick back in place, unaware his wife watched him through half-closed eyes.

❦

CRIMSON nodded and spoke with acquaintances while waiting while the traffic cleared enough for her to cross the street. The whirling dust left by horses and wagons going down Front Street eddied in the air, cloaking the milling crowd in a grimy brown. With the roundup completed, every rancher and their families from as far as one hundred and fifty miles away, came to Mobeetie for the fall court week festivities.

After checking for the room number, Crimson climbed the stairs and knocked. In a few moments, Honeysuckle opened the door. "Crimson, come in and talk real quiet. The kids are asleep."

After she closed the door behind Crimson, Honeysuckle drew her in her arms for a hug. "Crimson, it seems like ages since I've seen you. You wouldn't believe how much I miss you and so do the kids."

"I miss you too, Sis." Crimson released her sister and looked wryly down at Honeysuckle's stomach. "I see you didn't waste much time. When are you gonna learn to keep the spoon out of the kettle?"

Honeysuckle giggled and placed her hands over her extended belly. "I think every time Buck hangs his pants on the bedpost I get with child."

"When are you due?" Crimson asked, smiling.

"In a couple of months from my calculations. The baby will be big enough for traveling, and we figured me and the kids would follow Buck in a covered wagon during the cattle drive this summer. From there we'll catch a train and maybe see New York, then take another one as far as possible to our brothers' new ranch on the way back. We should be home in time for branding. At least that's our plan."

Crimson sighed. "Wish I was still going with ya'll."

"You still can." Honeysuckle glanced at the sleeping children.

"My, they've grown so much!" Crimson remarked, changing the subject.

"They sure keep me busy, let me tell ya. The boys haven't quite understood about having a little sister and why she's still not old enough for play time with them. Yet, every time I change her diaper, the boys run out the door screaming about the smell!" Honeysuckle's low laugh disturbed the youngest boy, and he turned over, facing the wall.

After the amenities were over, Crimson sat down in the ladder-back chair while Honeysuckle sat on the edge of the bed near the children.

Crimson avidly listened while Honeysuckle recited the children's little antics and the general happenings on the ranch. She added little to the conversation. What could she say without pouring out her troubles concerning her marriage and the frequent crying fits still attacking her? Honeysuckle had enough on her hands without worrying about her.

During a lull in the conversation, Honeysuckle speculatively eyed Crimson. Crimson had not said more than two words. "Something's bothering you, Sis. What is it?"

Chapter 23
Never Mess with an Angry Lady

CRIMSON stared at her clenched hands a few moments wondering how much to tell her sister. If she did not tell her something, Honeysuckle would keep on until she had Crimson telling her everything. Not that she minded divulging her issues with John—it was she would not be able to stand the *I-told-you-so-*stance. Deciding quickly, she answered, "It's nothing serious, really. It's…well…for several months I have been plagued with crying fits over stupid things, things that don't amount to a hill of beans."

Honeysuckle studied her sister, noticing for the first time the faint circles underneath her eyes. "When was your last monthly?"

"I wish that was it, Sis," she answered sadly, placing her hands over her flat stomach. "But I'm not with child." Perhaps if she had a child to love and cherish, her days and nights would not be so frustrating and lonely.

"You're sure?"

"Yeah, I'm regular as clockwork and that confuses me. If I'm not pregnant, then why these little fits? Sometimes I feel like I'm going out of my mind!"

Honeysuckle sighed, wishing she had a ready answer. She had worried herself nearly sick over Crimson's marriage, but it was out of her hands now. "I wish I knew. I feel like that all the time." She jokingly indicated her pregnancy, turning serious when her little joke did not bring the smile she hoped for. "Perhaps you're troubled over something else?"

Crimson shook her head, avoiding her sister's probing eyes. She was not really denying her sister's assumption as much as she was denying the problems herself. Honeysuckle had enough on her hands without adding hers. Besides, she and John were doing better though there was still an awkwardness between them.

Changing the subject, Crimson asked, "How's things at the ranch? Are ya'll still being plagued by rustlers?"

"Buck hasn't said anything, but by the way he's been acting, I think it's worse than ever."

"Does he have any idea who it might be?"

"If he did, they wouldn't have a snowball's chance in hell," Honeysuckle stated bluntly, her usually opened face hard.

Crimson lifted a finely arched eyebrow at her sister's choice of words. Honeysuckle was always the perfect decorum of a lady and her strong language was completely out of character.

They were silent a few moments, each lost in their own thoughts, the mentioning of the ranch bringing back Crimson's fears Landon was the one doing the cattle rustling. Crimson could only guess how much her sister knew. "Do you know Landon Wade?"

"Sure, I know Sky Eyes." Honeysuckle was suddenly alerted by the digressive subject. There had been a caressing fear underlying the way Crimson said Landon's name. "I heard he was in the area."

"Sky Eyes?" Crimson repeated slowly, meeting her sister's violet eyes.

"Eyes-of-the-Sky. It's his Indian name. I just shortened it." Honeysuckle held her sister's gaze, seeing her brow draw up in a studied concentration of surprise. The mention of the tormented boy of her childhood and the inadvertent instigator of her romance with Buck before she was captured by the Kiowas during the Red River Wars, Sky-Eyes was the one who found her and led her back to Buck. Her lips curved up in a soft smile thinking of the day as fresh memories poured over her.

Crimson missed the smile and blurted out, "What do you know about him?"

Brought back to the present, Honeysuckle shrugged. "Not much except he had a rough childhood. I was friends with him, but I guess mostly the friendship was based on sympathy on my part. I always felt such anger he was treated so horribly. In a way, I was relieved when his mother died, and he found his father."

She waved her hand, disavowing what she had just said. "I didn't mean it exactly the way it sounded. He was a tormented boy, angry at the world when I knew him. His mother was treated worse than he was. When she died, he left. I saw him a few years later, and I was happy he had found his father and was living there with him. Some of the anger and hatred had been diminished. I think he was treated as one of their own."

"You felt sorry for him?" Crimson asked, more in curiosity than questioning her sister's motivations. Her sister had stayed at home, caring for their mother and the sheep ranch while the rest of them were away at school. With Honeysuckle's monstrous duties, they had not really discussed outside affairs.

"Didn't you? He couldn't step out on the streets without someone either picking a fight with him or calling him names. He couldn't help who his parents were." Honeysuckle issued the question with a hint of anger in her soft voice. She had always hated the cruelty in which he was treated.

Crimson avoided the direct question with one of her own. "Wouldn't you say he grew up hating all whites?"

"Not all whites, I don't think, but most. Wouldn't you if you went through what he did?"

A curious frown on her face, Honeysuckle glanced at her sister. "Why are you asking?"

Shrugging, Crimson avoided her sister's too knowing eyes. "I saw him on the street and was wondering. More curious than anything else."

Honeysuckle's brow creased, watching her sister. "I heard a long time ago he was working at a ranch around here, but I ain't seen him yet."

◈◈◈◈◈

TAKING leave of her sister, the question haunted Crimson. She had carefully skirted around a direct answer, talking in vague tones, telling her sister little. Honeysuckle had inadvertently confirmed her suspicions Landon had a vendetta against whites. But the more she thought about it, the more confused she became. If Honeysuckle had been kind to Landon, why would he rustle their cattle? Or was he holding a grudge against her since she was friends with his worst tormentors? But then, if that was the reason, why didn't he stop after she left? She still wondered if he was the one who tried ambushing her. But why didn't he kill her when they were alone this spring?

She was so engrossed in deciphering the answer, she did not pay attention where she was going until she bumped into a warm, solid body. Bringing her eyes up for a hasty apology, she met ice blue eyes. "You! What are you doing here?"

The words were torn from her and her face filled with heat. She had been thinking so hard about him, then him suddenly appearing before her, she believed she had conjured him up somehow.

"I reckon the same thing you are," Landon remarked dryly, slowly sliding his gaze over her body. "I see you're still all in one piece."

His subtle reminder of him leaving her facing down her husband, brought a fresh blush staining her cheeks, and she tartly informed him, "No thanks to you. "You didn't stay around very long."

"I don't mess around with an angry lady pointing a rifle at her husband, especially when that lady ordered me to leave." A cynical smile pulled up his lips.

"No, you don't. For all that matters to you, I could have been killed." She was angry, more at herself than him, for he brought out her worse traits: anger, tears and lust. Chagrined with her thoughts, she whipped her skirt around and swept haughtily around him only to be brought up short when he grabbed her forearm.

She glanced scornfully at his hand, but he ignored it. "You think so little of me, Crimson? I watched your sod for days making sure Tom didn't harm you."

"Salvaging your ego, Mr. Wade?" She contemptuously lifted a mocking eyebrow. When he left so easily without a backward glance, she had momentarily despised him. A real gentleman would have stayed just in case she was still in danger. Wanting to hurt him for some reason she could not define, she spat, "You're a liar, a thief and a killer."

"I don't know why I bother with you. You never believe a word

I say." He released her arm like he had gotten hold of the hot end of a branding iron.

"You've never given me a reason," she hissed, rubbing her arm and covering the all too familiar weakness in her knees his nearness brought.

"I've tried, little spy." His soft voice carried a hint of sadness.

An idea forming, she lifted contemplative eyes to his. "I'll give you another chance. You can prove yourself."

"I don't need proving myself to you or anyone else, lady." His relaxed face of a moment before turned hard.

She stepped back, tingles of fear crawling up her spine. His eyes reminded her of a reptile—cold and unflinching. Mixed emotions fought inside of her; fear at how easily he had killed a man, yet fought a deadly duel protecting her, his cold, too penetrating eyes seeing more than they should, and the remembrance of how his kiss could weaken her with desire. He was never far from her reflections, always there haunting her. The strange man had two sides, and she desperately wanted the more tender side of him and the reassurance all her fears were unfounded. Unmindful she was pleading, she begged, "Please, Landon, I'll do anything."

His eyebrow lifting sardonically, he slowly undressed her with his eyes, remembering each lovely curve and indention, her statement intriguing him. "Anything?"

She flushed scarlet, interpreting his meaning, but her resolve was complete. If he was the one plundering her family's ranch, then maybe with this bargain he would stop. Hadn't she sacrificed herself for that very reason by marrying John, but for naught? It was worth a chance. She knew he wanted her, but was it enough? She lowered her eyes in shame. "Yes, anything."

He enjoyed her uneasiness, the way her face turned nearly the same shade as her hair and her complete submission. "What do you want?"

Her face a determined mask, she lifted her eyes to his. "Stop stealing Buck's cattle."

"I'd love to take you up on your offer, little spy, but I can't."

"Damn you!" Crimson cried, tears brimming in her eyes. She had shamefully offered herself, and she did not understand what hurt the worst—his refusing her request or rejecting her.

He grabbed her forearms and pulled her up within bare inches from his face. "Crimson, I'd like nothing more than taking you up on your offer, but I can't do as you asked."

"Are the cattle so important?" she snapped, hurt making her voice thick.

"You never will believe me, will you?" He shoved her roughly from him, fighting for control over his anger. "Don't believe me, but for your sake, go ask your brother-in-law if he thinks I would steal his cattle."

She studied his face through a haze of tears, the proud jut of his chin and the angry set of his mouth. "I will," she snapped, sharply turning on her heel and hurrying down the stairs to the dirt road.

Spotting Buck soon after she left Landon, Crimson shouted at him, waving for his attention while she waited for the passing wagon. After crossing the street, she had not made it up the boarded walk before Buck swung her into his arms and gave her a huge bear hug.

"How's my favorite sister-in-law?" he asked cheerfully. "Have you seen your sister and the kids?"

"I just left them." Crimson stepped back, nervously straightening her bonnet. "Can we talk?"

Buck scrutinized her serious face. "Let's get a sarsaparilla."

Releasing a sigh of relief that he did not immediately start firing questions, she nodded, then turned and stared across the street, unconsciously searching for Landon when a bright glint caught her eye. Staring open mouthed at the figure on top of the hotel she had just left, she caught sight of an unmistakable Stetson hat before she was suddenly thrown on the ground.

Buck rolled on top of her as an ear-shattering roar split the air and dust kicked up at their feet. The plate glass window of the store behind them shattered with the second shot and flying bits of glass sprayed them.

Confusion reigned in the street with women screaming and crying children suddenly dragged by their frantic mothers. Horses reared up, snorting in fear and pulling at the reins. A few succeeded in getting loose and ran down the street. Several men ducked behind buildings and watering troughs, whipping out their weapons in case more shots were fired.

What was in reality only a few seconds, seemed like hours with Buck's heavy body over hers, protecting her while he withdrew the Colt .45 from his belt. Her fear escalated sharply and a numbness seeped through her.

"Stay still, Crimson," Buck muttered in her ear, easing off her and glancing at the top of the building where the shot came from. A deathly silence permeated around them, but no more shots rang out. Buck and some of the other men made a cursory search, but whoever had fired at them was gone.

The people began venturing out onto the street again, and soon surrounded Crimson and Buck, firing questions and concern for their wellbeing. Buck stuck his pistol back into his belt and solicitously took Crimson's hand. "Are you hurt?"

She clasped his arm, frightened out of her wits and shaking like a leaf. "That shot was meant for me."

Buck placed his hand over hers and gave it an affectionate squeeze. "I doubt it. More likely it was meant for me. We're still havin' trouble with rustlers."

Denying his words, Crimson shook her head. She opened her mouth, the words almost tumbling from her mouth about everything that had happened before her marriage when her eyes were pulled toward the hotel. Landon came out of the doors, pulling his Stetson down over his eyes. Her confession froze on her lips and an iron band closed around her heart. Tears formed on her lashes and her mind silently screamed, *Landon, you tried killing me so I couldn't ask him!* Nothing in her life had crushed her so cruelly as this. She desperately needed to believe him, wanted to so much she had willingly given him the benefit of doubt this time, but now he proved all her suspicions were correct.

"Come with me and I'll take you to Honeysuckle." Buck took her arm and pulled her toward the street.

"No, I'm fine. Tell Honeysuckle I'm fine. I'm going back to my hotel room and rest. I'm a little shaken up."

"Are you sure? You know you're more than welcome," Buck insisted.

"I'm fine." Crimson forced a smile on her cold lips, hoping it would reassure him.

"I'll escort you to your hotel then," Buck announced in a tone brooking no refusal.

CRIMSON sat on the bed, her knees drawn against her chest and her arms wrapped around her legs. The tears readily forming in her eyes upon seeing Landon coming out of the hotel, froze inside of her. Coming up with the same conclusion, a dull ache sliced through her bruised heart; he had planned on killing her before she could ask Buck for the truth. More hurt by his betrayal than frightened, she wanted to believe him with every inch of her being, but he had proven untrustworthy.

The door opened, and she stared at it, unmoving, her eyes wide. If Landon came to finish the job, she would not put up a fight—there was no more fight left in her.

John and Harvey entered the room and a startled sigh of relief ripped from her.

"I heard ya got shot at," John remarked, speaking as if it were an everyday occurrence.

"No thanks to you," she retorted, her voice cracking with relief.

"Jist what in the hell do ya mean by that?" John stopped beside the door and glared down into her white face.

"You're never around when I need you, John. In fact, I haven't seen you since the day we arrived here. Where have you been?" She released her knees and straightened her legs, sliding off the bed.

"Where I've been ain't none of yore business. I jist came to make sure ya were unharmed." John's voice carried none of the tender concern a husband should have. His wife swept past him and stood in front of the window.

"I imagine you could have found out by the town gossip. Or are you here to convince everyone you are concerned about your wife?" Crimson snorted, his apparent disregard for her safety stinging her pride.

"Ah hell, what's the use? I try bein' nice to ya and ya throw it back in my face. There's no compromisin' with ya." John clenched his fists at his sides, red flushing over his ruddy face.

"I'm surprised you came." Her eyes green shards of glass and every line in her body defensive, Crimson crossed the room and stood in front of her husband where he had moved toward the bed.

"I wanna know who did it." John clenched his fists so he would not slap his silly wife. Whether she believed him or not, he was upset over the whole thing.

"Can't you guess?" Crimson asked caustically.

"Half-Breed," Harvey breathed.

John glanced over his shoulder at his partner, then looked back at Crimson. "Is he right?"

"For all you care, yes." She turned away from him and moved back in front of the window, the people below making no impression on her congealed mind.

"Damn!" John exploded. "I should of known." He followed his wife and swung her around toward him, tenderly caressing her cheek and frowning when she stiffened. "I'll take care of it, Crimson."

"What do you mean?" Her eyes narrowed in suspicion. What was he planning?

"Simply, my dear. I'll have a little talk with him, and if that don't do any good, I'll blow him away," John answered almost conversationally.

Crimson threw back her head and laughed, a low, hurt, scorn-filled sound. "Talk with him? How very thoughtful, John. I'm sure he'll willingly do anything you ask."

John's fingers crushed the tender flesh of her forearms, satisfaction filling him when she flinched. "Ya stupid little bi..." He stopped and released his hold. "Maybe ya should try understandin' what I'm up against, little wife."

"Yes, John, I can. If someone kills me, you'll be out on your ear without my family's good name protecting you. It's all you care about." The words meant as a taunt hit closer home than she realized.

John stepped away and turned his back toward her. It was useless arguing with her. As usual, she conveniently turned everything back on him. "Give it to her, Harvey."

Harvey handed Crimson a small two shot derringer and a box of shells. She took the small gun and stared at it. "What's this for?"

"Carry it everywhere you go for protection," John replied levelly, turning and facing her. "Ya know how to use it."

Crimson turned the derringer over in her hands, noticing the expensive pearl handle with her initials CR fixed there and the delicate engraved silver barrel. She was at a loss for words. John had never cared what she did or she imagined, if she lived or died. "I....I don't know what to say."

"Don't say anything. Jist use it if ya need it." John stepped back in front of her, lifting her face with the tip of his fingers, suddenly touched by the moisture sparkling on her lashes. Did it take so little for making her happy? Armed with that knowledge, he asked, "Do ya think I care so little, Crimson, that I would want ya dead? Yore my wife, for heaven's sake, and from now on, I want ya takin' precautions."

Her heart softened toward her husband for the first time. "Thank you."

John placed a soft kiss on her forehead, his smile triumphant. With his back toward Harvey, John pulled out his watch and quickly checked the time before clicking it shut and placing it back into his pocket. He motioned over his shoulder for Harvey to leave them. Pulling his wife into his arms, for the first time, he gently kissed her, then dropped his hands and unbuttoned her blouse.

"John," she breathed when he released her lips. "It's broad daylight. Shouldn't we wait until tonight?"

He did not stop but marched her backward toward the bed. "No, wife, I want ya now. Take off yore clothes, all of them. I wanna see ya naked afore me," he moaned, taking the derringer and the box of bullets from her hands and laying them on top of the dresser.

She did not comprehend why she slipped out of her clothes without arguing. This was the first time he had shown a small measure of gentleness with her. Standing in front of him, her clothes laying in the chair, she shivered as he slowly looked her over from head to foot, then followed with his hands over every inch of her bare body before guiding her toward the bed.

Chapter 24
Dealing with a Killer

JOHN dressed and with a soft chuckle, headed for the door. He had already spent more time than necessary with his wife. "I don't want ya venturin' out today. Stay in the room and I'll have supper sent up, so git dressed."

"Where are you going?" She rolled onto her side, fighting the tears coming into her eyes.

"Out."

She stared at the closed door, his short, clipped and totally useless word lingering after him. Burying her face into the pillow, she only felt hate and disgust for enjoying sex with her husband, especially remembering the last time Harvey had come to the sod when both thought she was asleep. Somehow knowing her husband liked having sex with men and women made her feel cheap, and in some ways, unworthy. She knew no matter how hard she tried, she would never be enough for him. Even worse, this was the first-time she had enjoyed sex with her husband and it left her feeling dirty knowing she was sharing her husband with possibly several sex partners. *What is wrong with me? Am I also perverted?*

TOM struck a match against his pants leg. The match flared before he cupped it and lit his cigarette. Shaking it out, he threw it on the ground. Leaning against the building, he took a drag, pulling the smoke deep into his lungs. Exhaling, he watched the wispy gray spirals drift toward the cold stars. The alley was cloaked in dark shadows, hiding the muted lights of Mobeetie. Dying campfires, like red gleaming eyes, dotted around outside of town where the people who came for court week camped along the outskirts after finding the hotels already full or the settlers could not afford them. An occasional cry and the scolding voice of a mother drifted on the wind and intermingled with the strident sounds of music and laughter from the saloons and dancehalls.

He had sent out subtle messages, notifying Half-Breed where they would meet, and having no doubt he would arrive for the rendezvous if only out of curiosity. The hatred between the two men had a long time festering and it would only end when one of them proved their supremacy over the other, which would only come after one of them was dead.

Staring off into the distance, Tom rubbed the back of his neck. He should have killed the sly devil long ago, but he was a tricky son of a bitch and all his attempts had failed. He could not always be so lucky, and one of these days when the breed's guard was down, Tom would get rid of him once and for all.

A wolfish grin pulled up his thick lips thinking about ending the breed's life. It was long overdue. He had enough competition gaining control over the dubious activities in the area and was slowly pulling together the different sects Gambler had started. Once they were organized, there would be nothing stopping their various so-called crimes.

He jumped when his name was softly spoken behind him. Damn! He had not heard the sly bastard approaching. Slowly turning, he faced his enemy.

"This better be on the level, Tom, 'cause if you've set up an ambush, you're a dead man," the voice warned.

"If it was an ambush, Breed, I wouldn't be puttin' myself in such close quarters with ya."

The breed nodded, satisfied. He seemed relaxed against the opposite wall, but his pose was deceptive. "What do you want?"

Tom dropped the cigarette on the ground and crushed it underneath the toe of his boot. "Leave my wife alone. Ya ain't got no call killin' her."

"I'm sorry I missed again. She's got the devil's own luck, but it can't last for long. And talkin' 'bout the devil's luck, how's Harvey?"

"He's alive though ya almost killed him," Tom retorted.

"A shame. He should of been dead. You must warn him about arguing with me over your wife," Half-Breed cautioned before chuckling.

"Ya know, Harvey reminds me of a trained dog following you around and obeying your every command. You gotta watch him, Tom. One of these days your dog's gonna come up and bite you on the ass."

The breed chortled over his little joke before saying in a low, serious voice, "Your wife knows too much and she's gotta die."

"She ain't got nothin' to do with our quarrel. She's completely innocent and doesn't know a thang 'bout what's goin' on," Tom insisted in a low voice.

"Oh, but she does. She's seen me many times, and I think she's already putting two and two together with your help. You've been agreeing with her about Half-Breed's activities," he sarcastically reminded.

Tom glared at him, feeling the coldness of his blue eyes on his face, the chill resembling someone walking over his grave and creeping along his spine.

Half-Breed threw his head back and laughed when Tom stiffened. "How do I know? You'd be surprised at just how much I do know. What I'm wondering is why you're so protective over your wife. She doesn't mean a thing to you. If she did, you wouldn't be so inclined of beating her every time she displeases you."

"Yore a slimy bastard!" Tom snarled.

"That's the nicest thing you said about me so far, Tom," the voice answered, amused.

"I'll kill ya if ya don't leave my wife alone," Tom threatened in a low, menacing voice.

"Such devotion," Half-Breed replied. "It makes me wonder why your wife means so much to you." He was silent a few moments before answering his own question. "Her brother-in-law's power? Maybe. But more likely she's considered a reward. Whoever owns her owns the rose of triumph." He chuckled at his own joke. "Yes, that's it. The crimson rose of victory."

Tom reached for his gun, determined to blow the bastard away when his words hit too close to the truth.

The sharp metallic click of a hammer being pulled back on a gun split the silence between them. Tom froze, his hand a bare fraction of an inch from the handle of his pistol. The fine hairs stood along the back of his neck, warning him while the disembodied voice drifted out toward him.

"Don't try it, Tom. I'll put a bullet through you before you clear leather."

Peering into the dark shadows, Tom slowly lifted his hands in acquiescence, then dropped them limply at his sides. An eerie feeling swept over him; the breed's form was completely swallowed in the darkness. One wrong move and he would be a dead man. "Alright, no gun play," Tom promised, a fine sheen of sweat covering his brow and over the top of his lip.

With his mouth churlish lifting, Half-breed released the hammer and replaced the pistol at his waist. "You may have more sense than I gave you credit for, Tom." He leaned back against the wall, deceptively casual. "Now, where were we? Ah, yes, your wife. You're a might touchy over her, eh Tom? I hit home with my remark." He sensed Tom stiffening and his sharp eyes, well-adjusted in the darkness, closely watching for any hostile movement.

"I warnin' ya, lay off her!" Tom tersely articulated. He shifted positions uneasily, gauging the breed's reactions in the darkness, wondering if he had made a bigger mistake in connecting with the bastard than he would have if he had laid an ambush for him.

"I've been going about this all wrong," the breed surmised. "Yep, instead of killing her, I should be claiming her as my own. That's what makes you the winner, eh Tom, owning Crimson Rose?" he asked conversationally, a touch of sarcasm underlying each word.

He continued voicing his thoughts out loud, not waiting for Tom's answer. "The perfect, sweet, innocent wife. Perhaps you should ask her about this spring. Ask her what happened before she came home and faced you down with a shotgun." His smile was cruel, sensing Tom's uneasiness.

"What do ya mean?" Tom asked hoarsely, his hands clenching in nervous jerks, fighting himself from going for his gun. His wife may be a stupid little idiot, but he had never seriously doubted her faithfulness.

"Ask her yourself, Tom. I'll be damned if I'm the one tellin' you." Tom's anger was a palpable thing and a cruel smile lifted Half-breed's lips. Anger made a man careless and he was not above adding more fuel. "Yep, just ask her. Ask her if she enjoyed her rendezvous by the creek. See what she tells you." He shifted positions in a stealthy manner, waiting in case Tom ignored his warning and went for his gun. He was disappointed when he didn't.

A red haze covered Tom's eyes, and he fought for control, visibly loosening his stance. "I will," he vowed softly.

Half-breed's disappointment did not enter his voice. "Do that. Now before we end this little chitchat, let me warn you, I still scout for the army now and then, and if you and your boys decide stealing any horses while you're here, never doubt I will lead them directly on the path you and your men take."

Tom threw back his head and laughed, a low, scorn-filled sound. "Ah, yes. I heard as much. Very convenient for ya, ain't it? One of the biggest rustlers in the Panhandle workin' for the army. Well, well, I wonder jist how much yore commandin' officer knows?"

A cold grimace passing for a smile crossed the breed's lips. "Don't say I didn't warn you, Tom. I will beat you at your own game anyway I can. In fact, I remember Major Larner was murdered in a very unusual way. Seems like he was stripped naked and taken to a deep gorge where he had his face and shall we say, family staff, were blown off." His brittle laugh floated across the alleyway. "Ah, yes, I do know about that. In fact, I know you're the one who killed him with the help of your whore, Jenny. I haven't proved it but give me a little time."

John unhurriedly left, the half-breed's savage, disembodied laughter following him. Crossing the street, the muted lights floated over the outraged furrows of his face and anger stiffening his mouth.

The tinny sounds of a lone piano, the brassy ones of a five-piece band and the discordant vibrations of voices filled the night air, drifting over Tom without making an impression. He entered the saloon, blinking rapidly against the lantern and candlelights nearly blinding him.

Ranchers, ranch hands, farmers and dubious characters enjoyed their night on the town and filled the saloon to capacity. The week-long court was a boom for business while drunken men, short on tempers, collided with regularity. A thick haze of smoke hung around the packed sweating bodies cursing, drinking and playing cards.

Tom sidled up to the bar and ordered a bottle of whiskey. Flipping a coin on the bartop, he grabbed the bottle's neck and transversed through the crush of people toward a lone table in the corner. The cruel tightening of his lips made the more sober men steer clear of him. Taking a long swig, Tom sourly eyed the occupants, the recollection of his conversation with the half-breed igniting his hair-trigger disposition.

Jenny plopped down in his lap, and he growled deep within his throat. Without a word, he shoved her onto the dirt floor. With the fierce expression tightening John's face, Jenny withheld her indignant tongue's waggle. Rising quickly, she dusted off the seat of her gown, her lips tightened with annoyance and turned, leaving him alone as did the others in the crowded room.

◦◦◦

UNABLE to sleep, Crimson lay staring up at the blackness covering the ceiling, every iota of today's happenings playing over and over in her tormented memory. She felt like a tiny dust particle swept along in a dust storm, lost and infinitesimal. Fixing bits and pieces together, she knew she was in the middle of something bigger, bigger and more profound than she was, but where it all led, she had no idea. Somewhere along the way, she had stumbled on something incriminating she was not aware of yet, but no matter how many times she replayed the past year and a half in her mind, she did not know exactly what it was.

The pieces of the puzzle did not fit. Is Landon a vindictive person, one who would kill for something that happened years ago? Or had she stumbled onto the center of some type of nefarious

243

activity? Was he afraid her questioning Buck would solidify his true nature? If Landon wanted her dead, why didn't he do it this spring when he had the chance? With the Indians leaving the reservation and roaming the Panhandle plains, her death would have been attributed to them.

She rubbed at her temples against the beginning of a headache, all her futile rationalizing going nowhere. Stumbling footsteps stopped outside the door of her room, and she eased over on her side and tensely watched the door. After several minutes of fumbling sounds and uttered curses, she relaxed, recognizing John's voice.

Carefully leveling her breathing, she hoped he believed she was asleep and would forgo him from waking her and performing her wifely duties. Her face flushed, remembering this afternoon and wondering if she really wanted another play of the same. Or would he instead revert to his typical ways, taking his pleasure and leaving her unfulfilled?

He stumbled toward the bed and the sour odor of whiskey and sweat assailed her nostrils. Through barely opened eyes, she detected his stocky frame outlined in the waning moonlight and caught her trembling bottom lip with her teeth when the figure stumbled closer. The mattress sagged heavily when he sat on it and after several seconds of fumbling and uttering curses, a match was struck before he lit the lamp beside the bed. The sudden light flared yellow in the room, forcing her eyes shut.

Without warning, he grabbed her shoulders, shaking her roughly, his whiskey-coarsened voice grating on her ears. "Ya damned two-bit whore, what did ya do with him? Answer me!"

Crimson's eyes flew open, revealing shock at his sudden attack, and her teeth rattled in her head. Resisting him, her body grew taut, her words coming out clipped and breathless. "Stop! Stop! I don't know what you're talking about!"

His fingers on her shoulders were like iron bands, unmercifully bruising the tender flesh. He stopped shaking her and licked his thick lips, his eyes red veined and dilated with his anger. "The damned half-breed, Landon Wade, ya damned two-timin' bitch. By the creek bed afore ya arrived back at the ranch. Were ya slippin' around with him afore ya married me? Damnit, Crimson! I'll kill ya if it's true. I'll kill ya for givin' the damnable half-breed what should have rightfully been mine!"

With the fierce, mottle-red face glaring at her, she cringed back against the pillow, her vision obscuring everything but him. His eyes were wild, lacking a spark of sanity. At first, she had no idea what he was talking about until memories of that cold afternoon replayed with vivid detail within her tortured brain. She held out her hands pleadingly, denying, "No! No! Nothing happened! I didn't..."

Something in her facial expression and eyes gave away part of her secret, a secret she had desperately tried burying. His eyes growing dark with rage, he knocked her hands away and fastened his hands around the slender column of her neck.

Her plea was cut off in mid-sentence with his thumbs pressing relentlessly against her windpipe. She bucked, clawing at his hands until her fingernails broke at the quick while she frantically fought to dislodge his grip around her neck until the lack of air made it impossible to fight any longer. Fighting for breath, tiny pinpoints of light danced before her eyes. Something perverse within her forced her to look above his head. She was dying and did not want his enraged face be the last thing she saw. As darkness began eating at the edges of her vision, she saw his shadow playing over the ceiling, grotesque and menacing, crouching over her.

Suddenly the pressure released. Crimson gasped painfully for breath while disembodied angry voices wove in and out of her hearing. After several minutes of drawing precious air into her tortured lungs, a wet cloth was placed against her throat and Harvey's concerned voice broke through the haziness of her hearing.

"Crimson, are ya hurt?"

She stared at him and numbly nodded, tears pricking her eyes at how close she had come to death. John stood behind him, his face still hard with rage, his meaty hands clenched at his hips.

Assured Crimson was alive, Harvey turned on John. "Ya stupid fool, I knew sumthin' like this would happen. Will ya ruin all our plans for sumthin' that lyin' breed told ya?"

Harvey's words hit her with a force that took her newly acquired oxygen from her lungs. Landon! He had told John about their almost consummation at the creek! Pain, piercingly hot, fractured every fiber of her being and erased everything good she ever thought about Landon.

In a startling, wild moment, she understood why John was so angry. Landon had told him something happened between them when in reality, it almost happened! But that was almost as bad. She had given him her most precious prize before she married John. And this was how he paid her back? Turning on her side, she closed her eyes against the tremendous aching inside of her, shutting out the angry voices still shouting at each other.

Chapter 25
The Devils' Deals

CRIMSON spent a restless night, the ache in her throat matching the one in her heart until she dropped off into an exhausted sleep, but her nightmares plagued her. She awakened a few hours later with the sun streaming through the white chintz curtains.

"Good, yore awake. How ya feelin'?" John frowned when she sat up, pulling the covers under her chin, her eyes wide and fearful.

"It's a little late for asking," she hoarsely countered.

"We gotta talk." His frown deepened when he touched her thigh and she stiffened.

"We have nothing to talk about," Crimson rasped, tears forming in her eyes. Her throat was dry and scratchy, and talking made the discomfort worse.

"Yeah, we do," John replied firmly. "And yore gonna listen."

If she could scream for him to leave her alone, she would. She did not care anymore about him or anything else, but her aching throat prevented vocalization of her words. She was, however, relieved the wild light in his eyes was replaced with calm rationality.

"Look, I know my anger got a little bad last night but I was drunk. Tell me the truth, is it true 'bout ya and the...half-breed?"

"A little?" she rasped, astonished by his description.

John self-deprecatingly shrugged his shoulders.

She realized in his own mind John was making amends for last night. The bitterness of Landon telling John about them was like a bitter gall in the pit of her stomach. Nothing really happened at the creek. She stopped in time. True, she had made love with him before her marriage, but why tell her husband? Assured his anger was under full control, she studied him a few more minutes before answering. Meeting his eyes squarely, she half-truthfully croaked, "Nothing happened, John."

John studied her for several seconds before nodding his head. "I believe ya."

"I guess it makes all the difference in the world since you nearly choked me to death last night," she sarcastically rasped.

"Ya have a right of bein' angry with me, Crimson. I acted afore I thought, but as of right now, I will make it up to ya. I'm sorry about last night and all the times I've treated ya badly."

A bubble of bitter laughter rose in her throat, but she quickly suppressed it. "You've said you were sorry so many times that I cannot believe anything you say."

John stared at a point above her head, running his fingers distractedly through his hair. She would not forgive easily this time. Words of repentance meant nothing to him, especially when he discovered how easy it was saying those simple words *I'm sorry*. Now he faced his wife who had figured it out. To regain her trust, his actions must speak louder than words.

"I've ordered us some breakfast. I thought a light broth would feel good on yore throat."

Her eyes wary, she nodded her thanks as her hand instinctively curved over the front of her throat.

He slipped his hand underneath the covers and dropped it between her legs. "Perhaps afterwards, we can make up. Would ya like that? Ya liked it yesterday afternoon," he cajoled, caressing between her legs.

A sly smile creased his lips when her legs slightly parted, giving him better access. "Perhaps we can do this afore we eat," he coaxed, ignoring the tears rising in her frightened eyes. "Yore my wife and it is my right whenever I want it."

"YOU LOOK pale, Sis. Are you sure you don't want the fort doctor taking a look at your throat?" Honeysuckle studied her sister, her brow pinched in worry.

Crimson protectively put her hand around the front of her throat. If a doctor examined it, he would see the bruise marks and no red throat, then possibly tell Honeysuckle. And that she must prevent at all costs. Honeysuckle would most certainly tell Buck, and with Buck's overprotective temperament regarding his family, all hell would break loose. She did not want to imagine how Buck would react. Besides, it was imperative Honeysuckle and Buck did not know about the shambles of her marriage. Perhaps in some ways, it was changing. She could only hope it was. "No, I'm fine. It's just a sore throat."

Both women looked up with the opening of the hotel room door. John walked in. "Howdy do, Mrs. Leathers. I'm glad ya come by to keep my wife company since she's feelin' so poor and all."

Honeysuckle nodded greeting, her smile tight, her eyes distrustful. She could not get over her dislike for her sister's husband. "I'd better be going. Buck's keeping the kids, and I figure by this time he's spanked Jake and Randy for their continued arguing and fighting, and Violet's probably bawling her head off 'cause she's hungry."

"If ya get a chance, come back and see Crimson later. In fact, why don't ya'll come out to our place and see her sometimes. I know she gits mighty lonesome out there," John replied.

Honeysuckle's eyes widened at the invitation. In the time he and Crimson had been married, John had never asked them to visit. "I just might do that." She placed a motherly kiss on Crimson's forehead and hurried out the door, her brow drawn into a frown over John's overt friendliness.

Crimson eyed John, like Honeysuckle, leery of his motives. He had been kind and considerate the last few days, and she wondered what his motives were. By the third day, she was more confused when he stayed by her side until she felt like screaming for him to leave her alone.

"Why are you treating me so nicely?" She watched his face closely.

"Yore my wife," he stated simply.

"It never bothered you before."

John shrugged, then leaned on the bureau. "Maybe 'cause almost losin' ya brought me to my senses. Hell, I can't explain it. I've been stupid and didn't realize jist how good of a wife I really had. I'm gonna make things up to ya, I promise."

Pushing away from the bureau, he sauntered toward her. Sitting on the edge of the bed, he tenderly took her hand and held her eyes with his. "Look, why don't we start over? I've been a lousy husband, I know, and I wanna try agin and make it up to ya."

She forced herself against cringing with his touch. He had treated her like so much dirt under his feet and tried choking her. And now he wanted a new start? With his tender administration during sex lately, she could not call it lovemaking, could she trust him? Could he change?

Chewing on her bottom lip, she broke his intense stare by looking down at her hands, uneasiness skipping along her backbone. Sensing dishonesty in his voice, it was all she could do not to scream at him to go bamboozle someone else. She was tired of the constant fights and everything that went with it. Although he had stayed a bit longer at their homeplace, the tensions between them had grown stronger. She hated when he demanded, yes, he never asked, but demanded she have sex with him, and at times physically forcing her into acts that were painful and degrading until the other day.

How could she ever forget that day? She had her first and only orgasm with her husband, then he tried strangling her that night. But that was not the only issue.

The pain of Landon's betrayal was like a sword slicing through her heart, and keeping a tenuous hold on her sanity, she desperately believed her husband could change. He had been very nice these last few days, but what else was lurking behind his actions? Regardless, she did want her marriage to work and knowing it would be harder now. She threw back the covers and smiled a tight invitation. "Alright, John."

☙❦❧

THE DRONING voices of the newly elected City Commissioners discussing sending off for Texas law books mingled with the soft rustling of women's skirts as they wiggled on the hard benches, the sounds a soft distraction, but not enough for forgetting the last few days. Uneasy and not understanding the changes, Crimson felt like she was living with another man; John had changed that much. But why? This was not the John she had married. When she invited him to her bed, he had been a considerate, tender lover. Though he did not take her to the same heights he had on that one afternoon, there had been no pain, only a slight discomfort which made it somewhat more acceptable. She did not understand why he took his time with her last night instead of his usual hurry, but in the end, she felt nothing, which puzzled her more. Was there only one time she truly enjoyed sex with her husband?

She glanced at her sister sitting beside her. Honeysuckle was solicitous and concerned about her apparent illness. And she had several times tried dissuading Crimson from coming today, but she could not face another day in the room with John waiting on her hand and foot. Sighing in resignation, Crimson closed her eyes. Nothing had made sense in so long, and she wondered if it was her.

Opening her eyes, her back stiffened with the sensation of someone watching her. Without turning around, she knew who it was. Landon Wade! She sensed his presence the same way she could sense a storm brewing during a calm. Her hands clenched around her handbag, feeling the comfort of the derringer inside it. Against her will, she turned slightly and met his mocking blue eyes. He cocked a half grin at her and barely touched his hat brim in greeting before removing it.

Hastily turning back around, her hand automatically settled on the high collar of her gown where her neck was still tender and bruised in ugly blue, chartreuse and yellow. Pinpoints of danger raced along her spine while loathing rose up, almost choking her. She blamed him for John's attack and his loose lips about something that almost happened between them.

Standing, she gave her sister a hasty apology, explaining she did not feel well as she first believed. Back ramrod straight, she left the throng of people and walked in forced, unhurried steps toward her hotel. Clearing a few buildings, she stopped short when Landon stepped out in front of her.

"Well, Mrs. Sullivan, I see you're better."

Her mouth grew taut when he sarcastically slurred her name. "You have no right speaking with me!"

Leaning against the wall of the building, Landon lifted a quizzical brow. "Oh? Didn't you have a talk with your brother-in-law?"

"You know damn well I didn't. You made sure we didn't when you took a potshot at me. Well, you did miss, Mr. Wade, but when you told John about the day at the creek, you nearly succeeded in getting me killed anyway! That would have made it all better. I'd been dead without you lifting a finger." She should walk around him and dismiss him with a toss of her head, but she wanted, no needed, this verbal assault with him.

His eyes widening, he nonchalantly studied her, watching her hand cover her throat. Sudden comprehension dawned in his eyes and his face became a hard mask.

"You don't deny it," Crimson railed, angry, hurt tears dewing her eyes.

"What difference would it make whether I do or not? You have already tried, convicted and condemned me. No matter what I say, you will never believe me. You never do," he replied cynically.

Crimson stiffened, her back becoming straighter. "I hate you!"

"Maybe," he drawled, "but I'm inclined believing you desire me more."

She knew it was true, knew with an uneasy certainty she loved him. She clenched her hands, quelching her craving of raising her hand and running her fingertips across the long, thick, sooty lashes framing his remarkable sky-blue eyes, then running it along his jaw where a muscle ticked in irritation. Embarrassed by her wayward thought, she blurted, "Why you insufferable brute! How dare you imply..."

"I dare very well, Crimson Rose, and you should have learned that by now."

There was a hard edge in his voice which should have warned her, but she was past rational thought. "Ah, yes, Sky Eyes," she said derisively. "Only a small man tries killing a woman."

Her hurtful words only brought a tight, crooked smile across his lips. "Why are you so angry all the time? What are you searching for?"

His sudden soft voice brought a flash of different emotions fleeing across her face. The question took her by surprise. What was she searching for? A husband who loved and cared for her, a home, her own children, yes, but though she had no children, there was much more missing. John did not love her. He was only using her, she realized with sudden clarity. Maybe that was what was missing, the love and caring she saw in her sister's marriage. But had not John changed these last few days?

Lifting suffering-filled eyes, she whispered, "I want my husband," though her heart cried out, *I want you. I want you to love me!*

Landon pushed from the wall, her green eyes and voice screaming out at him how foolish he was. Damn her, if she wanted her husband, then she would have him! Pushing his hat back with the tip of his finger, his mouth became a tight white line. "Well, Mrs. Sullivan, just keep going down this street, right on down near the end."

"To Feather Hill?" At Landon's nod, she searched his face, something in his voice and eyes crying a warning. She stepped past him, shaking off the desire of turning and running toward her hotel room, then hiding. Yet at the same time, perversely wanting to show him she was not afraid of what she would find. John hadn't left her side for days until early this morning. Surely he was not somewhere further down Feather Hill, the bad side of town.

Heading for the lower end of Mobeetie, she paced her steps in a slow, proud walk with her back stiff and her head held proudly. She felt his eyes boring into her back, daring her. As she crossed over into the fine line that separated upper and lower Mobeetie, her legs became leaden. Drunken laughter and discordant music floated out with each opening of the saloon doors.

Wary now of his words, she stopped when a couple stumbled out of one of the saloons. She had no doubt of their association with the man nuzzling the woman's neck. When he lifted his head and his gray eyes met hers, she sharply drew in her breath.

"What in the hell are ya doin' in this part of town?" John growled, unraveling his arms around the woman.

"I should have known your act was a lie." Crimson successfully hid the hurt piercing her heart. Twice she had been betrayed this week, by Landon and now by her own husband. Slowly, painstakingly, she began building a wall around her heart, protecting her from more unhappiness.

With the woman close behind him, John stepped off the boarded walk and staggered down the street toward her. Facing his wife, he grabbed her forearms in a tight grip, ignoring the pain crossing her face. "Spyin' on me, dear wife?"

"Lies, John, it's all you've told me from the very beginning." She fought back the unbidden tears.

"Ah, but ya are so gullible, my dear little wife. Do ya think a man would be content with your passionless lovemakin'? A man needs a woman with fire, not your spineless whinin'." John released his hold like the touch of her turned his stomach. "Go back where ya belong, Crimson."

His words stung the very depths of her soul. Without thinking, she pulled the derringer from her purse, her first thought of giving him back his present. Instead, she pointed it straight at his heart, intensely wishing she had the courage of pulling the trigger and wounding him the way he had her. "You've lied to me your last time, John. You promised you'd get rid of your whore. I told you if I ever caught you with her, I'd kill you."

"Don't be stupid! Ya ain't got the guts to kill me," John taunted, his tight grin daring her. His half-smile disappeared when the woman at his side stepped in front of him, protecting him with her body. He shoved her roughly aside. "I don't need your protection, Jenny. Git the hell out of here! I'll tend to my wife."

"Jenny?" Crimson cried, disbelieving. "That was a lie too, John? This is the woman who was supposedly killed in an accident?" A red haze covered her eyes, a haze of hurt, betrayal and anger. "Everything you've told me is nothing but lies."

"Give me the damned derringer!" John took a step toward her and grabbed the small gun held in her hand. The explosion shocked everyone into total stillness. His eyes widening, he slowly crumbled toward the ground.

"You stupid bitch!" Jenny cried, rushing toward John. "Look what you've done!"

Kneeling beside him and seeing the blood oozing from his side, Jenny screamed, "Somebody get the doctor."

"It was an accident," Crimson moaned, her body numb with shock, the derringer falling from her nerveless fingers. "I didn't shoot him. He grabbed the gun and it went off." A strange, unreal state swept over her. Some bystanders moved toward John and examined him, and she heard the proclamation the bullet grazed the fleshy part of his side.

A couple of men helped John into a sitting position, and he glared at her with such hate, she cringed inside. Slowly, meticulously, her gaze swept over the crowd which had some time during the ensuing argument surrounded them. Landon, Harvey, Jenny and several others. Her gaze held a silent moment with a man with the coldest blue eyes she had ever seen before passing over him and slightly skimming over the other people surrounding them. She spotted Mrs. Colby, a big, loud-mouth woman who was known as the biggest gossip in the state of Texas, sharply elbow her scrawny, henpecked husband when he took a step toward the crowd. The poor man doubled over, gasping.

Her shocked gaze landed back on her husband, who with Jenny's help, now stood on his feet, clutching his bleeding side.

"Are ya satisfied or do ya wanna finish the job?"

"You've lied over and over," she moaned, bending without thinking and picking up her derringer. Touching the cool ivory handle, she cringed. What if it happened again and she really did kill him? Doubling her fist over the gun, she stood upright, hiding the derringer in the folds of her skirt, the handle now burning into her flesh. Nausea swept over her and she released her hold on the derringer, feeling the small weapon slide down her skirt onto the hardpacked dirt street.

"I'll never forgive you for this, John," Crimson proclaimed before settling her gaze on the woman at his side. "And you, you two-bit floozy, if you value his life, you'll stay away from him."

Crimson turned and fought her way through the crowd, running toward her hotel room. Why had she uttered those last words? She did not care what they did, but everything was hazy and surreal. Though several people tried stopping her, she could not comprehend what they were saying, and waved them away.

After slamming her hotel room door shut, she grabbed the satchel beside the bed and began shoving her things into it. Never in her life had she imagined she could harm another human being, and actually injuring someone frightened her more than seeing the blood spouting from John's side. In her state of mind, she discounted it was an accident. Different emotions crowded over her, shame being the foremost, but her shame could not stop the hardening of her heart against all men and their lies.

A knock sounded at the door, and she did not look up. "Go away!" she yelled and continued packing.

The door opened, and much to her consternation, Harvey stepped in, closing the door behind him. "What ya doin'?"

"What does it look like, Harvey? I'm going home."

"Ya cain't go back by yourself," he argued.

"Like hell I can't! Go away. I don't need you."

"Yah, ya do more than ever afore. Look, Crimson," he coaxed, stepping closer and lightly taking hold of her arm, frowning when she shook it away. "I'll have the wagon hitched and go with ya."

"No, have the bay saddled. It'll be quicker that way." Crimson made herself soften toward him; he had done her no harm and she desperately needed help.

"I'll do that but only if I can go with ya."

"No, Harvey. Please just have the bay saddled and let me leave," she persuaded him with tearful, broken and pain-filled eyes, then nodded silent thanks when he agreed.

❧◎✿❦◎❧

THE HORSE and rider unhurriedly plodded toward the dim lights of Fort Elliot. His face a tight mask, Landon pondered the consequences of yesterday afternoon. The gossip of the unexpected run-in and shooting between Crimson and her husband was on everyone's lips. Her disappearance inflamed the gossip. There were varying rumors why she was not seen again during court week—her husband locked her up somewhere, she ran off with another man, she rode toward the north, et cetera, et cetera, et cetera. The point was—no one knew exactly what happened afterward.

He should have known better than provoking her, almost daring her exploration toward the lower end of Mobeetie, the infamous Feather Hill, especially when he was cognate of her stubbornness, her fearlessness of doing things her way. He accepted his responsibility and guilt in goading her, realizing he should have known she would bravely endure the criticism and inappropriateness of a lady seen in that part of town. His purpose was for her to witness her husband's true immoral character. Regrettably, his intent backfired. Above all, he knew she had a penchant for attracting trouble.

It tore at his gut she was stubbornly devoted to a man who never deserved her dedication. Faithful? Yes, she was faithful, even when he tried taking advantage of her crying that day at the creek, knowing her desire for him was as strong as his for her. Yet, if it had not been for the bobcat attacking the horses, she might have allowed him further exploration, but that was a big *might*.

In some ways, he admired her devotedness, though it irked him at the same time. His heart had warned him against her, yet he acknowledged he cared for her, cared way too much. She should be his, not the evil person she married.

Sharp regret tightened his lips. With yesterday afternoon ending in catastrophe, all the citizens talked about was Crimson shooting and threatening her husband. *You silly little fool,* he berated her silently. *Haven't I warned you before about those strong words?*

The music floating eerily on the night wind, the moon a bare sickle in the sky, producing little light, and one of the blackest nights he could remember. It matched his mood and wayward thoughts. An uneasy feeling had swept over him, and he left the dance early. It was the last night of court week and everyone would be headed home come morning.

He readily admitted missing Crimson's presence at the dance and had planned on dancing with her even if he had to force her. Whether it was to nettle her, speak with her or just plain hold her, he didn't know. All he did know was he wanted her in his arms again and feel her soft body against his.

Ebony's nicker brought him back from his bleak meandering. The horses corralled at the fort were restless, their stamping and whinnies breaking the stillness. Alerted, he stopped his mount and listened, his ears sharp from years of training. Suddenly, the horses broke free from the corral and the hurrahing of voices stampeding the animals.

Chapter 26
Crimson Rose of Triumph

LANDON kneaded his mount forward, his only thought—catching the rustlers and proving his suspicion of who they are. Closing in on the escaping horses, a man on horseback loomed in front of him. Landon drew his pistol and squeezed off a shot. The man jerked but stayed seated in the saddle.

The fast pace was dangerous, but Landon was hot on their tails. Detecting one of the rustlers outlined through the darkness, he squeezed off another shot. This time the man went down.

His stallion stumbled. Landon pulled on the reins, slowing his mount. It was madness racing a horse through the darkness with groundhog holes peppering the ground around them. The rustlers were riding a good distance ahead and leading the stolen horses, much to his chagrin, but good sense forced him to slow down. It was more important that his stallion not break a leg when it could be avoided.

Concentrating on guiding Ebony through the darkness, increased noises took a few moments to penetrate his consciousness. Crackling sounds, the cries of frightened animals, Ebony's sudden nervousness and the thick smell of something burning brought up his head. At first, he thought the orange glow on the horizon was the first fingers of dawn. Horror spread through him when the orange and yellow tongues of fire leaped forward, suddenly lighting the dark skies.

He sawed on the reins, halting the temperamental stallion, his eyes narrowed into mere slits as the yellow and orange monster spread in ever-increasing proportions. The town lay directly in the fire's path and the light wind fed its ferocious appetite. Turning Ebony back toward town, he raced back, alerting the inhabitants camped outside of town as he galloped by them.

Near Mobeetie, he hurriedly joined the posse already forming in the center of town. Most of the visiting citizens had left their horses at the fort, but they found enough mounts in town to form a sizable posse. Nearing the mounted riders, he yelled, "Prairie fire!"

Pandemonium reigned; women cried for their children and for each other as fear of the most dreaded disaster touched them. After several precious lost moments, the men: Landon, Captain Pierce, several army men and ranchers, Buck and a scout named Whiskey Joe, faced the scourge of the west.

Landon shot a glance at Whiskey Joe, experiencing an aversion to the scout. There was an indescribable intuition warning him if any crossed this man, he would show no mercy. Shaking off the impression, he knew they needed all available manpower.

The crackling roaring fire grew louder and frightened animals running for safety scattered the populous toward the small town's buildings. The heat from the fire grew until the distant fire nearly seared their faces.

The loud voice of a traveling preacher praying over the noise of the crackling flames, crying women and children and men cussing while working together against the conflagration, pleaded for God Almighty to send a rainstorm to defeat the flames. The traveling preacher's voice grew louder with each sentence but never ceasing until his voice became a hoarse whisper. A woman began singing songs of praise to the Almighty and others joined in as they set up lines and passed along buckets of water to the front firefighters.

Landon dropped a rope around a running cow, motioning toward Buck. "Rope its back feet!"

After several tries, they managed to wrangle the frightened animal spread-eagle between the horses. Landon drew his pistol and put a bullet through the animal's head. With Buck's help, they systematically halved the cow.

Slipping a rope around one leg of the halved carcass, Landon jumped onto his saddle and wrapped the rope around his saddle horn. They both dragged their portion, Landon riding in one direction and Buck in the other, hauling the cow halves across the leaping fire.

Seeing the effectiveness of it putting out the flames, other cowboys caught stray cows and did the same, working together against the blazes. Soldiers from the nearby fort joined the townspeople forming water lines when a couple of buildings caught fire from the wind-driven, flying sparks.

They fought through the night throwing buckets of water over the conflagrations, working together until exhaustion burned the muscles they used when passing the buckets. Women's cries filled the air, a wail of defeat, yet with underlying hope. Nevertheless, each kept working against the flames spreading.

The traveling preacher's voice hoarse, he never stopped praying. The people fighting the fire, sometimes raised their voices with him, pleading with God Almighty to save them.

Toward dawn, lightning snaked across the skies followed by the rumble of thunder. A sudden drenching rain swept across the land, moving almost as fast as the inferno, and soaking man, animal and the land in a heavy torrent flood.

Dawn broke and soon the sun smiled favorably upon them, celebrating with them the fire was under control. Women cried with joy and the men shouted, "Praised the Lord! *and* Hallelujah!" From the miraculous sweeping rain and using cows to put out immediate flames, the town received only minor damage. But with the loss of precious time, the fire also effectively covered the rustlers' tracks.

"It's useless following the horse thieves now," Captain Pierce stated, rubbing at his tired eyes and smearing black soot across his face, spreading it worse with the dampness of his uniform's sleeve.

"Maybe, maybe not. My guess is they'll head for the New Mexico border where there's a good market for horses," Landon stated, rubbing at his tired eyes, a sudden chill rising along his back.

"Whether they have or not, it's too late. I'm taking my men back to the fort. We'll eat, grab more weaponry and regroup before going after the thieves." Captain Pierce motioned for his men to mount up, ignoring Landon's sputtering argument.

Landon watched the soldiers ride off, along with several

mounted men, heading for their families already salvaging anything unburned within the camps. He angrily rubbed at his tired, burning eyes. His clothes bore burn holes, his hair was singed and his clothes were still damp, but he would not give up yet.

"The captain's right, Sky Eyes. It would be useless. Let's get some rest and head out later," Buck replied behind him.

"Maybe so, but I'm not giving up so easy. You can go with me now or go back, I don't care, but I am going on." Swinging into the saddle, Landon did not wait for Buck's answer. He kicked his heels in the stallion's flank and headed west.

After several minutes, Landon noticed there were no accompanying hoof beats behind him. He was alone in his haste of going after the rustlers. He could not really blame the men. They were all exhausted, but Landon's gut instinct whispered the horse thieves' names, and one especially.

The black, desolate plains stretched out before him in a mass of black emptiness, a fire just as hot as the prairie fire had been, burning through him and shouting for him to complete his mission and capture the men responsible, not only for rustling, but starting a deliberate prairie fire to cover their tracks.

✦

CRIMSON absently stirred the big pot of stew bubbling over the fire. The delicious aroma did not tempt her appetite. She had made the stew, more as an act of survival, an act of normalcy. It took a few minutes for the noise of an approaching horse to penetrate her consciousness. Resignedly sighing, she hung the spoon on a hook above the stove and headed for the door.

His face drawn in pain and white as death, John eased off his horse. Crimson rushed forward. "Get away from me, ya stupid bitch. I don't need yore help. If it hadn't been for ya, I wouldn't be in this fix in the first place."

She drew back her hand, her mouth tightening into a hurt, white line. Shrugging off her helplessness and regret, she turned away from him and stiffly walked back inside the sod.

John stumbled into the sod like he was drunk and sat down heavily at the table.

Crimson sat the bowl of stew in front of him and moved away. She wanted to say something, to apologize for what happened, but pride and hurt kept her silent.

She was brought up short when John growled deep in his throat and the bowl clattered against the fireplace. Hot bits of stew landed on her exposed forearms, and she hastily wiped the burning bits away before turning toward John.

"I don't need yore damnable food. In fact, I don't need nuffin' from ya. Ya have succeeded in makin' me the laughin' stock of town, damn yore hide to hell!" John clutched his side, his face growing whiter.

Red seeped through the white bandages, and she forcibly squelched her compassion at his apparent pain. He said he did not need her or her help, so let him wallow in his own pain. Turning and ignoring him, she cleaned up the mess. What could she say? Things couldn't get any worse between them, could they?

The day progressed into dusk, the tense silence between them so thick you could cut it with a knife. Crimson left the house and stood in the front yard, letting the breeze lift her heavy hair off her neck and cool the hurt anger on her face. With trepidation, she looked out over the prairie and saw the dust cloud hailing a rider. She automatically called out before thinking, "Someone's coming!"

John appeared at the door, leaning heavily on a rifle barrel, the butt end settling on the ground. He shaded his eyes against the brightness of the setting sun, his white face turning red when recognizing their visitor.

If Crimson was shocked at Landon's singed hair and the burn marks spotting his clothes, she did not show it by action or words. She silently stared at him, wondering what he was doing here and tensing when he stopped in front of them.

"Well, if'n it ain't the damned half-breed. What ya want?" John asked roughly, leveling the rifle at Landon.

"I'm taking you in on suspicion of cattle rustling," Landon stated calmly, leaning forward in his saddle, giving credence to his words.

John threw back his head and scornfully laughed. "Are ya now? Ya think I was rustlin' in my present state after my dear wife shot me? Don't matter anyhow. It seems to me I've got ya at a disadvantage, you bein' without a gun and all."

Landon's hand flew to his side, realizing too late that he must have lost his pistol during the fire. Whatever he was feeling did not cross the hard lines of his face. "I guess you do, Tom. Looks like I made this long trip for nothing, but let me warn you, Martin, I haven't given up. I'll see you hang before it's all over."

"Will ya now?" Laughter underlined each word John spoke. "Ya might come better equipped next time 'cause I won't go peacefully. Ya will have to put a bullet through me afore I submit to a necktie party."

When Landon did not reply, John continued, "Since this is a day for warnin's, let me issue one of my own. I'm feelin' a bit under the weather 'cause my wife," he nodded toward Crimson, "put a bullet through me. If I was more inclined, I'd kill ya on the spot, but...I'm a reasonably nice guy and I like havin' battles of wits with ya. But," His face grew hard, his lips a thick line, "if'n I ever catch ya on my property or around my wife again, I will kill ya."

"Back to the old battle, huh, Tom? So be it. It'll be who fires the first shot. Have no doubt, Tom, you'll die before me." With those last words of warning, Landon reigned his horse around and kicked his heels against his sides, riding back toward Mobeetie.

"Stupid son-of-a-bitch," John muttered to no one in particular. "I'll have his half-breed hide decoratin' my house afore long."

❦

CRIMSON stared out over the stark, winter-brown land. The icy November wind cutting through her wool dress chilled her bones. Her cold numbed hands made picking up cow patties or a stray buffalo patties hard to maneuver. Wood was a scarce and precious commodity. Cattle or bison refuse, though not the most pleasant smell, kept the fires burning hot. It was a job she did not necessarily like but one that must be done unless she wanted to freeze with the oncoming winter. Later, she would cut large stacks of tall, brown buffalo grass and make bundles out of them, substituting them with the patties.

Hefting the large basket in a more comfortable position on her arm, her mind wandered while she bent and plopped another patty into the basket. Three months had come and gone since the disaster at Mobeetie. The chasm between her and John had grown so wide nothing would bridge the gap. John had commandeered the bed after the accident, and she had made a pallet in front of the fire. Her body and bones screamed out against the hardness, and after all this time, she still rose stiff and sore.

She delicately shrugged her shoulders, expunging some of her dismay. John's wound had healed and he still waited around the ranch, waiting for something or someone she imagined or he would have already been gone. Whatever it was, she wished it would hurry and happen so he would leave her in peace. He continually taunted her, bullied her until she was near screaming at him, and at times, she almost wished she had killed him when his anger got the better of him and he beat her. She would have already left, but with the fall quickly turning cold, she would endure until warm weather arrived.

Heading back toward the sod, she shook her head, angry with her thoughts. She was only human, she rationalized, but it did not stop the guilt from piercing her traitorous thoughts. Her marriage was a travesty, a loony sham. And by now, everyone knew the truth of her marriage. So why try keeping up the pretense? Why shouldn't she just pack it in and leave before his anger ended up killing her?

With those last thoughts, she entered the sod with purposable steps. Placing the fire material close by, she stoked the fire and started supper. An hour later, John came in, washed his hands and sat down at the table without uttering a word.

Equally silent, she fixed him a plate, set it in front of him and poured them both a cup of strong black coffee. Ignoring the habit she had formed these last months of not sitting down with him while he ate, she sat in front of him and watched him shovel down his food while she sipped at her coffee. Stoking her courage, she began slowly speaking, "John, I've been thinking..."

He paused, his fork suspended between his plate and mouth. "Oh, since when have ya acquired the habit of thinkin'?" His surprise she spoke turned his remark into sarcasm.

Crimson ignored his taunt. "We don't have a marriage, never really did, and I have decided I'm leaving you and getting a divorce."

Red-hot fury shooting through him, he dropped his fork and it clattered against his plate. "Forget it, Crimson. Yore mine and ya ain't never gonna leave me!"

She drew back slightly with his venomous declaration before continuing undaunted, "You can't stop me. You can't stand staying here, though you have stayed here longer than normal, and when you do leave, I'm leaving too."

John pushed his plate away, losing his appetite. "That's where yore wrong, little wife. I can and will stop ya. Yore mine. I married ya for better or worse."

"Why? There's nothing here for either of us! We can't stand the sight of each other. Why don't you just go back to your two-bit doxy and leave me alone?" Crimson pushed back from the table and quickly stood.

No matter how hard she tried, she could not speak with him in a calm, level manner. "I'm not some kind of possession! You can't own me like you do this land or like some kind of livestock!"

John rose swiftly from the table, the bench falling and landing with a bang onto the hardpacked dirt floor. He spun her around, his hands on her forearms cutting cruelly into her tender flesh. Mottled-red swept over his face and his gray eyes narrowed. "But I do own ya, Crimson. I own ya just as surely as I do ever'thang else 'round here. *Ya are the crimson rose of triumph!*"

"What? The crimson rose of triumph? What are you talking about?" Crimson shrank back from him, pushing at the painful grip of his arms, the cruel twist of his lips frightening her.

"Yes, dear wife, the crimson rose of triumph. It took me a while to figure out why I was keeping ya around when I could of killed ya long ago. Like the half-breed said, whoever owns ya is the winner. Yore a symbol, a trophy for the best man, and I am the best man." He shook her, shaking his words into her head. "Ya will never leave me alive, Crimson Rose!"

She forced back the springing tears filling her eyes, the half-breed Landon again haunting her. He was her nemesis, the thorn in her side. No matter which way she turned, it always came back to him. "Why am I the trophy?"

He threw back his head and laughed, a low growling sound. "Very simple, Crimson. I am the head of the underworld around here, the syndicate as others call us. Yore from the class of the high dog, the respected parties. With ya at my side, I gain respectability."

Shaking her head, she denied his reasoning. "No! That brings me down to your level!"

"Not really, my dear. Ya see, nobody knows I'm at the head of the syndicate and who would they least likely suspect? Me, 'cause I have gained the respectability of yore family. No one would believe the great Buck Leathers family would have anythang to do with the underworld. Ya see, your brother-in-law has made quite a name for himself, quite the respectable man. It's the perfect cover."

"Whoever has me is the winner." She said it flatly, not really understanding his reasoning.

"You're all cowards for hiding behind a woman's skirts." The next thing she knew, she was on the floor, her cheek stinging from his sudden slap.

Lifting her hand toward her cheek, she glared at him, her shock briefly showing in her eyes. The sting in her face was nothing compared to the bitter taste in her mouth. Her voice came out level and unruffled, resigned. "I should hate you, John, for what you have done, but truthfully, I really don't care anymore."

He grabbed her shoulders, forcing her upright. "I can handle yore hate better, Crimson, not this, but it don't really matter anyhow. Whether ya hate me or ya don't care or if ya love me, ya will always stay by my side. That's what I've always admired and despised in ya, your stubborn, blind loyalty."

Shoving her against the wall, he spread his feet in front of her, leaving her no room to flee. "Ya see, dear wife, no matter what I do or what I have done or will do, ya cain't ever say anythang against me. It would go aginst yore grain, yore so-called rightness of thangs."

He caressed her cheek, feeling the warm silken flesh, undaunted when she cringed from him. "Yore misguided loyalty, Crimson, is sweet. I can do whut I want without worryin' 'bout ya. 'Sides, ya said it when ya proposed to me—a woman cain't testify aginst her husband."

"Don't be so sure, John. Right now, I don't care what happens with either of us."

"Ya cain't change your spots, Crimson. It's too late. Yore loyalty to family is too ingrained." He dropped his hand at his side, his face triumphant. "Naugh, ya cain't change."

Both hearing an approaching rider, John turned from her, and she sighed in relief. John took the rifle down from its spot above the fireplace and left the sod. She began shaking in delayed reaction. Just how much truth was in what he said? Could she tell somebody about John? And who would listen anyway? A man had prerogative over his wife, and it still was, more or less, like the stone age when a man could beat or kill his wife without anyone interfering. Who would believe her if she told them John was the head of the underground syndicate? They would all laugh at her. She had no proof, only his word.

The voices outside grew louder, angrier, dragging her from her unanswered questions with her curiosity pulling her toward the door. Opening the door a crack, she peered out. Harvey and John were squared off—Harvey with his hands clenched into fists and John holding the rifle on Harvey.

"We cain't go back into operation for a while. The damn law is on our trail. We lost one man in Mobeetie durin' the last job, and the other one who was shot, died on the trail. The newly elected sheriff must have gone back and formed a posse after the prairie fire ya started 'cause a few days later they were close behind us. The son-of-a-bitchin' breed, Landon was with them."

"Ya always did have a yeller streak down your back, Harv. If they was hot on your trail, ya wouldn't be here. Now, Colonel Goodnight is havin' a shipment of high-priced stock shipped in. Gather the boys and steal 'em," John ordered, his voice hard as steel.

"You stupid bastard, I won't do it! The only reason I'm here is 'cause I gave them the slip. The damned posse split up, and far as I know, I'm the only one who escaped. Some of our men were lucky enough to be shot dead, but the others were hung on the spot. Yore damned lucky we made it to New Mexico and had already sold most of the horses afore they caught up with us." Harvey was shouting at the top of his lungs, shaking his fist in John's face.

"Harv, if'n yore gonna be like a mewlin' babe, then leave here and don't let me see your ugly face 'round here agin or I'll kill ya!"

"That's fine with me, Tom, 'cause I ain't workin' for ya anymore nor be yore bitch when yore sources dry up." John's next words made him pause.

"I'll spread the word, Harv, 'bout what a yeller belly ya are. The operation ain't gonna like it, and ya know what happens to quitters like ya in this business. And as for ya bein' my bitch, that will never change."

Harvey slowly turned toward John, his face red with anger and a tinge of fear. He had a sinking feeling in the pit of his stomach. A coward died a coward's death, a slow, painful one the men in the syndicate devised. "I'll kill ya if ya do."

"How?" John taunted, "Ya will be dead!" Laughing, John watched Harvey leave.

When John came back into the sod, Crimson taunted, "Three times in just a short while, you've been threatened, John. How many more enemies have you made?"

Chapter 27
1882
Bargain with a Cast Iron Skillet

A POSSE of ten men, including Sheriff Cape Willingham and Deputy Sheriff Henry Brown, an ex-member of the notorious Billy the Kid's gang, stopped a couple of miles in a deep arroyo near Sullivan's place.

Big snowflakes fell from the leaden skies, cloaking them in the white fluff, frosting mustaches, beards, hair and clothing. The fiercely, gusting January wind had men holding their hats onto their heads with one hand and some who had no leather gloves, blowing on the other numbed hand, restoring a small measure of warmth.

Sheriff Willingham, a big man with blue eyes, laid his hand casually on the butt of the sawed-off shotgun ensconced in the scabbard hanging from the side of his horse. Never having learned to use a pistol, he depended on this lethal weapon.

He frowned at the blustery day, believing they should have waited for tomorrow and maybe the weather might have turned off warm again. The weather was unpredictable as the men it harbored, changing from day-to-day and breath-to-breath. This morning started off a warm, gentle, breezy day, then the clouds moved in and the rain soon turned to sleet, then snow. He wondered if he would ever grow accustomed to the fluctuating weather around here.

Shifting his considerable weight in the saddle, Sheriff

Willingham faced the men around him. "When we get closer, you will quietly surround the house. We know he's dangerous and armed. He'll probably resist. Just be careful. His wife will probably be there too, and I don't want her harmed."

The sheriff threw a particularly hard glare in Henry Brown's direction. Brown's whitish-blue eyes gleamed with suppressed excitement. Sheriff Willingham wondered if he had made the right choice for hiring him as deputy sheriff. Brown was known for his quick, out-of-control temper, but he was the most efficient man with a brace of pistols he knew. Willingham did what many other law officers did in lawless towns; hired a killer to keep other killers in line. Shrugging aside his doubts, the sheriff patted the warrant in his breast pocket and motioned with his head toward the Sullivans' homestead.

Before they had time to kick their heels in the horses' flanks, a gunshot reverberated through the snow-flurried weather. The sheriff's horse snorted and nervously pranced. Sheriff Willingham tightened his hold on the reins. "Sounds like it came from the Sullivan place. Forget about splittin' up. Let's go!"

Sheriff Willingham had and would see a lot of grisly sights in his lifetime, but for as long as he lived, he would never forget the sight meeting his eyes as he and the posse arrived at the sod. A beautiful woman, Sullivan's wife he presumed, stood staring down at the lifeless man at her feet, her lovely heart-shaped face as white as the fresh falling snow gusting around her, her waist-length, wavy mane of hair undulating like a dark red flag. In her finely-boned hand, she loosely held a derringer.

Blood slowly oozed from the jugular vein in her husband's neck, the ground underneath his head red with squirts of blood sprinkling the ground where the blood spurted five feet away, leaving crimson slashes in the pure snow. The victim's head angled awkwardly and his eyes, the same color as the heavy skies, sightlessly stared into the bleak, gray firmament.

Easing his heavy bulk off his horse, he barely heard the shocked mumbling men around him. In slow, reluctant steps, he walked toward Sullivan's wife. He did not look up when hearing another rider race across the yard and pull to an abrupt stop. Slowly walking toward the woman, he held out his hand, crooning softly, "Give me

270

the gun, Mrs. Sullivan."

The woman had not moved, only stared at her dead husband, and he wondered if she heard him. Repeating his order again, he reached out and gently forced the gun from her nerveless fingers. He noticed she shuddered, though she did not lift her head, and he wondered if his action of taking the small derringer from her hand had alerted her that she was not alone. Another shiver quaked her shoulders, and she lifted lifeless, green eyes containing no recognition within them.

He quickly scanned the ground around him, frowning when he saw all the footsteps, except his own, covered in white, and where the hoofprints of his posse were filled with big, white snowflakes, erasing all external tracks. Whatever he was hoping for, the evidence around him eliminated that this was an accident, and suddenly rendered his job a heavy burden. He released a deep, sad sigh. "Mrs. Sullivan, I'm arresting you on suspicion of murderin' your husband, John Sullivan."

In shock, Landon stared disbelieving at the scene before him as he eased off his horse. Crimson's deathly white face tore at his heart. The fiery girl he knew was standing so still, every emotion drained from her face until he wondered if it was the same person.

Instead of moving toward her, he reined in his wayward sentiments, noticing she only wore a woolen gown. He saw a shiver pass through her. She seemed unaware of the cold and stood with her arms akimbo, lifeless as a rag doll.

With long, even steps, he went inside the sod and pulled a quilt off the bed, then slipped the heavy black cloak from the nail beside the door, the small activity refusing to eradicate the appearance of her ghostly figure. *Crimson, why did you do it? I never thought you could kill your husband.*

Crimson had already been mounted on a horse, and he tenderly draped the cloak and quilt over her shoulders and tucked it around her arms and legs. She did not acknowledge the gesture or appear to know what was happening. Her face was set toward Tascosa, all coherence and spark of life missing from her lovely green eyes.

THE SKIES were a heavy gray, the ground frosted white and

the air too cold for snow. The wind's breath was colder than ice, whipping and slapping the young woman's cloak around her stiffly held frame. Her lips were blue with cold, her hands clutched beneath the cloak seemed frozen together, her heart-shaped face a soft ivory emphasized starkly against the black gown and cloak she wore. There was a haunting sadness, a loneliness, a quenched anger in her red-rimmed and swollen green eyes. She stood alone beside the six-foot-deep hole, and a man droned in a monotonous tone over the wooden box containing the body of John Sullivan.

From her peripheral vision, Crimson saw the different groups of people around the grave who had settled into the small town of Tascosa which was now a focal point of cattle herds driven through the Texas Panhandle toward Dodge City, Kansas. On one side were the townspeople who came to see a murderess, more than pay homage to the man being buried, then in a separate group at the other end was the riffraff of Lower Tascosa, also known as Hog Town, lending credence to John's boast of being the syndicate boss. In the last year, small businesses had set up shop along with various saloons, dancehalls and a shack settlement providing lonely cowpokes places for sexual activity with the soiled doves.

Only one person cried; Jenny, heaving great, rasping sobs with tears freezing almost as soon as they left her eyes. Behind Jenny stood a man Crimson had seen briefly before. He was one of the curious onlookers surrounding her and John during their argument and the unintentional shooting incident. The man's stance was rigid, his narrowed eyes cold and calculating, and his hooked nose winter-reddened. She suppressed the shiver his stern glare invoked.

Feeling cold as the icy wind, she turned her mind inward, blocking the sight of the people around her. She felt nothing—no sorrow, hate, love or regret. John's body was in the hastily built wooden coffin, and she flat did not care anymore. He had successfully killed all emotion she had once felt for him.

After a cursory prayer was said for John's soul, the people wandered off, and no one paid their respects to the widow, not wanting to be seen speaking with a murderess. Dispassionately watching the casket lowered into the ground, she waited until the last person left the gravesite. Tascosa had its fabled Boot Hill named after the one in Dodge City, Kansas. It was on top of a hill a couple of miles outside of town where several men had used pickaxes and shovels to dig a grave in the frozen ground.

She had been surprised so many people showed up for John's funeral on this cold, windy wintery day, but in her heart, she knew they only came to view her—the murderess. Oh yes, she had heard the whispered comments they said about her when they passed, how she had shot her husband before in Mobeetie and threatened to kill him if she caught him again with his doxy. Yes, John was often seen in Mobeetie, then in Tascosa visiting his huzzy. His wife must have found out and ended the affair once and for all.

Crimson turned from the grave and slowly walked back toward town. At the end of the hill, she came face-to-face with a distraught, furious Jenny.

"What are you doing at John's funeral, you murderer? You, of all people, should of stayed away." Jenny's voice, though tearful, held a deep, strong malice for the woman in front of her.

"Me, Jenny?" Crimson nearly choked saying her name. "I was his wife. If anyone should of stayed away, it should of been you. Major Larner's gun and holster was found in your quarters, and you're the one who spilled your guts about John's involvement, even helped him commit the bizarre crime."

"Why you...you...murderin' bitch! You have no right!" Jenny sputtered.

"Don't I? At least I was his wife. What can you say? You was his whore? Don't stand there accusing me. You will face judgement for murder the same as I." The burning fire in her eyes lent her anger on John's mistress. If it had not been for John's and his mistress' duplicity, she would not be in this predicament. Crimson disdainfully pulled her cloak closer against her thighs, avoiding Jenny's tainted touch when stalking past her.

Jenny's sharp intake of breath was loud as the blustery wind before she began cussing, using words Crimson had previously never heard but was assured of their meaning. She did not miss a step. Let the woman stew in her own juices. She had no right of judging her nor any of the people here. She would be accorded a fair trial the same as any other person.

Where had it all gone wrong?

The day before had started like any other; John taunting her and she withdrawn and ignoring him. Her silence hit a sore spot and John slammed her against the wall, hitting her several times in the stomach until she was bent over and heaving with pain. She had enough of his frequent thrashings and mistreatment.

Her stomach was bruised almost solid from his beating, and for most of the day, she managed to avoid him and his drunken temper. Finally, darkness came and John passed out on the bed underneath the quilt. He flopped over onto his back with his loud snore. Removing a small cast iron skillet from the stove, she moved quickly toward the bed.

Careful not to awaken him, she pulled the covers up tightly underneath his chin, then raised her nightgown up to her thighs before straddling his chest and sitting upon it with her legs pressed over his arms, holding them securely underneath the quilt. She jumped with his loud snore before she used the edge of the skillet against the side of his head, nudging him awake. She had to tap him several times before he awoke and stared groggily at her.

She lightly hit his forehead twice with the heavy iron skillet, emphasizing her warning, her voice low, harsh and filled with determination as he struggled to move. "If you hit me one more time, I will kill you by bashing your brains out. See how easy it is to capture you, John?"

She tapped his head a little harder with the skillet until he nodded his agreement. *"Do not ever touch me again!"* she growled warningly before she climbed out of bed.

The skillet banged loudly after she threw it back on top of the cast iron stove, barely glancing at him. He didn't move nor speak a word, only warily watched her.

She did not sleep that night, and after lunch when the weather seemed warmer, she left the house, anxiously wanting away from him. She grabbed two water buckets, arranged the handles over the ends of a carrying board and headed for the creek several hundred yards away. She had been so angry, she did not stop for her cloak. She could not face John again, not right now when her emotions were in turmoil. If he hit her one more time, she was terrified she really might kill him!

Needing water, she braved the freezing cold rain and walked toward the stream. The creek was down a steep hill and the wind at her back made the trip easy, though now the rain had turned into sleet that slashed across her face. The warmer weather had thawed the creek water enough to fill the buckets.

On the way back, the going was rougher with her fighting against the steadily rising wind that was now blowing snow against the filled buckets suspended on the yoke across her shoulders. Nearly at the top, she eased the buckets on the ground. The sudden snow did not stop her from perspiring with her exertions. She wiped her forehead before it froze on her brow, then placed her hands against the small of her aching back, stretching for relief from the heavy weight of water-filled buckets.

She heard a gunshot.

Leaving the buckets on the ground where she stood, she raced toward the house. The snowstorm had grown heavy and it quickly covered her tracks. She slid to a stop. All she remembered was John lying lifeless on the ground, his blood oozing out of a neck wound and squirts of blood around his prone body. She stepped closer, thinking she could help him when her foot twisted on something covered by the snow. She bent down, brushed the snow away and picked up the object. Her derringer! Where had it come from?

A strange gurgling sound came from John, and she shifted her gaze toward him. She must have gone into shock for she remembered very little afterwards.

With nothing but time on her hands, except when the law officers grilled her with questions, tiny particles of memory began trickling back.

"Crimson, are you alright?"

Crimson lifted her face, meeting azure-blue eyes. "Sure, Mr. Wade, I'm just lovely since being accused of killing John. We both know you are the one who killed him. I guess it suits your perverted whim for me being blamed for your crime. It gets rid of me without you dirtying your hands. You tried killing me twice before and failed. Now you've found a way that doesn't remotely point in your direction."

"You always think the worst of me, don't you, Crimson? Why do you blame me for Tom's death?" Landon's concern for the strangely controlled, young woman quickly edged at his anger. She had been a beautiful ghostly apparition, a wilting midnight rose standing alone on one side of the grave at the top of the hill and isolated from the groups of mourners who stood on the other sides with the preacher standing at the head. He fought his inclination of standing beside her so she would not be alone, but instead waited for her at the base of the hill. Now she stood before him like a wraith, accusing him of killing her husband.

"It should be easy enough to understand, Landon. I'm not stupid nor am I a murderer. It was very sly picking a snowy day and waiting until I left the house, then killing John. With the snow falling so heavily, there were no tracks. Ah, yes, very clever to double back and arrive only minutes after the posse arrived." The ice wrapped around her heart was cold as the winter wind whipping her cape around her. There was nothing left inside of her except the smothering unhappiness she had endured for the last two years. Men had built the wall around her heart—men who lied, cheated, stole and killed. They had all eradicated little bits of her, pieces which could never be replaced.

"Blame me if you must, Crimson. Tell the sheriff I killed Tom. Tell them all the things you have accused me of. You'll never be satisfied until you see me hanged and buried next to your husband. But let me warn you. You better prove your accusations."

Did she imagine the vibrating timbre of sorrow she heard in his voice? He spoke with such fury and sadness. She ran her icy hand across her eyes, wiping the sound away. He had no compassion, no love for anyone. He blamed all men for his childhood. "So, you did kill John."

"I admitted nothing, Crimson. I only said, accuse me if it will salvage your conscience. If you loved him so well, which surely you must have since you threatened to kill him if you found him with his mistress again, then point your finger at me." Landon watched her shiver, an uncontrollable gesture she could not stop. His fury at her accusation was tinged with his desire to comfort her. Damn her for the hard-headed woman she was. He could more readily accept her anger instead of this cold, unfeeling woman standing before him.

His eyes were the same color as a bright, cold winter sky, the nostrils of his broad nose flared whitely with his anger, she noticed. "I didn't love him. I didn't care whether he lived or died." Her plaintive spoken words frosted the air in a gray cloud.

Perhaps that's what upset her the most—this not caring. "Landon, God help me, I didn't care."

Landon could not stop himself from stepping closer and enfolding her into his embrace. Her mournful cry tore at the scarred strings of his own heart. She was stiff and unyielding, frozen as much on the outside as on the inside. "My God, Crimson, I thought you loved him. You were so jealous and I really thought you loved him."

He settled her head against his shoulder, feeling the quivers racking her body. "My midnight rose clothed in black with the glorious crimson hair, I will help you."

Crimson desperately wanted to lean on this strong man. But how could she when she knew he had killed John, and she was now facing false culpability for it? The heat of his body and his arms so securely wrapped around her brought the first faint flush of warmth which had disappeared days ago. An unfulfilled longing rushed through her, crying this man would mollify her, the man who was her nightmare and her pleasant dreams.

God, what is wrong with me? Where did I go wrong? Why am I so attracted to a man who wants me dead, who framed me for my husband's murder? So many unanswered questions, so many pieces of the puzzle refusing to fit comfortably together. Where would it all lead? Would she be hanged for a murder she did not commit?

With his arms wrapped around her, she could not think straight. His nearness always eliminated everything else from her mind except for him. Slowly, shamelessly, she lifted her arms, clinging to his comforting hardness, and the first tears since John's death, sparkled on her lashes.

"Who's the whore now, Mrs. Sullivan?"

Jenny's harsh, slurring voice spoke behind her. Crimson guiltily leaped away from Landon. She shook off his hand when he tried pulling her back. "Damn you! Damn you all!" she cried fiercely, pivoting on her heel and running the rest of the way back to town.

∽✦✦✦✦∽

"MRS. SULLIVAN, I'm Temple Houston. I'm the District Attorney for the 35th Judicial District of Texas. I will be your attorney."

"My name is Crimson. Please call me that." Crimson straightforwardly let the man know she did not want her name associated with being known as John's wife. Whatever happened, at least her marriage was behind her now.

"Please come in, Mr. Houston." She stepped back from the doorway and motioned him inside. It had been over a month since John's death, the most grueling month she had ever spent in her life.

She motioned him toward the table as she walked toward the stove. Picking up the coffee pot, she held it out toward him. "Coffee?"

"Yes, thank you."

After she poured two cups, she sat down one cup in front of him and motioned toward the sugar and cream containers on the table. Sipping her coffee, she studied him over the rim, watching him carefully through the steam. He was over six foot tall and a handsome young man with flowing, shoulder-length auburn hair. His gray eyes were sharp and intelligent. He looked too young to be an attorney, but he was probably a couple years older than she.

She almost smiled when observing his attire, wondering how lawyers usually dressed. He wore a tailored buckskin outfit, the trousers opened from the knee where his knee-high leather moccasins began, down to his feet. The pants were fringed with narrow ribbons of bright colors and matched the ribbons circulating the wide-brimmed sombrero adorned with a silver eagle, which he had laid on top of the table. A white-handled revolver was strapped around his waist. He was the son of the famed Sam Houston, defender and hero of Texas' fight for freedom from Mexico. "Did someone ask you to be my attorney or were you appointed by the courts?"

"I'm not at liberty in imparting that information, Mrs... ah...Crimson." His voice was deep and resonant. "All I can say is the same person who spoke to me also posted your bail."

Crimson shrugged dramatically. "I don't know why you'd wanna defend me. I've already been judged and condemned."

"The law says innocent until proven guilty." Temple studied the young woman in front of him. She was beautiful and resigned to a fate not yet determined, but the heart-shaped face held no traces of a cold-blooded murderer. If first impressions counted for anything, he would swear she was innocent. "Suppose you start from the beginning and tell me exactly what happened."

Chapter 28
Temple of Hope

CRIMSON covered her face with her hands and closed her burning eyes, feeling like she was in some kind of horrible nightmare and could not awaken. No matter how many times she tried forgetting or at least putting it behind her, the day kept repeatedly playing over in her mind, and she had hardly slept since it happened.

When she arrived in Tascosa with the posse, she had been blue with cold and in a deep state of shock. There was no jail for women, and the law decided they could not imprison her with male prisoners, and instead tied her to a support pole in the McMaster and Howard's General store. Several days later, they lodged her in the Exchange Hotel with a guard posted outside her door. They questioned her over and over for four days until bail had been posted, and she was allowed the freedom of leaving for home after the funeral.

Crimson rubbed at her temples, easing some of the headache away. If only Honeysuckle and Buck were not still up north, maybe they could have helped her. This way she did not know who her benefactor was.

Lifting dull, swollen green eyes, she began speaking, slowly at first, then it rushed out, a burden she happily placed upon someone else's capable shoulders.

"You told all this to the sheriff, and did he go back and check if the buckets were still near the stream?"

"Yes, but somebody must have gone back and moved them since they weren't there. The wind was blowing and it was snowing so hard by the time I reached John, the snow covered my tracks." She wiped her tired eyes, swiping at the terrible memories. "My God, they're blaming me! I did not kill John! I swear my life on it!"

"That's what we must prove, Crimson. The evidence is overwhelmingly against you. Your husband was killed with a derringer, the one bearing your initials, and you were holding it when the posse arrived." Temple's head drooped forward in deep thought. If she did not murder her husband, then it was a clever frameup. "It will not be easy since so many witnesses heard you threaten your husband and saw you shoot him."

"It was an accident. He grabbed the derringer and it went off," Crimson protested, earnestly capturing his gray eyes with hers, imparting the truth within them. "And besides, after the accident I dropped the derringer on the ground. I didn't have it anymore. Someone else must have picked it up later and killed John with it!"

"You're sure, Crimson?" At her affirmative nod, Temple Houston continued, "I'll speak with the people in Mobeetie and the ones who have moved to Tascosa to affirm if anyone witnessed seeing the derringer on the ground or if they saw someone pick it up. If they do, there should be no trouble having you acquitted, but to be safe, I wanna ask you some more questions."

"Alright, shoot." She placed her cup back on the table and blushed. "Wrong choice of words."

Temple smiled wryly. "I understand your marriage was rocky. Suppose you tell me about how you and John met, and about your marriage."

Like droplets of water, the words came out haltingly, then rushed out in a flood. Never had she told anyone the truth about her marriage. The only thing she left out was her last interaction with John and the iron skillet. No one would ever know about that incident unless she told them. After she finished, she glanced at Temple and saw his eyes snapping with anger.

"We may have a case there, Crimson. Justifiable homicide."

"I did not kill him!" she screamed, slamming her fists on the table, emphasizing her words. "No matter how many times he beat me, I never wanted him dead. Sure, I might have thought about it after he'd beaten me so bad at times I was unable to do anything for a week or more. Who wouldn't? But he was my husband for better or worse."

"I'm sorry. I did not mean it the way it sounded. You know it's going against you, especially if the prosecuting attorney finds out you married John knowing he was going under an assumed name. But if what you have told me about the derringer is true, maybe spousal abuse will not come up in court. However, in case we do have a trial, we will talk this over very carefully and be prepared." Temple hated he could not give her more hope. There was always the remote chance things would not work out as they planned. Before he left, he would check the grounds around her home. Maybe there were unsuspecting clues that were missing. Whether it was true or not about the derringer, he was inclined to believe her story.

He rose from the bench and picked up his hat, preparing to leave when she stopped him.

"Why was Sheriff Willingham and a posse here?"

Temple studied her for a moment, wondering why she did not know or if the happenings had somehow erased the posse's unlikely appearance from her mind. "Major Larner's Colt .45 and holster were found in a saloon girl's room. Faced with the possibility of being charged with murder, she confessed John's involvement."

"Jenny," Crimson put in the saloon girl's name. "She was John's hussy." She knew all this, but she wanted verification. Something about the whole thing puzzled her.

"Ah, yes, you reportedly had a run-in with her."

Crimson disdainfully shrugged it off. "What reason did John have for killing Major Larner?"

"That is something I haven't discovered yet. Even Jenny doesn't know."

"Mr. Houston, I think I know who killed my husband."

She hesitated and Temple gave her time to form her thoughts. From what she told him about John Sullivan, the man was not well-liked and probably more than one person had a motive for his demise.

Her hands wrapped around the coffee cup; the heat unable to penetrate the coldness enveloping her. She stared into the murky, black depths, wondering how to explain her suspicions. Slow bits had trickled back into her shocked awareness after the posse arrived until she began forming her own opinions.

Lifting her eyes, she slowly spoke, "I told you about Landon Wade and how he threatened John, but what I left out is, Landon wasn't with the posse. He arrived only moments afterwards. He would have had time to kill John and circled back around by the time the posse arrived."

"It's another possibility I will check into, Crimson. Please write down anything else you might remember and have forgotten. I'll be back in a few weeks." Temple placed the gray sombrero on his head and walked out of the sod.

Temple turned back around and added, "I've already arranged to have your court date set for early April." With a curt nod of his head, he walked away.

Crimson followed him, noticing he walked in short, nervous steps. She was placing her life in this man's hands. Did she trust him or any man? A fierce stab of self-preservation stiffened her spine. *I'll find out who murdered John one way or another!* Guilt sliced through her when she thought of how many times she had flirted with the ideal of John dying in Mobeetie, but feeling shamefaced about her wayward thoughts, she was determined not to pay for someone else's crime.

Watching Temple Houston ride off, a plan formulated in her mind. John had boasted about being the head of the syndicate, and what better place for garnishing information than working where the syndicate's primary control was headquartered. With law and order now in Mobeetie, the dregs of Feather Hill were driven toward Tascosa, the cowboy capital of the Panhandle, where there were rumors of the railroad that might be laid close by. The little place had grown with several stores, hotels, livery stables and gambling dens, which offered gaming rooms for faro, monte and poker. Gamblers, ladies of the evening and saloons had arrived in hordes in Lower Tascosa, appropriately known as Hog Town.

Walking back inside, she noticed John's personal effects still lay on the bed where she had thrown them. The belongings he had on him had been delivered after his coroner's examination. She could not force herself to sleep in the bed where she had only known pain and humiliation. Instead, she still slept on a pallet in front of the fire.

Morbid curiosity pulled her toward them. Sitting on the edge of the bed, she ran her fingers over the items: a pocketknife, several gold eagle coins, a tobacco pouch, cigarette papers and matches. She kept going back over the items, strangely feeling something was missing. Confusion poured over her until she drew back her hand and swept the items off onto the floor.

Lying on the bed, her arm covering her eyes, pictures of John came unbidden of their *supposed* honeymoon. Her hands clenched into fists, remembering the sting the first time he had hit her, and her cheeks tingled with the memory.

Rising with a startled groan, she remembered what was missing. John's pocket watch! The watch he so carefully kept her from studying too closely—the watch with the strange crouching mountain lion with emerald eyes and set in ornate gold.

✿

CRIMSON cursed her stiff, clumsy fingers. She was not very adept at sewing, but she ruthlessly continued working on finishing two dresses before she could put her plan into action. With the material across her lap, she left the needle dangling, placing her hands against the small of her back and stretched, easing the tension.

A slight shudder passed through her with the gusting, icy wind finding places in the sod house that crept through tiny cracks with chilling fingers. She carefully laid the dress on top of the table and put another batch of dried cow patties on the fire. Taking her shawl from the nail near the door, she wrapped it around her shoulders and stepped outside. There was a heaviness in the air. The blue skies of this morning had turned a leaden gray and white patches of snow dotted the brown land from the previous snow. With the winter starting so early this year, she knew it would be a very cold and snowy winter.

When the first flakes fell, she turned and went back inside. Shivering, she rubbed at her tired eyes, then picked up her sewing, but soon laid it on the tabletop and laid her head on her arms.

Crimson moaned against the icy shafts blowing through the cabin like the breath of Old Man North stirring the heavy tresses

284

falling down her back. Still groggy, she lifted her head from her arms and immediately spied the reason for the sudden draft. A man bundled up in a heavy buffalo coat, his hat and clothing a frozen mass of white, forced the door close behind him. Jumping upright, she turned, lunging for the rifle hanging over the fireplace when the man spoke.

"I won't harm you, Crimson."

She would know that voice anywhere. Slowly turning back around, she gazed at the white, snow-covered face and the sky-blue eyes still haunting her dreams night after night. "Landon, what are you doing here?"

"I was caught in the blizzard blowing outside. Do you mind?" He motioned toward the cheerfully glowing fire.

"Of course not." Reminded of his frozen state, she waited for him to pass, then helped him out of his heavy gloves, coat and hat, spreading them over the bench closest to the fire. "You need out of those clothes or you'll be sick. I'll get you some of John's."

Landon held his blue-appearing hands toward the fire, his face grimacing with the piercing tingles shooting through them with warmth slowly penetrating. He turned his head, watching Crimson rummage through a chest and collecting articles of clothing. She seemed unaware she only wore a white cotton nightgown and a pair of carpet slippers. The wild tresses of her auburn hair hung down her back, reflecting the red firelight. The coal oil lantern sitting on the table highlighted her lithe form underneath.

She turned and met the sudden blaze of his eyes, her pale ivory cheeks turning a dusky pink. Hastily draping the clothes over her arm, she closed the lid with a bang, discomforted with the heat of his gaze.

Taking the proffered clothes, he smiled crookedly when her cheeks turned pink and she lowered her head. The dusky pink on her cheeks deepening, she stumbled over her words, "I…I'll pour you some…some… coffee while you change."

Flustered over his sudden appearance, the sharp retorts she might have uttered were stunned inside of her. The rustle of clothing and the sizzle of snow droplets hitting the fire left her uneasy, embarrassed, but strangely compelled to turn her head and watch him undress. Instead, she poured two cups of steaming coffee, then dished out a bowl of stew. Hearing the bench drawn from underneath the table, she turned, and placed the coffee, stew, a plate of freshly baked bread and a crock of butter in front of him.

"Thank you, Crimson. You don't know how much I appreciate this. Why don't you join me?" He patted the place beside him on the bench.

Steadily avoiding his eyes, she sharply remembered the last time she saw him in Tascosa where he had held her so comfortingly, but briefly against him. Instead of taking the place he indicated, she sat in front of him on the opposite end of the bench where one end was turned closer to the fire and held his wet clothing. She drew in a shuddering breath, calming the upheaval of her nerves, and faced him.

With his strong hands bearing clean fingernails wrapped around the steaming cup, he watched her. "Aren't you eating?"

She shook her head, flipping back the fallen lock slipping over her eye. "No, I've already eaten."

The silence lengthening between them, she watched Landon devour the stew. There were so many questions, so many stinging things fluttering around her lips, but they were lodged in her throat, refusing to be said. She felt like a dummy, warily watching him.

He lifted his light blue eyes and raised his eyebrow mockingly, silently laughing when she blushed. "I've never seen you so speechless before, little spy. Cat got your tongue? Or are you curbing your acid tongue?"

His veiled sarcasm stung her into speaking. "Why are you here?"

"I told you."

She waved away his explanation. "Yes, yes, you were caught in a blizzard, but why did you come here, here of all places?"

"It was the closest," he stated matter-of-factly. "Ah, Crimson, my little midnight rose..."

Crimson cut through his softly spoken words. "Don't! Don't, Landon. For God's sake, don't."

Her bottom lip trembled, and she caught it with strong white teeth, sparkling moistness brightening the twin green pools in her face. Not now! she silently screamed. Not now of all times would she allow one of her unexplained crying fits. The confused core of her cried out for tenderness, but not from him, not from her enemy who held the strange power that melted the coldest heart within her.

Her hands clenching in her lap, she fought against herself, fought her desire of running to him and melting into his arms. Was she crazy? He was a thief, a liar, a murderer, and he had framed her for the murder of her husband. Was she some kind of deviant wanting him still? She turned her head and caught back a sob, fighting against these lonely, confusing sensations attacking her. Without focusing, she stared at the blurred images of the material on the table.

The bench scrapped loudly against the hardpacked, dirt floor; she did not look up. She felt him hovering over her like a phantom of blackness, the heat from his body shimmering over her. His very nearness sent a tremor through every nerve ending, a tremor of desire, confusion and hurt.

Landon stared down at the huddled, shrinking form perched at the end of the bench in front of him, thinking she resembled a lost little girl. He felt some of her pain and sympathized with her, for it corresponded with what he had felt for years. He often wondered about his attraction toward her. Her fiery temper? The loving care she gave her family? Her misplaced devotion and loyalty for her husband? Or like now when she reminded him of a stray puppy searching for someone ready to receive the ample love she so desperately wanted to share?

Kneeling beside her, he took her tightly held hands in one of his and tilted her face upward with the tip of his finger underneath her chin. "Crimson Rose, I did not kill your husband." He spoke each word distinctively, individually, making sure she understood the full impact of his words.

She drew in a shuddering breath, lost in the depths of calm, sky-dyed eyes. How many times had she wanted to believe him and then found out he told one more lie, and everything always pointed at him? "Why should I believe you?"

"I've never lied to you."

"Haven't you? All you ever told me has been lies," she spat, dismayed by the tears trickling down her cheeks.

Clutching her hand almost painfully, a muscle jumped in his jaw while his mouth drew into a tight line. "Maybe I'm being framed the same as you. Have you thought of that? My God, Crimson, if I wanted to kill you, I had numerous opportunities. Why do you persist in thinking it's me? Why?"

She trembled at the fierceness of his voice, the hard-edged, wounded sound. She tried drawing her hands away, but his hand tightened around hers, refusing. "Isn't it obvious? You are always around when I've been shot at. You're always there! Only you would have a motive."

Landon released a heavy sigh, the fervid glaze in his eyes unabated. "Damnit, Crimson, why in the hell are you so damned hardheaded? If I wanna kill you, I'd do it right now."

He felt her shrink away from him, which angered him more. "No, Crimson, enough is enough. I wanna help you. I too wanna find out who the killer is. Sure, I would have killed Tom given the right opportunity but not in the manner he died, but man-to-man, face-to-face."

Seeing the disbelief on her face, wounded him, but he would coax her into believing him. Tangling his hand in the untamed mass of hair, he pulled her face toward his and captured her unyielding moist mouth, grinding his lips against hers, then unexpectantly softened his kiss, molding the soft morsels with his until the firm lines of her mouth relaxed.

Releasing her hand, he gave into the temptation and entwined both his hands in the silken strands of her wild mane, holding her head while he kissed her. The vanilla she wore teased his senses, wiping all coherent thoughts away except for her nearness. She relaxed, moving her hands toward his shoulders until she ran her fingers through the back of his hair, giving into the turbulent sensations spreading over them both. Rising, he pulled her upright with him, enfolding her limp form and fitting her soft curves snuggly against him.

He covered her face with featherlight kisses across her cheek and her shell-shaped ear. "God, Crimson, you haunt my dreams," he moaned softly, massaging her slender shoulders. He had not felt this strongly about a woman since Sun-is-Setting. Capturing the pouting, swollen lips with his, he picked her up into his arms and walked toward the bed, then placed her gently on top of the covers.

Clinging onto his neck, she whimpered against his mouth, protesting against his intentions. The chaos of the last two years of her life tumbled away, leaving her helpless against the potent powers of this diversified man. He was hard and unyielding, yet she had seen him cry, the tears running like blood down his copper cheeks while singing during the lowering sun. He was tender and hard, confused and determined, and she could no more refuse him his desire than she could order the moon from following the sun. Each time he touched her, everything flew from her brain except for him, the feel, the musky scent all his own, his vibrating, sensual voice, only him.

But as he laid her upon the straw-stuffed mattress, she shuddered when John's taunting face rose before her. "No, not here. I sleep on a pall..."

Laying down beside her, he did not let her finish and drew her back into his embrace, capturing her mobile mouth once again, effectively cutting off her protest. He had waited so long and wanted her so badly, his fingertips trembled caressing her satiny cheek before entwining themselves again into her fiery hair.

All her imaginations and disturbing dreams could not compare with what she felt now with the tip of his tongue outlining the curve of her lips and tangling with hers, drawing her inner sweetness unto himself, his hands fondling her shoulders, then her breasts. The peaks rose against the palm of his hand and sharpened the intensity racing through her veins.

Her breathing quickening with her shallow breaths, he undid the buttons at the front of her nightgown and drew the material aside, baring her delicious fruit for his questing mouth. A low moan escaping her, he took the stiffened nub, suckling, his tongue making teasing circles, evoking her into greater heights. Her fingers weaved through his raven black hair, holding him motionless, silently begging him to make her complete once again.

Panting moans and soft cries rose above the crackling and sizzling fire, her blood pounding in her ears deafening the blizzard raging outside. Fingers of fire lashed at her lower belly, centering between her legs, and she rolled her hips closer toward his.

Chapter 29
Tangles of Life

LANDON pulled his mouth free from the delectable tidbit and kissed the wild pulse beating at her throat, his voice coming out harsh and breathless. "I feel like a moth attracted to your flame. Every time I'm near you my wings are singed a little bit more until one day, I won't fly away."

Crimson traced his face with her fingertips, the high cheekbones, the strong chin, lingering a moment before moving over his full lips, then over the heavy, straight black eyebrows and the long, thick lashes of his eyes. "Do you wanna fly away?"

His crooked grin was endearing, self-mocking. "Would it do me any good to stay? Will you ever believe me?" The puzzlement crossing her face was not the answer he wanted.

"I don't know. There's so much happening." Her eyes glistened with unshed tears while her body begged for his tender administration. She wanted to believe him, had always wanted to, but circumstances kept implying his guilt, preventing her from fully trusting him.

He tenderly wiped the stray tear falling down her cheek, almost groaning out loud with the symbol of her confusion. "When will Buck and Honeysuckle be back?"

Crimson did not question how he knew they were gone. Gossip traveled fast. "I don't know. They were gonna stop by Cotton and

Red's ranch in Wyoming before coming back home. Probably around spring roundup."

Capturing her chin with his hand, he kissed the corners of her mouth before staring straight into her eyes. "When they get back, you and I are gonna speak with Buck. He will tell you the truth about me. However, the first court week is early spring before the roundups. Let's hope they make it back before then."

She nodded, unable to think beyond this moment. "I'll never completely trust you until we do."

He released a heavy sigh, "I know," before capturing her lips once again.

Maneuvering her heavy cotton nightgown over her head and throwing it at the end of the bed, he quickly slid out of his borrowed clothes. The heat of his body warmed her, toasting her hotter than the fire burning cheerfully on the other side of the room. His hands and mouth loved her, seeking out hidden spots, bringing intense pleasure rippling like the blowing snow outside, the storm inside matching the intensity of the blizzard surrounding them in a cocoon of solitude and warmth.

She ran her hands along the smooth, sinewy back, feeling the shape of his shoulder blades and the ridges of tendons. He was bringing back the intense sensations she had experienced with him before her marriage with John, coaxing her into a pleasant lull of senses. She followed the dictate of her hands, letting them wander over the silken flesh of his smooth chest and the hardened crest of his nipples.

He coaxed her higher and higher into an almost forgotten realm of sensuality, teasing her flesh with such powerful emotions, she felt any second now she would melt completely into him, becoming one for all times. His hardness pressed against her thigh like a searing rod, branding her as his.

Her fingers lingered on the heated flesh of his chest before lowering toward the puckered scar on his side. Trembling, she moved her hand downward and captured the essence of him. He moaned when she tightened her hold and moved up and down the hardened shaft.

Her breath caught in her throat as he twined his fingers in the curly mass of hair covering her womanhood, a wayward finger touching the soft folds tauntingly before stroking the pouting flesh. When he touched the throbbing center, a cry emitted from her and her hips rose against his hands. She opened up for him like a morning rose unfolding its petals and welcoming the summer warmth while capturing the morning dew. Her lips trembled, her hips quivered under his searching hands until she released her hold on his manhood and pulled him on top of her.

"Please, please," she moaned, rolling waves of desire sweeping over her. "Make love to me."

Landon released the dusky red crest and positioned himself at the entrance of her being. Her fingernails dug into the flesh of his back, the pain mingling with pleasure. Entering the moist center, he shoved home, riding her slowly, then picking up speed and galloping them both toward fulfillment. Her moans and sharp cries matching his own, they rode toward the center of the sun, erupting in blinding lights of heat and pleasure so intense they exploded into tiny fragments before falling slowly back to earth.

Their breathing ragged and shallow, Landon kissed her closed eyelids and moved down to the wonderment of her kiss-swollen lips. A fine sheen of perspiration dotted her upper lip and glossed their naked bodies. He lay beside her, pulling her close against him, holding onto her as if he let her go, she would disappear once again into his dreams. He kissed her cheek and her lids fluttered open, her lips curving into a smile.

"Thank you for showing me what it is to be a whole woman again," Crimson sighed softly, her eyes heavy-lidded with sated prurience.

"Thank you? What an odd thing to say." He caressed her cheek, his heavily lashed eyes narrowed in amusement. "If I make love to you over and over again, will you still thank me?"

He tickled her ribcage, and she giggled helplessly, enhancing the marvelous thing they had just shared. The tangy, salty, musky smell of their lovemaking saturated the small sod and mingled with the unique aroma of cow patty-fueled fire.

Landon nuzzled her neck, licking the salty moistness of her skin, delighting in this soft purring kitten she'd become within his arms and who seemed intent on making love all night.

She gave into her earlier yearning and dropped her hand again between his thighs, taking hold of his manhood still wet with their lovemaking. He sharply drew in his breath, hardening with her touch, a feat he had not thought possible so soon afterward. Her fingers were soft and gentle, coaxing a rise with firmness, her husky voice prompting him to teach her the fine arts of love.

"Love me, Landon. Teach me to please you. Show me, make me believe everything is perfect for a little while."

◝◟◉◜◟◝◉◞◟◝

CRIMSON slowly opened her eyes, a sigh of contentment passing her lips. The smoldering embers lit the room in a faint red glow. The wind whistled eerily through the sod, finding places of sneaking in and chilling the room while she lay toasty warm in Landon's arms. She gently, so as not to awaken him, turned and watched him, memorizing his face all over again. Sleep gentled the tense lines, giving him a boyish appearance with his long, sooty lashes lying like shadows upon his upper cheeks and his mouth slightly open.

Seeing him relaxed in sleep, it was hard believing he could kill with as much compunction as killing a coyote. But he could, she reminded herself. Then why was she so unafraid in his arms, so content? Everything was right between them with the wildly blowing blizzard wrapping them in a world of their own. John had been dead for less than two months, and oddly, she felt no guilt for what she and Landon shared last night.

Placing a light kiss on his mouth, she smiled when his eyes fluttered open. Focusing on her sleep-softened face, his own blazed with renewed hunger. Her fiery auburn hair was tangled underneath his head and wrapped around her slender shoulders in an interlacing curtain. Her lips were full and moist, begging to be kissed. Entangling his fingers in the hair at the back of her head, he pulled her forward and captured them, molding them with his own, teasing her inner mouth with his tongue. Her arms slipped around his shoulders, tracing the patterns along his back and down toward muscular tight buttocks, pulling him closer and feeling him hard against the softness of her stomach.

Heated blood rushed through her veins, tingling just underneath

293

the surface as he resurrected her need for him again. His hands were everywhere, bringing a fiery response rushing through every pore of her being. He filled a craving, a burning need plaguing her from her first awareness of being a woman, her first awareness when she spied him bathing in the cold stream.

Landon was tender and loving, teaching her the full benefits of being a woman and showing her how to please him until they both burst into a brilliant world of total release. Cuddled within his arms, the fine sheen of sweat cooling with the icy fingers of the wind blowing through the cracks of the sod, she was whole, languishing in contentment. With his arm wrapped around her shoulders, her head tucked against his chest, she snuggled closer, fingering the puckered scar on his right side. "How did you get this?"

"From a raid into Mexico. I ran into a blade meant for my friend, Flies-Like-an-Eagle."

She acknowledged his bravery and the simplicity he told it without asking more questions, but she also wanted to know more about him. His whole life after he left Salina, Kansas was wrapped in mystery. "Do you wish you were still with them? The Indians?"

"Yes." His answer was short and simple, relaying more in one little word than most men could have explained in a whole sentence.

"Why did you leave?"

Turning his head so he could look into her eyes, he wondered if he should tell her. He tried pushing his past at the back of his memories, wanting to forget and live one day at a time. The sincerity in her emerald eyes gave him courage, and in simple words, he explained his past, something he had never told anyone about his life with the Kiowas and Sun-is-Setting.

After he finished telling her the whole story, he turned toward her, surprised by the tear running down her cheek. In awe, he captured the silvery droplet with his index finger and licked the saltiness. "Why do you cry?"

"It's so touchingly sad. You must have loved her very much." She stroked his jaw, conveying her sorrow before bringing her mouth against his, kissing away some of his hurt.

He accepted her kiss only for a few seconds before every muscle in his body grew taut. With a furious flip of the covers, he was out of bed and threw on his dried clothes.

Staring at him, her mouth opened in surprise and confusion, she too rose from the bed and began dressing. "What's the matter? Did I do something wrong?"

"Nothing." His voice was short and clipped, carrying a hint of anger. "I'm just hungry," he added a bit more softly.

"You have a funny way of showing it," she grumbled, knowing full well it was not the reason for his hasty departure from her bed.

An angry tick working in his jaw, Landon built up the fire. How could he explain talking about himself and Sun-is-Setting reminded him of his vow of never getting too close to another woman? He had already become too involved with her, cared too much and he was afraid, deathly afraid, if it transcended any further, he would be condemning her to death. But damn it, he did care, cared more for this fiery-haired, fiery-tempered young woman than he should. He should have walked away from her long ago, but something intangible, some fine, silken web kept pulling him back.

He heard her slam the pots and pans around the stove, clearly conveying her own fury. Damn! he thought dryly, chucking another dried cow patty into the fire. A perfect end to a perfect night, he sardonically pondered.

His thoughts in turmoil, he sat at the table, torn apart by wanting to stay and knowing he should leave. She needed his protection against outside forces and from himself. He stared glumly at the black material on the table while he absently fingered it. It took a few moments for him to realize it was a dress she was making, and when he did, his temper exploded. He grabbed the material and sprang from his seat, reaching her in one giant stride. Grabbing her arm, he swung her around, holding the dress up with one hand and shaking it in her face. "What in the hell is this?"

"A dress," she stated calmly, her insides shaking and her heart pounding so loudly she was afraid he could hear it.

"That's not what I meant, and you know it. At first, I thought you were making a dress for mourning, but no damned mourning dress is cut this low. What are you planning, Crimson?" He grabbed her upper arms, his face awash with barely controlled anger.

"Let me go!" Crimson managed through clenched teeth.

"Not until you answer me. What are you planning?" The stubborn set of her uplifted chin infuriated him and his fingers cut a little deeper into the tender flesh of her arms. Landon had a vague idea of what she was intending, making him more determined to find out the truth.

The coldness of his eyes pierced through her like icicles, and she cringed. She hated him, she reminded herself, then why did she melt into his arms with his first touch? She pulled back, breaking his hold. "Why should I tell you? I can't trust you, Landon. I'll never be able to trust you. Though we had sex, it doesn't give you the right to question me."

"Sex? You call what we shared together last night just sex?" he asked in a low, almost growling voice.

"Yes. What would you call it?"

"Making love."

"Making love," she mocked him, lashing out and suppressing her love for him. She realized loving him would only end up lacerating her heart, and she did not want the pain—the constant replaying of her unreachable dreams. She must deny this love! "There is no love between us. So how can you call it making love?"

"You're an infuriating, stubborn woman, Crimson. If you wanna call what we shared together sex, then so be it. But let's not digress from the subject. What are you planning?" he inquired, furious she somehow, with her simple statement, dirtied what they had shared together. He imagined there was more between them than just sex, though he cried out against those emotions.

"It's none of your business, Landon. We might have slept together, but that doesn't make me trust you," she angrily spat, more infuriated with herself than she could ever be with him.

He heavily sighed and ran his fingers through his hair, rumpling his straight black mane. He locked eyes with her. "You have no one else who you can trust right now except me, Crimson. Are you planning on becoming a dancehall or saloon girl?" With her not answering, he softly placed his hands on her forearms, asking, "Are you?"

She shook his hands away, placing her clenched fists on her hips, screaming, "Yes! Yes! I will not be hanged for something I didn't do! And it's the only way I can find out who killed John." There, she said it. Let him do what he wanted with the knowledge.

"No!" His harshly shouted word had a final ring to it.

"You can't stop me, Landon. I will find out who killed John or bust a gut trying. Even you think I killed him. I saw it in your eyes. Well, I didn't kill him, but I will find out who did."

A rush of guilt flooding through him, Landon dropped his hands at his side. He turned and stared into the dancing fire, his voice coming out strained and guilt-ridden. "You're right. At first, I did think you killed him, but there was something wrong with it all. Everything was too pat, too perfect."

Turning back around, he wanted to pull her into his arms, but realized it would be a mistake. "After you were taken in and gave your account of what happened, I believed you. The sheriff and a deputy came back out here and checked around, especially for those water buckets you said you left on the hill near the creek. The buckets weren't there—they were outside by the door."

He motioned with his hand toward the wall near the door. "I could have sworn when I came in here and grabbed a quilt before the sheriff took you in, those buckets had not been there. Something kept nagging at me, kept pestering me like a blue heel fly in springtime about what I'd seen. It took me several days before I figured out what it was. At Mobeetie, after you had shot Tom." He emphasized Tom, silently demanding her to call him by his real name, not John.

"At first, I thought when you bent down, you had picked up the derringer before you ran away, then a glint caught my eye. When I looked at the ground, I spied your derringer lying there. Instead of immediately picking it up, I watched you. After you disappeared around the building, I went back and the derringer was gone. I didn't think much about it then. In fact, I completely forgot about it. When I remembered it, I knew for certain you had not killed Tom."

"You could've picked up the derringer and killed John with it. You had ample chance and opportunity. You arrived a few minutes after the posse, so why should I believe you?" She glared her accusation, her distrust of him coming back with full force. "It was all your fault the confrontation between John and me took place anyway."

A flash of repentance crossed his face before he schooled it back into his normal blank lines. "Yes, it is, Crimson. I regretted it from the beginning, but you were so jealous, so protective over him. I was forcing you to see what type of person he really was. I asked what you were searching for, and you said John, so I only directed you to him. If I had known what would happen beforehand, I would have never done it."

"Your apology is too late, if an apology it is. If it hadn't been for you, I wouldn't be in this fix in the first place. Landon, I'm scared. I've never been so scared in my life. I can be hanged or imprisoned, and I won't go! I'd rather take my own life instead. That's why it's so important I find out who killed him." She instinctively raised her hand and cupped the base of her throat already feeling the noose slowly tightening around it. She already had a good indication of what being hung felt like after John strangled her.

The frightened tremor of her voice tore through him sharper than the icy fingers of the north wind slipping through the crevices of the sod house. "I swear on my honor you won't hang, Crimson, but you cannot endanger your trial. Temple Houston is the best lawyer in these parts, and if anyone can prove your innocence, he can."

"How do you know who my lawyer is? I never mentioned him." There was something in his voice, the self-mocking, half smile lifting his grim lips making her more suspicious. "Answer me," she ground out between clenched teeth.

He broke their eye contact and glanced at a spot above her head. He had inadvertently given away something he had meant never to tell her. "I spoke with him."

"You? But why? Even you thought I killed him." She stared at him in astonishment.

"Yes, at first when I spoke to him, but I knew if anyone could get you off, it was him. I tried to hire him, but he's the District Attorney and was appointed as your lawyer. There was no one else here helping you since your family is not here." He met her eyes again, impressing his sincerity upon her. "Tom deserved dying no matter who killed him. I know now you didn't do it, and I didn't, but it leaves any number of people who could have picked up your derringer. Think, Crimson. Who else was there? Who else had a reason of wanting him dead?"

"I don't know. John..."

"Tom, Crimson," Landon interrupted harshly. "Call him by his real name."

"Fine. Tom. Tom mocked me about him being the syndicate boss, so it would leave the door wide open to any number of people. Harvey threatened to kill him too, but it was in the heat of anger. Tom and Harvey have always been best friends. They grew up together." She rubbed at her eyes, picturing who was present that day. Many people had gathered around them, some she knew, some she did not.

"Speaking of Harvey, where is he?" Landon looked around the room like he was hiding somewhere within the sod.

Chapter 30
Sex Education

"I DON'T know. I hadn't seen or heard from him since the day he threatened Tom. He's probably gone on one of his numerous business ventures, any which would have him gone for months at a time. But I really don't think Harvey would of killed him." Crimson's eyes grew crystal hard, remembering another incident in Mobeetie. Pointing her finger accusingly at Landon, she ground out, "You nearly cost me my life by telling Tom about the day we were interrupted by the bobcat."

"No, Crimson. I didn't tell Tom or anyone else about our moment." Why was everything falling back on him? How could he impress her to trust him? Who else would know what almost happened between them, and why were they framing him? There were too many unanswered questions, and he would find the answers, but not at the expense of letting her compromise herself before the trial.

He gently grasped her shoulder, lifting her chin with a finger and looking into her eyes. "Promise me, Crimson, you will not do anything foolish. Promise me you will not go to Hog Town or any of the lower parts of Mobeetie or Tascosa."

"I can't promise you, Landon. I must find out who killed Tom." Her voice was soft, low but filled with determination.

"Dammit, Crimson! Will you endanger everything? Let me and

Temple Houston find out who killed him. We're working on something now that will possibly guarantee your freedom. Don't put everything in jeopardy by doing something foolish such as working in Hog Town. Your trial is in a little over two months, the first full week of April. Promise me, Crimson, and I promise you will not pay for Tom's killing."

She searched his eyes. Something in them and the tone of his voice prompted her belief in him. "Alright, Landon. I promise I won't do anything until after the trial."

Releasing her shoulders, only partially satisfied with her answer, her suspicious voice stopped him from moving away.

"What are ya'll planning?"

He avoided her eyes. How could he tell her he was playing on a bet Tom was wanted in several states, and they planned if they could not find out who the real murderer was, to prove she had committed justifiable homicide? She would never forgive him if the charges were dropped this way, and there was always the question of why he had not come forward before now knowing Tom was wanted by the army. He did not know why he waited so long except there was no proof. All the wanted posters had been burned in the fort fire. "Just some hunches."

"What kind?" She watched an impenetrable mask slide over his face and knew he was hiding something. "Did it have something to do with him killing Major Larner?" He gave her a curt nod. "What reason would Tom have for killing Major Larner?"

"That's what we're trying to find out." Whether she was satisfied with his answer didn't matter for he would say no more. He grabbed her hand and gently sat her beside him on the bench. "We have something else to worry about. If it comes out you married Tom knowing he was going under the assumed name of John Sullivan, your marriage will become null and void, and it's gonna look bad for you."

She blanched, a sinking feeling beginning in the pit of her stomach. In a little girl's voice, she asked, "But what can I do? Now when the women pass me, they pull their skirts away or cross the street like I carry a plague."

"I don't have a ready answer for you. Why did you marry him?" He squeezed her hand in reassurance.

"He lied! He lied about Jenny!" In a halting voice, she told him Tom's story about being wrongly accused of murder in Illinois. She did not tell him the real reason for marrying Tom—she was afraid of him, Landon Wade, the only man she loved.

After she finished, he pulled her into his arms and planted a light kiss on her forehead. "For all your fiery emotions and knowledge, you're still a gullible little girl, but let's hope it works out in your favor." He entwined his fingers in her hair, holding her head against his shoulder while staring sightlessly at the far wall. Her information was another clue he would work with Temple Houston in finding any information, warrant or knowledge about the ordeal, if true. He just hoped it all panned out before the trial. If it did not, all could be lost. The information and proof they wanted traveled slowly, and he hoped it came back quick enough so she would be acquitted for Tom Martin's murder.

The blizzard's force was weakening and blew itself out by midnight, wrapping them in its sparkling whiteness. It resembled daylight outside with the full moon reflecting on the high drifted snow. There was an uneasy truce between them, each wondering what the other was planning after they parted company.

It took several days before he could push the door open and feed the animals. By the time he reentered the sod, he was covered with snow. She helped him undress, but instead of giving him dry clothing, she wrapped a quilt around his shoulders and backstepped him toward the bed. With him cuddled underneath the quilt, she slipped her nightgown and carpet slippers off, and joined him. With his freezing form against hers, she shivered and her nipples drew taut. "Lovemaking or sex, I will always want you."

"So much you'll let me put my cold feet between your thighs?" Landon growled, flipping Crimson over on her side and turning his back toward her.

"Yes," she murmured, then drew in a sharp breath when he angled his feet between her thighs, wiggling a heel against the bush between her legs.

"Landon!" she squealed, moving away.

"Shush. Warm my feet, then warm the rest of me, little spy, so we can take a trip or two back to heaven," he teased, massaging his heel against the top of her thighs.

With a giggle, she moved her thighs apart, giving him better access. He smiled while moving a big toe upward and heard her soft intake of breath. "Have I found a new way of making you want me? You are already wet."

"Hurry and warm your feet. There are other places I want warmed up."

With a chuckle, he moved his feet away and turned around, spooning her back, his hand searching for the place between her legs. "Like this?

"Humm…exactly."

≪∞≫

CUDDLED against Landon with his arm around her shoulder, Crimson glanced once at the dying fire while lightly racking her fingertips across his chest and stomach. Her voice low, she timidly asked, "Can I ask you some personal questions?"

"How personal?" He caressed her shoulder.

"Not so much personal for you. Just some questions about something that's confusing me."

"What kind of questions?"

"It's about sex. No one has ever talked about sex or allows questions, so I am confused," she whispered, blushing.

Landon turned on his side, keeping her close against him, then brushed stray tendrils of hair from her face before meeting her eyes. "You can ask me anything and not be embarrassed about it. If I don't know the answer, I'll tell you."

Releasing a sigh, she closed her eyes before opening them again, but could not meet his. "Can…uh…can two men have sex together?"

His arms tightened around her as he glanced at her with surprise. "Yes. Are you wondering how or only wanna know if it is possible?"

"Not how, please no, not that! However, can you explain a little about it? And if men like sex with each other, can they also like sex with a woman?" She brought shocked, curious eyes up to his, her blush deepening. With his deep sigh and the tightening of his body against her, she wondered if he would answer. Time seemed to stop as she waited.

Taking another deep breath, Landon brushed his fingers against her cheek. "Perhaps you need to understand something about a normal man. From the time they enter puberty until probably death…well let me rephrase that. I believe males are fascinated with their little peepees the day they are born, and when they get older they think a lot about sex. A lot!" he emphasized, smiling as her fingertips traced down the center of his chest to his belly button, then along the strip of hair leading downward. With the immediate hardening of his shaft, he softly chuckled. "As I was saying, men think about sex most of the time, I think."

He felt her smile while her fingertips skipped around his erection and slipped between his legs, exploring his hairy sac, and he elicited a soft moan.

"Go on," she crooned, enjoying the feel of the wrinkled sac around the twin balls and how the sac drew up with each of her caresses.

'Yes, men can have sex with other men and women."

"But why?"

Landon chuckled, enjoying her exploration of his body and her small, soft hand cupping his shaft. Her slow, firm movement up and down his rod was enough to distract him from answering her question. He lay on his back and opened his legs further, giving her better access. "If you are trying to sidetrack me, you're doing a great job."

"I thought it might make it easier for you. I'm curious how some things work. It would help if someone would answer my questions about sex instead of acting like it's horrible and embarrassing."

He lifted his head and kissed the top of her head. "Oh, I'll gladly answer your questions, but afterwards, I will ravish you."

"Promises, promises," she giggled.

With a slight chuckle, he tried ignoring her hand playing upon his body. "There are few good women who live in the west, and they are usually married women, except those women sometimes have a grown daughter or two living with her. The others are considered soil doves who have sex with men and get paid for it. These are not the type of women men will marry. The problem is, men cannot make it to a brothel every day or once a month and pay for sex. Most likely, it's months before a man can pay for a prostitute. Most men desire lots of sex since that is the subject most of us think about. The more sex, the better. A female partner is rarely available, so some men will occasionally have sex with other men. You probably know that men have get-togethers for dancing and drinking when no women are available. Some men will dress up like a woman or put some type of ribbon on his arm indicating he will be the female partner, and some make it known he will have sex with another man."

She nodded against his shoulder, indicating she understood. She marveled at his hardness in her hand, especially the iron stiffness and smoothness of his skin. She slipped her fingertip over the slit on top of the bulbous head, a drop of precum wetting her finger. With his sudden intake of breath, his hips lifted with her coaxing, giving her a power she was only now understanding.

"There are men who travel in couples. These men are lovers, and they move from ranch to ranch after the cattle drives to hide their preference, usually after the other men catch them in their indiscretion and belittle or abuse them. That's the best way I can describe it without going into detail. Now, what has brought on these questions?"

She stopped moving her hand, a blush flushing her face and neck. "I heard a conversation between two men who thought I was asleep."

"And who and what was said?" he prompted, his body tensing. "And why were you asleep with two men?"

Confusion lifting her brow, she sharply glanced at him. "Harvey came one night when John and I were asleep. John got up and I pretended I was still asleep. Anyway, I heard them whispering. When Harvey was about to leave, John, I mean Tom, told Harvey he needed and missed his ass and mouth. He made him go with him to the barn. He said he hated my ass."

He drew back and stared down at her face. "When was this?"

"Before court week. John, er Tom, we weren't getting along then." She stopped her hand's movement on his shaft and met his eyes, her blush deepening. "Have…have you ever had sex with a man?"

Bursting out laughing, he pulled her tighter into his arms and squeezed her, patting her rear end. "No, Crimson, never. And I love your ass. I'd take it over anybody's. Besides, my right hand does come in handy every now and then when no woman is available."

He cupped one of her plump nether cheeks and caressed it, slipping a finger toward the tight puckering between her buttocks. "Now, would you like me taking yours?" Proving his point, he captured her lips with his, his finger slowly moving into her tight anal sphincter.

"No. Tom hurt me when he tried to do it the first time. When I wouldn't let him use me that way, he beat me really bad that time. I wouldn't let him try again."

"I would never hurt you, Crimson. Trust me. If you don't want it that way, then I will respect your choice."

<hr />

LANDON plodded through the high snowdrifts as he fed the animals one last time before taking his leave, when he preferred staying with this redheaded, hot-tempered, beautiful woman for another week or so. They argued, made love, talked, laughed and made love again. It was a dream come true lying in bed so often cuddled together or exploring each other's bodies, finding new ways of pleasing each other. He might hate Tom with a passion, but he was benefitting from Tom's teaching Crimson about sex.

Bundling up against the freezing temperatures and dreading the long trek back to Tascosa, Landon watched her draw a shawl tight around her chest. Tying the leather belt around his fur coat, he pulled her against him and captured her pouting mouth with his. The now familiar tingling began in his loins, and he wished he did not have to leave so soon.

Tangling his fingers in the curtain of her fiery auburn hair, he brushed feathery light kisses along her jawline across her ear. "Promise me, Crimson, you'll stay here until the trial. I'll bring you all necessary food supplies." When she did not speak soon enough, he closed his arms more securely around her, cupping her buttocks and bringing her up against him. "Promise me, Crimson!"

She cocked her head backward, glaring at him through narrowed eyes. "I gave you my word, Landon, but how do you know you can trust me?" Why did he persist? Didn't he realize she did not fully trust him or Temple Houston's efforts of freeing her from the murder charge?

He kissed the tilted corner of her angry mouth, suppressing a grin. "If you give me your word, you won't break it. That much I do know about you. Your word is your bond."

Shading her eyes against the glare, she watched him ride off, morosely thinking, yes, my word is my honor. Why did he make me promise?

∾❀❀❀∾

IT HAD been a long, hard winter. The snow dotted the land in dirty white patches, but there was an air of spring about with the brave green shoots peeping from underneath the brown landscape. Staring out into the endless distance, Crimson tugged at a loose tress escaping from the haphazardly rolled bun. She coiled the strand around her finger, gnawing on her bottom lip. She had never felt so alone and lost in her entire life. Her family was far away, and the people she thought were her friends, did not come around. The only ones she saw were Landon and Temple Houston when they made infrequent trips; Temple to ask questions or reinforce something she had already said a thousand times before or give an update on his plan of defense. Landon brought her food supplies, usually staying the night or two and taking what she so freely gave him.

Running her fingertips across her lips, she savored those times. Those were the only times she did not feel lonely, and whether she wanted it or not, he did make her feel loved. Nothing made sense anymore. Nothing! Especially not the beginning of trust she was developing for him.

She pushed the stray lock into the bun at the back of her neck and sighed. Landon. He was her island in the vast sea of endless plains, him the rock of Gibraltar and she the doubting Thomas. However much she wanted to believe him, she could not put her complete trust in him. There were still too many unanswered questions, too many circumstances pointing in his direction.

Landon could have very easily killed John. What evidence did she have he didn't? His word? But could she trust his word? Could she trust him? And if he did not kill John, she should be finding out who did, not staying here falling deeper into depression with each passing day. Why had she promised him she would stay at the ranch? Why? The whole situation was hopeless. She just knew in her heart she would be found guilty. The evidence was too strong, too damning.

She half turned toward the sod when a spot in the distance caught her eye. Her heart drummed in her chest, a pleasant tingling erupting in her stomach. Landon! She vividly remembered all the times she spent in bed with him. He filled a deep-seated need within her, fulfilled the emptiness that had so long been a part of her life. But as the figure grew larger, a sinking began in her stomach. It was not Landon. She could tell by the way the man sat his horse.

A heaviness grew around her heart, but nevertheless, she waited, wondering who would be coming out this way. She tugged at her earlobe, fighting the desire of running and hiding from the distant visitor. She could not tolerate more bad news.

Recognizing Harvey, her welcoming smile was strained. Not that she wasn't glad for company, it was the tension coiling up inside of her like a deadly rattler. After answering his hail, she waited impatiently for him to dismount.

"What brings you here, Harvey?" There was an edge to her voice.

"No welcomin' hug, Crimson?" he queried, a bland look on his face. "I guess not. I thought we were better friends but sounds like ya ain't too pleased with me bein' here." Harvey laced the reins around the hitching post without taking his questioning eyes from hers.

"We were never close enough for hugs, Harvey."

"Ah, guess not. Jist cain't figure out why yore acting so unwelcomin'." He drew up in front of her, noticing the dark circles under her eyes and the way her body tensed when he held his hand toward her.

She looked off into the distance, a faint blush covering her cheeks. "It ain't you. I'm under a lot of pressure." She turned from him and motioned toward the sod. "Come on in and have a cup of coffee."

Closing her hands around the coffee mug, she studied Harvey through the steam. "What are you doing out here? Last time you were here, you threatened John."

"So, ya know 'bout that, huh? I had my reasons. 'Sides, I heard John was killed and ya were accused of his murder. Thought I'd come out here and give ya my support. God only knows what John put ya through." *What a good-lookin' woman she is*, he thought, studying her closer. It was nice not seeing bruises along her face for a change. Maybe she had been John's wife, but the path was now clear for him to make his own advances. She had been without a man for months now and probably would welcome his attention.

"I didn't kill him."

"Didna say ya did. John had a lot of enemies, any one of them who would want him dead. It's part of the reason why I'm here. I'll help ya find out who killed him." Harvey placed his coffee mug on the table and reached his hand out toward hers. He was nonplussed when she ignored it and took a sip of the steaming black brew.

"And you think you know who killed him?" Her voice came out a bit sarcastic.

"I got a inklin' who it might be. I'm gonna dig a little further and find out for sure. Trust me, Crimson."

She shook her head, biting back a sharp retort. Didn't he realize she did not trust anyone?

"Lighten up, Crimson. I'm offerin' my help in any capacity ya need. Did ya think I wouldna help?" Harvey pushed his cup toward the center of the table, a frown wrinkling his forehead while watching her reaction.

She looked away, somehow dissatisfied with his offer of help. There was something about the way he offered it, something in his eyes warning her. "You could of easily killed John, Harvey. You had as much reason wanting him dead as anyone else."

"Perhaps, but have ya forgotten Tom and I grew up together? Do you honestly think I could of killed my best friend?" He smiled tightly when she looked down at her clenched hands.

"I guess not," she agreed softly, glancing back at him. "I'll need your testimony. I need all the help I can get."

"Name it and it's yores."

"One thing before you go. Where have you been all this time?"

Harvey had already risen and was walking toward the door. "New Mexico. Sold the last herd." Stopping at the door, he pulled a handful of gold eagles from his pocket, counted off several hundred dollars and handed them to her. "That's Tom's part. It's now yorens."

She stared at the heavy gold coins in her hand, the memory of Tom and Harvey's last argument playing over in her mind. "Didn't you and Tom sever your partnership?"

"Well, we did, but I decided against it. In the end, the cost was too great."

Chapter 31
A Twist of Words

CRIMSON looked around the sod, imprinting it on her memory. It may be the last time she ever saw it. She really didn't know why— it only held bad memories, especially of abuse and loneliness. Landon was silent, giving her the last few moments to prepare herself before they headed into Tascosa for the trial. She turned and met his eyes, silently nodding her readiness.

Landon stepped nearer, taking in her proper black dress and the severe hairstyle bringing out the sharp angles of her face. She gave the appearance she was going to her own hanging, and it bothered him. He cupped the sides of her face, rubbing his thumbs along her high cheekbones, wishing he could shield her from the strain and uncertainty of the trial. There was so much evidence against her it would probably display her character in an unsavory light. His only hope was for the information on Tom Martin, alias John Sullivan, that Temple Houston required, arrived before the trial ended. Whether it did or not, he knew he'd never allow her imprisonment or be hanged for murder.

He searched for words of comfort, but none seemed appropriate. Instead, he pulled a few strands from her tightly coiled bun and let them curl around her face. "It softens the severity, little spy. We want you looking your best and not like you're attending a funeral."

Hoping for a smile, he ran his index finger along the curve of

311

her lips. *She's too grave, too resigned*, he thought, brushing his lips across her forehead. "Don't worry. I made you a promise, and I'll keep it come hell or high water."

She captured his hand and planted a frightened kiss in the palm before moving it back against her cheek. "Hold me, Landon. Please hold me."

He pulled her slender form tightly against his. Trembling like a frightened deer in his arms, he breathed in her vanilla scent tainted by the faint scent of fear. Her head rested on his chest, and he laid his chin on top. "There will be many more times I'll hold you. Just remember, I'll do the right thing for you no matter what it takes." Giving her a reassuring hug, he took her elbow and assisted her into the wagon before sitting beside her and taking the reins. It would take several hours before they reached Tascosa.

Crimson drank in the greening landscape, memorizing each detail for future reference. The rolling hills, the arroyos, the mesas, the way the whippoorwills sang—everything. There was sadness in her lingering eyes, a premonition of worse things coming. She was putting what little trust she had left in a man whom she suspected of many foul deeds. She still was not totally convinced he was not behind some of them, but she had no one else. Where was her family? They should be here by now. Landon stated he had sent a telegram, wiring them to come home as quickly as possible. Had they received the telegram or had Landon lied?

Landon glanced uneasily at the still figure beside him. Her face was drained of color, her hands clenching the bottom of the seat so tight her knuckles were white. If only he could give her some of his strength or something she could look forward to, at least some type of reassurance. Nothing he could say or do would lift her spirits. She had sunk too far into depression.

The streets of Tascosa were a beehive of activity and there was a festive air about it. The streets were teaming with horses, oxen and mule teams, buggies, buckboards, wagons, sun-tanned plainsmen, home seekers and bone-pickers who savaged unwanted household items and resold them. The Equity Bar was packed with people witnessing the various judging sessions. A burst of laughter came from the bar before being silenced by an impatient banging.

Crimson tensed beside Landon, glancing uneasily in the

direction of the saloon. A couple of women walked along the street tugging some crying children along behind them. They stopped and stared at Crimson, pointing accusing fingers at her. She could not hear what they said, but she could imagine it. 'Look, there goes a murderess. Killed her own husband, she did.'

She glanced down at the pressure on her arm before shifting her eyes to his warning face.

"Overlook them, Crimson. They can't hurt you."

"They've already hurt me, Landon. They've judged me guilty."

Landon fought his yearning of embracing her in the middle of the street, but it would only increase the gossip. Her words were softly spoken, carrying a sharp edge of pain. If he could only soothe away her fear, promise her everything would resolve itself. And yet, he also fancied throwing her into the wagon and racing away toward the sunset so she could avoid the trial. However, his hands were tied. His honor was no less than hers, and yet there was a limit with his honor. Just as he had promised her, he would never let her be convicted for John's murder. No matter how much Tom deserved his fate, he wished he were still alive so Crimson would not be suffering for his sake.

After lifting her from the wagon, he took her elbow and led her toward the Equity Bar. The stiffness of her walk, the grim twist of her lips and the paleness of her face were unnatural. Squeezing her elbow reassuringly, he whispered, "Don't give up. I promise everything will be alright."

She stopped in midstep and turned, staring sadly into his sky-blue eyes. "You can promise me the moon, Landon, but can you deliver it?"

"I don't make promises lightly." His eyes grew hard at her subtle question, clearly conveying her doubts he could or would prevent the court's decision.

"I can't promise you the moon, but I can promise you I am making every effort of freeing you." She turned her face away from his, and he gripped both of her arms, forcing her to meet his eyes.

There was a harsh edge darkening his voice, "Don't doubt me, Crimson Rose. Don't ever doubt me or underestimate me. I made you a promise and I will keep it. Just don't doubt me."

She searched his determined eyes, piercing their depth for his soul. His eyes resembled the deep summer sky, promising continuance and calm weather. How much trust could she give him? He was slowly chipping away at the stone around her heart, leaving it bare. Without any defense, she would be open for a greater hurt, a pain which she could not bear if she lost him. He was all she had. Grabbing his hand, she held it firmly. "Will you testify about not seeing those water buckets in the sod?"

He turned his face from her and stared out over the town without seeing it, an angry tick jumping in his cheek, his voice carrying a brittle edge, "I'm a half-breed, Crimson, a nonperson. I am not allowed to testify for you or anyone else ever."

"But why..."

Facing her, his eyes granite hard, he clarified, "I'm a dirty half-breed. Have you forgotten?"

She looked down at her feet, a blush of shame for her people showing on her face. "Then I don't have a chance, do I?"

Grabbing her shoulders, he shook her, her sad, resigned voice cutting through his heart. "Don't give up! Will you let them defeat you? You with your strong pride and temper? Don't you give up now!"

Meeting his eyes, she realized for the first time they were both outcasts, yet his words prompted the pride he spoke of within her. Nodding, she stiffened her spine and walked into the courtroom.

The Equity Bar was overflowing with people from the surrounding area attending the court trial of the first woman in the Texas Panhandle tried for murder. A sudden babble arose when people recognized her, and Crimson felt their accusing stares and stinging words. A faint blush creasing her cheeks, she made her way toward Temple Houston and sat in the chair beside him.

❧◦❧◦❧

WHILE the sheriff and the posse members gave their testimony, Temple doodled on a piece of paper in front of him. Only when the prosecution called Mrs. Colby, the town gossip of Mobeetie, forward for her testimony, did he lift his head.

Temple glanced at Crimson, noting the way she held her head high, her chin lifted in defiance and her hands clenched so tightly in her lap, her knuckles were white. She sat stiffly, her back several inches from the chair's back. The bloodless quality about her face and lips proclaimed her fear, but also her determination of facing judgement. Temple was just as resolute in proving her innocence.

A.L. Neal, the prosecuting attorney, began questioning Mrs. Colby. "How well do you know the defendant, Crimson Rose McFarlin-Sullivan?"

"Knowed her since she was knee-high to a grasshopper."

"Would you say Mrs. Sullivan has a quick temper?"

"A quick temper? She's got a temper that'd blow a keg of gunpowder sky high. Ever' time she and her family came into town, you could bet she'd be in some kind of trouble. I've seen her get into a out-and-out brawl with boys, the kind you get down in the dirt and fight. Headstrong, that's what she is. I always knowed one day she'd get into trouble with that temper of hers." Mrs. Colby focused her disapproving, squinched eyes on Crimson.

Directing his questions at the witness in front of him, Mr. Neal leaned on the bar. "Can you point her out?"

"I object!" a voice from the observers shouted. "Ever'body in these here parts knows Miss Crimson."

Laughter burst from the audience, and Judge McMasters banged his gavel against the bartop. "Brody, this here is a respectable court and just because everybody knows Miss Crimson, it's still a matter of record for Mrs. Colby to point her out. If I have another outburst from you, I'll fine you for contempt of court."

"If'n that's the way you want it, Judge. We're jist wantin' to hear the good parts quicker." There was another burst of amusement.

The judge banged on the bartop again. "Another outburst like that and you'll all be thrown out into the street. Can't have you disruptin' my court."

With the stern warning given, the courtroom settled into silence.

Neal repeated his question, and Mrs. Colby pointed at Crimson. "That's her, shore is." Mrs. Colby quickly nodded her head several times, sending her many chins a'waggling.

"Isn't it well known Miss Crimson has been cohabiting with a mixed breed named Landon Wade?"

Mrs. Colby nodded vigorously while answering Neal's question. "Well, I would think so. Ever' time I seened Crimson the last year or so, she was talkin' with the breed. I heard they were co... whatever you called it, since her husband's death."

"I object, your honor. Mr. Neal is leading the witness, and Mrs. Colby's statements are a matter of conjecture, not established fact," Temple boomed.

"Sustained. Redirect your question, Mr. Neal."

"Your honor, Mrs. Sullivan's association with the half-breed Landon Wade may very well bear looking into. I intend to show the court her true character," Neal argued.

"Unless you can produce facts about the matter, contain your remarks and questions, sir," Judge McMasters ordered.

Neal nodded curtly and pivoted toward Mrs. Colby. "During court week last fall, you stated Mrs. Sullivan and her husband John had an argument in Mobeetie, in the section of town known as Feather Hill. In your own words, please tell the court what you saw and heard."

Mrs. Colby, thoroughly enjoying the court's full attention, elaborated on how Crimson had found John with one of the saloon girls, enumerating how she also threatened to kill him, not once but twice.

"Let me get this correct, Mrs. Colby. You stated Mrs. Sullivan's exact words were, 'You've been lyin' to me, John and you promised you had gotten rid of her. I warned ya if I ever caught ya with her, I'd kill you,' then she reinforced her words by shooting him?"

"That's what I remember, give or take a word or two. She told the saloon girl if'n she wanted him alive, then she'd stay away from him. A sure threat if you ask me."

"That's all, Mrs. Colby." Neal shot a triumphant look in Temple's direction before taking his seat.

Temple threw his pen down on the tabletop, walking back and forth in short, jerky steps, his gold mounted spurs jangling, his head drooped forward in deep thought. He presented a flamboyant figure in his black suit with the bright yellow flowered vest, a crimson Mexican sash around his waist, and a red silk neckerchief around his neck. At his hips were a pair of silver-plated and ivory-handled revolvers holstered in a silver studded belt. Though he dressed ostentatiously, he was known for his quick wit and keen mind. He had also, on more than one occasion, proven himself a man fast with a gun and deadly accurate, a combination most men steered clear.

Temple stopped in front of the witness and pierced her with his sharp gray eyes, his resonating booming voice drawing the court's undivided attention. "Mrs. Colby, you stated you've known Miss Crimson since she was knee-high to a grasshopper. When did you and your husband move to Mobeetie? Was it more than two years?"

"Gettin' right particular, ain't ya, Mr. Houston?" Mrs. Colby asked, her face flushing red.

"Answer the question," Temple drawled, slapping his hand lightly against the table.

Mrs. Colby released a deep sigh that carried across the room. "Nah, a little under."

"Were you acquainted with Miss Crimson before you moved here?"

"Nah," she answered, her face growing hard and the red coloring her face deepening.

"Then how could you know Miss Crimson since she was knee-high to a grasshopper? Were you exaggerating? I will say she's not very tall, but she's definitely taller than a grasshopper for the last couple of years. I know we live in Texas where everything is bigger, but does that also include specific timelines?" Temple leaned forward, his voice deep and soft but carrying well over the court audience.

"That'll be your opinion, Mr. Houston. I ain't exaggeratin' much. Who uses such language anyway such as exaggeratin'." The crowd burst out in laughter, and Mrs. Colby glared at them for chuckling at her expense. Her fists clenched her brown skirt along her thighs as she scowled at the attendees.

"So, to be clear for the jury, please estimate how many times you have been in the presence of Miss Crimson?"

"Enough to know 'bout her temper," Mrs. Colby grumbled, her eyes narrowing within her flaming red face, embarrassed and angry over being caught in a blatant lie.

"Since the jury now knows the true fact, which they probably knew anyway because Fort Elliot wasn't established until 1874 and Mobeetie didn't apply for a post office until 1879, you couldn't have known Miss Crimson well enough to make a reliable judgement of her personality. Correct?"

"I'll have you know I'm very good at judgin' people's character, Mr. Houston, and don't ya be sayin' otherwise." Several snickers erupted over the court.

"So, have you only lived in Mobeetie around here?"

Still angry, Mrs. Colby stated with a low volume voice, "Ya mean Buffalo Dung?"

"Buffalo Dung or Sweetwater. I don't believe the true meaning of Mobeetie has been established," Temple corrected.

The court loudly guffawed with the judge banging on the bartop. "Order in the court! This ain't no comedy skit!"

The amusement increased with the judge's declaration. After it calmed again, Temple leaned closer to Mrs. Colby. "Mrs. Colby, what were you doing in Feather Hill? It's not a part of town where respectable women are found, is it?"

"*I am a respectable woman*, Mr. Houston, and don't you go a'thinkin' otherwise. The day Crimson shot her husband was the first time I ever got near the place." Mrs. Colby glared at Temple. Respectable woman indeed! She'd tell him a thing or two!

"Just answer the question, Mrs. Colby."

"I had planned on it, Mr. Houston. Now don' be gittin' all crochety on me." She waved away his pointed statement and adjusted her hat before answering. "Well, most people here abouts knowed me and my husband own the dry goods store. When I seen Crimson talkin' to that half-breed Landon Wade, I naturally got curious, 'specially when I could see they were arguin'. Ya see, I'm jist a naturally curious type of person."

Scoffing cackles erupted, breaking Mrs. Colby's testimony, and some male stated loudly, "Yeah, sure thing as bein' a busybody gossipmonger."

She glared around at the packed courtroom, effectively silencing them. "I knowed Crimson had up and married another man. It weren't proper for her a'talkin' with another man without her husband with her. I peeked my head outta the door and saw Crimson angrily stalkin' off toward Lower Mobeetie. Mr. Wade was a'follerin' right behind her, and I follered too. That's when I saw her husband John come outta that saloon with one of dem women."

"In other words, your insatiable curiosity prompted you to follow Mrs. Sullivan?" Temple asked before he shot a disbelieving glance at the jury.

A low mocking snort came from the audience and was quickly hushed when Mrs. Colby glared, her small eyes sparking anger. "Those are fancy words, Mr. Houston, but that's 'bout the size of it."

"Mrs. Colby, how many children do you have?"

"I object, your Honor. How many children Mrs. Colby has, has no bearing on this case," Neal interjected.

"Your honor, I beg the indulgence of the court. I will bring in some vital information, which has an indirect bearing on this case."

"Sustained," Judge McMasters declared. "Answer the question, Mrs. Colby."

Mrs. Colby drew back in surprise, her eyes wary. "Why I have nine kids, four boys and five girls."

"Nine children, quite a brood, Mrs. Colby, and probably a hard job in handling them adequately, in which case you do well."

"Why yes, I think so."

Temple leaned closer, speaking only to her in a conversational way. "Do you remember the first time I questioned you about this case while gathering evidence?" At her affirmative nod, he continued, "Please tell the court what happened while I was there."

At her blank stare, he elaborated, "It was a muddy day and you had just hung out your laundry."

Understanding dawning on her face, she directed a disapproving scowl toward her children seated along the west wall. "Well, I had warshed all mornin' and jist hung out the warsh on the clothesline that my husband had rigged up for me. Two of my sons there, Phillip and Charles, were chasin' a pig that had gotten out of its pen. The little rascals chased it right into my nice, clean clothes, pullin' down the clothesline and tramplin' it all into the mud. Every last piece, mind you. I thought I'd never git it all warshed again."

"I assume you punished them for their deed, but for the record, what did you yell at them?"

If Mrs. Colby wondered how Temple's question was pertinent, it did not dampen her moment of glory. "Why, what I always tell 'em. Let me tell you, I was ready to kill the little brats. Lord only knows what a mother goes through."

"I assure you, most of us do, Mrs. Colby, but I don't think most parents want to kill their children over that type of misdeed. However, please answer my question," Temple interrupted.

"Don't git feisty, Mr. Houston, I'm a'comin' to that." Mrs. Colby cast Temple a sharp look, one she might have shot at her own children for being disrespectful.

"I grabbed them both by the ears and told 'em I was gonna throw 'em down and stomp their guts out, then I was gonna beat 'em to death wid 'em." She shot a fierce look at her sons, angry all over again.

Temple faced the jury. "Let it be recorded Mrs. Colby stated she was so mad she threatened to throw them on the ground and stomp their guts out, then beat them to death with the entrails."

A nervous twittering broke the silence. Judge McMasters had a hard time keeping the smile from his face though he pounded the bar with the gavel.

"You jist twisted my words, Mr. Houston. What I said was jist a matter of speech. Why I couldna no more kill one of my children than I could make it rain. What I said was said in the heat of anger," Mrs. Colby clarified, glaring at Temple while her hand distressfully fluttered against her chest.

"In the heat of anger, Mrs. Colby? Don't you think Mrs. Sullivan might have said those things to her husband *in the heat of anger* and *as a matter of speech*?" Temple glanced at Crimson before turning the force of his burning eyes on Mrs. Colby.

"Why, I suppose, but she did shoot her own husband 'cause I saw it."

"But are you positive that's what you saw? You stated John Sullivan reached for the derringer and Mrs. Sullivan pulled the trigger."

There was a tense silence, waiting for Mrs. Colby's reply. Uncertainty settled over her face before the lax lines tightened and she nodded. "I'm sure of what I saw."

Temple stepped in front of the judge. "If it pleases the court, I will demonstrate that what Mrs. Colby thinks she saw isn't necessarily what happened."

"You have the court's permission."

"Thank you, your honor." Temple slipped out of his black jacket, carefully folded it and laid it beside his gray sombrero with the rattlesnake band onto the round card table where Crimson sat. At the other side of the bar, he took the derringer and held it toward the jury. "I have here exhibit A, the alleged murder weapon."

Walking toward Mrs. Colby, he stopped directly in front of her and held the small gun toward her. "Now, Mrs. Colby, you stated John Sullivan reached for the derringer, and Mrs. Sullivan pulled the trigger. We will demonstrate a different scenario for the court's benefit. Please stand and act like you are Mrs. Sullivan and I'll pretend I'm Mr. Sullivan."

Mrs. Colby dubiously took the derringer, holding it loosely and uncertainly.

"Relax, Mrs. Colby. The derringer won't bite you." The courtroom erupted in laughter and Temple bit back a grin.

After the laughter settled down, he showed Mrs. Colby how to properly hold the derringer. "For the record, your Honor, you notice Mrs. Colby is holding the derringer with her finger on the trigger. My intent is to demonstrate and show the court how Mrs. Sullivan did not pull the trigger, but it was jerked from her hand, causing the derringer to unintentionally fire."

As soon as his last words were spoken, Temple suddenly grabbed the gun. A loud explosion split the silence. Temple was thrown backwards and landed with a solid plunk onto the hardpacked dirt floor. The jurors, judge and several people of the court dived for cover. Realizing Temple lay unmoving, several men rushed forward.

Chapter 32
Thorny Rose

TEMPLE sat up groggily, waving away their help. Rising, he assured the court he was unharmed. Without the court being aware, he had secretly loaded the derringer with blanks earlier that day. Waving at the black powder marks on his yellow vest, he boomed, "As the court has witnessed, Mrs. Colby accidentally pulled the trigger when I grabbed the derringer."

"Mr. Houston, was such a demonstration necessary? You have scared the wits out of Mrs. Colby and a better part of the jury." The judge pointed at the faint Mrs. Colby, her hand pressed against her bosom, her face deathly white.

"I humbly beg the court's pardon, but yes, it was necessary for demonstrating what Mrs. Colby thought she saw was not necessarily what happened."

Judge McMasters pounded on the bar. "Court dismissed and will be reconvened after lunch. We all need our wits about us to continue after Mr. Houston's demonstration."

Crimson sat frozen in the chair, a feeling of unutterable loss filling her. All the evidence so far had been damning and her association with Landon was condemning her more. For the first time, she finally understood the stigma attached to being an Indian half-breed.

A man tapped her on the shoulder, and she barely looked up,

numbly taking the white piece of paper the deputy sheriff handed her. The loss feeling grew more pronounced after she read it. She closed her fist around the note, a lone tear escaping down her cheek.

"Crimson, I'll escort you to your hotel." Temple reached for her hand and stopped halfway, noticing the tear on her cheek. He took her hand and gently forced it open. Taking the note and reading it out loud, his brow puckered in a frown. "Harvey sends his deepest apology for being unable to testify for you. Seems he was called away on urgent business."

She looked up, her voice barely above a whisper. "I'm truly lost now. My last friend will not be testifying for me."

Temple took her elbow and led her from the court/bar. "We haven't lost, Crimson. Not by a long shot."

❧❦❧❦❧

LANDON sat upon his horse on Boot Hill above the collection of rough-built adobe and wooden gambling halls and drinking businesses, with the end of the street and behind said buildings, containing dilapidated tiny shacks housing prostitutes. He searched the stark landscape for a hard-riding rider, but no flying dust appeared, and his heart sank lower.

He had stood at the back of the saloon during the trial and listened to the testimonies, each word piercing deeper into his heart. The testimonies were brutal and condemning, questioning her character, and specifically the threats she made against her husband. "Dammit, Crimson, why did you let your temper and loose words get you into this fix?"

Sweat broke out over his forehead and his stomach clenched with his gloomy thoughts. *My little spy, I've wronged you. It was not my purpose of falling in love with you. I'm a non-entity—half a man. I cannot testify for you because of my mixed blood. And if proof is presented we have spent nights together after your husband's murder, it will surely increase your condemnation.*

With the sunlight warming his face, he lifted his hands heavenward and cried, "Help me, Great Spirit, father of my people. I am neither Kiowa nor white, and the ties with my people were forever severed. It was a white man's kindness that brought me back

323

from the depths of despair. I still felt half dead until I met Crimson Rose. I have claimed her as mine, but death may claim her if she is convicted. Is this my lot in life—to love and lose? Will I never be accorded happiness? Must she die also and share my fate? Grant her freedom and I will gladly give up my life so she might live in peace and happiness. I beg thee, Great Spirit, take my life instead of hers."

His plea was met by deathly silence. Not a bird chirped, not a blade of grass rustled. An empty void spread out before him, and he had never felt so alone. Shaking his fists toward the sun, his harsh voice was absorbed by the many hills surrounding Tascosa. "Must you continue punishing me? Save her life! You took my mother. You took my Kiowa lover, Sun-Is-Setting. Must you take Crimson Rose too? Let her live in tranquility and I will forever ride out of her life, if this is your will!"

❦

CRIMSON sat silent, still as a marble statue, and stared blindly at the delicate red rose in its first bloom Temple had laid on the tabletop in front of her. With the testimony continuing, she briefly wondered why Temple had brought the rose.

Pedro Romero testified Crimson had lost her temper during many of his bailes, which she and her brothers attended. With an apologetic glance, he spoke about the last baile she attended and the fray she got into with Billy the Kid and one of his henchmen, Charlie Sorrel.

One of the immigrants who had stayed and homesteaded in the area, explained how Crimson and her brothers rode in and rescued the wagon train from attacking Indians. It was also noted Crimson had her horse shot out from under her. It should have been a point in her favor if Attorney Neal had not turned it around, exclaiming it proved she knew how to use a weapon and possibly shot another person during the Indian attack.

Other witnesses testified she shot John in Mobeetie but were divided in what they saw. Some testified she picked up the derringer and some claimed the opposite.

With the last testimony, the silence was soon broken by the spectators' animated debate, discussing the last pieces of information. A tense hush filled the room when Jenny Brown was called to the stand. Her testimony was one Crimson dreaded the most.

"You're saying you and John Sullivan were lovers?" Neal asked.

"I said I loved him and would have married him if he'd of asked me. Instead, he married her jist so he could git in good with her family." Jenny accusingly pointed a finger at Crimson.

"How long had you known John before he married his wife?"

"Knowed him for years, since afore he changed his name."

"He changed his name?" Neal seemed shocked at the new evidence Jenny unwittingly supplied.

Jenny grew uncomfortable and shifted uneasily in the chair.

"Remember you're under oath, Miss Brown," the judge reminded sternly.

Jenny nodded her head, her voice cracking with her short answer. "Yes!"

"What was John Sullivan's real name?"

Jenny looked over at Crimson before answering. "Tom Martin." She pointed again at Crimson, a hard, satisfied expression falling over her face. "She grew up with him."

An excited babble filled the court room. The judge banged on the bartop, shouting for order. When the noise died down, Neal remarked, "Tom Martin. Then Crimson Rose McFarlin Sullivan married him knowing that he was going under an assumed name."

Pointing a finger at Crimson while facing the jury, Neal shouted, "That makes her marriage null and void. She knew, members of the jury, and married him anyway, knowing he was going under an assumed name. How much more must be proven against Crimson Rose McFarlin?"

Temple's head jerked up and he jumped from his chair. With hands clasped behind his back, he paced back and forth in front of the court, then turned sharply on his heel and faced Jenny. "You are charged with an accessory to murder. You admitted you suspected John Sullivan killed Major Larner. And yet you stand here and accuse Mrs. Sullivan of marrying a man she grew up with, though you have no proof. You stated you would have married him under the same circumstance."

"Yes, yes! A thousand times, yes! I loved him!" Jenny tearfully shouted.

Temple nodded his satisfaction with his point made. Crimson fervently prayed the earth would open and swallow her. All her dirty laundry was being brought out and displayed before the whole Texas Panhandle.

Mr. Temple faced the jury and stated, "Gentlemen of the jury, there is no proof Miss Crimson Rose McFarlin married John Sullivan or married him under his real name, Tom Martin. All information was destroyed in the fire, which burned both Major Larner's and the post adjutant's offices, along with other buildings at Fort Elliot the night Major Larner was murdered. Therefore, the court cannot declare her marriage null and void without proof she married him under an assumed name."

Crimson testified on her own behalf, staring out over the court with fierce pride. Temple led her into talking about her life with John and how he had beaten her. Her voice shaking, she tearfully told her story, carefully leaving out her real reason for marrying John and her suspicions of Landon.

"So, let this be clear for the court, when was the first time John beat you?" Temple watched Crimson swallow hard against the memory.

"Our wedding night," she stated quietly.

"And when did the beatings end?"

"The day before he was killed." Crimson met Mr. Houston's gaze, hers wide open, the pain apparent in her eyes and face.

"How severe were the beatings, Miss Crimson?"

"Sometimes I could not move or walk for several days. Sometimes the injuries were so severe I was unable to do much for a week."

"That's a lot of beatings, gentlemen of the jury." Temple glanced toward them, his gaze meeting each juror's eyes, imprinting the information of John's unnecessary violence into their final consideration. He also directed her toward John's statement he was head of the cattle rustling syndicate and other areas of her life with John.

Crimson did not know why she did not implicate Landon during the latter questioning. She had a golden opportunity, but the words would not come. Under Neal's harsh cross-examination, her story never changed. She could not testify regarding which name she married John under for she never saw the information written down before or after the marriage.

❧⁂❧

A.L. NEAL stood in front of the jury and gave his closing statement. "As you can see, your honor and gentlemen of the jury, the defendant willingly admitted how she and her husband fought from the beginning of their marriage," Attorney Neal proclaimed. "

"She also stated she fought back. Is not a wife subjective to her husband? And she was never submissive. She threatened to kill him not once, not twice, but three times. She herself spoke about the time he became angry when he caught her with a half-breed, a dirty savage, though she explained Indians were in the area."

Neal pointed an accusing finger at Crimson. "Crimson McFarlin had the motive, the opportunity and the skill to kill her husband. She shot her husband with the derringer he gave her, gentlemen of the jury. Sheriff Willingham and the posse found her standing over her husband with the murder weapon still in her hand. Remember, hell hath no fury like a woman scorned, and if you have been listening to the testimony given today, you will find Crimson Rose McFarlin-Sullivan guilty of the murder of John Sullivan, aka Tom Martin."

While Attorney Neal made his closing statement, Crimson sat with her hands clenched in her lap. She jumped when he pointed a finger at her, cringing under his accusation. The feelings of the court were running high and she felt their eyes burning through her back.

I'm not guilty! she wanted to scream. *I'm not!* She clenched her teeth, the muscles jumping from her firmly clenched jaw until she fought back the urge of screaming it out loud.

There was an expectant air in the bar-courtroom, each person anxiously waiting for Temple's closing argument. Temple was a genius criminal lawyer who, like a master artist, played upon the emotions and minds of the men. He also had a reputation for having a genuine reverence for women.

Temple walked in front of the jury, his resonating voice filling the courtroom. "*My God, my God, why hast thou forsaken me? Why art thou so far from helping me, and from the words of my roaring?*

O my God, I cry in the daytime, but thou heardest not; and in the night season and am not silent."

"Our Lord is merciful as written in the scriptures and states, *But thou art holy, O thou that inhabitest the praises of Israel. Our fathers trusted in thee: they trusted, and thou didst deliver them. They cried unto thee, and were delivered: they trusted in thee, and were not confounded.*"

"Look at her, gentlemen. See the bloom of youth on her cheeks like the dew on the morning rose. She has raised up her voice unto the Lord begging for a just trial and freeing her from being unjustly accused of cold-bloodedly murdering her husband, a man who beat her, belittled her, committed adultery and treated her worse than he did his animals. By a man whom the posse was nearby with an arrest warrant in their pocket for his unspeakably cruel murder of Major Larner."

"Like the delicate rose, she was a gentle, loving wife fulfilling her husband's every need, and like the gentle rose, our Master hath given her thorns for protection, thorns that pierced the skin when brutally plucked. Her husband violently plucked those petals until she almost withered and died."

Temple reached for the red rose he had laid on the tabletop and stood in front of the jury, every eye riveted on him. His voice, heavy with compassion yet laced with righteous anger, exhibited the rose with its thorns before crushing the delicate head in his hand and scattering the petals over the jury. "Like this did her husband tear her asunder, bruising the tender petals and throwing them into the wind, willing her death underneath his cruel hands. Ah, look closely at her, gentlemen. As her name proclaims, she is a delicate rose, a beautiful crimson rose."

"Her home is here where the sunrises are filled with splendorous colors, the land of gentle golden sea of grasses, the sunset a burst of gold, crimson and purple. The stars are but a hand stretch away. She is a rare rose in the wilderness—and her family like yours. No! Not like yours for her family is in deep despair, racing home by train, wishing they were at her side—knowing her life and future are in your hands. Her sister weeps for her little sister, assured of her innocence, praying for the real murderer be found and her name cleared. This tender rose will wither and die in prison—taken from the family and land she loves—the ugliness of prison forever dimming the light of life from her lovely meadow green eyes. Can you in good conscience condemn this delicate rose on circumstantial evidence?"

"*Blessed are the merciful: for they shall obtain mercy. Blessed are ye, when men shall revile you, and persecute you, and shall say all manner of evil against you falsely. Woe unto you, scribes and Pharisees, hypocrites! for ye pay tithe of mint and anise and cummin, and have omitted the weightier matters of the law, judgment, mercy, and faith; these ought ye have done, and not to leave the other undone.*"

"Lo, like the beautiful rose, our God in Heaven gave his gentlest creatures thorns for protection. Her anger, as heard on this day, was mostly directed at the injustice of some remark, someone else less fortunate or in protection of her family. Our Lord sayeth, *Greater love hath no man than this, that a man lay down his life for his friends.* And yet, she fought for the lives of immigrants—strangers when they were raided by Indians. Ah, there's another question. Have you, gentlemen of the jury, ever known Indians attack at night? Oh, no! Perhaps they were white men dressed as Indians, stealing the poor immigrants' livelihood. So, I remind you, *what greater love has a man than that a friend lay down his life for him?*"

"Gentlemen, *let him without sin cast the first stone.* Break the suspense; dry those tears; bind up these broken hearts, for now no power but you can do so. This noble duty done; each hour of life thereafter will glow proud with this recollection!"

There was an awed hush mixed with a few sniffles after Temple Houston finished speaking. Most of the people were aware he took the Bible out of context but were still affected by the way he put them together in defense of Crimson Rose McFarlin-Sullivan. Judge McMasters, caught up in Temple's oratory, took a few minutes before he banged on the bartop and dismissed the jury for deliberation.

≈⦅♥⦆≈

CRIMSON sat nervously in the chair, the strained pressure she was under showing in her dull green eyes. The jury finished their deliberations in less than an hour, and her future was in their hands. Silently watching the head juror stand, a buzzing began in her ears as he handed the judge a slip of paper.

After the judge read it and handed it back to the juror, the juror declared, "We, the jury of Oldham County find the defendant..."

"Stop!" came the shout from the doorway.

Crimson jerked around, her eyes widening when she saw Landon waving a handful of papers. Temple hastily stood and motioned Landon forward. "Your honor, I beg the court's permission to study the papers before the jury gives its verdict. We have been waiting for some evidence that would bear greatly on the verdict."

"Proceed, Mr. Houston."

Crimson distractedly rubbed her earlobe while Temple and Landon spoke in low murmurs. Her curiosity, like the rest of the court, was piqued. Temple glanced at the papers Landon handed him, his brow drawn up in a frown.

In short, confident steps, Temple walked toward Judge McMasters and presented him with the new evidence. They spoke in low monotones for a few moments while the judge examined the stack of large, printed papers.

The people attending court whispered among themselves, their voices growing louder from wondering what type of information was so important, it interrupted the reading of the verdict. The judge banged on the bar, quieting the still rising voices.

After all was silent, the judge, his voice loud with his proclamation, stated, "Mr. Houston, Miss Crimson, please stand. We have new evidence that puts a different light on the whole case. Tom Martin, alias John Sullivan, and J.T. Markman are wanted dead or alive in four states for murder, one of them for a judge's daughter in Illinois and she was with child. The army wants Tom Martin for the theft of twenty thousand dollars in gold, numerous horses and mules and for the murder of three men on a wagon detail. And that is partial evidence presented by these papers. Tom Martin, also known as John Sullivan, is wanted dead or alive. The proof is overwhelmingly against Tom Martin. This evidence, combined with the warrant and his attempted arrest, is irrefutable. Whether Mrs. Sullivan killed her husband or not is irrelevant. Whoever killed Tom

Martin is exonerated by these wanted bills, which are considered government and law enforcement notifications."

Judge McMasters looked down at the standing Crimson. "Mrs. Sullivan, you are cleared of the charges of murder. You will also be rewarded the bounty monies quoted on each." The judge tipped his hand containing the information toward Crimson.

His face foreboding, he instructed the jury, "Gentlemen of the Jury, in view of this new evidence, I am warning you, no member of this jury shall breathe a word of the determined verdict. If any word reaches me, you will be heavily fined and serve a prison term."

Banging on the bar, he shouted, "Court dismissed!"

Crimson stared blankly at the departing judge, uncomprehending what had happened. The buzz in her ears grew worse until everything was dreamlike. She remembered Landon bursting in at the last moment, but everything from there failed to register in her tormented brain. She slowly focused on the person shaking her shoulders, not understanding the words he was saying. Temple's face was wreathed in smiles while repeating the words.

"You're free, Crimson. You're free."

"Free?" she asked numbly. "Are you sure?"

"Didn't you hear? Whoever killed your husband has been exonerated, whether it was you or not. The wanted posters proclaimed he was wanted dead or alive."

A hard shudder ran through her, quaking every bone in her body. Temple took her arm and led her outside, glancing with puzzlement every so often at her. She stopped in front of Landon, speaking softly, uncertainly, "I'm free?"

Landon's crooked smile filled her vision. He nodded, thanking Temple before taking her arm. "Yes, little spy, you are free just as I promised."

The last few words finally penetrating her understanding, she jerked her arm back, a snarl on her lips, hissing, "Free, Landon? I'll never be free. I'll never know if the jury found me guilty or not. The people around here are looking at me suspiciously. Free, Landon? I'll never be free from the stigma of killing Tom, not until I find the person who really did it."

"What more are you wanting, Crimson? You have been exonerated of Tom's murder. Let it go." Landon was taken aback at her fierce words. Her stubborn, headstrong ways were reasserting themselves. He realized the plan she had made before the trial was still on her mind. "Don't go looking for trouble. If you carry out your plan, things will only get worse. Let it go, Crimson!"

"Never! Not until I find the real murderer. Landon, you didn't clear me of the murder charge, you just postponed it. As long as it's never proven who killed him, there will always be whispers and rumors I did it." There was a fanatical glow in her eyes and her cheeks, pale for so long, flushed with color matching the flame color of her hair. She glared at him. *Did he not understand?* Apparently not, for a muscle jumped along his jaw and his eyes grew hard as the winter sky.

All the hurt, mistrust, anger and disillusionment rose inside her, suffocating any reasonable relief she might have felt. Her fingernails biting into the palm of her hand, she scathingly quizzed, "Are you waiting for me to thank you, Landon? You'll have a long wait before I do."

She pivoted sharply on her heel and marched down the street, one destination firmly planted in her mind.

Chapter 33
Midnight Rose

LANDON watched her stiffly walk away, frowning when he noted her direction. *Don't do it, Crimson*, he silently begged. He should follow her and dissuade her, pick her up and carry her away. He shook his head against the notion, quenching the impulse. It was just as well they left each other on these terms. Her anger and determination would keep her from missing him. He had made a promise and would leave forever, staying out of her life.

"Landon, I'm glad she's free."

Landon slowly acknowledged his boss, Kerby Olsen. "I'm taking off."

His eyes were hard, distant and something else lingered there that Kerby could not identify. There was a final note in his voice, and he realized Landon meant something else entirely than going back to the ranch. "Come back when you get ready, Landon. The job is always open."

Shaking Kerby's hand, Landon's eyes strayed toward the disappearing figure. "So long, Mr. Olsen." Landon mounted Ebony and touched the brim of his hat in farewell before kicking his heels against the stallion's sides. He rode out of town, not once looking back, leaving his heart with the fiery-tempered, distrustful Crimson Rose.

CRIMSON hesitated a few seconds before entering the Lazy Day dancehall. She pulled on her earlobe, then gathered her courage around her like a suit of armor. Pushing the door open, she stepped inside and walked directly toward the woman sitting at one of the tables. "I need to talk with Dancin' Lil."

"You're lookin' at her, honey. What can I do for ya." Dancin' Lil's hennaed hair and heavy cosmetics ineffectively covered her lax age lines.

Crimson hesitated a moment, the uncertainty she felt rising back within her. Visibly stiffening her spine, she stated, "I need a job."

"Do ya, now? Why would a gal like you be interested in a job here?" Dancin' Lil motioned toward the empty chair in front of her. "Have a seat. Want something from the bar?"

"No, thank you," Crimson demurred, sitting down. After she was seated, she looked Dancin' Lil straight in the eyes. "Do I need a reason why I wanna work here?"

"A girl like you? Yes. I can see you're quality. Your manner says a lot and your dress ain't made out of cheap material. What are ya wantin', honey?"

"A job," Crimson stated simply. "I can dance, dance as well or better than the next. Are you gonna give me a job or should I go somewhere else?"

Dancin' Lil unabashedly studied the young woman in front of her, not missing the hard gleam in those great green eyes or the determined set of her chin. She was a real beauty with her dark auburn red hair, eyes that could melt a man, if she would loosen up a bit, and a body visually perfect for the lonely cowhands to enjoy. She'd be an asset, and she'd be ill-advised if she let her walk out. "Sure, honey, you got a job. When ya turn in your tickets at night, I'll count them and give ya half of what you make. What you make after hours is yours. You gotta have a name, a fancy name, too."

Crimson pursed her lips, only one name slipping past her lips. "Midnight Rose."

"Perfect, honey. Now that all the details are settled, do you gotta a place to live?"

"No, do you have any ideas?" Crimson had not thought about living arrangements. Her main objective was getting a job at the dancehall.

"Sure. One of my gals doesn't need it anymore. She's essentially jailed at the hotel. More than likely, she'll be leaving the Panhandle if she ain't sent to prison. It'll cost you five dollars a month."

"Show the way," Crimson remarked, more lighthearted than she felt.

～◎✌◎✌◎～

LONG before closing time, Crimson's legs ached and her feet were swollen, and she seriously doubted she could walk in the morning. She had never considered dancing for hours on end would be so tiring. She did admit most of the men she danced with were respectful, though her subtle questioning had not given her any clues of who killed Tom.

Groaning inwardly, she smiled as Jesse, an LX ranch hand, handed her a thick stack of tickets.

"Ma'am, heard you're callin' yoreself Midnight Rose. I think it's a mighty good name. Wanna tell ya how sorry I am 'bout the trial. Cain't see a woman like you bein' accused of murderin' a low-down rotten polecat like yore husband."

"You knew John?" Crimson asked, suddenly alert.

"Knew 'bout him, ma'am. What I did know, I didna like, and sure didna wanna know him better. I jist tellin' ya he got what he deserved."

As he danced her gracefully around the room, Crimson returned the young man's smile. In the harsh, unsettled Panhandle, there was still a youthful innocence about him. She found him pleasant and respectful, wondering before she decided on this action how the men would treat her. So far, there had been no problems except for a few suggestions for an after closing rendezvous.

"Ma'am, do you think you're doin' the right thing by bein' here? I mean, a woman like you shouldn't be in a place like this. Ain't fittin'." Looking down into her beautiful green eyes, Jesse was seriously concerned for her. He had never met a woman so pretty and graceful as she.

"I have good reason, Jesse. Let's just leave it at that." Crimson's voice was pleasant enough, but there was a hard, final edge in her voice, effectively cutting off any discussion on the matter.

"If'n ya say so, ma'am. I jist wanna tell ya if ya have any problems, call on me. I'll help ya, ya hear?"

"That's very nice of you, Jesse. Thanks, I'll think about it." Crimson smiled up at him, and Jesse missed a step, his heart flip-flopping madly, suddenly in love with the bewitching woman in his arms.

Recognizing the harsh, belligerent voice beside them, Jesse abruptly stopped them dancing.

"So, you're Dancin' Lil's new gal, Midnight Rose." He pushed Jesse to the side. "Get on with ya, boy."

"Now look, McCullar, wait your turn like ever'body else," Jesse sputtered, his newly discovered love giving him the courage to face the meanest man in town.

"That so, boy?" Before anyone could guess what was happening, McCullar jerked his pistol out of its holster and slammed the butt end against Jesse's head, knocking the young man on his knees. Too shocked at first to react, Crimson watched McCullar hit Jesse on the head again. By the third blow, Crimson's shock disappeared and she threw her body against McCullar, knocking them both to the ground. Her nails extended like a cat's, she raked them across his face, screaming her outrage.

The music and dance forgotten, several men pulled them apart. Holding onto Crimson was like holding down a captured bobcat. She shook off their hands and knelt beside Jesse, smoothing back his hair from his head and barely refrained from launching into McCullar again when her fingers came back bloody. She was unaware when several men, guns at ready, forced McCullar from the dancehall.

"Oh, Jesse." Crimson swallowed the sob rising in her throat. Jesse lay unmoving, blood streaming down his face. Someone forced her on her feet, and she unsteadily watched some men pick up Jesse and carry him into the back room.

"Doc's on his way, Crimson. Come with me and have a drink."

Recognizing the voice, Crimson turned from watching them carry Jesse away, and stared at Harvey's face. "Harvey?" she barely got out, fighting back tears.

"Yeah, Crimson. Sorry ya saw a cowpuncher's shampoo. McCullar's famous for givin' 'em." He slipped a comforting arm around her shoulders and led her toward the bar.

After he ordered whiskey, Crimson spoke half angrily, the worry still apparent in her voice. "I thought you was away on business."

"I was. I rushed back as soon as I could, hopin' I wouldna be too late. I paid a fine for missin' the trial, but all the same, I'm glad ya got off free. What I was a'wonderin' is, why are ya here in this place?" He offhandedly flipped some coins on the bar and pushed one of the filled-whiskey glasses toward her, searching her face for the answers.

"I'm gonna find out who murdered John. Until I do, everybody will think I did it." Her chin lifting defiantly, she waved away the whiskey he held toward her.

Harvey drank her whiskey, then quickly finished off his. He took her elbow and led her out the door. "We cain't talk here. Show me where yore stayin'."

Crimson did not refuse. She had enough of the dancehall tonight. Her small hut was over the hill and they walked in relative silence. Entering the one room shack, she lit a kerosene lamp. The room leaped into a yellow glow, chasing away the deep shadows. Motioning toward one of the rickety chairs, they sat down at the table.

"Ya ain't gonna find out who killed John here, Crimson. Ya know as well as I do who killed him." Harvey leaned back in the chair and searched her face.

"Who, Harvey?" There was something dubious about the way Harvey broached the subject and had Crimson on guard.

"Half-breed."

"Landon?" Crimson asked, her voice clearly conveying her disbelief.

"The very same," he remarked offhandedly. "Somehow, I'm gittin' the impression ya don't believe me. Let me assure ya, Crimson, he did kill John regardless of what ya think."

"Just how do you know?" Doubts about Landon's character were once again forming in Crimson's mind. What did she really know about him?

"It oughta be simple, Crimson. He's been behind ever'thang from the beginnin'." Uncertainty crossed her face, and he reached across and laid his hand on top of hers, unperturbed when she jerked it away. "It ain't fittin' for ya workin' in a dancehall. Ya know, I've always cared for ya. I've admired ya for ages. Why don't ya marry me and I'll protect ya and prove Half-breed killed John."

She shook her head, a numbness passing over her body. "No, Harvey. I won't marry you."

"Think about it, Crimson. I've been in love with ya for a long time. Will ya at least think 'bout it?" he asked again.

"There's no need, Harvey. The answer's no." She quickly changed the discussion, something from the trial bothering her. "Who is J.T. Markman?"

Harvey's face hardened and he looked away, his jaw clenching. "Don't know."

There was something elusive about his answer and his refusal to look at her. Before she could think about his reaction, she blurted, "You're J.T. Markman, ain't you?"

"It's better you don't know," he grumbled, standing. With a short quirk of his head, he left.

It was his reaction to her question that affirmed he went under the name of J.T. Markman. Undressing, she slipped into her narrow bed, her thoughts in such turmoil, she was unable to sleep. Her heart cried out against Harvey's accusation. Could he prove Landon killed John, er Tom? But why did he pay for her bail out of jail? *Landon, please don't let it be you! Please!* her heart cried out, but Harvey only brought back her suspicions once again.

❧

FIRMLY ensconced in the little shack, Crimson glanced about her, her heart feeling it had been roped and pulled in two completely different directions. She was furious and hurt by the outcome of the trial, and against her will, she railed against Landon, damning him and loving him for his decision. While dressing, she grimaced, her heart crying out that Landon had not prevented her from this plan she had decided on, though she realized at the same time no one could have stopped her.

I'm free, Landon, and you have ridden out of my life. Is this all I meant to you, a convenient lay, a trifling acquaintance? Where is your proclamation I am yours? Where are you? She clenched her fists so she wouldn't strike the mirror in hurt anger. She had overheard some cowboys talking about Landon riding out of town and no longer working for the KO ranch. So where was he?

Viciously inserting the last pin in her hair, she stalked out of the wobbly shanty, the unanswered questions and the rendering of her heart playing havoc with her emotions.

Though it was still too early for customers, she entered the dancehall and made her way toward a little blonde-haired woman who had befriended her on her first working day. From the beginning, she realized Rovin' Wendy had an aptitude for stretching the truth, but she was pleasant and diverting company. Her veiled questions had not revealed the answers or clues about John's murder, and she was hoping Wendy, in her own way, would be the key of answering those questions.

Sitting at the table, Crimson noticed Rovin' Wendy nursed a whiskey, a far away, sad expression upon her pixy face. Ever touched by another's misfortune, she laid her hand on top of Wendy's. "What is it, Wendy? Do you wanna talk about it?"

Pulled away from her tortuous thoughts, Rovin' Wendy had trouble focusing on Crimson. When she did, the words she often uttered before found a new release. "My man, Gambler, if he hadn't been killed, I wouldn't be here now by myself and I wouldn't be makin' a livin' like this."

Crimson's heart did a mad flutter with the mention of Gambler's name. Probing gently, she prompted, "Tell me how he was killed."

A hardness came into Wendy's eyes. "He was killed by a half-breed. He provoked him."

"Ah, damnit, Wendy, why don't you admit the truth for once in your life? He was careless in cheating at cards. Landon Wade had every right of killin' him," one of the girls sneered at the table beside theirs.

Rovin' Wendy swept her hand and knocked the whiskey glass from the table, her eyes revealing her distress. "No! No! Landon Wade couldna of killed Gambler! He wanted to be my protector and I know he couldna of done it!"

"Don't be a little nincompoop. Of course, Landon killed him for cheatin'. I was there and I saw it happen. I've been tellin' you the truth for a long time."

Rovin' Wendy covered her ears, tears streaming down her cheeks and ran out the door while screaming, "No! No!"

Crimson sat frozen, one of her deepest fears answered. *Landon! You did kill Gambler!* Holding back her tears, her eyes burned, like a vice crushing her heart so painfully she had trouble breathing.

One of the girls touched her shoulder, concerned for the sudden colorlessness of her face. "Don't worry 'bout Wendy. She's had trouble reconciling the fact for a long time. She just doesn't wanna believe her man was a cheat."

She handed Crimson her whiskey glass. "Here, drink a little of this and get a hold of yourself. The customers are comin' in."

Crimson mindlessly took the glass and sipped it. The fiery liquid burned down her throat and landed with scorching confusion within her stomach. She wiped the tears from her eyes the whiskey brought and laid the offending glass down on the table. The potent liquor put the needed color back into her cheeks. Before she could dwell on the startling turn of events, a cowboy approached her and handed her several tickets.

⌇◎⌇⌇◎⌇

COTTON stood at the doorway, a rush of anger flushing across his face while watching his headstrong sister dance with an awkward cowboy. He admitted she was a fetching picture with her hair in an elegant coiffure, curling tendrils softening the lines along the side of her face and a crimson rose with a background of black velvet in her hair. Pinpoints of livid lights swept across his eyes when he spied her scandalous attire—the elegant dress of black satin, the sleeves a full, quarter length ending into long black gloves and the skirt pulled back into a small bustle, clearly outlining her shapely form. The bodice was cut into a deep vee with a red rose settled in the deepest part, drawing attention to her ivory breasts, which fairly spilled around the edges of the gown.

In two long strides, he was at Crimson's side, pulling the cowboy away from her. The cowboy sputtered at the intrusion but was quickly hushed by the dangerous glint in Cotton's eyes. "Try it, cowboy, and I'll put a bullet through you. This is my little sister and I'll not have her sullied by the likes of you."

The cowboy backed off a step, Cotton's hard, unyielding stance giving him a moment's hesitation. The man meant exactly what he said, and since he was not adept with guns, he shrugged before walking off, mumbling under his breath.

The momentary shock wearing off, Crimson threw her arms around Cotton's neck. "Oh, Cotton, you don't know how glad I am to see you. I thought I'd never see you again."

Cotton stood implacable under her sisterly hug, then grabbed her by the arm, his fingers like iron, and pulled her toward the door, unhindered by her angry retort and sudden digging of her heels into the hardpacked dirt floor. "I don't wanna hear it, Crim. You are comin' with me. The family's waitin' for you at your little hut."

The embarrassment and anger quaking through her, resembled a hard blowing wind. Her family! Oh Lord! For them finding her in this situation was beyond comprehension, and it kept her quiet as Cotton led her outside and toward her small shack.

Her lips trembling, she opened the door. She had barely stepped inside when she was enfolded in her sister's loving embrace. The tears she had held back for so long burst out in a rush. Both sisters cried wrapped in each other's arms until Buck separated them and gave Crimson a quick hug, then barraged her with questions.

"Give her a chance to breathe, Buck," Honeysuckle sharply ordered her husband, sitting Crimson next to her on the bed.

"My God, look how's she dressed! Cotton found her in a dancehall! And you say give her time to breathe? I'll give her time to breathe after I bend her over my knee and bust her bottom," Buck retorted, his face mirroring Cotton's annoyance when seeing her scandalous dress.

Honeysuckle affectionately squeezed Crimson's hand, shooting a quelling glance at her husband.

"You can't leave her alone for two seconds without her gettin' into some kind of trouble," Cotton harshly stated, pulling a rickety chair closer toward the bed.

"You shut up too, Cotton! All we've heard is gossip. Now both of you be quiet and let her tell us what happened." Honeysuckle rarely raised her voice, but this time she was determined her hotheaded men would listen and listen well to Crimson's side.

Crimson drew in a shuddering breath, clasping the shawl

341

Honeysuckle placed over her shoulders. Pulling it in front of the exposed parts of her breasts, she faced her family and launched into her story, leaving out nothing. She began with her first meeting with Landon, but carefully left out how they had made love, until the present. She answered a question here or there when Cotton or Buck interrupted and cleared up some detail. The rest of the time, they remained silent, their faces growing red with suppressed fury after each infliction she voiced regarding John's actions toward her.

"Damn the son of a bitch! I never trusted him! If you had listened to us, you wouldna of suffered through this whole blasted thing!" Buck rose from the chair and paced in front of them, banging his fist against his opened hand.

"I didn't know he would be like that, Buck, honest I didn't. We were in school together and were best friends. How could I have known? Besides, I did it so Landon would stop rustling your cattle," Crimson cried in distress, dismayed by the tightening of Buck's and Cotton's jaws, reading in their expressions if John had not been killed by parties unknown, they would have done it themself.

Suddenly, Buck threw back his head and laughed, breaking the tension in the room. "Oh Lord, Crimson, if you had only voiced your fears before you married the bastard, Honey and I could have cleared up the misconception. Landon is one of our dearest friends, and he would never rustle our cattle. I definitely know he wouldna kill you."

Crimson sat stunned for a second before her heart hardened against Landon once again. "But he killed Gambler!"

"With damned good reason, I suspect," Buck shot back. "Don't go judging, Crimson. Landon's a good man if a confused one."

"But that didn't give him the right..."

Buck sharply interrupted, "With good reason, Crimson. You said yourself he caught Gambler cheating, and if I'm any judge of character, I imagine Gambler shot first."

"It doesn't explain what you're doing in those whore's clothes and in a dancehall," Cotton curtly barked.

"Cotton!" Honeysuckle cried, her hand fluttering to her breast, shocked at his choice of words.

"Well, it's the damn truth," Cotton snorted, glaring at his little sister.

342

Crimson shrank back slightly, an embarrassed red rushing across her face. She glanced around the shack, avoiding his eyes. "Where's Red?"

"Don't change the subject, Crim." Cotton pulled the chair up closer, his knees touching hers.

Honeysuckle shot Cotton a pointed glare and answered Crimson's question. "He couldn't come. He had to stay on the land he and Cotton are homesteading. If he left, they would of lost their land."

"The little scamp had a shotgun marriage," Cotton interrupted, wanting the amenities quickly over. "He got a little chit with child, and her father brought over a shotgun and a preacher."

Waving his hand and dismissing his brother, he began his questioning again. "Now answer my questions. What are ya doing wearing that and working in this part of town?"

Crimson's chin lifted in unconscious rebellion, her eyes narrowing. "There was no other way. I will not go through life with people thinking I killed my husband. You can't stop me *and* I will find out who did."

"Oh, but we will stop you," Cotton resolutely replied, pointing his finger at Crimson. "Buck and I will take over, and you will go back to the ranch with Honeysuckle."

Chapter 34
Plucking a Rose

CRIMSON shuddered, the trial haunting her and the opposing attorney pointing his finger while proclaiming her guilty. Without thinking, she slapped Cotton's hand away. "Don't you ever point a finger at me," she warned in a deadly voice. She jumped from the bed and walked toward the other side of the little hut, her body visibly shaking as she gained control over the sudden irrational fury erupting inside her.

Taking several deep breaths and stiffening her spine, she walked back in front of them and stared both in the eyes. With an angry huff, she threw Honeysuckle's shawl on the bed and placed her fists on her hips. "Before this farce goes any farther, I want you to look at me and listen well. I am a woman grown, capable of deciding and doing what I think is right. I love you both dearly, but you cannot tell me what I can do or how I do it. I will find John's killer any way I see fit, and if you don't like how I go about it, tough."

Both men rose at the same time, their faces hard masks. Cotton was the first to speak, his voice cynical and reprimanding, "You won't ever change, will you, Crim? You'll drag all our names in the mud so you can get revenge."

"That's enough!" Honeysuckle shouted, flying off the bed and planting herself firmly between Crimson and the men. "Do you hear me? I have heard all of this I'm going to. Both of you get out of here and go check on the kids at Roscoe's. Scoot!"

Cotton opened his mouth, but Buck laid his hand on his arm, stopping him. He glared at his wife, seeing the fierce protective expression on her face, which proclaimed nothing would change her mind. His glance firmly conveyed he and Honeysuckle would have words later. "It may be best we leave now and let our tempers cool, Cotton. Come on." Guiding Cotton toward the door, he shot the women a pointed look.

Crimson went limp after hearing the door close behind them. Honeysuckle led her back to the bed where they sat down and she affectionately squeezed Crimson's hands. "I can't condemn or condone what you are doing, Sis. Who knows? Maybe if I was in your shoes, I'd do the same thing. I ask only one thing—if you need help or need to talk, come find me. If you had of told us of your suspicions earlier, we could of saved you a whole lot of heartache."

A tear slipped down Crimson's cheek, followed by another, then another until she was sobbing uncontrollably. She did not resist when Honeysuckle enfolded her into her arms and let her cry.

Honeysuckle soothed her sister, stroking the back of her neck, tears flooding her own eyes. "There's more to it than what you've told us, Sis. You're in love with Landon Wade, ain't you?"

Crimson left her sister's comforting embrace and sniffed, wiping the tears from her cheeks and her runny nose. She silently took the handkerchief Honeysuckle handed her and blew her nose before answering. "Yes, I love him. That's what hurt so much, thinking he was rustling cattle and wanting to kill me."

Honeysuckle gave a low laugh and compulsively hugged her sister again. "He would never hurt any of us, much less you."

Crimson stared off at the far wall, the hurt she had been suffering clearly showing in her eyes. "He's gone, Honeysuckle. He rode out after the trial and I'll never see him again."

"My baby sister has grown up," Honeysuckle said sadly before giving Crimson another affectionate squeeze. "We'll talk in the morning when tempers have cooled. You rest now."

Crimson opened the door for Honeysuckle, and both were shocked when Cotton nearly fell inside from leaning against the outside door jamb.

He spoke first. "I'm waiting on Honeysuckle to guide her back.

Couldn't very well let her walk around here without a escort."

"That's very considerate of you, Cotton." Honeysuckle took his arm and gave Crimson a cheerful wave goodbye.

Cotton coolly met Crimson's glare. "I'll be back."

"It won't do you any good."

"We'll see."

Crimson stared at the closed door, a multitude of different emotions rushing through her, mentally preparing herself for the argument she knew was coming.

Cotton did come back in short order, and they argued and fought, their voices rising in heated anger. She was sure the whole town could hear them. Finally, having enough, knowing neither were going to change their minds, she begged, "Meet me halfway, Cotton."

Cotton glared at his stubborn sister, his hands clenching and unclenching in front of him, fighting against taking her by the shoulders and shaking some sense into her. "How?" he asked suspiciously.

"I will finish what I already set in motion. If it will clear your conscience some, then help me find the killer."

Cotton wanted to argue the point again, but all his reasoning had gotten him nowhere. At least this way, he could keep a watchful eye on her. With strong misgivings, he scurrilously replied, "I'll think about it."

❧

"SHE'S hell-bent on this damned plan of hers," Cotton snarled. "She hasn't changed a damned bit. It's her way or not at all. She had the gall of asking me to meet her halfway."

"And did you agree?" Buck asked, looking up from the beer he had been twirling in his hand.

"Told her I'd think about it."

Buck shrugged his massive shoulders. "Ain't much we can do about it, except..." He launched into a plan. After he finished, he asked, "Agreed?"

"If you think it will work, I'm all for it." Cotton would try anything just to keep his sister out of trouble and the lower end of

Tascosa's Hog Town. He had hoped marriage would calm her down, at least pierce through her hard head.

"Take Honey and the children back to the ranch while I'm gone. We'll leave Crimson on her own for a few days and hope she don't get into any trouble while we're away. We'll both be back by then, but you know Crimson. A few days and God only knows what she'll stir up by then." Buck finished his beer, nodding toward the door. "Best get started."

❦

CRIMSON walked toward the Drink Emporium and the job she found distasteful but was determined she would discover the truth who really killed John. She must clear her name or she would never be able to lift her head with pride again. She had been more than a little surprised her family had not forced her back home, much less arguing about her life's choice. She was thankful they did not. Nothing they could have said would have changed her mind, but what surprised her the most was when all of them left town. She did notice one of the ranch hands watching over her whenever she was at work. Bothered only a little, she was thankful for the protection. He had stopped more than one man's forced attention on her.

Shaking her head, she wondered what her family was planning. It was unlike them not pressing the issues and letting things go quite so easily. Whatever it was, she was sure she would not like it. They were just as headstrong and stubborn as she.

Landon, why did you leave? she silently screamed. Why couldn't she forget him? She had just about reconciled herself in believing he was not responsible for John's death, but Harvey's visit brought those doubts back more strongly than before. Regardless of her family's reassurance he would not harm them, he could have been the one who killed her husband.

And Harvey? He was another problem. He hung around, watching every move she made, pressing his suit and simply refusing no for an answer. An unpleasant shiver swept through her. He was a small comparison against Landon, her enemy, her love. Never again would she marry a man without loving him, if she could love another man.

347

She hated admitting she was in love with Landon, his mixed blood making no difference. Yet, she cursed his mixed blood when she saw the town's reaction and accusations against him. *You walked out of my life forever and forever I am doomed to love you.*

Forcefully dragging her thoughts away from Landon, she waved at the pregnant Mexican woman walking past her. The sound of horses coming down the street and the riders' boisterous voices loudly rumbled through the town, disturbing the peaceful day. The riders were apparently drunk and probably headed for a bar in town.

She recognized Frank Leigh, the foreman of the LS ranch. As he rode by a flock of ducks preening in the water, he pulled out his gun and shot the head off a duck as he and his men passed. The young Mexican woman she had greeted screamed, then fell on the ground in a faint. The men laughed and raced down the road.

The gunshot shattered Crimson's nerves and the scream screeched through every nerve ending when watching the duck's head splatter blood and tissue. There was a commotion behind her, and she assumed it was the young woman's family rushing toward her. After assuring herself the Mexican woman was unharmed, she headed for the Drink Emporium, her clenching fists grabbing at the sides of her gown.

Nearing the Drink Emporium, she spotted Sheriff Cape Willingham run at a half-trot from the rear of the saloon, his sawed-off shotgun in the crook of his arm. Leigh dismounted, his reins and cigar in his left hand, his right hand free, and unaware of the sheriff yet.

Willingham stepped out on the street, his shotgun raised at Leigh's chest, his finger on the trigger. "Leigh, hand over your weapons. We've had enough of your insultin' the law for one day."

Leigh did not reply. He turned, put his free hand on the saddle horn, leaped into it without touching the stirrup, and landed in the saddle. His right hand flew over his holster and his fingers closed around the handle of his pistol.

Before he could free his six-shooter, Willingham emptied both barrels of buckshot into his side, blowing him out of the saddle. The horse bolted, racing down the street past the sheriff. Leigh's companions kicked their heels against their mounts' flanks and followed it, wisely bypassing any more trouble.

Badly shaken from watching the bloody scene, Crimson turned around and raced back for her hut, realizing she could not possibly work in her present condition.

Morbid curiosity brought out the townspeople, many of them rushing past her. A few tried questioning her, but she numbly shook her head and continued walking fast, frantically hurrying home. Perhaps there she could shut out the world and what she had just witnessed.

As she topped the hill, she became aware of a fast-moving rider behind her. She edged off the road. Barely turning her head, she was caught by surprise when the rider headed straight toward her. Before she could leap out of the way, the rider swooped down and caught her by the waist. He threw her face down across the front of his saddle and raced out of town.

Crimson lay stunned, the breath knocked out of her, the saddle horn digging cruelly into her pelvic bone and jamming against it each time the horse hit the ground. She fought for breath, the pungent, salty smell of the animal filling her nostrils, the sweat stiffened hairs stinging her face and the ground swiftly flying past her vision.

Chilling fear kept her from fighting at first, then with a savage snarl, she kicked her legs and pounded her fists into the animal, desperately fighting for her freedom. The hard pressure of a hand against the small of her back effectively held her struggling form in place. She raised her head, her lips pulled back in a feral snarl, and tried biting her abductor's leg. Each time the horse's feet hit the ground, it jarred her teeth in her mouth, hitting so hard against her captor's leg bone that her teeth felt like they were loosened. Her captor growled, pulled her partially upright and cuffed her on the side of the head, dazing her.

It seemed like hours before the man slowed his mount and hailed some men up ahead. With frustrated patience, Crimson drew a ragged breath, lifted her upper body and sank her teeth in her captor's thigh right above the knee.

The man yelped in pain, striking her against the side of the head with his open palm. Her fright and anger were so strong, she did not feel pain. She sank her teeth deeper into his thigh's flesh and the next blow was so hard, it snapped her teeth through the skin. Biting off a bloody chunk of the man's thigh, blinding pain exploded through her head and tears formed in her eyes. Shaking her head like a ferocious lioness, she spat blood from her mouth onto the hardpacked dirt. There was a sharp tug at the back of her gown and the next thing she knew, she was viciously hitting the ground.

"The damned bloody bitch bit me!" he cursed, his face screwed up in pain, reaching for the place where she had bitten him. His leg went numb and his hand came away sticky with blood. "The damned savage bit a hunk out of me! Give me some damn whiskey! The bitch's probably got rabies."

Crimson fell on her back, the air knocked out of her. She struggled for breath, unable to sit upright. Finally able to pull in several deep breaths, she yelped outraged and flipped over onto her knees with her palms planted firmly on the ground. In grim satisfaction, she watched a man named Frank hand her abductor a flask of whiskey. "Serves you right, McCullar," she taunted bitterly. "You nearly killed Jesse."

"Shut up, bitch," McCullar ground through clenched teeth, pouring a liberal dose of whiskey over the wound and biting back a scream when the whiskey burned the flesh. Yanking off his neckerchief, he tied it around the bloody bite, then pulled his six-shooter from the waistband of his pants and aimed it at Crimson's head. "I oughta kill ya."

Her hair had come loose during the wild ride, and she haughtily tossed her hair over her shoulder. She glared at him, frightened out of her wits, but derisively sneered, "Go ahead and kill me, McCullar. Only a sorry snake in the grass would shoot a woman. You're such a coward, you only beat a unsuspecting man over the head with your gun."

McCullar eased out of the saddle, cocked the hammer of his pistol and aimed it at her head.

"Go ahead," she challenged bitterly, pulling her shoulders back defiantly. Her shock and fury made her beyond reason or care for her own safety, though a cold sweat broke out on her forehead.

"McCullar! That's enough!" The one called Ben warned.

Her eyes green fire, Crimson turned toward the man who spoke, noting there were three men counting McCullar. She studied them, memorizing their faces.

McCullar slowly eased the hammer forward, his face a mask of fury. "I'd kill ya if I hadn't promised I'd bring you in alive."

"What the little wildcat needs is a tamer," the other man called Frank said, his brown eyes lasciviously watching the rise and fall of the ivory breasts fairly spilling over the top of her black gown.

Seeing the same expression before in John's eyes, Crimson grew taut, every muscle in her body ready to spring away if he came toward her. "You touch me and I'll kill you," she grated harshly, meaning every word.

"Half-breed picked a live one," Ben snorted.

The air left her lungs at the mention of Half-breed. Drawing in a quick, painful breath, she warily watched the men, her mind screaming against Landon. Frank jumped from his saddle, his face hard, his eyes filled with lust and his intent clear. She jumped to her feet, spun on her heel and ran with the tight skirt of her gown in one hand and her steps short and awkward.

Her hair was like waving a red flag in front of a bull. Frank caught the streaming mass, sharply pulling it. Her head snapped back, jerking her off-balanced. He caught her before she fell and roughly turned her around. Shoving her up cruelly against him, he wrapped his arms around her, catching her far elbow with one hand and at the same time, locking the other arm. Throwing back his head and laughing pitilessly, he lowered his mouth toward hers while releasing one hand and fastening it on her breast, his fingers digging mercilessly into the tender flesh.

Crimson gagged, his foul-smelling breath cutting off her precious air. Twisting her head, she kicked out at him, but he had her in such a hold she was almost helpless. He released her breast and caught a handful of hair, jerking her head around and holding it while capturing her lips in a bruising, punishing kiss.

She screamed her outrage against his mouth, fighting him with every ounce of her strength. She squirmed and twisted in his arms and clenched her teeth together, but he forced his tongue past them. She felt the bulge of his loins against her stomach each time she squirmed, trying to break his hold.

The invasion of her mouth was too much. She clamped down on his tongue and brought her knee up at the same time. He screeched, releasing her so suddenly she stumbled and fell, landing on her bottom. She instinctively threw back her arms, catching herself against the fall, the rocky ground scratching and cutting the palms of her hands. Momentarily stunned, she grimly watched the man clutched at his groin and spat blood out of his mouth simultaneously.

"Grab her, Ben," McCullar demanded.

Seeing Ben running toward her, she jumped up, spun around and scampered away. Something knocked her to the ground and she landed face forward, her teeth cutting into her lip and dirt filling her mouth, nose and eyes. Her arms were jerked violently behind her back and a rope was tightly wrapped around her hands. As she was jerked upright, she spat blood and dirt at the ground, almost choking when the man pushed her toward McCullar.

"Damned bitch, you're a vicious little savage and I ain't gonna have no more trouble from ya." With a wolfish grin, McCullar slammed his pistol's handle against her head.

Explosive pain and brilliant stars flashed through her head and everything went black.

"I hope the hell ya didn't kill her, McCullar," Ben growled. "Half-breed ain't gonna like it."

"If you wanna fight the little bitch, then you find a better way. I've had enough." McCullar threw a baleful glance at the other man. "Go help Frank so we can get the hell outta here."

◦◦◦◦◦

CRIMSON groaned, her head feeling like a bass drum someone was beating upon. Her lips were swollen and stiff from dried blood, her mouth so dry it felt like a herd of buffalo had been stampeded through it. She tried moving, but every muscle in her body screamed in protest and blinding pain shot through her head when she opened her eyes. Quickly closing them, another groan escaped her. She rubbed her face against something scratchy beneath her and struggled, realizing her hands were tied securely behind her back. Lying face down, she opened her eyes again and focused on her surroundings. A feeling of deja vu pierced every nerve ending when she perceived the hide walls.

Damn him! she silently cried. Damn his black soul! He's brought me to an Indian camp. She shut her eyes, denying her surroundings, denying the bitter agony tearing at her heart. *How much more can you hurt me, Landon? How much more before I die of this mental torment? Are you determined to break my spirit? I'd rather you'd physically cut out my heart instead of this!*

She fought back the stinging, bitter tears forcing past her eyelids. *No, I won't cry! I will not grovel at his feet and beg for my life.* Ruthlessly, she fought against her building heartbreak and the tears filling her eyes. Hearing someone enter the tepee, she kept her eyes closed, forcing her tears back.

"Well, wildcat, I see you've finally come around. Half-breed's ready for ya."

McCullar's voice sounded above her and she stiffened, willing herself motionless. She could not face Landon! Could not until she gained control over her wayward emotions!

"Ain't gonna do ya no good playin' possum. I know you're awake."

Hearing him step nearer, she refused to open her eyes. A scream nearly escaped her when her tied hands were grabbed and she was roughly and painfully jerked upward. Her eyes flew open, hate crystal clear in the misty green depths. "You're a dead man, McCullar. My family will find you!"

McCullar sneered, jerking her tied hands upward toward her shoulder blades. A grunt of pain escaped her, bringing him mild satisfaction. "Cain't say yore a docile bitch. Don't matter no how, Half-breed's gonna take care of ya."

He grabbed the tangled mass of hair at the back of her neck, shoved her head down and pushed her through the tepee flap.

Chapter 35
Wilted Rose

THE SUN was burning away the early morning mist that hung over the land, dissipating her pride and will to live with it. In her peripheral vision, Crimson noticed the curious stares the Indians cast her while McCullar half-dragged, half-pushed her toward another tepee. With her head down, she was shoved through the tepee's opening, her wrenching heart a mass of tormented agony. Of everything she imagined Landon had done, this would never have been one of them—him capturing her and submitting her to cruelty. Her eyes a dull, lifeless green, she stared at the ground, avoiding looking at the man waiting for her inside.

"The rose of triumph looks a little wilted this mornin'."

The frigid tone of a man's voice sent warning through her body as she lifted her head and peered into pitless blue eyes. Her heart skipped erratically with the mingle of joy it was not Landon, then clenched with dread. The man's merciless eyes fastened on hers and the malicious tilt of his mouth sent a fresh wave of trepidation settling between her hunched shoulders.

"Who are you?" She forced the question from her compressed lips, feeling breathless.

The man's mouth pulled back into a mocking sneer, and he waved his hand negligently. "The little rose doesn't recognize me, McCullar. Tell her who I am."

"Whiskey Joe or known by most as Half-breed," McCullar introduced, a chilling smile on his thin lips.

"Half…" Crimson stopped, confusion sweeping through her. "I…I…don't understand."

"Ah, no? What a shame." Whiskey Joe curtly waved McCullar out of the tepee. After McCullar left, Whiskey Joe slipped the knife from its case hanging at his side and abstractedly cleaned his fingernails. He walked around Crimson, crudely examining her, taking in the tangled mass of auburn hair, the dirt smudges across her nose and bruised cheek, and the dust marked and torn black satin gown. He was most interested in the white expanse of breasts pushing prudently above the gown's decolletage. "You're beautiful in a pale sort of way. It's almost a shame after I tire of ya, I'm gonna let the dogs have ya."

"Why? What have I done?" she cried, fear lodging uncomfortably in her throat and making her voice squeaky. The cold steel of his knife blade skimmed across the exposed tops of her heaving breasts and cold sweat popped out over her body.

"Little rose, tonight I will enjoy debauching every nuance of your body." He grabbed her arm tied behind her back and cut the rope binding her hands.

Drawing in a quick, shuddering breath, she rubbed her wrists and shook her arms, gritting her teeth against the stinging of restored blood flow and piercing pain shooting through them. "Why kill me?" she asked through gritted teeth, fighting the tears threatening behind her eyeballs.

His rough hands dropped on the top of her shoulder blades, and he shoved her on the ground into a sitting position. There was the pressure, then the sound of material ripping and the rush of hot air along her barely covered leg.

A nasty smile uplifted his thin lips. Her gown had ripped along the seams and exposed her petticoat. He crouched on his haunches in front of her, still playing with the long, wicked-looking knife. "Too many questions, little rose, but I shall answer them for ya. It will be a pleasure watching the expression on your face when I do. You've become a thorn in my side, Crimson Rose of Triumph. You've been digging deeper with every question you ask. It wouldn't be long before you'd started whoring in your desperation of finding Tom's killer. With your beauty and talent of turning men's heads, someone would open up and spill their guts about my business to get between your sickly white thighs." He ran the cold, sharp steel under the edge of her petticoat, then with an upward motion, slit the material from her ankle toward her upper thigh, his eyes cold and a snarky smile lifting one side of his mouth.

"The truth?" Panic filled her, racing from the top of her head and down through her toes with the knife lightly laying on her upper thigh. She glanced at him in confusion, then her face suddenly cleared.

"It was you trying to kill me all this time!" she accused, studying him. He was about the same height as Landon, slender with coal-black hair and blue eyes, but the resemblance ended there. Landon's nose was broad whereas Whiskey Joe's was hawk-like, and Whiskey Joe's icy blue eyes lacked a spark of humanity. Glancing around the tepee, she spied the same type of Stetson hat Landon wore, hanging on a pole. At a distance, mistaking Whiskey Joe and Landon would be easy, and in describing them, the descriptions would have been much the same. "But why?"

"You're a smart gal, little rose, but I'll tell you just so ya won't die not knowing." A wolfish grin split Whiskey Joe's narrowed mouth. Sitting and crossing his legs in Indian fashion on the buffalo robe, he waved his knife in front of him, indicating the grounds outside.

"These are my people, the Comanches, the white ones call us. Being of mixed blood, I came and went as I pleased. I met Tom, that bastard husband of yours, in Kansas. We recognized a ruthlessness in each other. It was your lover Landon who did us both a favor by killing Gambler. Gambler had been organizing the underground, but with his death, the struggle started between me and Tom. Ah, I've gotten ahead of myself."

Crimson stared at the savage in front of her, relieved Landon was innocent mingled with the cold fingers of fear squeezing her heart. Terror-stricken, she was assured too late of Landon's innocence, and surely as she was still breathing, she was staring death in the face.

Lupine-blue eyes glared into hers, immobilizing her with their intensity. A heartless grin pulled up his razor-thin lips when she shrank back from the point of his knife. "Cringe, little rose, I smell your fear."

He ran a thin tongue slowly over his lips. "It also changes the smell and taste of your sweat. A headier draught I've never smelt before. I will taste you, little rose, with much pleasure. You will give me what ya so freely gave Landon before it's all over. When I tire of ya and after my dogs have ya, I shall end your miserable life."

"But why? I don't understand. I've done nothing to you." Her voice came out high and squeaky. This could not be happening! She swallowed hard, forcing down her steadily rising panic. Calling from the very depths of her soul, she searched for the few remaining strings of defiance within her.

Whiskey Joe, seeing the change in her facial expression, threw back his head and sniggered, a potent deadly sound. "Yes, little rose, draw on your reserve of stubbornness. It will take you much longer to die, but..." He ran the blade across her cheekbone, "after I am through with you, you will be cowering from everyone's touch. You will have a painful death either while or after my tribe and my men take their own pleasure from my leftovers."

He grabbed a tangled tress and pulled her face cruelly toward his, his foul-smelling breath nearly choking her. "I will crush your great pride. You've had the devil's own luck. Ya shoulda been dead a long time ago." He licked his lips in anticipation of when he would have her and how she would beg for her miserable life.

"What do you mean?" she squeaked, tears filling her eyes when he pulled her hair sharply.

He released the curly, tangled mass and leaned back, his ever-watching eyes observing each fleeting expression on her heart-shaped face. With a sudden, quick motion, he tore off his shirt, smiling pitilessly when she cringed backward. Pointing at a scar on his upper forearm, he growled, "See this? This is from our first encounter."

Whiskey Joe snarled at the puzzlement across her face. "The immigrant wagon train? Remember, little rose? I wasn't expecting a fierce she-demon rushing out of nowhere riding hell-bent for leather into the fray. Ya shot me, creasing my arm. I woulda killed ya if your horse hadn't reared."

"You!" Crimson breathed, the night coming back clear as if it were yesterday. How could she have ever forgotten those cold blue eyes? She unconsciously leaned forward, staring at his face.

"Yes, me. It was my first encounter with you. You and your brothers put questions into the citizens' mouths, which none had ever been there before. I swore then I would kill ya, little rose. You kept appearing more and more frequently, asking too many questions about Half-breed, and then the fool Tom up and married ya."

"Ah, the day you went riding along the lonely stretch, I shoulda pulled you off your horse and devoured ya like your lover did later, then killed you, but instead, I took a shot at you and your fool horse bolted. I shoulda hit ya and thought I had when you laid so damn still. Tom and Harvey heard the shot too. Harvey, the dog's own fool, didna like it and argued with me over it. The fool pulled a gun on me."

"You're the one who shot Harvey, not..." She did not finish, the last two years becoming crystal clear.

"Of course, I shot him. It was afterwards I realized I hadn't hit ya and you weren't asking about me, but another half-breed. Tom was no fool when he let you believe it was Landon Wade. He knew there was a attraction between the two of ya. You believed the worst of Wade while feathering Tom's nest. What he didna realize at first was he was also aiding me. It was easy enough letting the people think Half-breed was Landon and he was part of the underground, especially since I went outta my way and bought a hat like his. It woulda worked too if your brother-in-law hadn't known better and started his own investigation."

"I did watch you, kept you constantly within my sights. Saw ya meeting Landon in the abandoned sod one day, watched Tom beat ya after you married the fool. Yes, little rose, I saw it all. Saw you enter the Kiowa encampment with your half-breed. Saw you near the creek where ya ignored your wedding vows, your naked body gleaming like the purest ivory against the gray sky."

He licked his lips again, relishing the memory of her nakedness, the long, smooth limbs joined at the apex by a thick patch of curly, auburn pubic hair. "Your half-breed was a fool letting ya refuse him after the bobcat interrupted your tryst. I woulda forced ya into completing what ya started."

With each word he spoke, another piece of the puzzle was neatly inserted. Her fear was so great, she did not feel any embarrassment he had seen her naked. She had never felt so helpless in her life. With perverse curiosity, she sat spellbound while he answered most of the questions that had been bothering her for so long.

"In Mobeetie when ya was gonna ask your brother-in-law the truth about Landon, he pushed you down before my bullet could hit ya."

"You're the one who shot at me," Crimson interrupted harshly, her fingernails digging into the palms of her hands. She suppressed a shudder, realizing just how many times she had been his target.

He was unruffled by her spurt of anger. "Yes, and that was when I learned how Tom truly felt about you. Tom was a fool. He hated and loved ya at the same time. He had trouble separating the two. You are the rose of triumph. Whoever owns ya owns respectability. That's what ya meant, respectability, a show of winning. It was then I realized taking ya from him would make me triumphant, make me the winner, the head man of the syndicate. But I had one advantage over Tom—I was scouting some for the army. It played very well with my plans and gave me the jump on whatever Tom was doing, but before I could carry out my plans, someone else killed him."

"You...you...didn't kill him?" Crimson stammered. "But who did?"

Whiskey Joe nonchalantly shrugged his shoulders. "Who cares? Tom got what he deserved. If they hadn't killed him, I would of."

Crimson rubbed her temples, unanswered questions still playing havoc with her mind. "John...uh...Tom hated breeds of any kind. How could you work so closely with him?"

"Simple enough. I provided a service he couldna get from anyone else. We met in Kansas, like I told ya, only he challenged me. When I beat him at his own dirty game, he attained a grudging respect for me. We were planning on taking another load of cattle from the L Heart range the day the tornado... shall we say, ya got raunchy with your half-breed. I recognized you and had to keep ya from recognizing me. I planned on killing ya and would of if you hadn't met up with your half-breed."

"Why are you telling me all of this? I had no idea it was you instead of Landon doing these things." It was John stealing her family's cattle all along. How could she have been so blind, so stupid?

"Ya were asking too many questions. It was just a matter of time before ya asked the right person and he spilled his guts about me. Ya were stupidly smart, little rose, by going undercover and leaving the dancehall to work at the Drink Emporium instead. Ya didn't realize how close ya were getting. The Drink Emporium is where I carry out most of my business. Your name couldn't of been anymore stained by ya working on that unsavory side of town than it already was. People expected it of ya. You see, most of them are not satisfied ya didna kill him. Whoever set ya up and framed you for the murder of your husband didn't take into consideration your breed would pay your bail and encourage the district attorney to dig deep into Tom's past."

"All this time, I've accused Landon of these things," Crimson mumbled, speaking more to herself than him. Her teeth gnawed at her trembling bottom lip as she fought against the tears popping into her eyes.

"What do you intend to do with me?" She wished she could call back the question as it left her mouth, and watched Whiskey Joe lick his cruel lips, a glint of pure evil sparkling in his eyes.

Whiskey Joe stood and walked behind her. Grabbing a length of hair, he yanked her head back, his knife tracing the exposed mounds of her breasts above her bodice. "Don't cringe too much, little rose, or I might accidently cut off those lovely white breasts." With a quick movement, he slipped the point of the knife at the low center of her bodice and sliced the material down to her waistline.

Crimson froze, aware of the sharp blade against her flesh. Whiskey Joe pulled back the sides of the bodice with the tip of the knife and exposed her full mounds.

"You shall be my whore until I tire of ya, little rose, then I shall torture ya and make ya pay for all the sleepless nights you've given me."

Terror kept her from moving a muscle and barely breathing as he ran the point of the knife around an impudent nipple. She who had laughed fear in the face and defied it, was frozen motionless with it. She had no thoughts, only wishing she were free. Freedom had never seemed so far out of reach.

"Whiskey Joe, Flies-Like-An-Eagles' band has arrived and the Comanches are askin' fer ya to join 'em in welcomin' 'em," McCullar said, grinning widely at the display of her breasts.

Whiskey Joe released her hair and slipped both hands over her breasts with his knife still held in one hand, and painfully squeezed them while saying casually against her ear, "We'll finish this later." Sheathing his knife, he ordered, "Take her back to the other tepee and set guards in front. We don't want our little rose plucked from our midst."

McCullar pruriently grinned, grabbing Crimson by the arm and pulling it sharply behind her. Crimson cried out as hot pain sliced through her shoulder. After Whiskey Joe left the tepee, McCullar grabbed one of her full breasts and squeezed, licking his lips. "Little bitch, I shall teach ya what it is to have a real man atween yore thighs."

Crimson ducked her head as red covered her face, neck and breasts, and suppressed the cringe running through her body. When she lifted her leg for an awkward back-kick, he brought her arm up toward the middle of her back. "Don't try it, bitch or I'll break yore arm."

McCullar pushed her out of the flap into the opened encampment while tears of pain, fury, embarrassment and fear blinded her. She kept her head down, feeling curious eyes watching them as he forced her back into the tepee she had regained consciousness in. Her arm was pinned behind her back and he still cruelly fondled her breast, the other exposed in plain view.

He shoved her inside and she landed face down. McCullar stood over her, straddling her prostrate form, his mocking laughter falling unpleasantly on her ears. "Later, bitch, I shall have ya after Whiskey Joe finishes, but 'til then, I gotta put in my presence at the Injuns' powwow."

McCullar pulled back the flap, then turned back around, warning, "If ya try leavin', the guards will stop ya. And when they do, they won't stop with jist takin' ya back here. They'll rip off the last of yoren clothin' and line up fer their turn 'cause they like watchin' each utter humpin' a white lady."

With a twisted smile, he licked his lips, enjoying watching her frantically cover her breasts. "Yep, after the tribesmen and the rest of us git our first round with ya, the bastards will have to tie a board behind their asses so they don't fall in for the second rounds." His cruel, suggestive laughter trailed behind him as he left the tepee.

On her hands and knees, Crimson crawled toward the farthest leather wall and huddled there, her thoughts on Landon. *Landon, I am so sorry I never believed you, forever doubting what you told me. I drove you away. I'll never feel your arms around me again nor tell you how much I love you. The words will be forever locked into my heart and will die with me. It's too late to change the past and the future is a black spot in the distance. They're gonna kill me.*

No! her mind screamed. *I'll not die so easily!* Her fierce pride rose within her, shattering the stifling fear overcoming her during her encounter with Whiskey Joe, the half-breed behind all her troubles.

Fiercely, she tore a wide strip from what was left of her petticoat and bound her breasts, covering them from lustful eyes. With them covered, she felt more at ease, more herself. She would not die so easily, she decided. *I will escape!*

❦

THE SUN lowered closer toward dusk, and the tepee became suffocating, the heat prickling sweat along her back and neck. Crimson huddled against the tepee wall, discarding each plan that crossed her mind. Flies-Like-An-Eagle! Isn't this the Kiowa band Landon is from? Surely, he would help her! No, she decided. He was more interested in trading for her, and besides, she would be caught before she could reach him. What could she do? She must find another way out of here!

With the sun sinking in the western horizon, she glanced around the tepee, searching for a weapon, anything she might use as protection. There was a forlorn, neglected air about the tepee though a ray of light pierced through one of the seams. The first gleam of hope erupted in her breast. Edging closer to the sewn edges, she plucked the leather threads free with her fingers.

Every time a noise sounded outside, she jumped and moved in front of the opening. After what seemed like hours, she managed to tug the threads free until she had a place large enough to crawl through. The waning light outside was gray, and if she escaped, not only did she have to worry about being recaptured, but also hunger and thirst. However, dying from exposure was preferable than dying at the hands of Whiskey Joe.

Thinking of hunger, her stomach growled, reminding her it had been a couple days since she last ate. She barely thought it when the flap opened, and an Indian entered bearing a bowl of some kind of food. She sat straight up, her back covering the hole in the tepee she had made. The Indian guard sat the bowl down several feet in front of her, grunted something, then left.

Soon as his back disappeared through the flap, she grabbed the bowl and ate like she had never eaten before. She ate so fast, she did not taste the concoction. Her main objective was having something in her stomach before escaping.

The drums started up, the pounding reverberating through every pore in her body. Darkness covered the land, enclosing her in its protective shield and giving her courage. If they were having a powwow, it would keep them busy. The main issue was escaping at the right time.

She shivered, forcing fear from her mind. She would rather die first than be caught! But her escape would be tenuous. She had no water or food and the nights were still cool. She could take one of the buffalo robes on the floor, but the heavy robe would impede her escape by weighing her down. She was better off risking the weather.

The minutes ticked by in her mind until she heard the drunkenness erupting around the village—men laughing, arguing and calling for another drink. Easing her head out of the ripped seam, she cautiously glanced around her. She saw no one around. Sucking in her breath, she crawled out of the tepee.

On tiptoes and a prayer, she edged out of the encampment, praying her black dress would cloak her in darkness. Ducking and dodging, she raced out onto the prairie, a prayer still upon her lips. She held her breath, but no alarm was raised. Taking courage, she ran, stumbling and falling, praying for safety and some type of protection.

Chapter 36
The Challenge

WITH THE wind riffling through his raven black hair and the clean air filling his lungs, Landon gazed around him. He lifted his face toward the sun, the rays warming his face and falling over his bare chest. In the distance, the whippoorwills sang their mournful song, the squirrels chattered in the trees and the cicadas chirped undisturbed.

His gaze was far-reaching, soaking in the way the rolling plains met the endless blue skies. He memorized each detail: the golden grasses mingled with the greenery of spring, the prickly pear cacti and the ocotillo plant cacti or coachwhip, a cluster of slender, thorny stems, the flower clusters at its tips opening in a brilliant scarlet panorama, the cottonwoods along the creek and riverbanks, their leaves green and silver, the wild fruit bushes with white flowers and the trees opening with tiny green buds. The land, a forever changing landscape of rolling hills, flat plains, deep canyons of starkness— canyons of exquisite colors, bear grass with stalks of white bulbs, trees and all types of wildlife. There were the thousand hills area around Tascosa, arroyos and mesas with weather ranging from the deepest blizzards to the harshest drought. A land that was mistress to no one, defying any man to tame her.

In this savage, beautiful land, he became a man, a man loving unstintingly and the love returned by a woman who understood his

364

need of being accepted—Sun-is-Setting. Her face was overshadowed by another, a crimson rose of passion. His heart ached leaving this place—this land which called to his very soul, a savage prairie, more cruel and demanding than a woman. Crimson was like this land, changing, demanding, hot and cold, and bearing a fierce love any man would be proud of receiving.

Lowering his arms, a muscle jumped erratically in his cheek. He should have left already, but her presence here was powerful as the land, holding him motionless and rooted. He made a rash promise to the Great Spirit, but his love for the fiery, strong-willed woman overrode all else.

He looked at the abandoned sod, memories of the tornado that precipitated his and Crimson's first lovemaking, pleasant and heart-rendering. A gentle smile curved the grim corners of his mouth as he remembered the fingers of the sun playing across her naked body. The wind repeated her fierce words of anger, her sharp cries of rapture, her murmuring sighs of fulfillment. It was all here pressed in invisible time.

The wind whipped away the half smile, bringing brutish reality in its wake. For nearly two weeks he had camped at the abandoned sod, fighting with his need to leave and his desire to stay. The Texas Panhandle was his home, the only real home where he ever lived freely. This was home—he had lost his heart here both times, women from both sides of his mixed blood; one red and the other white. He slammed his fist against the wall, the pain exploding in his hand, but the pain was nothing compared to the one in his heart.

What spell had she cast over him that overrides the Great Spirit where he cannot keep his promise and ride out of her life forever? Even the wind moans her name, Crimson Rose, over and over again. The sod was a painful reminder of her, and no matter how much he tried, he still had trouble leaving. "Damn!" he exploded, slamming his fist into the wall again. "I cannot love you, Crimson!"

There was a bitter irony where he had fallen in love with a wild creature, a woman whom he swore he would leave if she were freed, a woman who meant more than his life. But he must leave, must before he inadvertently caused her death. Why was he so cursed? Was his mixed blood the cause?

Hearing Ebony nicker, every muscle in his body grew taut. The sun burned into his bare back, the copper skin drinking in the blessing. He slowly turned around, shading his eyes and watching a single rider approach.

"Sky Eyes," Buck greeted, reining in his horse and dismounting. "Been lookin' all over the country for you. Didn't expect to find you here on my own land. I'd decided this would be the last place I looked 'cause something about Crimson kinda mentioned being here during the tornado. She changed after that." He did not mention in his search for him, he had nearly given up before he remembered Crimson's claim she sat out the tornado here. It was a slight shot, but he had nowhere else to look.

"Buck," Landon warily returned the greeting, reaching for his shirt and pulling it over his arms and shoulders before buttoning it. "I was just packing up and heading for New Mexico."

"Then I caught you in time." Stepping near Landon, Buck casually held his horse's reins in his hand.

"It's time to say goodbye, old friend." Landon cursed his rotten luck. Why was Buck looking for him? His very presence boded ill, contradicting what he should do.

"Never thought you'd run out on a job, Sky Eyes. You were hired in good faith," Buck sonorously replied, their being friends delineating any tact he might have shown to another man.

"I got my reasons."

"Perhaps. I hate seeing you leave when you're getting so close. 'Sides, I got another problem on my hands and need your help." Buck blithely observed Landon, hoping his approach was the right one. He glanced over the starks plains and rolling hills, pushing back his hat with his fingertip.

"Sorry, Buck. I've got business elsewhere." A bitter gall lodged distastefully in his mouth at his blatant lie.

Buck continued looking out over the rolling hills. "You know she's in love with you."

"Who?" Landon asked in disinterest as his heart did a quick turn with unreasonable excitement.

"Crimson."

Landon shrugged like it was none of his concern. "That's rather hard to believe. She's always had a low opinion of me."

"She's changed her opinion, Sky Eyes. Told her myself the truth about you, how we'd been friends for ages. Wouldna of matter if I had told her or not 'cause she's in love with you. But if you're disinterested, guess I'll find someone else who'll help me get her out of trouble. Ran into one of the ranch hands I sent to keep a eye on her, and he told me she quit her job at the dancehall and is now working at the Drink Emporium." Buck's lazy, offhanded conversation had the desired effect.

"What?" Landon shouted, cold fury tightening his jawline.

"Yep, it's a shame too. She's stubborn and won't listen to any of us. She's got the hardest head I ever come across. Her rashness is gonna get her killed and there ain't a damn thing I can do about it. She may be my sister-in-law, but she's a grown woman like she says, and I can't force her back to the ranch with me."

Landon regretted his shouted word almost as soon as it left his mouth. In sarcastic dispassion, he asked, "What do you think I can do?"

Buck faced Landon, his fingers rasping the two-day old whiskers along his chin. "She's in love with you, and I think she'll listen, especially since you're in love with her too."

Landon glanced sharply at Buck, not denying or agreeing with him. He had admitted it himself earlier. "I can't." He glared angrily at the sod, his prayed promise becoming feeble compared with Crimson's danger, but he was honorable and a promise was a promise.

"You'd let her commit suicide?" Buck's scorn was apparent in the hard glance he shot Landon. "It is suicide letting her continue like she is."

Feeling his resolve weakening, Landon blithely admitting he had stuck around this long, searching for an excuse not to leave. His main worry was the Great Spirit retaliating and taking Crimson away from him by death or some other means. "What can I do? She doesn't listen to me anymore than she does you." Irony edging each word, he fought against the urge of jumping on his horse and racing toward Tascosa and Crimson.

"You're a smart man. You'll find some way."

"Alright, I'll do it for you," Landon brusquely agreed.

"Not for me, Sky Eyes. For Crimson and yourself." Buck shrewdly watched for his reaction and was satisfied when Landon gave him a curt nod.

Buck mounted his horse while Landon stood impassive. He had given his promise he would try and discourage Crimson from her suicide mission of finding John's murderer.

Buck leaned forward, the saddle leather creaking. "Dissuade her anyway you can, Sky Eyes."

He pulled his mount around and stopped. In the distance, a cloud of dust swirled in a steady line. "A rider's comin' up fast. Got a bad feeling it's trouble." As he and Landon waited for the rider, both recognized Cotton.

Cotton frantically waved his hat. He rode hard all the way until just a few yards from them and pulled his mount up sharply, the horse rearing. "Crimson's disappeared. Had some trouble in town and nobody's seen her since. The hand we had watching her says when the trouble began, he stopped to see if they needed help. He saw Crimson head back toward her shack, but she ain't there. Can't find her nowhere. One of the Mexicans said he saw a man riding hard toward her and pull her in front of him, then headed outta town. That was two days ago."

"Damnation!" Buck exploded. "I knew we couldn't leave her by herself. Come on! We gotta find her!"

Landon had already mounted with Cotton's first words. Without waiting for the others, he kicked his heels against Ebony's side and headed for Tascosa, his heart beating fiercely against his ribcage, Crimson's safety tantamount in his mind. They nearly rode their horses into the ground racing toward Tascosa, each in their own pit of hell worrying about Crimson's safety, each blaming themselves for her danger. Reaching Tascosa, they paid for new mounts at the stable, asked a few questions, then headed in the direction the Mexican pointed.

Landon was quick to pick up the trail. "Three men, four horses. They headed south toward the Comanche camp. It's a day's hard ride from here. Let's just hope we reach her in time."

◦◦◦◦◦◦◦

CRIMSON had no idea how far she ran when the stitch in her side became too great. There was no sign of the campfires, but she still did not feel safe. She sucked in a painful breath and continued walking, holding her arms across her chest against the chilled night air. The farther away she was, the better off she would be. She walked and walked, cringing at the night sounds, dreading the darkness where she could barely see where to place her foot, and so tired, it was an effort to put one foot in front of the other.

Dawn permeated the land with the first purplish rays of the sun rising in the east. She threw open her arms, welcoming the new day for freedom had never seemed so sweet. She twirled around, relishing her sense of accomplishment too soon. On the second turn, she saw a rider swiftly bearing down on her from the north. A fearful cry escaping her lips, she jerked up the front of her gown and ran, forcing more speed when hearing the rider close behind her.

She was plucked up so suddenly, she was running in mid-air. With a scream of rage, she attacked her captor, pulling them both onto the ground. The shock of hitting the hardpacked dirt only lasted a split second. She launched into a violent attack, grimly pleased with her fingernails digging into the man's face.

"Damn bitch!" McCullar growled, bringing back his fist and slamming it against the side of her head.

Lights exploded before her eyes, dazing her, and her body went limp. McCullar straddled her hips, forcing her arms above her head, his face a bare inch from hers, and growled, "Bitch, this will be the last time ya fight me."

Releasing his hold, he grabbed the band of material across her breasts and pulled, the material ripping in his hands. Licking his lips, he lifted enough to jerk the bottom half of her skirt up around her hips, a cruel smile lifting his grim lips with the tearing of her dress.

His intent clear, she shook her head, moaning while he freed himself, forced her thighs open and positioned his engorged penis head at the center of her womanhood. She stiffened underneath him and he was unable to penetrate her. Her hand closed around a rock at the same time he angrily grunted, and she brought it down hard against the side of his head, hitting him time and time again.

McCullar grunted with her fierce pounding of his head before falling on top of her. Her fear was so intense, she did not realize he was motionless. She kept bringing the rock down repeatedly on his head, crying out in rage and fear. Her arm grew tired before she realized he was not moving. With an outraged cry, she pushed him away from her. Rising swiftly, she glared at him, nearly becoming sick when spotting the blood running down the side of his face.

"Oh my God, I've killed him!" Throwing the offending rock down, she glanced wildly around her.

There was no one else coming. McCullar's horse was several yards away patiently munching grass. Tearing a strip from her remaining slip, she bound her breasts once again. Crooning softly, she cautiously walked toward the horse. Grabbing the bridle, she put her foot in the stirrup, mounted it and kicked her heels against the gelding's side, heading south toward Tascosa.

❦

"LOOK, there's someone up ahead riding fast. My God, it's Crimson. It's gotta be her!" Cotton shouted.

Landon kicked his heels against his mount's sides, racing toward the desolate figure, his heart joyfully singing she was safe.

Crimson lifted her head, fatigue lacing every muscle. Watching the riders quickly approaching her, her fatigue was forgotten and choking cries tore through her throat. She turned the horse sharply back toward the opposite direction. The animal was as tired as her. It had been ridden at a fast pace all night. The horse stumbled, righted itself and kept going, giving his heart for the rider on his back.

She heard the encroaching rider and fear penetrated through every fiber of her being. Without warning, she was plucked from the animal's back into the rider's lap. Panic erupted through her. She fought tooth and nail, crying her outrage, her arms flailing against her captor before they were caught in a hard bind, and the man's voice finally entered her tormented brain.

"Crimson, Crimson. Stop! You're safe! I won't hurt you."

She stilled momentarily, then turned her head toward her abductor. "Landon!" she moaned, the pent-up tears she had held for so long coming in great racking sobs.

Landon cradled her, lying his head on top of the wild mass of hair, his heart crying out against the display of terror he saw and felt. "It's over, little spy. You're safe."

370

Suspicious moisture gleaming in his eyes, Landon barely looked up as Buck and Cotton came to a tearing halt beside them.

"My God, Landon. What happened?" Buck asked, guilt tearing at his guts.

Landon sent him a sharp glance; the cold depths of his eyes would have made a lesser man cringe with fear. "I don't know, Buck, but when I do..." He let the end of his sentence hang, the savageness in his harsh voice clearly conveying whoever did this was a dead man.

Though Crimson cried until there were no more tears, she felt safe in Landon's arms for the first time in weeks. Landon eased them to the ground, keeping his arms securely around her. It took a while before she could tell them what had happened, hiccupping every so often from the strength of her crying. "He shot Harvey too and Harvey was protecting me!" she ended.

She did not see the tightening of Landon's jaw or the erratic muscle beating there. Blinding jealousy exploded through him at the mention of Harvey. Landon released her and started for his horse, his purpose plain; head for the Indian encampment and kill the half-breed Whiskey Joe.

Crimson grabbed at his shirt sleeve, frantically pulling him back. "No, Landon, they'll kill you!"

He ignored her frenzied plea until she whimpered, "Please don't leave me, Landon. Please!"

"She's right, Sky Eyes. We need a plan before we go gunning for this Whiskey Joe. Our first obligation is getting Crimson fed, cleaned up and safely in Tascosa before we go traipsing into a beehive."

Landon half turned and glared at Buck. "Then you take her back. I'm settling this once and for all."

"I never counted you for a fool, Sky Eyes. You need time to rationally think this over, and in your present condition, rational you ain't," Buck grimly reprimanded.

A muscle worked in Landon's jaw, torn apart by wanting revenge and securing Crimson's safety. Her clinging hands and wide begging eyes finally won. "Alright, but Crimson's riding in front of me."

"Fair enough. At least we can be assured she won't get into any more trouble for a while," Buck agreed solemnly and deadly serious.

Cuddled lovingly in Landon's arms wrapped around with her riding in front of him, she slept most of the way back to Tascosa, the blanket Cotton had covered her with shielding her near nakedness. They entered Tascosa through back roads, staying away from prying eyes. Stopping in front of her small shack, Landon would not give up his precious load while dismounting. Cotton opened the door while Landon carried her inside and tenderly laid her on the bed.

Crimson opened her eyes. Seeing Landon's concerned face above her, she smiled, all her previous troubles disappearing. "Is there any way I can get a bath and something to eat, please?"

"I'll get her a plate of food from the Exchange Hotel, then head home. Honey will be sick with worry by now," Buck stated, already heading out the door.

"I'll carry in the water, Landon, if you'll heat it." Cotton picked up the bucket near the door with Landon's nod.

"I've never had a man wait on me before and I don't know how to act," Crimson tried teasing, her eyes filling with tears.

"Enjoy it, little spy. This may be the last time it ever happens."

Clean and fed, Crimson slipped into a nightgown and crawled into bed, falling asleep as soon as her head touched the pillow.

Landon and Cotton sat at the small table talking in low voices while she slept. "One of us has to stay with her at all times," Cotton said softly, glancing at his sister's sleeping form. "I don't trust her as far as I can throw her. Part of her questions were answered, but we still don't know who framed her for John's murder, and knowing her, she ain't gonna rest until she does."

"I agree and I'll be damned if I let her go back working as a saloon girl." Landon frowned at her sleeping form, at the same time, relieved for her safety, yet angry with her for putting her life in danger.

"Crim's as hardheaded as they come. We're gonna have trouble with her. You can bet on it, but if we join forces, you and I, we can find out who killed John. Agreed?" Cotton asked. At Landon's affirmative nod, Cotton stuck out his hand and they shook on it.

"Crim may be as stubborn and balky as a mule, but she's my sister and I love her. I want what is best for her. And if we stick together, we can clear her name, and in the process, clear my family's name. I ain't gonna leave until I do," Cotton declared, his violet eyes hard.

Landon poured them both a shot of whiskey, suspiciously asking, "What are you getting at, Cotton?"

"Well, Crim's in love with you, and I figure you're in love with her. She's like a wild thing, I grant you, and there ain't many men who can tame her, but you're different. These last few days, I've grown respect for you. What I'm saying is, if you wanna marry her, you got my blessings." Cotton took a sip of whiskey, watching Landon's face.

Landon downed his drink, then looked over at Crimson, a muscle working in his cheek. "I can't marry her, Cotton. Thanks for the offer."

"Why the hell not?" Cotton asked heatedly.

Landon tore his gaze away from Crimson and glanced at Cotton, the bitterness apparent in his eyes. "I'm a half-breed, half white, half Indian or have you forgotten?"

"I don't give a damn what you are! You could be purple for all I care. I ain't a man who usually says things like this straight out, but I've met many men and there ain't many who can hold a candle to you. Buck's one man I've got great respect for, you're another. My sister loves you, and I ain't gonna sit here and let her get hurt again. I don't know what kind of grudge you got about your mixed blood, but I don't have any and neither does my family. If you're the man I think you are, then you won't either. I'm telling ya straight out, if you love her, then marry her. If you don't, then get the hell outta her life."

"Are you offering me a challenge, Cotton?" Landon asked in a deadly voice.

Chapter 37
Snap of a Finger

"CONSIDER it what ya will. I'm just telling ya if ya love her, marry her and hell take the consequences. My main objective is making sure Crim is happy and settled afore I leave again. After she married that bastard Sullivan, I thought he might settle her down. Little did I know he turned out to be a crooked bastard. With you, I am certain ya can tame her and make her happy. There ain't many men who can do that. If you're using your mixed blood as an excuse for not marrying her, then let it be on your conscience if she winds up in trouble again. The next man may end up killin' her," Cotton ground out, impressing the importance of his words on Landon.

"Your family's very loyal to one another," Landon sarcastically remarked.

"You're damn right, and if ya become a part of our family, we'll give ya the same type of loyalty and expect the same from ya." Cotton was not pulling any punches. If this was the only way he could guarantee Crimson's happiness, then so be it. Let it fall on his head.

"Crim and I have fought all our lives, fought as only a brother and sister can, but there were times I wanna beat some sense into that mulish head of hers. I still loved her and protected her. I'm doing the same thing now. I can't go back to Wyoming until I know she's settled down."

Landon poured another liberal dose of whiskey and downed it before glancing over at the gentle expression on Crimson's sleeping face. He had fought with the pull of his mixed blood all his life, but what the hell! He did love the little wildcat, and if her family didn't care about his mixed blood, then why should he?

Sticking out his hand, he sheepishly announced, "If she'll have me, I'll marry her and settle your mind at the same time."

Shaking Cotton's hand, he blithely added, "She's gonna be fit-to-be-tied knowing we've planned her future."

Cotton's answering grin was enough.

◦◦◦◦◦◦

CRIMSON awoke with the feeble yellow glow spilling out from the lamp setting on the table. A smile lifted her lips seeing Landon at the table asleep with his head on his arms. She eased from the bed and gently touched his head.

Landon instantly snapped awake, orienting himself to his surroundings. Aware of Crimson beside him, he grabbed her by the waist and pulled her onto his lap, then nuzzled her neck.

Wrapping her arms around his shoulders, she entwined her fingers in the thick black hair at the nape of his neck, meeting his lips with a fierceness that took their breaths away. She had been frightened and her life in jeopardy within Whiskey Joe's hands, but she loved this man holding her, and she would make up for lost time. Disengaging her mouth, she whispered huskily, "Come to bed with me."

His answer was a low, satisfied growl deep in his throat. He rose with her still in his arms and deposited her tenderly on the covers. There was nothing bashful about Crimson who crouched on her knees and pulled the nightgown over her head, then lay down while watching him swiftly slip out of his own clothing. She invitingly raised her arms toward him. "Love me, Landon."

Quickly shucking his clothes off, he joined her on the bed. Pulling her naked form across his lap, he fiercely possessed her lips, his fear and gratitude apparent with his commanding kiss. One hand clasping the side of her head and the other resting along her waist, he leaned his forehead against hers. "Don't ever do that again,

375

Crimson. I don't think I could of lived knowing you were hurt and had suffered."

"You came back," she whispered. "You came back for me?"

He pulled back enough to capture her eyes with his and domineeringly growled, "You are mine, little spy. Make no bones about it this time. You are mine."

He kissed her swiftly and passionately, branding her for all time as his own. He softened his bruising kiss, plundering the velvety inside of her mouth, and then nibbled along her jawline to her ear.

Tangling her hands in his hair, she jerked his head back so she could look into the blazing light in his eyes. "Yes, Landon, I am. I love you."

Capturing the stubborn tilt of her lips, he branded his possession into them. Pulling back, he growled, "I feel the same and tomorrow we'll make it permanent."

She pulled his head back when he tried kissing her again, asking in a shocked, happy voice, "Are you asking or telling me we're getting married?"

He laughed, his crooked smile endearing. "Take it any way you like, little one. Tomorrow, we are getting married." He caressed an impudent breast and heard her breath catch in her throat. "You are mine," he repeated.

"Yes, always," she earnestly agreed, running her hands over the sinewy ripples along his back.

With very little tenderness, they took each other, giving and receiving, climbing the very heights of passion, branding their love into each other's bodies. Crimson whimpered, cresting the peak. Breathless, they lay in each other's arms.

When their breathing was back to almost normal, Crimson flipped over on top of him, running her hands down his chest. "Now, my Indian breed, we shall do it properly."

Lowering her head toward his, she teased him with the very tips of her breasts on his, licking at his mouth and holding his arms down at his sides. "I will love you, Landon, as you have loved me."

She gently moved her hips in a circling motion on top of his, feeling him harden against her. She lowered her head and took his man nipples in her mouth, tenderly chewing and sucking, going from one to the other while her hands caressed the muscled bulges of his arms. She slipped her full length down his body, kissing the taut, smooth flesh all the way down his chest to the thin line of hair beginning at his belly button and dipping into the center near his thighs.

Landon growled, her sweet torment too much. His loins tightened and strained, and he almost lost control against the soft mound of her breast. He grabbed her hair and forced her back up, taking fierce ownership of her mouth and flipping her onto her back. "So, little one, you wanna tease me. Let me show you how it feels."

He lowered his head and took the rose-colored bud, suckling it until it grew hard. With teasing swipes, he caressed the nub, softly pinching it and kissed along the undersides of her breasts. She moaned as his hands caressed the other before one hand slipped along her side and settled at the thick auburn curls at the junction between her thighs. His finger grazed the pouting flesh, slipping in between the swollen lips and stroked the stiffened center of her being. He nibbled her flesh from one side of her to the other, especially over the small pouch of her stomach, all the way down where his finger cuddled. With a feral groan, he gently forced her legs apart before opening the pouting nether lips and touching the center with his tongue.

Crimson moaned out loud, the exquisite sensations racing through her veins faster than a strike of lightning. As he feasted upon her lower regions, her legs crossed over his shoulders, her hands fastened in the soft length of his black hair, holding him in position. Delicious, forbidden thrills tingled every fiber of her, starting from the very tip of her toes to the top of her head and centering where his mouth gently suckled her. His hands massaged her buttocks, holding her hips upward and accommodating him with one impudent finger teasing at the nether opening.

Her head tossed on the pillow, her low moans of pleasure filling the room, her pubic area grinding into his mouth as blinding lights and intense ecstasy swept over her within the pentacle of passion.

Landon lifted his head and smiled his lopsided smile, the glistening dew of her sex on his face. "That shall teach you to tease me again, Rose of Passion." Rising, he gently opened her thighs and positioned himself at the entrance of her desire. Pushing inside, the silken depths closed around him, pulsating against him. He tangled his fingers in the curly tresses, holding her head still and crashing his mouth against hers, letting her taste herself on his lips.

He moved slowly at first, stoking the banked fires back into a full blaze inside of her. Her hands squeezed his buttocks, and she felt the muscles tighten and relax. He plunged deeper and deeper, filling her depths. Like a faint rumble at first, the sensations grew steadily more intense until they both met stroke for stroke, picking up speed and flying toward the very stars into heaven.

Easing off her, he pulled her satiated form up against his side, her head nestled in the crook of his arm. He buried his face in the soft mane of her hair. "I love you, little spy."

It felt so good, so right, being in his arms, her body snuggled up perfectly against his hard length. "And I love you, my darling, fierce savage."

"At first light, we'll find a judge and have him marry us, then we're heading for your place," Landon gruffly told her.

Her lips hardened into a stubborn line, she lifted her head and moved away from him. "No, Landon. I will not leave until I find out who murdered John."

"Tom, dammit, Crimson. His name was Tom. And you will leave here as my wife. I don't wanna hear any more about it." Landon lifted on his elbow and stared into her determined face, his voice a harsh assurance she would do as she was told.

She rolled from the bed so fast he did not have time to stop her. She stood at the side of the bed, her hair a streaming mane of tousled curls, her hands on the rounded sides of her hips, the soft ivory mounds of her breasts heaving in anger. "How dare you tell me what I can and cannot do! I will stay until I find Tom's murderer!"

With a savage growl, Landon jumped out of bed and caught her, pulling her down beside him on the bed, flipping her over until the pale globes of her bottom lay upright across his knees. With his forearm securely positioned at the small of her back, he easily held her there as she fought him like a wild cat. With the flat of his hand, he slapped one side of her posterior to the other, watching the white skin turn pink, then an angry red, punctuating each word he spoke. "How many times have I told you *I do dare*, Crimson!"

She howled with each descent of his hand, her bottom stinging like the fiery depths of hell and tears streaming from her eyes, falling onto the hardpacked dirt floor where her hair streamed down and wiped them up.

Furious with himself as well as with her, Landon pushed her off his lap onto the floor. Why did he do that? The answer was simple; she provoked him once too often. His eyes cold as a blue northern, he glared at her. She crouched on her knees in front of him, rubbing her stinging backside, her eyes shooting green fire. Even incensed, she presented a tantalizing picture with the curly tresses hanging down her back, one insolent lock circling around a rose-colored nipple, her full breasts heaving with rage, her small waist flaring out in slim, curvaceous hips. His eyes locked on the tight curly mass between her thighs, brazenly beckoning like a red beam. He licked his lips, the cold depths of his eyes blazing with renewed passion.

Seeing his expression quickly change and the hardening of his manhood, she ground out through clenched teeth, "You half-breed bastard, I wouldn't marry you if you were the last man on earth!"

Landon leveled his eyes to her jade green ones, the fire in his eyes quickly extinguished. "I am the last man on earth, Crimson, who'll put up with your hardheaded, damnable temper. And if you don't watch your language, I'll bust your bottom again."

"You wouldn't dar..." Stopping in mid-sentence, Crimson bit into her bottom lip, wishing she could pull the words back. He had shown her too many times he would; her smarting posterior reminded her.

"Yes, Crimson? I wouldn't what?" Landon goaded, waiting for her to finish the sentence. Tensing, he had no desire of breaking her pride or combustible temper, only her learning how to control it.

"I hate you!" She briskly rubbed her bottom, never taking her stormy, mutinous glare from him. Before she could dodge him, Landon reached her in one step, pulling her up against him. He pushed her on the bed, straddled her hips and held her arms above her head.

"Shall I show you how much you hate me, Crimson?" he threatened, then lowered his mouth to hers, punishing her with his hard, demanding kiss. He caressed her flesh with one hand while holding her arms above her head until it felt like molten lead flowed through her veins. He teased her with his hardness, exploring every nook and cranny of her beautiful body once again, bringing a flush of desire pinking her skin.

As her heated whimpers grew more intense, he flipped her on her stomach, lowering his head and kissing the still reddened posterior cheeks. Slipping his arms under her stomach, he lifted upward, moving her until she crouched in front of him. "You have a beautiful ass, Crimson Rose," he groaned, still moving his hands over her bottom before moving behind her and kneeling between her outspread knees.

"Shall I show you how much I love your ass?" he growled, caressing her firm butt cheeks.

"No," she groaned, her hips squirming under his hands.

He chuckled before positioning his hardness at her heated, moist entrance, barely shoving the engorged head inside. Her soft moan encouraged him, and he pressed another inch inside her. "Now, little spy, let me show you how much you hate me. But before I do, I'm tired of your hate and I'll be damned if I listen to it anymore."

"Just shut up and make love to me," she fiercely replied, shoving her backside against him.

Grabbing the sides of her hips, he held her motionless. "Not until you tell me, Crimson. Tell me the truth," he demanded hotly, moving a little more inside of her, reaching across her waist and lowering his hand between her hairy junction, stimulating her desire.

She groaned through gritted teeth, her body on fire and only he could put it out. He was holding her motionless, refusing to satisfy this savage blaze coursing throughout her entire being, raging through her burning more fiercely than a red-hot branding iron. He had won, she knew, aware of his pelvic heat mixing with the heat from her still smarting buttocks. "Lord help me, but I do love you, Landon. I love you!" she screeched hoarsely as he filled her completely.

They took each other with a stormy fervor, erupting in exquisite ecstasy, the heat as blinding and hot as an exploding star. Landon lay across her back, easing his weight from her, the afterglow completely draining their strength. He tenderly kissed her shoulders and along her neck. "You are mine, little spy, and we are getting married."

"No," she refused half-heartedly, half in stubbornness, "not until I find Tom's killer. I haven't changed my mind, Landon, and I never will."

He eased off her and turned her over on her back, leaving a heavy leg across hers and his arm around her ribcage before moving his hand and fondling her breast. "For once in your life, be sensible. Cotton and I will find out who murdered Tom. We will have a much better chance than you. At least give me reasonable doubt."

"Reasonable doubt?" she asked caustically, turning around in his arms so she could look into his eyes. "I've given you a reasonable doubt, but I found out you killed Gambler and how you asked his mistress to be yours."

"I what?" He shook his head like an enraged lion. "I never asked Wendy to be my mistress. She asked me."

"That's not what she said."

"Ah, you are jealous, little spy," Landon teased, cheered at the thought.

"Don't get off the subject," Crimson snapped. She was jealous, she uncomfortably realized, and she did know Wendy's penchant for stretching the truth. "You still killed Gambler."

"I never lied to you, Crimson. I never told you anything about it. But before you judge me too harshly, let me tell you what really happened," he stated, his voice mirroring his seriousness.

He tightened his hold, his lips a bare fraction from her mouth, his eyes coolly boring into hers, reaching into her very soul, demanding she listen to the truth of his words. "Your so-called friends are bad as egg-sucking dogs. You wouldn't believe me when I tried telling you. Sure, I had a grudge against them, a big grudge for what they did when I was growing up. But..."

Placing his finger over her lips, he stopped her from interrupting when she opened her mouth. "I never went out with the intention of killing them. Whether you believe it or not, I do not enjoy killing, and I damn sure don't go out with murder on my mind. Well, I take that back. Yesterday I could have very easily gone into the Comanche camp and killed Half-breed—Whiskey Joe, whatever you wanna call him, for what he did to you."

Tightening his grip around her waist, he imprisoned her when she tried wiggling free from his grasp. "I saw them one day when I was headed toward Tascosa, all three of them. I knew their plans would stir up some kind of trouble. I had already heard about

Gambler's tenuous hold on the syndicate and his cheating practices at the Silver Saloon. I cornered him into a poker game with the intent of proving he was a cheater. That would have been enough to get him run out of the Panhandle. I had succeeded, but he drew on me first. He left me with no alternative but shoot him."

"Why should I believe you?" she bit out brittlely, tensing beside him. "You lived with savages for years, and I know they kill without mercy."

"Damnit, Crimson," he harshly exploded. "When are you gonna trust me? Until you do, our marriage will never work."

He pushed away from her and sat on the edge of the bed, running his fingers through his raven-black hair. "Yes, I lived with the Kiowas, but when I left, I left that part of my life behind. I'm living in the white man's world, your world."

"You changed just like that?" she asked tartly, sitting beside him and snapping her fingers.

"No, not like that," he grated, snapping his own fingers.

"It took time, but I never purposely went out with murder on my mind. You forget I was first raised in the white man's society and bore the brunt of the white man's cruelty. I was treated with respect by the Kiowas or at least by most of them," he finished a bit bitterly. "I fit nowhere, Crimson. I am only half a man."

"Like hell," Crimson cuttingly interrupted. She was intensely aware of his secret pain. Kneeling in front of him, she grabbed his hands in a hard grip and stared deeply into his sky-colored eyes. "If I ever hear you say that again, I'll cut your heart out. Do you hear me?"

A faint smile curving his grim lips, a sparkle appeared in his eyes. "Will you, little bloodthirsty savage?"

Straightening her spine with pride, she gave him an answering smile. Was she really any different? She was fighting for her pride the same as him. She accused him of being a cold-hearted murderer when she had felt the same desire, but her secrets were out in the open. He was still an enigma. "No more putting each other or ourselves down, Landon. We've both got skeletons in our closet, but you know more about me than I know about you. You're a cunning devil, and I wanna know more about you—how you always know what's going on."

He glanced at her, his face showing doubt. There was a deceptive softness in the depths of her meadow green eyes, which could just as quickly turn into hard chips of glass. "Oh hell, I might as well tell you the truth."

Pausing, he wondered if he was doing the right thing, then with a hell-take-the-consequences attitude, he told her, "I've been secretly working for the Panhandle Cattlemen's Association. Buck and Kerby Olsen are the ones who recommended me for the job. My main job is discovering who the criminals are stealing cattle around here."

Her voice filled with shock, her hands tightened on his. "You? Why didn't you tell me before?"

He turned, his face censorious. "You wouldn't have believed me."

Pushing her hair back from her face, she dropped her sight to her clasped hands. No, she would not have believed him. She was too convinced he was behind all her troubles. "I...I'm... sorry, Landon," she stammered apologetically.

He touched her chin with the tip of his finger and lifted it so he could look deep into her eyes. "It's behind us now, little spy. We must start with a fresh slate." He kissed her briefly, then rose. "Get dressed and we'll go eat."

They had barely finished dressing when Cotton burst through the door. "We need to talk, Landon." He shot Crimson a harried glance, then added, "In private."

Chapter 38
Hidden Secrets

HER MOUTH tightened with aggravation. Crimson knew Landon would order her out of her own shack. "No secrets, huh?" she retorted. "Oh, alright. I'll go outside."

She stomped out the door, slamming it behind her, reminding them she was not thrilled with being left out of the conversation. She knew it had something to do with her and she should be told the worst of it. Leaning against the door jamb, she listened to their indistinct muffled voices, though she could not make out a word they said. She heard the patter of footsteps running toward her and spotted Rovin' Wendy, her small pixy-shaped face tight and frightened.

Wendy stopped in front of her and quickly grabbed Crimson's hand, her eyes beseeching. "Midnight Rose, please, I need your help."

It was Rovin' Wendy's apparent distress and agitation that pulled Crimson away from the conversation behind the door. "What is it, Wendy?"

"Please, come with me. Please!" Wendy pulled on her hand, her voice ending in a shrill note.

Crimson threw a disparaging look toward the closed door before agreeing. She would find out what was going on between Landon and Cotton later. There was no way she could refuse Wendy's call for help. Rovin' Wendy had befriended her when no one else would.

They were breathless by the time they reached Wendy's small shack. Dusk had set in, throwing the surrounding shacks into a haunting gray light. Wendy threw open the door and rushed inside, Crimson right behind her.

Wendy pointed at the bed and the large figure draped with a threadbare blanket. "He's been hurt real bad and I don't know what to do for him. His head is bashed in, there are scratched marks on his cheeks and his thigh is infected where someone bit a hunk out of it. Ben and Frank brought him in—said he had been ambushed. Who would do a such a thing?"

Crimson stiffened, glaring down at McCullar's inert body where his large form dwarfed Wendy's bed. The left side of his head was swollen almost beyond recognition and the other side still bore Crimson's fingernail marks. She swallowed the bile rising in her throat, her stance taut as a strung bow. "McCullar... I would," she acidly scorned.

Wendy turned swiftly on her heel, her mouth wide open with astonishment. "You? But why?"

"He abducted me and took me to Whiskey Joe in the Comanche camp with the intent of him and his cronies killing me—that is after they had their fill of me and my charms, but I escaped." Crimson's lips turned into an ugly sneer, her loathing for the unconscious man plain. "I escaped and he found me. He was assaulting me and I found a rock and hit him over the head with it over and over until I thought he was dead. God help me, but I actually wanted him dead."

Wendy stared at her aghast, uncomprehending the extent of Crimson's hostility. McCullar groaned. She quickly knelt at his side and grabbed a wet rag from a bowl nearby. Tenderly washing his face, she glanced back at Crimson, her purpose of first going to Crimson not abated. "He still needs help, Rose. Please, will you help me? He's gained consciousness twice and he didn't recognize me or Ben or Frank. He can't talk. I'm scared, Rose. Please."

Staring down at McCullar, pure hatred swept through Crimson, the begging Wendy having no effect on her. She had heard about people with amnesia where they forgot everything and had to be taught the fundamentals of speech, eating, walking—everything she now took as a natural part of life, but this kind of amnesia was rare.

"No, Wendy, I can't help you. I can't understand why you wanna help a low life like him. I'll go get the sheriff and inform him where McCullar is and tell him what happened."

Wendy's eyes begged Crimson to relent, but Crimson was irrevocably committed to ending McCullar's cowboy shampoos. And her determination would not have changed if McCullar had not opened his eyes and stared at her through dull, pain-ridden, blank eyes. He groaned and pointed at his head. Crimson turned away, unable to watch the pathetic man. "Wendy, I won't get the sheriff, but I can't help you. Find someone else."

Dropping the rag in the water bowl, Wendy hugged Crimson. "Thank you, Midnight Rose. I'll make sure he never harms anyone else again. Thank you!"

Crimson walked out the door and closed it softly behind her. Darkness had set in, covering the land in black velvet. The soft yellow lights shining out of the distant adobe and wooden houses, a pleasant murmur with a burst of laughter chiming through the night air, assured her people did survive and were happy.

She sighed heavily, frankly admitting she was relieved of not informing the sheriff of McCullar's crimes against her. Her name was black enough, and with all probability, he would not believe her anyway. It was Wendy's open heart weighing her down the most. For all Wendy's faults, she needed a man to replace Gambler, a man she could call her own. And who was she to deny it even if the man was not worth the refuse on her shoes? Maybe with luck, McCullar would completely forget who and what he was. She hoped he would become a changed man for Wendy's sake.

❧❦❧

HE STOOD in the deep shadows against the outside of the saloon, the tinny strains of the piano, the chink of glasses, rambunctious voices and bursts of laughter seeping through the walls, then the sounds were gradually muted with his subtle movements until the only sound was his harsh breathing. The darkness effectively hid him from a casually thrown glance. He clutched the shotgun with sweaty palms, his upper lip beaded with perspiration. The summer breeze did nothing to cool the oppressive heat laying over the land, shimmering in the sun during the day and laying like lead during the night, stifling him.

He ran his sweaty palm down the side of his breeches, then switched hands and did the same with the other one. He was gonna kill that damn half-breed. The man was too dangerous now! *I've worked too hard getting where I am,* he railed against the star-studded sky.

Tensing, he heard soft footsteps walking down the street. Drawing in a quick, settling breath, he positioned the shotgun and waited. When the figure appeared within eyesight, he eased the trigger back and fired off two shots in quick succession.

The half-breed's body jerked several times before he fell on the ground, dead before he could draw his weapon. A satisfied smile lifting the grim lips of the ambusher, he slipped around the back of the saloon as the first curious citizens ran outside.

He entered through the back door, ran to his room and hid the shotgun. Within minutes, he was rushing out of the front door like he had been inside the whole time and mingled with the crowd gathering around the half-breed's body.

❦

CRIMSON stood indecisive, half listening to the singing cicadas, wondering if she should go home or head for the restaurant in town. Gunshots shattered the silent surroundings. Doors opened, spilling light out into the darkness, and she was rooted in place as townspeople rushed past her, calling out, "What happened? Who got shot?"

The normally subdued town burst into a babble of voices, resembling a busy beehive. A heavy feeling of dread weighed down her limbs, refusing her mind's command to move. The voices rose in a mingled, fevered pitch, but one thing was carried on the night air clear enough for her to understand. "Somebody ambushed Half-breed."

She was running before she knew it, her heart beating erratically, a cold sweat popping out over her forehead. Half-breed! *Is it Landon? Please God, don't let it be Landon,* she silently pleaded. Her stomach roiled in sickness, her ears buzzed like a million bees

387

lodged inside her head and her breathing labored. A crowd of people gathered around something in the street, the expressions on their faces cast in a pale glow from the lanterns playing over the area in front of the Drink Emporium.

Panicking, she fought her way toward the front, rudely elbowing the people aside, desperately needing to establish whose body was lying in the street. "Let me through!" she demanded half crying, fighting back the demon beast of fear rising within her. A few people looked at her with sympathy, a few with distrust and dislike, but she did not see any of it.

Suddenly, someone stepped out in front of her and grabbed her, pulling her against a hard, muscular chest. She blindly fought him, crying out for Landon, her ears buzzing. "Let me go! I've gotta get to him!"

The man shook her until the pins holding her hair came unloose. Her hair fell in glorious disarray down her shoulders, obscuring the paleness of her face. "No, Crim, be still for God's sake!" he shouted at her.

Crimson stopped her frantic struggles and looked up into Cotton's face, numbly staring at him, tears flowing in rivulets down her smooth cheeks. "Cotton, I must see him!"

He pulled her into his arms, letting her cry against his shoulder and preventing her from getting closer to the bloody body, her terrified face cutting through him like a razor-sharp knife.

"Crim, it's not him," he soothed against the curly mass of her hair.

Gripping fear crushing her heart, she shook her head against his shoulder. "I can't bear it if it is, and I can't believe you until I see for myself," she moaned, her heart wanting to believe him but her mind refusing. "Let me see for myself."

With a heavy sigh, Cotton knew when she had made up her mind on something, nothing would dissuade her. With his arm securely around her shoulders, he pushed through the crowd until they reached the inner circle of bodies. The yellowed lights from the windows and the open door of the Drink Emporium spilled out and mingled with the lanterns held by the citizens of Tascosa, the soft light highlighting the reddish-brown walls of the adobes.

Disinterested in the follies of men, brilliant diamond stars and the half-moon looked down on them, gentling the careworn, leathery faces of men. Trembling, she clenched her hands as her brother took her upper arms and pushed her in front of him, softly demanding, "Then look, Crim."

Biting hard into her lower lip, she swallowed against the bile rising in her throat, the bitter bilious taste settling with harshness in her mouth. The body lay in a pool of black blood, the lanterns revealing huge holes and bloody masses in his stomach and chest. With ghoulish curiosity, the people stared at the body and talked among themselves.

With a ragged sigh, Crimson saw it was not Landon but Whiskey Joe. She grabbed Cotton's shirt front and buried her face against his chest, asking faintly, "Where's Landon?" She was so relieved, she was weak and gratefully thanked God it was not him lying in the dusty street.

"I don't know, Crim." One arm across her shoulders, he pulled her back from him and led her from the press of people. In a split second, he fully realized his sister was a grown woman and the extent of her love for Landon. Whether he could tame her wild spirit was yet to be determined, but he'd lay his last dollar in Landon's favor. "I found out Whiskey Joe and his cronies were in town. That's why I interrupted you—to inform Landon."

"You don't think..." Crimson could not finish the question, something inside of her revolting at the idea.

"No, he didn't ambush him, Crim. You oughta know better," Cotton gruffly censored, subtly warning her not to carry the thought through.

She looked up at him, the light catching the strange silvery whiteness of his hair and saw the truth in his violet eyes. Impulsively, she gave her brother an affectionate hug. Cotton returned it, then tenderly forced her away, looking over her shoulder. "Landon, we were worried 'bout ya."

Crimson spun on her heel and stared into the beloved face she thought she had lost forever before running into his open arms.

Hugging her firmly against him, breathing in the faint scent of vanilla in her hair, Landon felt her fear and was comforted by the knowledge she did care for him.

"Please hold me and never let me go," she cried against his

shoulder. "I thought I had lost you." She lifted her hands and tenderly cradled his face, feeling the strong, leathery jawline as she pulled his head down. Kissing him fiercely, she pressed her full length against him, her love deep and strong, and everlasting as the distant skies.

Landon wrapped his hands in her hair, needing her against him. "You were frightened it was me lying there?"

"Yes. I thought I had lost you just when I had found you," she exclaimed with deep concern underlying each word.

"Enough to marry me in the morning?" Landon softly asked, waiting tensely, afraid the attack on her vanity when he spanked her this morning would affect the answer he most wanted.

"I love you, Landon, more than life itself, but I can't marry you until my name is cleared."

His fingers tightened in her hair and he grew taut against her, his anger palatable, conveying itself in every line of his frame. He spoke curtly, his lips thinning into a tight white line, "You'll always put something between us, Crimson, one more obstacle to overcome before you'll consent to be mine. And if we don't find the killer, will you still place it between us?"

An iron band tightened around her heart, making breathing difficult while her temper rose with his. Couldn't he understand she wanted to marry him free of the stigma of murderess? Tom had soiled her with a mockery of a marriage, a marriage declared null and void by the attorney, Mr. Neal. Did he honestly think she wanted him while one more stain was added to her name? The symmetric beauty of her heart-shaped face grew flinty, her eyes diamond-hard emeralds. "You don't understand, Landon, and until you do, there is nothing more we can say." She sidestepped him and stepped away.

He grabbed her arm and swung her back around, his stance rocklike. "There is more, little spy. I will find Tom's killer and present his head to you on a golden platter. It is what you want, ain't it? And you, my dear, are going back home. Your very presence here creates problems, unintended danger, and makes it harder for Cotton and me. We cannot be constantly worrying over your safety."

His hold on her arm tightened. "For your information, Half-breed was here for you. I was gonna meet him in the saloon face-to-face. I would of killed him if he did not swear he would leave you alone."

From his pocket, he withdrew her derringer Tom had bought her and held it out toward her. The intricate silver wrought barrel and ivory handle with her initials in silver seemed to glare at her in the feeble light. "Take it," he ordered firmly.

"No!" Crimson could not suppress the shudder sweeping through her. The gun had brought her nothing but trouble, and she would be damned if she took it back.

"I said take it," he ordered again, his voice brooking no refusal. "Mr. Houston got your derringer back from the court. Now take it!"

She gingerly took the small derringer, the ivory still warm from his hand. If she were braver in the face of his present fury, she would have thrown it back in his face, but something about his lean, hard body warned her if she did, he would have no compunction turning her over his knee, flipping her skirts over her head and spanking her in front of the citizens of Tascosa. She was not foolish enough to risk the embarrassment.

"It's loaded, ready to use if you should need it. Put it in your purse and carry it with you at all times. Do you hear me, Crimson?" His fingers bit into the soft flesh of her arm. She winched under the pressure, but he refused to release her until she agreed.

"Yes, I hear you."

◦◟◎ᐧ◠◎◜◎◦

GLANCING around the sod house, there was an oppressive feel about it. This was the first time Crimson had been back since the trial, and had in fact, never expected to come back. A musky scent permeated the inside, and the furniture and bed were covered with dust and cobwebs. While Landon brought in her bag, she rolled up her sleeves.

The air permeating with anger, Landon dropped her bag on the floor close beside her. "Stop cleaning a few minutes so we can talk."

"What more is there to say, Landon? You're already forced me back here knowing how much I hate it here." She kept cleaning the collected dust over the stove, refusing to face him.

"Damn it, Crimson!" he growled, moving toward her bent form and grabbing her shoulders, forcing her upright before turning her around.

"Don't touch me!" she snarled, pushing against him, the dusty rag still in her hand and now against his chest.

"Wrong move, sweetheart," he growled, taking the rag and throwing it across the room, then turning her around and forcing her upper body across the table. Before she could react, he had shifted the bottom of her skirt over her waist. Holding her down with one hand, he used the other to smack it against the white orbs of her bottom.

"Landon! Don't you…" Before she could move, he smacked her behind several more times, the stings forcing a cry from her lips.

"When will you learn, Crimson?" he growled, smacking her several more times before smoothing his hands over her reddened bottom cheeks.

"I still hate you," she sniffled.

A crooked grin lifted one side of his mouth as he ran his hand between her legs and felt the wetness there. "Let me see again how much you hate me," he answered, unbuttoning his pants and letting them slide down at his feet. Moving between her legs, he forced them apart and shoved into her moistened tunnel. Rocking his hips against hers, he pulled her buttocks tighter against him. "I'll stop after you've cum several times before I leave, and each time, you will tell me whether you hate me or love me."

Damn him, she thought. *He always wins!*

Landon did not stay long afterwards, but calmly pulled up his pants and buttoned them. Crimson was still angry, but she did change her tune about hating him several times. Their tempers were too volatile, too near the surface for wagering much conversation between them.

After bringing in a couple of buckets of water, he confronted her. "I never want to hear how much you hate me again, Crimson. You either love me or you hate me. Make up your mind while I'm gone. If you tell me you hate me again, I will leave and never come back. Do you understand, Crimson? Once more and I'll never come back!"

With a hard kiss of warning on her sullen lips, he mounted and sternly admonished her to stay at the house.

Oh, he thought he had won. He should know her better. She

spent the day furiously cleaning, working against the pent-up rage rushing through her. She was determined she would find Tom's murderer with or without him.

The thick silence of the sod dissipated her thoughts. She hated this sod and the memories it bore. The brief, stolen moments with Landon in this room could not appease her conscience. Past voices of hers and Tom's raised in anger echoed inside her head, bringing back the pain, the depression and the misery she suffered during the time she spent with him. She covered her ears, willing the sounds away, but the voices refused to be stilled. Throwing her arms out, she screamed, "No! I wanna forget!"

Silence met her shouted words.

Drenched with sweat, she ran her arm across her forehead, then shook her head, feeling ridiculous for her shouted words. It was a hot summer day, but outside there was a freshness in the air, the smell of living things. She glimpsed the fireplace from the corner of her eye, a glimmer of the past replaying in her memory of Harvey coming in the dead of night and softly knocking on the door. Assured she was asleep, he and Tom spoke in low voices, most of what they said was muted. Through the narrowed slits of her eyelids, she had watched Harvey hand Tom several gold eagles. After Harvey left, Tom pulled out a loose brick from a high spot along the hearth and removed a metal box.

Life with Tom had never been easy, and there had been so much more on her mind, she had completely forgotten about the incident. With curious trepidation, she neared the cold fireplace, bent slightly backward and lifted on her tiptoes. With her fingertips moving across the rough surfaces around the approximate area she remembered Tom had pulled out the brick, one of the bricks shifted slightly underneath her searching fingers and a mist of black soot spilled on top of her.

She moved the closest bench toward the fireplace and stepped on top, her face a study of concentration, her teeth pulling on her lower lip, while she eased the brick out and laid it on top of the cold ashes.

The hole where the brick had been, was dark inside. She rubbed her fingertips together, hesitant of sticking her hand inside the hole. She hated small crawling creatures, especially spiders, and thinking about encountering one in the dark hole effectively kept her from reaching inside.

Sighing in disgust, she stepped off the bench and retrieved a lantern from the table. With trembling fingers, she succeeded in lighting it, and stepped back onto the bench with the lamp in her hand.

Lifting it, light cast shadows inside the hole, clearly revealing something inside. She did not see anything moving, so gathering her courage, she set the lantern on the table before pulling the heavy metal box out of the enclosure. The box took both hands and was surprisingly heavy. She nearly dropped it before stepping off the bench. She set it down on top of the table with a loud bang before opening the lid, mildly surprised it was unlocked.

The lid fell back and revealed a stash of silver and gold inside. She gasped in astonishment. "Tom, whether you like it or not, you have left Landon and me a accidental gift, a new beginning after I clear my name, if there is anything salvageable left of our relationship," she stated into the silent room.

Chapter 39
Playing with Fire

OPENING her drawstring purse, Crimson's gaze landed on the small pearl-handled gun. She clenched her hand over the derringer, her reactive instinct encouraging her to throw it against the wall, but something stopped her. Instead, she filled her purse with some of the coins, then dumped the rest into a saddlebag. At the bottom of the box was a folded yellowed sheet and a lone key she assumed fitted the box's lock.

She tentatively took the sheet with trembling hands and opened it, smoothing the sheet across the tabletop and scrutinizing the information printed there. Her face tightened with sudden anger. It was a wanted poster from the army wanting Tom Martin dead or alive for robbery, theft and murder.

Folding the poster, and for some reason she could not explain, put it inside her purse. Drawing the strings closed, she turned and gasped. Harvey stood in the doorway, watching her with narrowed eyes, his arms stretched between the door frames.

"So, ya found the wanted poster. Ya know Tom murdered Major Larner. He was the only person who knew about it." Harvey stepped inside, blocking the only way out of the sod with his body.

"You scared me, Harvey. What are you doing here?" Crimson breathlessly asked, still clutching the drawstring of her purse. There was a strange glint in his eyes, the gleam sending shivers tripping along her spine.

"Why did you take up with the half-breed? I love ya, Crimson." He stepped nearer, hurt sounding in the intonation of his voice.

"Harvey, you'd better go. I'm fixing to leave and I don't wanna be late in meeting Landon." Glibly lying, she recognized an intensity in Harvey's eyes, and it unnerved her.

"Oh, Crimson? And what time are ya meetin' him?" Harvey asked sarcastically, seeing through her lie.

"I haven't gotta watch. Perhaps you can tell me what time it is," her voice strained with her bid for time. She had no explanation why he frightened her so. Maybe it was his sudden appearance that put her on edge.

"What's the matter, Crimson? Ya have no reason to be scart of me. Didna I jist tell ya I love ya?" Harvey lifted his hand to touch the side of her cheek and darkly frowned when she shrank back. "Really, Crimson, we've been friends for a long time. Why the sudden fear?"

A wry smile slightly pulled up her lips with his soft reprimand. Why should she fear him? They had been friends for years. "I don't know. I was unaware you were watching me from the door and it startled me."

"That's better, Crimson," he replied in satisfaction, reaching inside his coat and pulling out a pocket watch. He flipped the top open and announced, "It's jist four thirty. It will be several hours before the breed realizes ya ain't comin'."

Crimson stared at the watch, mesmerized by the distinct design on the front. The gold watch's inner casing was intricately carved and the front design bore a crouching mountain lion with emerald eyes. She never heard his last words. "You! It was you all along who killed Tom! Why, Harvey? He was your best friend!"

Chillingly glaring at her, his stance sinister, he harshly laughed, "My best friend? He was the lowest scum of the earth."

He waved the watch in front of her nose. "See this watch? Yes, it's the one Tom had, but do ya know how he got it? No?" he asked when she remained silent.

"I'll tell ya then. It was several years after Tom left Salina that we met again. We were both fifteen and were makin' our own way in this rotten world, but I remembered a childless aunt and uncle livin' in Illinois. What better place for a roof over our heads and possibly work? We hadna been there long when my aunt threw a big party for their twenty-fifth anniversary and all the neighbors for miles around came. My aunt gave this watch to my uncle for a anniversary gift. See the inscription?" Harvey held the watch out toward her.

Inside, written in beautiful script, was the inscription *To my loving husband, Elisha James, with love, Nelly.*

"Tom stole it?" Crimson asked sharply, suddenly feeling ill.

"Stole it?" Harvey growled menacingly. "Let me finish the story, Crimson, then you decide."

He stepped closer, watching her through half-lidded eyes, reliving some terrible memory. "My aunt and uncle didna have any children and treated us like their own kids. Uncle Elisha promised us the farm after they died. Maybe it was the promise startin' the whole thing. I don't know. We'd worked there for a few years and Tom was workin' the furthest boundaries of the farm. I went into town and picked up supplies. It was near dusk when I got back. When I saw smoke hangin' in the distance toward my uncle's farm, I whipped the mules into a run, but it was too late. The farmhouse was nothin' but a mass of charred, smokin' ruins. Tom was bent over my uncle's body and beside him was my aunt's bloody body. Tom claimed when he saw the smoke, he dropped ever'thang and came a'runnin', only he arrived too late to save them. My God, I actually believed him!"

While Harvey's story unfolded, Crimson stood motionless. She felt a deep, abiding sympathy for him, hearing in his voice the depth of his love for his aunt and uncle. She compassionately listened, not interrupting.

"I couldna stand the thought of farmin' the land after the way my aunt and uncle died, so I sold it and divided the money atween us. I never dreamed Tom was responsible for their deaths, not 'til the day I came here and saw he had my uncle's pocket watch."

He waved dismissively at the knowledge Tom killed his aunt and uncle and diverted from the topic. "Ya see, in Mobeetie when ya accidentally shot Tom, I picked up your derringer from where ya dropped it. Me and Tom, well, we weren't gittin' along too well and so I never had a chance to give it back afore then. I only came here that day 'cause Tom and I had some unfinished business. I was also plannin' on takin' ya away. I knew he wasn't far from gittin' rid of ya. Ya didna know, but Tom tried gittin' me killed twice after we broke off our relationship, did ya, Crimson?"

"But why didn't you give it back when I was packing that day?" Crimson asked, carefully sidestepping around him.

Harvey shrugged and continued his conversation as if she had not spoken. "No, ya wouldna of known. Tom didna tell ya anythang."

He waved his hand, dismissing the whole thing. "I watched ya leave the sod with some water buckets and decided I'd confront Tom while ya were gone. We had a fierce argument. And Tom pulled the watch from his pocket and ordered me to leave, said he had important business. Ya can imagine my surprise when I recognized my uncle's watch. I asked him why he had it, and do you know, he jist laughed at me, told me how he killed my aunt and uncle, then set the house on fire. He called me a fool 'cause I believed him aforehand. Afore I realized it, I pulled your derringer from my pocket and shot him in the neck. I wasn't plannin' on droppin' the derringer when I grabbed the watch and took off."

"You set me up!" Crimson accused.

Harvey shook his head, denying her accusation. "Not I. I found out later Whiskey Joe watched the whole thang. He's the one who put the water buckets inside yore house. Oh, but I got him back for settin' ya up. I ambushed him in Tascosa. He was gonna take ya agin and I couldna allow it. I've worked too hard havin' ya for myself."

The information regarding Half-breed was unnerving. "You knew all along? You let me take the blame for killing Tom. I could of been hanged for your crime," she bitterly cried, distracted from her bid of running.

He tiredly shrugged his shoulders. "I was scared and I didna wanna be hung."

"Scared?" she ground out resentfully. "You didn't have the guts to testify for me."

"I'm sorry. I couldn't testify 'cause I was afraid somehow the truth would come out. I'm not exactly guiltless in the crimes Tom committed. I know I should of come forward when I heard Tom's killin' was ruled a justifiable homicide, but what was the use? It was over and done with. I shoulda kilt him after he killed Jennifer. It would of saved us both a lot of grief."

Crimson edged closer toward the door when he uttered his last words. A sense of danger still lurked around him, but when he mentioned Jennifer, she stopped. "Jennifer? Jenny?" Was it possible there were two different people named Jenny or Jennifer?

"Yep, he killed her jist as surely as he would of kilt ya. Ya see, several years ago, we went back to Illinois. Tom got a job workin' for the judge in Vandalia as a carriage driver and I got one workin' in the stables. Tom had charm when he wanted to, and Jenny, the judge's daughter, liked men, any man. Tom and Jenny were sneakin' around and seein' a lot of each other. The only problem was, I was also meetin' up with her. Jennifer got with child and said it was Tom's. She made a bad mistake when she accused him of fatherin' the child. Tom messed around for years and no woman ever got with child by him. He had mumps when he was younger and they fell down to his privates. It must of rendered him unable to git a woman with child." Harvey moved closer toward Crimson and bent his head near hers.

"Tom exploded and beat her, called her ever'thang under the sun, then took a knife and kept stabbin' her. He killed her, Crimson, kilt the woman I loved and my unborn child. I weren't gonna let him do the same with ya. Ever'thang I ever cared about somehow Tom managed stealin' it from me. I was determined I weren't gonna let him keep ya and destroy ya too."

As possessive madness laced his words, Crimson edged toward the door. Deciding on taking a chance, she picked up her skirt and made a run for it.

Harvey caught her before she reached the door. Clasping her arm in an iron grip, he dragged her back. "No, Crimson, you ain't gonna leave me. I'm takin' ya with me and yore gonna marry me."

"Be sensible, Harvey. There's a lot of women willing to be your wife. Besides, Landon will hunt you down and get me back," she warned, struggling against his grip and still clutching her drawstring purse. She felt the added weight of the derringer but knew she couldn't get it out with his hold on her. It was too risky.

"That's a chance I gotta take. I ain't 'bout to give ya up agin," Harvey replied unruffled. "And too, there ain't no other woman I wanna marry. 'Sides, there ain't a decent single woman for hundreds of miles 'round here. Maybe that's what men find so attractive 'bout ya 'sides your beauty, which coupled with your relationship with Buck Leathers, makes it doubly desirable."

Crimson glanced futilely around the room, searching for a way out of his grasp. He was mad! Utterly mad! "I thought you only like men, Harvey, especially Tom."

"Ah, so ya know 'bout that. Let's say yore dead husband was a gud cock sucker. We'd played wid each other when we were kids, and when there were no women around, me and Tom pleasured each other."

He pulled her against his body, the hard imprint straining his pants obvious against her stomach. "Feel this, Crimson. It ain't a hard-on for a man but for ya. I'm sure yore mouth is much sweeter than Tom's ever was and yore pussy finer than his ass. 'Sides, Tom and I only did what some cowpokes did, use any hole available even with another man." He ran his free hand down her back and cupped her bottom cheek.

Crimson jerked out of his hold, her face flushing red, one of his hands still holding onto her arm. His fingers loosened ever so slightly, and taking a chance, she lunged for the table, grabbed the still lit lamp and threw it. Harvey deflected the lamp with his arm, knocking it toward the bed. Kerosene spilled across the room, and suddenly, the whole sod was ablaze. Harvey grabbed her arm before she could run past him. "Wanna die together, Crimson?"

He motioned at the fast-licking flames. The roof beams caught on fire and quickly spread across the furniture. The heat, smoke and crackling blaze ate at her nerves. Her eyes stung and teared up as racking coughs tore through her.

"It's yore choice, Crimson. Die here with me or leave with me." When she did not answer quick enough, he grabbed her around the neck, holding her motionless in front of him, her back against his front.

"Answer me!" He grabbed the flying strands of her hair and sharply pulled her head back, the action stinging her scalp.

"I don't wanna die, Harvey." She had trouble speaking—smoke was billowing around them.

"Good girl," he replied in satisfaction. Not releasing his

strangling hold on her, he grabbed her saddlebag of gold before walking them out the door. The roof fell in only a split second afterward, showering them with sparks.

Harvey pushed her none too gently further out into the yard, stopping in mid-stride when a voice commanded, "Let her go, Harvey!"

Harvey increased the pressure on Crimson's neck, drawing his gun at the same time and leveling the barrel against her head. "Don't be a fool, breed. If ya try shootin' me, ya might hit her, and if ya don't, I will. Now, if ya want her alive, ya will throw your gun over here." He motioned with his head at the ground in front of him.

Crimson nearly cried out loud when she saw Landon standing several feet in front of the burning sod, his pistol aimed at them, a muscle fiercely working in his cheek, his eyes hard and cold. Her eyes pleaded with Landon when Harvey jammed the muzzle of the pistol against her temple, his arm around her neck nearly choking her.

Landon glared at Harvey, his stance deceptively loose-limbed, debating whether or not to risk shooting at Harvey's exposed head. Crimson watched him with fear-widened green eyes, her face white as snow. With a disgusted, futile-ridden growl, he threw his gun several feet in front of his boots. "You haven't won, Harvey. I'll come looking for you and hound you to your white man's hell until I find you."

Throwing Crimson away from him, Harvey leveled his gun at Landon. "We'll meet in hell then, breed, 'cause yore gonna die."

Crimson caught herself on her arms a few feet away from Harvey. Not thinking, she rolled on her stomach, her purse still attached to her wrist, and pulled the drawstrings open. She did not have time to pull the derringer from it but closed her finger on the trigger, aimed and shot Harvey twice through the purse at the same time he fired at Landon. In horror, she watched Harvey's eyes widen in shock, then crumble on the ground, her bullets entering between his ribs.

Taking a chance with his own life, Landon dove toward his gun, the bullet from Harvey's gun hitting his shoulder while he was in mid-motion. Grabbing his gun and rolling, Landon lifted his weapon only to watch Harvey slump toward the ground.

Within seconds, Crimson was up and running to Landon's side. He struggled to stand and blood spread in a wide circle around his shoulder. "Landon, you're hurt!" she cried.

"I'm fine. It's just a flesh wound," Landon assured her, crooking his uninjured arm around her and pulling her up against him.

Laying her head on his shoulder and encircling his waist with her arms, heart rendering sob broke through her near shock. "I killed him, Landon."

"Hush, little spy. You saved my life. Remember that." Landon pressed his face against her hair, pulling her tighter in his one-arm embrace.

A muffled groan broke through the sound of her sobs. Crimson lifted her head and looked at the prone form of Harvey, seeing the blood stains wetting his shirt. Pushing away from Landon, she knelt by Harvey's side. "Why did you do it, Harvey? You should of known if you killed Landon, I would hate you for the rest of my life."

Opening dull eyes and grabbing her hand, a trickle of blood ran down the corner of his mouth. "I loved ya, Crimson." He drew in a rasping breath, then did not breathe again, his eyes staring sightlessly, the light of life extinguished forever.

Landon stumbled toward them, took her by the arm and lifted her upright. Pressing her face against his shoulder, he replied softly, "It's over, Crimson."

Numbly nodding with tears flowing down her cheeks, she drew comfort from him, accepting the knowledge if she had not fired when she did, Landon would be dead instead of Harvey. She could not bear the thought of losing him when they had finally found each other. "Yes, it's over."

She pushed back from him and rubbed the tears from her face, all business now. "I'll get your wound bandaged before you lose any more blood."

While she cleaned and bandaged the wound on his arm from a shirt she discovered in his saddlebags, she asked, "Why did you come back? I thought you were in Tascosa. I thought I'd never see you again."

"You can thank your brother for me being here in time. He'd gone to the sheriff and told them about Half-breed and his cronies abducting you. After the sheriff arrested Ben and Frank, they talked like there was no tomorrow, spilling their guts about Half-breed and how they had seen Harvey enter the back door of the saloon only moments after the shooting. Cotton put two and two together and came up with Harvey, only he had seen him leaving town a couple of hours before that. I met Cotton while I was riding back to Tascosa."

"But where is he now?"

"I sent him back for help. Buck was meeting us in Tascosa early this afternoon. I suspect they'll be arriving soon."

Crimson sat back on her haunches, observing her handiwork. The walls of the sod caved in, drawing their attention. "I always hated that sod. I'm glad it's gone."

With Landon's arm around her shoulder, they sat on the ground, watching the sod finish burning. Glancing back at Harvey's prone form, the memory of J.T. Markman flashed through her mind. "Do you remember the judge speaking about J.T. Markman? I believe it was a name Harvey used."

"Why would you think that?"

"Well, when I asked Harvey, he would not meet my eyes nor answer. It just seemed logical since him and John were usually together."

Landon ran his hand up and down her arm, thinking about the wanted posters. "You might be right. The man identified as J.T. Markman had a beard. When we take Harvey's body into town, I will ask him to recheck the poster and verify if it was him. They *were* wanted dead or alive."

He felt her shiver and quickly understood her fear. "Crimson, I will tell the sheriff I killed Harvey. It'll be better that way and save any more taint to yours and your family's name."

She nodded agreement as they watched the sod burning until there was nothing left but embers and the fireplace. Her jaw hardening, she scooted out from underneath Landon's arm. "I don't want anything left of this place."

Before Landon realized what she was planning, she ran toward the shed near the corral. While she was inside, Cotton and Buck rode up, took the scene in with a glance and dismounted. Before either could question Landon, Crimson came out of the shed, dragging a large sledgehammer behind her.

Heading for the chimney, she ignored their questions. It took all her strength to pick up the heavy hammer and slam it against the brick. Over and over, she drew upon her inner anger for more strength hiding deep within her. One last swing was all she could manage, and she had not done much damage. With the last blow, a hole was made in the sod brick. Suddenly, a shower of gold began pouring out.

"My God, gold eagles. There must be thousands of them," Cotton exclaimed excitedly.

"Government money," Crimson replied grimly. "Fill up your saddlebags. I'm taking them to the fort."

"You must be crazy, Crim!" Cotton let the gold coins fall into his hands and filter through his fingers.

"No, Cotton. It's blood money, money Tom killed for and I ain't gonna have it." She guessed there would be a huge reward for its return, and besides, she had coins inside her purse and saddlebag. It was enough to give her and Landon a new lease on life. With the combined monies along with the reward money from the wanted poster, they could buy some land, an inheritance for their children, and start living and loving each other to the fullest.

Landon draped his arm around her shoulder. "While we are at Tascosa to deliver Harvey's body and tell the sheriff what happened out here, shall we get married?"

"There's nothing stopping us now. Besides, it might be better sooner than later since I'm carrying your child." She smiled into the sky-blue eyes piercing into hers. His dark, coppery skin was tanned almost black, his eyes a startling contrast.

Smiling, he pulled her into his arm and lowered his head. "Guess we'll go into Tascosa today and get it done. What I want to know is, why are you just telling me?"

She pulled his head toward hers and passionately kissed him. Moving back a little, she whispered, "Couldn't tell you, Landon. You would have never let me work at the dancehall." With a slight, mysterious smile, she whispered, "We made a lot of heat this winter waiting for my trial, remember?"

He whispered back, "Yeah, and we'll make more. You know, I do like paddling your beautiful ass and you deserve another for hiding your pregnancy from me." He grinned down at her, his eyes lighting with his smile. "I think you like me paddling your ass too, don't you, love?" Without waiting for her answer, his lips said more than any words could.

Crimson felt the heat between her legs and the moisture erupting there. Between kisses, she murmured, "Only when you finish and kiss it."

Life would never be easy between them, but if she had not taken Harvey's life, she would never know the strength of their love. If she had it all to do over again, she would do the same thing, for she could love no man as passionately as she loved him.

www.ingramcontent.com/pod-product-compliance
Lightning Source LLC
Chambersburg PA
CBHW052107030426

42335CB00025B/2874